Public Economy and Urban Governance in China

Series Editor

Baijun Wu, East China University of Science and Technology, Shanghai, China

This book series aims to promote the research in innovation-driven development of public economy and urban governance in China, and ultimately the social governance model based on collaboration, participation, and common interests enhancing the foresight, precision, and efficiency of urban governance. Focusing on the urban governance of Chinese top megacities, this book series combines economics and sociology and explores a new way to solve problems of social governance concerning urban public goods supply mechanism, innovative models of social governance, as well as critical urban development issues like public safety, infrastructure and environmental pollution.

Baijun Wu · Maogang Tang · Zhen Li

Effective Supply Mechanism of Urban Public Goods

ECUST PRESS

Springer

Baijun Wu
School of Business
East China University of Science
and Technology
Shanghai, China

Maogang Tang
School of Business
East China University of Science
and Technology
Shanghai, China

Zhen Li
School of Public Finance and Taxation
Nanjing University of Finance
and Economics
Nanjing, China

Translated by
Xiaoying Bao
Shanghai International Studies University
Shanghai, China

Mengyun Zhao
Shanghai International Studies University
Shanghai, China

ISSN 2948-1872 ISSN 2948-1880 (electronic)
Public Economy and Urban Governance in China
ISBN 978-981-96-2607-6 ISBN 978-981-96-2608-3 (eBook)
https://doi.org/10.1007/978-981-96-2608-3

Jointly published with East China University of Science and Technology Press Co., Ltd.
The print edition is not for sale in China (Mainland). Customers from China (Mainland) please order the print book from: East China University of Science and Technology Press Co., Ltd..

This Springer imprint is published by the registered company Springer Nature Singapore Pte Ltd.
The registered company address is: 152 Beach Road, #21-01/04 Gateway East, Singapore 189721, Singapore

Preface

For Series of *Public Economy and Urban Governance in China*

After more than 40 years of rapid development, China's economy and society have undergone profound changes. One notable feature of this transformation is the increasing importance of the public goods sector as a driver of national economic growth. In response to the global financial crisis in 2008, the Chinese government made significant investments in public infrastructure to combat economic recession, sustain economic growth, and maintain social stability. Alongside urbanization and population policy reforms, the government has also increased its investment in public services such as education, healthcare, security, and social welfare to address the rising demand for social welfare. As a result, the supply of economic and social public goods has become a vital component of the overall social supply system. In some years, public goods investment has been the primary driver of marginal economic growth.

Although the overall social framework and power dynamics have remained relatively stable, new social forces such as the immigrant class, the middle-income class, and the private capital class have emerged and grown increasingly influential, reshaping China's social structure and profoundly affecting the distribution of social interests. Additionally, as China adopts an increasingly market-oriented and socialized production system, the lifestyles, thoughts, needs, and demands of the public are evolving, making it difficult for the government to accurately assess their needs, preferences, and behaviors, thereby challenging the effective delivery of public services. Furthermore, the changes in production methods and the expansion of economic activities beyond the traditional administrative boundaries have enhanced social mobility, posing a significant challenge to the traditional top-down administrative management system. This necessitates a restructuring of social governance mechanisms to better align with modern political and economic development.

The ongoing social and economic transformations pose considerable challenges to making accurate predictions about future development. However, by examining changes in the political system, certain patterns in socioeconomic evolution can be identified. Throughout human history, advancements in technology and production methods and market expansion have provided the economic foundation for individuals to overcome environmental constraints and pursue prosperity. Nevertheless, the expansion of the private goods sector complicates efforts to ensure equitable and secure development for all. In contrast, the public goods sector, whether in a planned or market economy, consistently enhances shared social welfare. The supply of public goods and services highlights the distinct roles and social impacts of the private and public sectors, underscoring the need for a rational allocation of resources, as imbalances between public and private good supply may lead to economic and social inequality. While the private goods sector often generates more wealth, it can also exacerbate environmental degradation, wealth inequality, and social disparities. Conversely, the development of the public goods sector, though enhancing social welfare and security, is often accompanied by resource misallocation, inefficiency, bureaucratic privileges, and administrative monopolies. Consequently, ongoing efforts have been made to develop systems that regulate excessive competition, negative externalities, and address wealth disparities in the private sector while improving the efficiency and social benefits of the public goods sector.

Global economic development trends indicate that, as the economy grows and incomes rise, the public goods sector expands significantly in both asset scale and its share of total social supply. It is playing an increasingly vital role and enjoying a higher position in socioeconomic development, reflecting both the current realities and future trends. In comparison to the development patterns of the public goods sector in other countries, China's rapid development in this area since its reform and opening up mirrors broader socioeconomic transformation. However, it is crucial to recognize that, in a rapidly changing socioeconomic environment, the growth of the private goods sector will continue to be shaped by technological advancement, market dynamics, and institutional development. The public goods sector faces its own challenges, which include:

1. Effective resource allocation: One key question is how to allocate social and economic resources between the private and public goods sectors. This requires a thorough understanding of the economic and social needs, alongside a well-designed mechanism of resource allocation. This balance should meet the demands of both sectors while fostering sustainable economic growth and more social welfare so as to realize the dual objectives of economic efficiency and social equality.
2. Effective supply of public goods: It is crucial to address both theoretical and practical challenges of understanding the actual needs and preferences of Chinese people and take measures to involve the public in the selection and decision-making processes of public goods projects. Public goods supply depends not only on the system and mechanism of a country but also on its political, technological, market, and cultural contexts. At the core of this issue is the design of its political and economic system. To break the traditional "all-in-one" government governance and adopt a more people-centered approach, the central government

must clearly define its role, deciding what responsibilities to retain and what to delegate. Empowering grassroots governments and granting more autonomy to social organizations will enable them to play a larger role in social governance. Furthermore, the government needs to reform the existing public goods supply mechanism and explore new cooperative approaches involving multiple stakeholders, tailored to China's national conditions.

3. Building a collaborative governance structure: Another challenge is to create a social governance structure featuring "joint contribution, joint governance and shared benefits", and establish a social governance community in which "everyone has a role, contributes and shares in the benefits". This entails building a governance system integrating the efforts of the government, social organizations, and the public, all under the leadership of the Chinese Communist Party, and in addition, public participation in community governance must be encouraged to foster a sense of responsibility and engagement at the grassroots level and enhancing the skills and capacity of community workers and participants is also crucial to ensuring effective governance.
4. Innovating grassroots governance: To do so, it is necessary to position grassroots governance as the foundation and focus of national governance, as well as the fundamental part of China's governance system and the modernization of governance capacity. The government should address the "idling" of grassroots governance by strengthening institutional framework and using legal tools. A governance model should be established that accommodates diverse governance subjects, reducing bureaucratic administration in community institutions and their activities. Efforts should be made to "de-administrate" grassroots organizations and allow them to function more independently. Additionally, it is important to build an operating system for grassroots organizations to enhance their capacity to mobilize resources, provide public services, and participate in public decision-making processes.
5. Using new technologies: New technologies such as the internet, big data, and artificial intelligence should be leveraged to innovate public goods production and supply, enhance public service efficiency, and improve grassroots governance capacity. This entails the constant improvement of laws and regulations to enable public service departments to legally and effectively use information technology to better understand the needs of the public for goods and services. Access to comprehensive data will enable more informed decision-making and provide technical tools to monitor public service performance to achieve the goal of efficient resource allocation and supply.

With these understandings of China's socioeconomic development and structural changes, the Research Institute of Social Sciences at East China University of Science and Technology (ECUST) has gathered a research team dedicated to exploring issues on public economy and social governance. With a particular focus on grassroots society and the microeconomic level, the team aims to provide close observations and in-depth analyses of China's socioeconomic development within the broader context of its social and economic transformation. In recent years, a group of young scholars at ECUST specializing in public economics, sociology, and public management have been committed to researching public economics and grassroots social governance. They have undertaken numerous international collaborations and national research projects, mainly on the following three themes:

1. Fundamental theory of public goods development and its application in China. The research emphasizes interdisciplinary research. Integrating various research paradigms to explore the structural relationships and internal mechanisms between public economy and social governance during the process of social development;
2. New forms and methods of public economy and social governance in the age of new technologies, such as the internet, big data, and artificial intelligence;
3. Empirical research and field experiments in public infrastructure, public services, and community-level governance to uncover valuable practices with Chinese characteristics, aiming to identify valuable practices that reflect distinctive Chinese characteristics, critique classical theories, and expand the theoretical landscape of public economics and governance.

This book series offers a preliminary summary of the research findings, with each volume exploring different aspects of these research themes. It explores public economy, social governance, and social policies through interdisciplinary studies, grounded mainly in public economics and public management theories and addressing critical issues in public economy and social governance and policies. The five volumes in the series on public economy include:

1. *Research on Effective Supply Mechanism of Urban Public Goods.* The book reviews the theories and literature on public goods supply, examines China's public goods supply mechanisms and their reform outcomes, and provides empirical analyses on financing, production, and distribution in urban infrastructure and public services;
2. *Research on Urban Infrastructure and Economic Development.* The book examines China's achievements and challenges in infrastructure construction over the past 70 years, using theories of fiscal decentralization and comparative institutional analysis to reveal how infrastructure influences regional economic development. It explores the impact of China's infrastructure development on market integration, open development, and improvements in people's living standards through econometric analysis, while proposing innovative infrastructure supply models in light of political economic theories;
3. *Research on the Mechanisms and Methods for the Effective Supply of Environmental Public Goods.* This study investigates the supply mechanisms of environmental public goods, with a focus on the role and behavior patterns of households in environmental governance. It positions households as key actors in environmental protection, incorporates intergenerational factors into the analysis framework, and builds a theoretical model for effective supply using three methods of environmental public goods value assessment;
4. *Research on the Spatial Distribution Characteristics and Comprehensive Capacity Evaluation of Urban Public Services.* With big data, the book conducts

a comprehensive analysis of the development processes, resource scale, spatial distribution and service capacity of urban public services, evaluates the factors influencing urban public services, and proposes optimizing strategies;

5. *Research on the Multilateral Collaborative Governance of Urban Shared Platforms.* The book explores the public nature of private goods within the shared economy, reviews the development models, governance experiences, and operational mechanisms of urban shared platforms both domestically and internationally, and proposes a governance framework that prioritizes self-regulation, government oversight, and social assistance. The research breaks the traditional restrictions on the supply of public goods in cities and makes a groundbreaking study on the revolutionary changes in the public consumption and production model of private products in the new technological environment.

The five books take infrastructure, environmental protection, pollution control, and other major urban public goods and public services as research objects, analyze the characteristics and internal operation mechanism of China's urban public goods supply, and put forward institutional reform proposals and policy suggestions for the effective supply of public goods.

The series includes another five volumes on urban social governance. They are:

1. *Research on Urban Immigration and Public Governance.* The book examines urban governance in the context of urbanization and explores how to shift from immigration control to immigration services to improve governance and help immigrants integrate into urban life more quickly;
2. *Research on the Urban Public Safety Risk Prevention and Control System.* The book addresses the frequent occurrence of urban public safety incidents and systematically analyzes the sources and types of urban safety issues. It offers a thorough examination of the causes of urban safety risks and explores effective mechanisms for risk prevention and control, ultimately proposing an urban safety risk prevention system;
3. *Research on the Social Mechanisms for Resolving Urban Grassroots Conflicts and Disputes.* By taking the rapidly developing People's Mediation Organizations as an example, the book analyzes the practical demand, functional positioning, organizational networks, operational mechanisms, and development logic of social forces involved in resolving grassroots conflicts, aiming to develop the governance mechanisms for a "Chinese-style risk society";
4. *Research on the Construction of an Integrated Service Model in Urban Community Governance.* With the grassroots governance practices in Shanghai as an example, the book examines various aspects of grassroots social governance, such as street system reforms, government-purchased services, the development of community social organizations, the role of social forces in governance, and the capacity building of community workers, The book analyzes new challenges in grassroots governance, identifies the underlying social and structural causes, and explores innovative elements, processes, and critical aspects of modern grassroots governance, offering new ideas for constructing a grassroots governance system and practical model for megacities;

5. *Research on the Development and Operation of Urban Community Foundations in China.* The book focuses on urban community foundations through empirical analyses of their growth environments, localized characteristics, governance structures, and functions within an administratively driven framework and explores the development pathways and operational mechanisms of grassroots social organizations in China's political system.

This book series was published during the COVID-19 pandemic, a time when China and the world faced a significant public health crisis in about 20 years after the SARS epidemic. The pandemic has once again underscored the critical importance of respecting natural laws and prompted reflection on the effectiveness of public health system reforms, the limitations in the current social governance structure, and the implementation of public policies. China's effective control of the epidemic demonstrates the strong mobilization and response capabilities of grassroots community organizations during public emergencies, highlights the need for a multilateral supply mechanism that involves social organization and public participation as key elements in social governance reforms, and proves once again the importance of building an effective public goods supply system.

The publication of the book series has been made possible with the support of the Chinese National Publishing Fund and Shanghai Publishing Projects for Universities Serving the National Strategies. We would like to extend our gratitude to the East China University of Science and Technology Press for its support and to the editors for their dedication and hard work in bringing this project to fruition.

Shanghai, China Baijun Wu
May 2020

About the Book

The public goods sector has emerged as an important component of China's economy, significantly influencing its economic and social welfare development. The book explores the theories related to public goods supply, focusing on resource allocation and supply mechanisms involved. It examines various supply approaches, including governmental, market-based (private), and social (voluntary) supply mechanisms as well as multi-stakeholder collaborative strategies and conducts a comparative analysis of public goods supply and the corresponding reforms of supply mechanisms in different countries. On the basis of the research, the book introduces a model elucidating the relationship between public goods supply and economic growth, providing empirical evidence of how urban public goods supply impacts economic growth in China, and examining the realities, institutional reforms, and development trends of public goods supply in Chinese cities. It highlights the distinctive features of public goods supply in Chinese cities, identifies challenges, and explores the key factors influencing supply mechanisms. The book categorizes urban public goods into two areas: urban infrastructure and public services, examining their evolution, supply mechanisms, and performance. With a particular focus on the decision-making mechanisms in China, the book explores public policies governing the supply of urban public goods and assesses the factors influencing these policies, ultimately providing recommendations for improving supply effectiveness and policy decisions.

Contents

Chapter 1
Introduction

1.1 Research Background and Questions

The evolution of modern urban cities is both a result and a crucial indicator of a nation's economic advancement. The economic advantages of cities generally arise from the concentration of economic factors and the positive externalities generated by economic activities. People choose to live and work in cities not only for occupational opportunities but also for the conveniences offered by urban environments, such as social interactions, access to healthcare, cultural and educational experiences, and more comprehensive social security. These advantages stem from two main sources: the concentration of spatial resources and the public infrastructure and services provided by cities, which are classified in economics as public goods. A variety of public goods form the foundations of urban socioeconomic activities and the welfare of residents, making them critical indicators of a city's level of socioeconomic development.

After the founding of the People's Republic of China in 1949, the low level of economic development led to the allocation of the majority of resources to industrial system development, resulting in significant limitation of the capacity for furnishing urban public goods and failure to meet even the basic needs. Through the 1980s, investment in urban public infrastructure and social services remained minimal, leading to shortages of both private and public goods for urban residents. Moreover, under the planned economy system, the supply of urban public goods was predominantly dictated by administrative planning.

Since 1978 when China began its reform and opening up, driven by the forces of economic development zones and urbanization, cities have evolved rapidly as engines of economic growth. Local governments have redefined cities as centers of regional economic development, breaking away from their previous politically driven urban roles. This shift has strengthened the economic functions of industry, commerce, and services, leading to fundamental changes in urban spatial structures that align with the needs of urban industries and residents. At the same time, the structure

B. Wu et al., *Effective Supply Mechanism of Urban Public Goods*, Public Economy and Urban Governance in China, https://doi.org/10.1007/978-981-96-2608-3_1

of the urban system has shifted significantly. China's urban system has evolved from a city-centered model with isolated intercity relationships to one dominated by urban clusters, urban belts, and central cities. Particularly in recent years, the reform of the household registration system has fostered multilevel urban development, with large cities expanding and small to medium-sized towns developing distinctive characteristics. Amid this rapid urbanization, the supply of both economic and social public goods has greatly improved, with their composition tailored to urban demands.

This book explores the evolution of urban public goods supply in China since the founding of the People's Republic of China and analyzes the factors shaping this supply. The study reveals that the demand driving the supply of public goods has shifted across different periods, accompanied by changes in influencing factors. We classify the development of urban public goods in China into three stages:

The first stage is the planned economy period. During this period, the primary goal of China's economy was to build an industrial system, with resources mainly directed toward industrial sectors. The cities functioned primarily as hubs for government administration and industrial growth, with less emphasis on meeting the needs of residents. Consequently, urban public goods were severely underfunded, with most of the limited investment directed toward industrial infrastructure, leading to severe shortages in public services.

The second stage is the post-reform and opening up period. With the acceleration of industrialization and urbanization, cities have assumed increasingly important economic roles, especially with the rise of economic development zones and the migration of rural labor into cities. This shift generated an urgent demand for public infrastructure and services. Statistical analysis indicates that since the late 1980s, investments in urban public infrastructure have still been aimed at economic growth, much like in the planned economy period. However, the speed and scale of construction during this phase were unprecedented. The critical distinction between this period and the planned economy period lies in the expanded set of factors influencing public goods supply. Critical infrastructure and public services necessary for urban life, such as transportation systems, communication networks, energy supply (water, electricity, gas), public health, and basic education systems, saw continuous development. Institutional factors, including land-use rights transfer, the fiscal management system under the tax-sharing system, and local government land financing, play a vital role in funding urban public goods.

The third stage began around 2008. In response to the global financial crisis, the Chinese government implemented proactive fiscal and monetary policies to maintain economic growth stability. With the slowing of international and domestic private product demand, the growth rate of private sector industries declined. In this period, increased monetary, fiscal, and land resources were allocated to the public goods sector, which showed strong demand potential and lower elasticity. The surge in public sector investment and output helped stimulate sustained economic growth. In recent years, China has seen remarkable growth in public infrastructure projects funded by both central government investment and local government initiatives. This strategy of using public investment to counter economic downturns mirrors anti-cyclical policies in Western countries during the 1930s, 1950s, and 1970s, as well as Japan's post-war economic development. While this approach has shown significant short-term effects, the long-term impact on economic growth remains a topic of ongoing debate among scholars.

In China's economic development, the increase in urban public goods supply, before the 2008 financial crisis, was largely driven by internal demands of industrialization and urbanization. After 2008, however, the driving force behind public goods sector development shifted toward supporting broader economic growth objectives. Currently, the factors determining investment scale and project construction in the public goods sector include:

(1) Economic growth goals. Investment in the public goods sector is a tool to promote economic growth that is aligned with the development of urban industries and the growing demand of residents.
(2) Evolving socioeconomic strategies. Changes in national socioeconomic development strategies and a shift toward more inclusive growth have increased the demand for social services, particularly in areas such as social security, public health, basic education, and social welfare, becoming a major driving force for public goods sector growth.
(3) Local government debt management. Large-scale public infrastructure investments have left local governments with heavy debt burdens. Consequently, the public goods sector is closely linked to local government debt, with continued investment in projects necessary to secure financing from financial markets and ensure local governments' budget and debt interest payments.

The public goods sector has become a leading force in driving national economic growth alongside the private sector. Some public infrastructure and social service industries have even become some of the fastest-growing sectors, contributing significantly to economic expansion.

The expansion of the scale of public goods sectors and their increasing socioeconomic impact have transformed urban production conditions, lifestyles, and physical landscape in China, presenting the following research topics for understanding both current and future trends in China's economic and urban development:

(1) The economic characteristics of public goods, such as foundational nature, social publicness, and public welfare, are essential for the operation and development of modern cities. However, public goods investment is often large-scale, with long payback periods, and many investment projects are non-profit or yield minimal returns. The inflexibility of the social welfare system means that any reductions in welfare can carry significant social risks. Consequently, sustaining a high level of public goods supply requires robust public financial resources, which is challenging for middle-income countries to sustain. The conflict between national income, public financial capacity, and public goods expenditure, triggered by the expansion of the public goods sector, can lead to economic imbalance and inefficiency. This type of scenario has occurred before, such as in Europe in the 1970s and in Japan in the 1990s. Thus, it is imperative to consider whether positioning the public goods sector as the primary driver of

economic growth and committing substantial resources to it may exceed China's economic capacity. While rapid growth in the public goods sector may yield short-term economic benefits, could it ultimately weaken long-term economic potential? Additionally, questions arise regarding how future debt payments and ongoing maintenance costs of public infrastructure will be managed.

(2) The investment efficiency and operational efficiency of public goods tend to be lower than those of private goods, despite higher initial investment and operating costs. Investments in public infrastructure are especially driven by the development needs of the private sector. In this context, it becomes vital to determine the optimal scale of resources allocated to the public goods sector over a given period. On the other hand, an excessive emphasis on the development of the private sector may lead to a severe public infrastructure shortage and hinder public welfare advancement. Therefore, balancing the development of the public and private goods sectors within the national economic framework is critical. However, determining the appropriate scale for both sectors and effectively allocating resources poses significant challenges to the studies of economic growth theories.

(3) In public economics, the non-exclusivity and non-competitiveness of public goods often lead to distorted demand signals and behavioral deviations due to externalities and the "free rider problem". Consequently, assessing the true demand for public goods becomes challenging, complicating the effort to balance public goods supply with demand. Especially in specific political system contexts, factors such as regional competition and administrative assessments influence decisions, and local governments may even face binding debt obligations; suspending new public projects can lead to a crisis of debt from prior projects. Therefore, in economic practice, balancing the supply of public goods with limited public finances and matching the supply structure of public goods with social demands remain persistent challenges. Currently, in the supply of urban public goods in China, urgent public goods and services issues such as public health, primary education, and environmental governance have remained unresolved for a long time. Meanwhile, a large number of funds are allocated to image projects such as lighting and greening projects, and large squares, oversized high-speed rail stations, and airports that not only require massive investment but also impose a heavy financial burden on local governments for future operation and maintenance costs. Therefore, it is imperative to objectively assess the supply capacity and effectiveness of various public goods based on the economic and social development of different cities and the actual needs of residents. Public goods planning should focus on optimizing the structure of public goods supply, prioritizing critical projects, and effectively allocating resources to the most pressing public projects.

(4) Given the nature of public goods, private capital is generally reluctant to invest in non-profit or low-return public goods projects, making government investment essential for construction and operation. However, limited public resources often result in an inadequate supply of public goods relative to societal needs. Since the 1980s, the privatization and marketization of public goods sectors worldwide

have demonstrated that, under sound legal frameworks and institutional arrangements, private and social capital participation in public goods sectors can yield greater economic and social benefits than state-run models. With the advances in engineering technologies and management methods, formerly integrated public infrastructure projects can now be divided into different subsystems for construction and integrated operation. As financial markets have matured, the public goods sector has gained access to new financial tools and clarified property rights through property rights and management systems, transforming traditional modalities of public good investment, production, and delivery. Certain public facilities and services, while maintaining their public functions, have shifted to private or quasi-public ownership. Similarly, some traditional private goods, under certain technological and market conditions, have begun to perform public goods functions. These shifts have led to transformations in public goods investment, production, and distribution, prompting reforms in public goods supply systems. The most salient transformation is the diversification of supply mechanisms, evolving from the traditional solely government supply model to a cooperative supply system involving government, market, and social actors. This raises the question of how to design supply mechanisms based on the attributes, systems, and operational requirements of different public goods to enhance the effectiveness and efficacy of the urban public goods supply.

(5) Unlike private goods, public goods' actual demand and utility are difficult to measure. Without a price mechanism, it is challenging to capture the genuine preferences of demanders and establish a mechanism that reflects demand preferences, thereby complicating the evaluation of individual utility and total social benefits associated with public goods. Without accurately obtaining demand information from enterprises, the public, and social organizations, it is difficult to determine the overall social demand for these goods, which complicates the task of designing a reasonable supply structure. This raises further questions: In the absence of effective mechanisms for expressing consumer demand preferences, how can we evaluate the economic and social benefits of public goods, or assess the individual utility of their consumers? How can we evaluate the social benefits of public goods supply, especially when considering factors like the universality of public goods supply or fairness of distribution, and time? Additionally, can advances in technology and modern market institutions help overcome the challenge of capturing consumer demand preferences for public goods through institutional innovation?

Continued exploration of these issues opens numerous avenues. Economists, public administration scholars, and political scientists are engaged in ongoing research concerning these topics, frequently posing new questions and proposing solutions. Remarkably, some researchers have broken through traditional research paradigms in theory and opened up new research fields with innovative research methodologies and ideas, leading to ongoing achievements in public goods theories and providing more mechanisms and market tools for the supply of public goods. Moreover, models like Public–Private Partnerships (PPP) exemplify a shift from conventional supply mechanisms, offering flexible alternatives within a diversified supply mechanism. These advancements provide both a solid theoretical foundation and practical insights for further research into the effective supply of public goods.

1.2 The Significance of Research

Theories in public economics on the research on public goods can be traced back to ancient Greek philosophers who recognized the public nature of certain goods. Adam Smith later articulated unique economic activities in national economies that exhibited public attributes and highlighted the functions of non-market sectors in society. Arthur Cecil pigou, 1920, also explored the externalities involved in producing and consuming goods, addressing the intrinsic characteristics of public goods. In 1919, Lindahl introduced the concept of public goods and attempted to explain the resource allocation and supply–demand balance. Following Lindahl, scholars such as Samuelson, Musgrave, Buchanan, and Ostrom have built upon this foundation, developing research frameworks and theoretical systems for public economics and expanding the scope of research to incorporate insights from economics, political science, and public administration, which enriched research paradigms and deepened the study of public goods.

Despite the richness of theories in public economics, many theoretical challenges remain unsolved. As noted above, these issues are from the complex political and economic relationships inherent in public goods and the public goods sector, and to date, we still lack suitable methods and tools to observe and simulate their underlying mechanisms. Neoclassical economics, based on self-interested behavior, explains individual behavior in economic activities, but has made limited progress in studying collective public economic behavior. Paradigms and methods from new institutional economics and public administration offer valuable guidance for tackling fundamental issues in public economic theory and exploring the complex systemic issues within the public economy. Moreover, technological advancements- represented by the internet, big data, and artificial intelligence- have provided ample information for studying public economic issues. The development of financial markets, innovations in financial instruments, and reforms in public sector institutions have also laid the foundation for diversifying public goods production, distribution, and consumption methods. These developments enable us to analyze and understand the supply processes and internal mechanisms of public goods from fresh perspectives.

This book aims to summarize and review existing public economic theories and practices. Given the breadth of issues involved in public economics research, we primarily focus on the supply of urban public goods, particularly on supply mechanisms, with the aim of exploring which supply mechanisms are effective under specific political and economic conditions. The book also examines the evolution of China's urban public goods supply mechanisms and summarizes the lessons learned. This research offers several implications:

(1) In economic research, the characteristics of public goods such as non-rivalry, non-excludability, and externalities, and influenced by behaviors such as the "free rider problem" and "overcrowding problem", complicate the achievement of a supply–demand balance that maximizes benefits for individuals and society. Therefore, some scholars have attempted to approximate societal demand for public goods through external conditions, such as majority voting and "voting by foot" mechanisms. However, these strategic approaches often lack rigorous theoretical foundations and are challenging to implement in practice due to numerous prerequisite conditions. Nevertheless, actual economic activities suggest that by decomposing the supply process of public goods based on their complexity and systemic nature, separating components with different economic characteristics, some steps can exhibit pure public characteristics, while others may have clear property rights and distributable economic surplus, resembling private goods in terms of excludability and competitiveness. This decomposition can ensure that certain public infrastructure and public service projects meet public needs while weakening non-excludability and enhancing their competitiveness. Different supply methods can be employed, such as various investment, production, distribution, and operation approaches. To some extent, we may call this the internalization mechanism of public goods externalities, which could improve the efficiency of public goods supply and provide a more straightforward means to measure the actual preferences of public goods demanders. This book intends to explore these aspects through an analysis and summary of public goods supply practices.

(2) Public goods supply mechanisms are generally categorized into government supply mechanisms, market (private) supply mechanisms, and multi-stakeholder cooperative supply mechanisms. However, each mechanism has its institutional, technical, and market foundations, along with real-world constraints. By clearly defining these constraints and the appropriate environments for different mechanisms, we can better analyze their strengths and weaknesses. This analysis can also explore the application of various mechanisms to different public goods projects or even stages within the same project. Such an exploration would not only deepen theoretical understanding but also provide practical insights.

(3) The supply of public goods in China has long been dominated by government planning and fiscal investment. In times of shortages, a low-level supply–demand balance was maintained through household registration restrictions and reduced welfare levels. Today, the situation has significantly improved, with laws and regulations involving governments, enterprises, social organizations, and individuals in the supply of public goods across various fields. However, the use of market mechanisms and government-society cooperation is still in its early stages. Many marketized or socialized public goods projects focus mainly on financing or shifting government responsibilities. In some areas, such as education and healthcare, the boundaries between private and social interests are unclear, and supervision mechanisms are underdeveloped. For certain quasi-public goods, such as urban infrastructure, the government continues to invest,

build, and operate in an administrative manner, resulting in inefficiencies. Therefore, through empirical studies of public goods in various urban sectors, we can objectively assess the effectiveness of existing supply mechanisms and their problems, systematically design effective public goods supply mechanisms, and promote the formulation and implementation of regulations related to the legal, economic, technical, and market aspects of public goods supply.

(4) Since the 1970s, advances in information and communication technologies, including blockchain, big data, and cloud computing, have fundamentally transformed the way data are collected, transmitted, stored, and processed, reshaping government functions, facilitating the evolution of urban social governance and public goods supply. In particular, new technologies and big data offer richer and more accurate information to inform decision-making, allowing public services to become more precise, personalized, and equitable for urban residents. As networked societies continue to develop, cities face rising levels of volatility, complexity, and ambiguity, posing significant challenges to urban security and governance. Traditional management methods, such as administrative regulation and experience-based methods, are no longer adequate for the dynamic realities of city life. Therefore, new questions arise about how to systematically apply new technologies like the internet and big data to the public goods sector, and what changes these technologies may bring to public goods supply mechanisms, which open new avenues in public economic research, offering opportunities to construct theoretical frameworks and develop new models for public good supply in the digital era.

1.3 Contents

The book delves into the supply mechanisms of public goods, providing an in-depth review of public goods supply theories, with a particular focus on empirical research on the supply mechanisms of urban public goods in China. Through a comparative analysis of foreign cities, it systematically examines the changes in the supply level and structure of public goods in Chinese cities, as well as the development of public goods supply systems and mechanisms. It also observes how the government-led supply mechanisms have evolved during China's transition from a planned economy to one that fosters market-based mechanisms and multi-stakeholder cooperative supply mechanisms, revealing the characteristics of urban public goods supply in China and assessing the effectiveness of these mechanisms. The book also emphasizes urban public infrastructure and public services, analyzing the supply mechanisms for these two areas. It views urban public policy as a distinctive form of public goods, assessing its role as an external factor affecting the supply of urban public goods.

The contents of this book are as follows:

In this chapter outlines the research background and questions, presents the research theme, discusses the significance of the research from both theoretical and practical perspectives, sketches the research content and framework, and summarizes the main viewpoints.

Chapter 2 analyzes the historical trends in urban public goods supply in China since the founding of the People's Republic of China in 1949. It reviews the reforms in public goods supply systems and mechanisms, identifies the existing problem, and explores possible paths for reform.

Chapter 3 offers a theoretical analysis of urban public goods supply mechanisms and, combined with the actual situation of urban public goods supply in China, conducts empirical research. This chapter focuses on analyzing the factors influencing supply mechanisms and empirically evaluates government, market (private), and multi-stakeholder cooperative supply mechanisms within the Chinese context. Finally, it proposes a performance evaluation system for these supply mechanisms.

Chapter 4 addresses the financing mechanisms for urban public goods. It reviews the evolution of China's financing mechanisms, calculates the investment levels, and analyzes the investment structure of public goods. It also examines government fiscal investment mechanisms, market financing mechanisms, and public–private partnership (PPP) financing mechanisms. Additionally, using the rrr model (Government-Market-Society) as a case study to analyze its functions, implementation conditions, and legal regulations, discussing the development potential of multi-stakeholder cooperative supply mechanisms and their significance for the adequate supply of public goods.

Chapter 5 analyzes the current development status, category structure, and essential characteristics of urban public infrastructure. It empirically investigates the factors influencing urban infrastructure construction in China. The chapter also conducts empirical research on the factors influencing urban infrastructure construction, discusses the financing and operational mechanisms for urban infrastructure in China, analyzes the performance of government, market (private), and multi-stakeholder cooperative operational mechanisms, and proposes reform ideas and policy recommendations.

Chapter 6 focuses on urban public services, discussing the connotation, attributes, and characteristics of urban public services, analyzing the system of urban public services and the development status of urban public services in China. It examines government, market (private), and multi-stakeholder cooperative supply mechanisms for urban public services. Empirically analyzing the performance of these mechanisms and offering policy recommendations for reforming urban public service supply mechanisms.

Chapter 7 focuses on public policies related to the supply of urban public goods. It systematically reviews public policy theories, analyzes the key factors influencing public goods supply policies, and examines the characteristics and decision-making mechanisms of China's public goods supply policies. The chapter identifies the challenges in policy formulation and implementation, with a focus on public education, health, and social security policies. It assesses the impact of public policies on service supply and views public policies as a unique category of public goods. From a broad public policy perspective, the chapter discusses the choices and decision-making mechanisms shaping public policies for the supply of urban public goods in China.

1.4 Conclusions and Perspectives

The book aims to offer new insights and empirical analysis of the supply of urban public goods, with a selective summary of existing theoretical research and empirical analysis on public goods supply systems and public economic activities in Chinese cities. The following is the introduction of some of the key viewpoints.

1.4.1 Understanding of the Concept of Public Goods

Through a review of the evolution of public goods supply theory, this book analyzes the characteristics of non-rivalry, non-excludability, and externalities of public goods. We found that different disciplines have extended the meaning and scope of public goods based on these fundamental characteristics, offering different definitions. However, as public goods and services diversify, the core meaning of public goods seems increasingly ambiguous. This ambiguity manifests in the uncertainty of the scope of public goods supply, where some goods benefit society as a whole, while others are limited to collective or group settings. Certain public goods can even change their traditional supply scope through institutional arrangements, potentially expanding or restricting their target recipients and thereby modifying their public nature. Moreover, traditional public goods can be broken down into sub-projects through property rights systems, financial systems, or technical means. These sub-projects often take on strong private product attributes, though maintaining their public or social benefit overall. A more prominent phenomenon is the emergence of platform-based or co-creative economic activities under technological revolutions. Although inherently private, these activities exhibit strong public functions. Given these increasingly complex economic activities and the mix of public and private functions in product supply, we believe that the essence of public goods is no longer determined by who supplies them or whether they possess obvious non-excludability or non-rivalry. Instead, it depends on whether they have significant social and public functions. In other words, whether a public good is paid for or supplied in limited quantities, its fundamental nature is determined by its function, impact, and societal role. Thus, the determining characteristic of a good's public or private nature is its social and public utility.

1.4.2 Socioeconomic Contributions of the Public Goods Sector

The significance of public goods supply to socioeconomic development is undeniable. However, considering the scarcity of socioeconomic resources and the economic benefits and welfare effects of public and private goods, scholars have different views on the relationship between public goods supply and economic development. By analyzing relevant research, we find that these differing viewpoints stem primarily from the perspectives and evaluation criteria used in the studies. Generally, we consider the economic efficiency of the public goods sector to be relatively low, particularly under state-owned systems where production efficiency tends to be poor. However, when examining the contribution of public goods to investment-driven growth and GDP, the empirical analysis in this book demonstrates that the public goods sector contributes to the economic growth of the cities in eastern, central, and western China. In particular, public infrastructure construction has provided foundational support for improving the productivity of the manufacturing and service industries. Through heterogeneity analysis, we found that the growth effects of public goods vary across cities with different levels of economic development. Eastern cities, with relatively higher levels of economic development and well-established public infrastructure and services, have accumulated a large stock of public capital. Therefore, the potential to stimulate economic growth solely by increasing public sector funding is weakening. In contrast, the central and western cities, with lower levels of economic development and lagging infrastructure and services, exhibit higher output efficiency and elasticity from public capital investment compared to eastern cities. Thus, the contribution of public goods supply to economic growth in these regions is relatively higher, and increasing public sector investment is conducive to economic growth. However, it should be noted that this analysis is limited to the relationship between public goods investment and GDP growth, does not account for the output efficiency of individual public goods investments, and does not carefully analyze how public goods supply improves per capita social welfare.

This quantitative analysis reflects the policy effects of China's balanced regional development strategy. Over the past 20 years, with the implementation of the Western Development, Central China Rise, and Northeast Revitalization strategies, the central government has mobilized substantial construction funds through fiscal transfer payments, land-use indicator trading, and special bonds for public infrastructure construction. This has led to rapid public infrastructure development in the central and western regions, significantly narrowing the gap between these regions and the economically developed eastern areas. Likewise, the nationwide provision of public services, such as public health, education, and social security, has greatly improved the balance of public goods supply across regions. These fiscal and public goods supply mechanisms have significantly reduced regional disparities in public goods provision in China.

Another heterogeneous quantitative analysis from this book shows the varying impacts of economic and social public goods on economic growth. Empirical results from both national and regional cities indicate that economic public goods have a significantly positive impact on economic growth, particularly in central and western cities rather than in eastern cities. This positive effect is attributed to two main factors: (a) Economic public goods generate public capital investment, thereby promoting economic growth; (b) Economic public goods, such as urban infrastructure (transportation, energy, communication networks), benefit from economies of scale and network effects, producing spillover benefits for economic growth. Our analysis confirms that the supply of economic public goods in China positively and significantly affects total factor productivity.

Conversely, our analysis shows a negative relationship between social public goods and economic growth in national, eastern, and central-western cities. This suggests that, at China's current stage of economic development, social public goods expenditures may crowd out investments in private and economic public goods, thus negatively impacting GDP-based growth. Moreover, it highlights the difficulty of accurately measuring the effects of public goods supply on immediate and long-term resource allocation efficiency. Further analysis reveals that social public goods positively affect total factor productivity, but the effect is not statistically significant. Model predictions suggest a U-shaped relationship between the proportion of social public goods expenditures and economic growth. As development progresses, increasing the supply of social public goods, such as education, healthcare, and social security, can reduce precautionary savings and boost consumption, fostering technological innovation and high-quality economic growth.

Evaluating the social benefits of public goods remains a long-standing challenge. Based on the above analysis, we can roughly determine the contribution of public goods, particularly economic public goods, to economic growth. However, given resource scarcity, public and private goods investments are substitutes, offering different utilities to consumers. Thus, determining the overall contribution of public goods to national economic development is a key challenge, puzzling researchers and policymakers. Although an ideal analytical model is lacking, the book highlights several factors to consider: (1) The issue of present investments and future construction costs in public goods projects. From rough calculations, we find that starting infrastructure construction earlier can lead to lower overall costs and higher long-term returns; (2) The scale effect of public infrastructure and services, which suggests that completing projects in a short period can lower operating costs and achieve cost–benefit balance; (3) The social welfare effects of public goods supply. Recent investments in transportation and communication systems in China have improved social convenience and environmental welfare. However, it is difficult to fully capture these welfare effects in economic growth models. Therefore, public perception and recognition of public sector development, as well as improvements in social welfare, are important variables in evaluating public goods' impact.

1.4.3 Evolution and Decision-Making Mechanisms in Public Goods Provision

Economic reforms in China have been crucial in achieving remarkable economic milestones, with studies highlighting the private sector's significant post-reform growth due to a comprehensive market mechanism. Similarly, the public goods supply mechanism is experiencing a paradigm shift from government provision to market-driven and multi-stakeholder collaborative supply models. Furthermore, a consensus remains elusive within academia and the political sphere concerning reforming public goods provision mechanisms. Theoretical ambiguities require clarification, and a rigorous assessment of the efficacy of various mechanisms in practice is imperative.

1.4.3.1 Trends in the Evolution of Public Goods Supply Mechanisms

Analyzing public goods reform in various countries reveals a primary focus on transforming supply mechanisms. There is a notable shift from a government-centric approach to a more market-oriented one. While some countries emphasize privatization and market-oriented supply, others continue to depend heavily on government investment. These countries encourage social capital participation in the construction and operation of public goods projects, thus adopting a collaborative model between government and social capital. Most nations invite social organizations and third parties to aid in public service delivery. Although this approach has shown limited success in addressing funding shortages, it effectively promotes the selection and realization of social benefits in public service projects. As economies evolve and the lines between public and private goods blur, there is a growing diversification in the mechanisms employed for public goods provision, with market-driven approaches gaining around.

In China, attempts have been made to adopt market-oriented mechanisms under private property regimes in some public goods sectors. However, various constraints limit these efforts from becoming the dominant supply method due to the relatively minor role of private and social organizations in the national economy. Their limited participation hampers the necessary market forces for these mechanisms. Additionally, China's developing country status and unique challenges require significant government intervention in establishing an economic system for public goods. The prevailing system constraints and the long-standing dominance of the government create a path dependency that resists the incorporation of private and social capital.

From a reform perspective, China's current approach favors promoting market-oriented mechanisms while maintaining some governmental control. One prevalent method is the development of public infrastructure through government and social capital cooperation (PPP models). Nevertheless, many local initiatives primarily address funding issues rather than reforming supply mechanisms or enhancing project efficiency. Some projects have shifted too far towards commercial interests, straying from the public-focused goals of such initiatives. Despite increased government oversight of PPP projects, challenges remain. As the reform of public goods sectors in China progresses, adopting a multi-stakeholder cooperative model appears inevitable, as international practices indicate. There is a pressing need for China to develop robust legal frameworks and regulations to govern public goods sectors and to standardize the behaviors of all entities involved in government-social capital cooperation.

It is generally accepted among academics that the future design of supply mechanisms should vary according to the category of public goods. For essential services such as national security, foundational research, and environmental protection, the government should remain the leading supplier, depending on national economic capabilities and strategic priorities. Conversely, there is significant debate regarding the appropriate supply mechanisms for quasi-public goods such as health care, education, and transportation. The impact of these services on societal welfare, human development, and social stability is profound, particularly in sectors like education, health care, and public housing. Despite over 30 years of reform efforts since the 1990s, challenges continue to mount. Currently, China employs a dual-track system that combines government-provided public services with private and social capital contributions. However, maintaining dual mechanisms in the same market often leads to conflicts and competition, posing significant regulatory challenges in reforming the provision mechanisms for these quasi-public goods.

1.4.3.2 Decision-Making Mechanisms in Public Goods Supply

In the provision of public goods, decisions regarding the planning, investment, and production of specific goods and services are critical in shaping the structure of the public sector and the societal benefits it delivers. In China, regardless of whether public goods are supplied through government, market (private), or hybrid mechanisms involving multiple actors, the government invariably plays a pivotal role, especially in overarching planning and specific project decisions. Theoretically, in a democratically robust context, the government should act as a representative of public interest, guiding supply planning and setting project objectives and functional requirements. However, in practice, establishing and developing urban public goods projects in China are frequently subject to political and economic influences. A critical issue in these decision-making processes is that China's mechanism has yet to evolve from an empirical approach to a modern, scientifically grounded approach. Currently, public decision-making tends to be insular, with limited engagement from relevant stakeholders. Therefore, China urgently needs to adopt advanced modern public decision-making theories, techniques, and methods, transitioning from reliance on departmental experiences to evidence-based approaches. This includes overhauling the operational mechanisms of the public sector and moving away from using administrative directives as the primary tool for public goods provision. Establishing a scientific, transparent decision-making mechanism for public goods, led by the government and reflecting public needs and desires, is particularly critical. International experiences suggest that extensive public consultation in public goods projects' planning, decision-making, approval, construction monitoring, and acceptance phases is beneficial. Including a wide range of social representatives, project beneficiaries, and community members in these processes significantly enhances the impact and effectiveness of public goods projects.

1.4.4 Funding of the Public Goods Sector and Sustainable Development

1.4.4.1 Challenges in Funding the Public Goods Sector

Acknowledging the critical role of public infrastructure and services is essential for societal development. Under principles of social equity, continuous public goods provision through institutional arrangements is necessary to enhance social welfare. Comparative studies on the public goods sector in economically advanced countries reveal several challenges that emerge as the sector develops: significant financial pressures on governments, especially in those predominantly responsible for public goods provision, lead to severe fiscal crises that are difficult for many countries to manage; governmental administrative structures may hinder market competition in the public goods sector, leading to inefficiencies and higher costs; and rising government spending on public goods indirectly results in high tax rates, diminishing business competitiveness and personal welfare levels, often precipitating changes in government due to tax burdens. Addressing these funding and financial challenges is imperative for the sustainable development of the public goods sector. Since the late 1970s, many countries have reformed their public goods sector by adopting market-based supply mechanisms, primarily driven by funding pressures. This is a cautionary example for the development of China's public goods sector; for its sustainable advancement, it is crucial for China to carefully resolve the funding issues related to new projects and the ongoing financial needs of its existing public goods infrastructure.

1.4.4.2 Solving the Public Sector Funding Dilemma Through Supply Mechanism Reform

Despite the pronounced financial challenges within China's public sector, some scholars argue that the era of massive investments in public goods might soon conclude due to shifts in the economic growth environment. They anticipate a slowdown in public infrastructure project investments and a significant reduction in investment scales, which will gradually alleviate the substantial fiscal liabilities previously incurred by the government. However, this book presents a different perspective. By examining the public goods sectors in advanced economies and approximating existing assets' initial estimates, it is asserted that the government's fiscal pressure may not ease quickly, even with reduced investment sizes. The inefficient governmental expenditures on public services and the extensive responsibilities of infrastructure operation, maintenance, and upgrades continue to place significant burdens on public spending. Consequently, finding effective management mechanisms for the expansive public sector remains a critical challenge for the nation's future economic development. Drawing on international practices, although a few countries have experienced relieved fiscal pressures later in their public sector development through private sector growth and increased tax revenues, most have navigated financial crises via systemic reforms. Therefore, the resolution to the public sector's funding issues relies on continuous progress in systemic reform. By leveraging modern technology and the conditions of financial markets, reforms in property rights systems and institutional mechanisms within the public sector should be implemented. Encouraging participation from enterprises and social organizations in managing public sector projects, implementing early reforms in state-owned enterprises, and partially transferring infrastructure property rights to private and social capital are essential steps to reduce government fiscal pressures and improve the efficiency and quality of public goods provision.

1.4.4.3 Fostering Diverse Mechanisms for Public Sector Investment and Financing

Since the reform and opening up, China has witnessed a consistent rise in urban public infrastructure investments. Significant investments have also flowed in non-economic public goods sectors such as education, healthcare, and social security, positively impacting residential welfare and social stability. Recent empirical studies highlight that alongside the rapid expansion of investment scales in urban public goods, the mechanisms for investment and financing have also noticeably transformed. Initially fully financed by government funds at the start of the reform era, the investment landscape has progressively transformed into a complex mechanism that includes fiscal government investment, land finance, private and social capital investment mechanisms, and public–private partnerships (PPPs).

The transformation of public goods investment mechanisms has been partially driven by fiscal system reforms. Before the reform and opening up, central finance funded economic and social development projects, including those in the urban public goods sector. After implementing the tax-sharing system in the 1990s, both central and local governments assumed varied economic and social development responsibilities. Local governments became responsible for funding basic urban public infrastructure and public services, including education, health, and social security, alongside national infrastructure. This responsibility shift has made it challenging for local governments to balance fiscal revenues and expenditures, leading to severe budgetary imbalances. Furthermore, to achieve higher regional economic growth targets, local governments needed substantial infrastructure investments to enhance the investment and production environment, at times leveraging public infrastructure investment as a growth catalyst. This dynamic between central and local fiscal systems and the investment motivation led to a proactive investment drive among local governments, resulting in various government debts exceeding repayment capabilities. In economically developed regions, land revenue outpaced general financial tax revenue, while economically underdeveloped areas have long depended on fiscal transfers from the central government. This complex fiscal relationship between central and local governments, alongside the challenging debt pressures faced by local governments, necessitated reforms in public goods investment and financing.

Consequently, China began moving towards a market-oriented reform in its public goods investment system.

Despite these changes, the debt issue remains unresolved, and a sustainable and efficient investment and financing mechanism for urban public goods remains unestablished. Thus, accelerating reforms is essential, adjusting the fiscal relationship between central and local governments, optimizing central fiscal transfer payment methods, engaging the financial market as a platform under weakened land finance and financial capabilities, extensively incorporating social capital, and improving the public goods investment and financing structure. Strengthening fiscal budget constraints, advancing local government investment management system reforms, implementing fiscal budget performance management, and ensuring a comprehensive budget supervision system that integrates internal and external oversight are essential steps forward.

1.4.4.4 Addressing Internal Economic Circularity in Public Goods Sectors

The public goods sectors face significant financial challenges, as previously mentioned. From the perspective of the relationship between economic growth and resident welfare, it is crucial to address the difficulty in enhancing welfare through extensive public infrastructure investments aimed at sustaining growth. This is particularly challenging when there is an imbalance in the supply–demand structure and a lack of effective operational mechanisms. Often, the economic benefits from numerous infrastructure projects do not adequately reach residents but instead create an internal economic cycle within these sectors, which can crowd out private sector opportunities. This scenario was especially apparent during China's planned economy period, where state investments in heavy industry led to a closed loop of investment, production, and consumption within these sectors, failing to benefit household economies or enhance welfare. Relying solely on heavy public infrastructure investments for economic growth may perpetuate these cyclical inefficiencies. Therefore, effectively resolving these issues must be a priority in the future development of China's public goods sectors.

1.4.5 Operational Efficiency and Mechanisms in Public Goods Sectors

As investment in public goods projects has grown, China's public goods sectors have accumulated significant assets. The effective allocation of these assets, enhancement of operational efficiency, and fulfillment of public goods functions are pressing issues that have yet to receive adequate attention from the government or society. Urban public goods sectors are predominantly managed by state-owned enterprises and public institutions, resulting in inefficiencies and high operational costs. Many public service-oriented enterprises operate at a loss, relying on government subsidies. The fees for public services are rising, burdening ordinary citizens. Additionally, government dominance in managing public infrastructure and services hinders the entry of private and social capital. Even when policies permit participation due to subsidies, market monopolies, and price distortions by state-run units. Recent large-scale urban public infrastructure projects have increased population aggregation, enhanced transportation and information capabilities, and introduced significant safety risks and frequent major accidents. While cities construct modern facilities, they often lack modern operational capabilities, especially in comprehensive safety management in large urban areas. Governments have emergency plans, but administrative departments typically operate in silos without effective coordination for information sharing or unified action. In public goods supply, services are intimately connected to user demands. Service delivery often enhances service levels directly dependent on service providers' responsiveness, professionalism, and attitude. Under the current administrative system, most public services in China are provided by governmental institutions or state-owned enterprises, often resulting in poor service quality and a bureaucratic approach to management.

Consequently, the primary focus of future development in China's urban public goods sectors should be establishing effective operational methods for public goods projects. Drawing on profitable insights from international public goods sector reforms, most infrastructure and public service projects in this sector should adopt market-oriented operational mechanisms. This includes operating privately funded, government and social capital cooperation projects in a market-oriented manner, as well as those invested in by the government and state-owned enterprises, utilizing tactics such as government subsidies, outsourcing services, and service purchases. Over the past two decades, China's urban public infrastructure and public service sectors have undergone reforms in marketization mechanisms, incorporating enterprises and social organizations through government service purchases and commissioned operations. These methods have significantly advanced the market-oriented supply of public goods.

This book's research proposes three key reforms to improve the functioning and service quality of China's urban public goods. Firstly, overhauling the existing administrative management system is essential. This would involve eliminating the operational privileges and market monopolies held by administrative departments, state-owned enterprises, and public institutions to foster a competitive environment. For projects unsuitable for market-oriented operations, implementing an internal competition mechanism through a scientific performance evaluation system is necessary. Secondly, the property rights system for public infrastructure projects should be updated according to the specific conditions. After project completion, private and social capital can be introduced through mechanisms like build-operate-transfer (BOT). Thirdly, a legal framework must be established for managing and operating urban public goods, providing clear regulation for the behavior of commissioners and operators. Lastly, the level of public infrastructure operation and service quality relies heavily on the expertise of the operators. Government public sectors should incorporate market mechanisms into human resource management to revise knowledge structures, appointment methods, and evaluation criteria, enhancing professionalism and service awareness.

These points stem from the research in this book and address primary concerns. The related themes will be further explored in subsequent chapters. In recent years, scholars have devoted considerable attention to the mechanisms behind public goods supply, leading to many innovative findings. Nevertheless, not all research is comprehensively incorporated. Further explorations on China's public goods supply are expected to expand across disciplines as theoretical research seeks to address practical challenges in economic and societal development. For instance, optimizing the allocation of public goods resources in urban–rural integration, ensuring the systemic operation of urban public infrastructure, and addressing major safety issues in large cities, all demand interdisciplinary studies. Moreover, given China's unique economic development path and institutional framework, it is essential to construct a theoretical framework for public goods supply that aligns with Chinese characteristics. this framework, grounded in modern public goods theory and China's realities, should clarify the relationships between government, enterprises, and social organizations in the public goods sector. It should also elucidate the intrinsic mechanisms by which the market can play a decisive role under government governance. This approach will ensure the effective supply of public goods, improve social welfare and support a scientific and equitable path toward shared prosperity.

Reference

Barro, R. J. (1991). Economic growth in a cross section of countries. *The Quarterly Journal of Economics, 106*(2), 407–443.

Chapter 2
Evolution of Urban Public Goods Provision Mechanisms

2.1 Introduction

Since the founding of the People's Republic of China in 1949, the economic and institutional mechanisms of Chinese cities have undergone significant transformations, leading to substantial changes in the systems and mechanisms for providing urban public goods. During the planned economy period, the government, public institutions, and state-owned enterprises primarily managed the provision of urban public goods, which was characterized by a highly administrative approach. However, since the economic reform and opening up in 1978, and with the gradual establishment of the socialist market economy system, the main entities involved in urban public goods supply have diversified. Social organizations and private enterprises have increasingly participated in this system, which remains government-led but is now market-oriented. This chapter traces the historical development of China's urban public goods supply system, focusing on the shift from a government-dominated to a market-oriented approach. It provides a comprehensive analysis of the evolution of government, market, and multi-stakeholder collaborative supply mechanisms in this process. Considering the close link between the reforms of the urban public goods supply system and fiscal reforms, this chapter also explores the evolution of the public fiscal system.

2.2 Reviews on Urban Public Goods Supply

Urban public goods are locally provided public products within urban spaces and have a significant impact on modern urban economies. As socioeconomic conditions and technology advance, the nature and scope of urban public goods are constantly changing. To analyze the historical context of urban public goods supply in China,

B. Wu et al., *Effective Supply Mechanism of Urban Public Goods*, Public Economy and Urban Governance in China, https://doi.org/10.1007/978-981-96-2608-3_2

it is essential to comprehend the shifts in the definition and scope of public goods and to utilize consistent metrics for assessment.

This book proposes several perspectives for measuring changes in public goods supply: first, through government fiscal expenditures on public goods sectors, such as public health and medical expenses within the budgets of central and local governments; second, by using the intermediate outputs from public expenditure, such as the number of hospital beds per thousand people or the quantity of medical staff; third, by assessing the public services received by consumers and the related benefits, using indicators like life expectancy to measure public health levels. However, this approach represents a broad measurement method (Jia & Lu, 2010; Shu, 2010). For historical comparative analysis, this book adopts the first method, utilizing fiscal expenditure indicators of public goods sectors to track changes in public goods supply over time.

Chinese cities have a long history and distinctive attributes, which traditionally served as political and military power centers. Therefore, the infrastructure construction, production, life supplies, and city service supply have been shaped by government fiscal policies. In modern times, except for a few port cities like Shanghai and Qingdao, where industry and commerce took root, government influence remained significant in shaping public facilities and services, even in cities with modern industries.

After the founding of the People's Republic of China, urban economies focused primarily on industrial system construction under the planned economy system, with limited fiscal funds invested in the private goods sectors and minimal investment in public goods sectors. Non-economic public goods were provided through administrative planning mechanisms. Still, due to low supply levels and limited projects, even urban areas prioritized for these resources experienced a severe shortage of public goods, falling short of residents' actual needs. After the economic reforms, the urban economic system underwent transformative changes. Resources in cities began to be allocated through market mechanisms, while cities continued to maintain a leading role in driving national economic development. With the rise of special economic zones and urbanization, urban economies rapidly expanded, serving as the engines of growth. This expansion also spurred rapid growth in the public goods sectors, especially those supporting industrial development, such as infrastructure. In terms of public goods supply mechanisms, the abandonment of the planned economy system paved the way for new mechanisms, encompassing government-led, market-driven, and multi-stakeholder collaborative approaches to public goods supply.

2.2.1 Urban Public Goods Supply During the Planned Economy Period in China (1949–1978)

After the founding of the People's Republic of China and an initial period of political consolidation and economic recovery, the country completed its transition to a socialist planned economy from 1953 to the end of 1956. During this planned economy period, the central government directed economic resources through administrative planning, centralized funding, and mandates controlled production, distribution, consumption, and investment. National fiscal revenue and expenditure consistently accounted for around one-third of GDP. Government fiscal expenditure rose from 6.805 billion yuan in 1950 to 112.209 billion yuan in 1978, with an average annual growth rate of 10.52% (see Fig. 2.1).

Despite the rapid increase in government fiscal expenditures, the public goods supply in urban areas remained limited. This was due to the government's control over the decision-making, funding, production, and distribution of public goods, as well as its direct planning of private goods supply (Gou, 2016). The priority given to heavy industry relegated urban public goods to secondary importance, making significant improvements difficult (Wang et al., 2009). As shown in Table 2.1, from the first to the fourth Five-Year Plans, the investment in public infrastructure and social services sectors remained a small share of the national economy. For instance, industrial investment accounted on average for 55.28% of total societal investments, peaking at 61.40% during the second Five-Year Plan, while the highest proportion of investments in sectors such as scientific research, education, health, social welfare, and municipal utilities did not exceed 10.70%, and it dropped below 5% during the third Five-Year Plan, and when including transport and telecommunications investments, it weighted up to 27.10% during the first Five-Year Plan. Considering the political and economic environment at that time, if excluding railway investment, those three

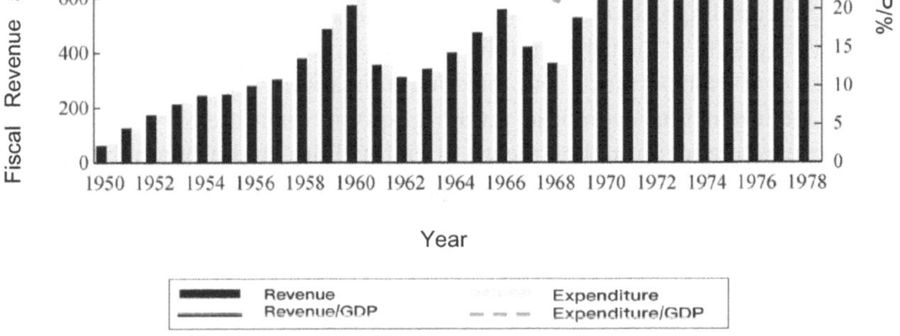

Fig. 2.1 National fiscal revenue and expenditure and their proportion of GDP (1950–1978) (*Data Source China Statistical Yearbook*)

investments peaked at 16.30%, and declined to a low of 7% by the third Five-Year Plan.[1]

Several characteristics emerge from the shifts in the structure of government fiscal expenditure:

(1) Economic Construction: During the planned economy period, economic construction expenditures accounted for the highest share and showed an increasing trend, even exceeding 70% between 1958 and 1960. This indicates the highly centralized nature of the planned economy, where the government-controlled resource allocation and prioritized rapid industrialization in fiscal spending.
(2) Social Education: Expenditure on social education remained relatively stable during this period, ranging from 10 to 18%, slightly above the level of low-income countries.
(3) Defense Spending: Defense spending was relatively high and fluctuated significantly, averaging up to 40% between 1950 and 1953, influenced by the international environment, which gave the budget a semi-wartime status. Subsequently, the share of defense spending in the budget significantly decreased, stabilizing at around 20% after 1961. Fourthly, administrative management spending remained stable and slightly declined, maintaining between 5 and 10% after 1953 (see Table 2.2).

When classifying public goods into economic and non-economic categories, infrastructural components, such as railways, highways, telecommunications, and power supply systems, are considered economic public goods. Conversely, education, healthcare, social security and employment, scientific research, culture, sports, media, and environmental protection fall under non-economic public goods. Despite their significant social impacts and externalities, non-economic public goods have typically been undersupplied over the long term.

During the planned economy period, the government allocated investments in economic and non-economic public goods across various sectors. Therefore, corresponding data can be derived from the primary investments of each economic sector and analyzed according to two categories: economic and non-economic public goods. Specifically, investment in urban public goods is measured by excluding railway investments from transportation and telecommunications expenditures. In contrast, investment in urban non-economic public goods is quantified by investments in scientific research, education, healthcare, social welfare, and urban public utilities.

As shown in Fig. 2.2, during the planned economy period, the proportions of investment in economic and non-economic public goods remained relatively stable, ranging from 5 to 10%. Specifically, regarding urban economic public goods, such as urban infrastructure, its share of total investment across all sectors remained around

[1] During the planned economy period, railway investments had a unique political and economic background, primarily serving the "Great Leap Forward" and "Third Front Construction" strategies. As a result, the role of railways as public goods, particularly as urban public goods, was diminished (Rong Xinchun, 2009). Consequently, this book excludes railway investments when analyzing the structure of public goods supply during the planned economy period.

Table 2.1 Basic construction investment in various sectors of the national economy (1953–1975)

Sector	First five-year plan period	Second five-year plan period	1963–1965	Third five-year plan period	Fourth five-year plan period
1. Total national investment/100 million yuan	549.98	1186.67	403.74	914.71	1680.37
Industry	250.26	728.30	210.18	541.51	977.97
Construction industry	21.54	16.30	8.91	17.38	28.57
Geological resources exploration	14.36	14.25	1.68	4.57	11.76
Agriculture, forestry, water conservancy, meteorology	41.83	135.71	74.46	104.27	173.08
Of which: water conservancy	25.51	94.45	42.35	69.52	119.31
Transport and communications	90.15	163.30	53.78	150.01	317.59
Of which: railways	59.16	104.16	33.95	112.50	173.08
Commerce, catering, services, and material supply	21.40	24.12	10.44	21.04	50.41
Scientific research, education, health, and social welfare	44.58	46.39	24.05	27.44	55.45
Urban public utilities	14.43	27.55	12.31	17.38	33.61
Others	51.43	30.75	7.93	31.11	31.93
2. Proportion(total national Investment = 100%)/%					
Industry	45.50	61.40	52.10	59.20	58.20
Construction industry	3.90	1.40	2.20	1.90	1.70
Geological resources exploration	2.60	1.20	0.40	0.50	0.70
Agriculture, forestry, water conservancy, meteorology	7.60	11.40	18.40	11.40	10.30

(continued)

Table 2.1 (continued)

Sector	First five-year plan period	Second five-year plan period	1963–1965	Third five-year plan period	Fourth five-year plan period
Of which: water conservancy	4.60	8.00	10.50	7.60	7.10
Transport and communications	16.40	13.80	13.30	16.40	18.90
Of which: railways	10.80	8.80	8.40	12.30	10.30
Commerce, catering, services, and material supply	3.90	2.00	2.60	2.30	3.00
Scientific research, education, health, and social welfare	8.10	3.90	6.00	3.00	3.30
Urban public utilities	2.60	2.30	3.00	1.90	2.00
Others	9.40	2.60	2.00	3.40	1.90

Data Source China Statistical Yearbook (1981)

5% until the third Five-Year Plan. Although there was a slight increase during the fourth Five-Year Plan, the proportion remained relatively low at 8.60%. This was largely due to the prioritization of heavy industry, which meant that urban infrastructure development was often relegated to a secondary status, resulting in long-term underdevelopment. Meanwhile, they became the primary investors in infrastructure, but their focus on cross-regional and significant projects led to a lack of diverse funding sources, ultimately causing a shortage of construction funds. Regarding urban non-economic public goods, the special political and economic climate during the third and fourth Five-Year Plans caused significant setbacks in the education, healthcare, and culture sectors. As a result, investment and development in these areas faced considerable challenges, keeping the proportion of investment in non-economic public goods around 5% of total economic investment.

Throughout the planned economy period, the government lowered living expenses and social security costs through controlled policies of low wages and low prices to ensure the smooth implementation of the priority development strategy for heavy industry. It also standardized salaries and living standards nationwide to reduce social security costs for state-owned enterprises and administrative institutions. Under this highly centralized financial system, the government budget focused on basic infrastructure, operating under a unit supply system based on unified government standards. This system was mainly managed by state-owned enterprises or institutions where urban workers were employed, leading to a simple, low-level, state-controlled public service system (Yu, 2011). For example, individual units primarily administered social security, with health and welfare expenses entirely covered by the employing entity. State-owned enterprises primarily funded these expenses from

Table 2.2 Structure of fiscal public expenditure by function unit: 100 million yuan

Year	Total expenditure	Economic construction expenditure	Social and cultural expenditure	National defense expenditure	Administrative management expenditure	Other expenditure
1950	68.05	17.36	7.55	28.01	13.13	2.00
1951	122.07	35.11	13.44	52.64	17.45	3.43
1952	172.07	73.23	21.11	57.84	15.49	4.40
1953	219.21	87.43	32.44	75.38	19.72	4.24
1954	244.11	123.58	34.61	58.13	21.62	6.17
1955	262.73	137.62	31.89	65.00	21.54	6.68
1956	298.52	159.14	45.96	61.17	26.60	5.65
1957	295.95	163.04	46.42	55.11	22.70	8.68
1958	400.36	278.86	43.54	50.00	22.72	5.24
1959	543.17	389.33	58.60	58.00	30.00	7.24
1960	643.68	460.71	86.95	58.00	31.39	6.63
1961	356.09	210.01	61.25	50.00	27.14	7.69
1962	294.88	152.64	51.73	56.94	21.91	11.66
1963	332.05	174.12	51.45	66.42	23.86	16.20
1964	393.79	209.99	66.09	72.86	26.22	18.63
1965	459.97	254.11	62.70	86.76	26.34	30.06
1966	537.65	309.43	67.06	101.01	26.59	33.56
1967	439.84	244.03	60.83	83.02	22.95	29.01
1968	357.84	166.03	47.88	94.09	22.91	26.93
1969	525.86	295.52	49.77	126.18	29.82	24.57
1970	649.41	392.61	52.22	145.26	32.00	27.32
1971	732.17	418.30	63.80	169.47	37.62	42.98
1972	765.86	431.96	75.31	159.39	38.93	60.27
1973	808.78	468.27	88.57	145.39	38.59	67.96
1974	790.25	460.93	95.02	133.39	39.76	61.15
1975	820.88	481.66	103.55	142.46	41.81	51.40
1976	806.20	466.22	120.06	134.45	43.38	42.09
1977	843.53	493.73	119.43	149.04	45.18	36.15
1978	1122.09	718.98	146.96	167.84	52.90	35.41

Data Source China Statistical Yearbook (2000)

production costs or employee welfare allocations, while administrative institutions, military units, and social organizations drew from their budgets. Many enterprises and administrative institutions also operated affiliated schools, hospitals, and libraries that served as collective welfare for employees. It is important to note that during this period, the investments and profits of state-owned enterprises and institutions

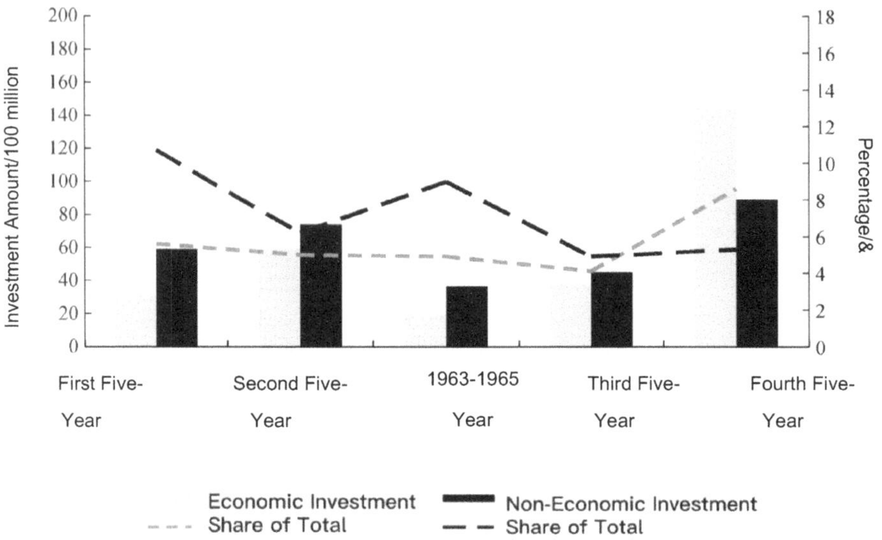

Fig. 2.2 Proportion of investments in economic and non-economic public products (1953–1975) (*Data Source* Calculated based on relevant data from *China Statistical Yearbook*)

were centrally allocated by the government, essentially making their social security expenditures part of government spending.

2.2.2 Urban Public Goods Supply After the Economic Reform and Opening up (1979 to Present)

During this period, cities utilized development zones as engines for development, investing significantly in public infrastructure to attract domestic and foreign capital for industrial production. Meanwhile, to create a conducive business environment for the development of the urban industrial economy and to provide basic living facilities for the influx of rural labor, the real estate industry emerged as a foundation for the rapid expansion of urban commerce and services. Correspondingly, the urban public goods sector also developed rapidly, achieving improvements in both "quality" and "quantity" (Wan & Wang, 2019). As shown in Fig. 2.3, in terms of the overall scale of public spending, national fiscal expenditure increased from 128.179 billion yuan in 1979 to 22,090.41 billion yuan in 2018, representing a 171.32-fold increase, with an average annual growth rate of 11.41%, overall higher than the GDP growth rate.

However, examining this progression in phases before the tax-sharing reform reveals that the fiscal responsibility system caused incentive distortions (Deng & Tang, 2011), leading to a yearly decline in the proportion of national fiscal revenue and expenditures to GDP. From 1979 to 1994, fiscal revenue as a percentage of GDP

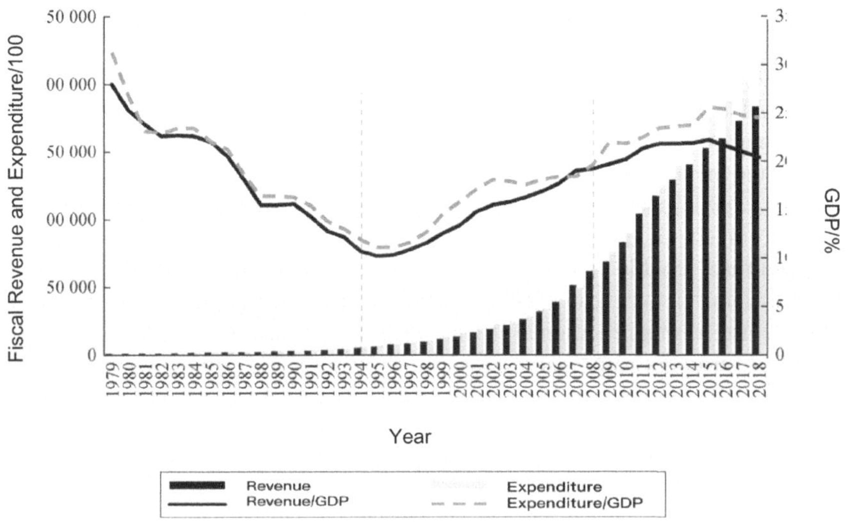

Fig. 2.3 Fiscal revenue and expenditure and their proportion of GDP (1979–2018) (*Data Source China Statistical Yearbook*)

fell from 28.22% to 10.83%, and fiscal expenditures as a percentage of GDP from 31.55% to 12.02%. Therefore, although there was some growth in urban public goods supply during this period, it lagged behind economic growth. After the tax-sharing reform, there was a significant enhancement in national fiscal capacity. From 1994 to 2018, fiscal revenue as a percentage of GDP rose from 10.83% to 20.36%, while fiscal expenditures rose from 12.02% to 24.54%. As a result, urban public goods saw considerable overall development, and differentiation in the supply structure began to emerge. In 2008, affected by the global financial crisis, the government implemented proactive fiscal policies, increasing the national fiscal deficit, with a fiscal gap exceeding 3.75 trillion yuan in 2018. Especially to stabilize the economy and maintain high economic growth rates, post-financial crisis China heavily invested in the construction of public infrastructure, with infrastructure construction scale continuously expanding, and investments in public infrastructure and public services by local governments being carried out on an extraordinary scale. Further analysis will be conducted in the subsequent below.

2.2.2.1 Urban Public Goods Supply During the Period of "More Fiscal Autonomy of Local Governments" (1979–1993)

During this period, the fiscal system broke away from the highly centralized fiscal authority, expanding local government fiscal autonomy. As shown in Fig. 2.4, from 1979 to 1993, local fiscal revenue increased from 91.504 billion yuan to 339.144 billion yuan, with an average annual growth rate of 9.81%; local fiscal expenditure also increased from 62.671 billion yuan to 333.034 billion yuan, with an average annual growth rate of 12.67%.

From 1979 to 1984, local fiscal revenue peaked at 80% of national fiscal revenue, averaging 70.65%; however, local fiscal expenditures accounted for less than 50% of national fiscal expenditures, averaging 46.71%. From 1985 to 1993, the share of local fiscal revenue in national fiscal revenue remained elevated, averaging 68.22%, while local fiscal expenditures rose sharply to an average of 66.14%. This period of fiscal system reform, characterized by "the central and local governments dividing revenue and expenditure", enabled local governments to establish autonomous fiscal regimes, severing the link between local fiscal authority and responsibilities. Although this fiscal system reform strengthened fiscal constraints, it also led to the factual localization of government responsibilities (Tsui & Wang, 2004). In the supply of urban public goods, local governments sought to gradually lessen their public affairs burden amid increasing fiscal and administrative powers. Although this alleviated the fiscal burden on local governments, it also required a rise in the supply of local public goods. During this period, as local government fiscal revenue primarily came from industrial enterprises, their revenue growth also depended on the development of enterprises, and personal income tax was not the main source of fiscal revenue for local governments (Zheng, 2010a, 2010b), thus local governments lacked incentives to provide non-economic public goods to the public. Demand for urban public services was also low during this period; despite limited social security for urban workers under a dual welfare system from the government and employers, basic welfare protections were available. Following the reform and opening up, the overall income level of urban workers has augmented. With the marketization of the economy, urban

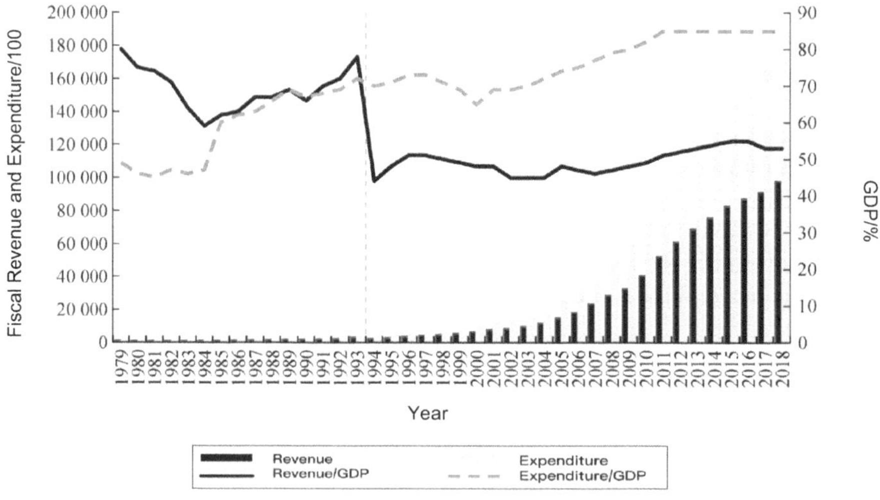

Fig. 2.4 Local fiscal revenue and expenditure and their proportion of national fiscal revenue and expenditure (1979–2018) (*Data Source China Statistical Yearbook*)

residents are increasingly concerned about employment opportunities and income enhancement, resulting in lower demands for the urban environment and essential public services. This political environment has facilitated urban development with an economic growth focus.

Taking medical insurance as an example, in the early 1980s, local governments began reforming the medical insurance system to ease fiscal burdens by linking public medical expenses to individual contributions. However, the socialization of medical insurance in China remained relatively low under this system (see Table 2.3).

As shown in Tables 2.4 and Figs. 2.5, the structure of public goods supply saw a decline in the proportion of capital construction expenditure within local fiscal spending, dropping from 29.84% in 1979 to 8.31% in 1993. A primary contributory factor was the trial of the "from grants to loans" policy for capital construction in 1979, which changed the non-repayable government budget grants for capital investments. Until 1991, local governments also faced restrictions on infrastructure investment and project decision-making, with central projects representing over 50% of overall investments (Wei, 2002; Zhang & Zhou, 2007). As to the expenditure on science, education, culture, and health, measures such as restoring the college entrance examination system in 1977 led to a noticeable increase in expenditure, stabilizing at around 26% of total fiscal expenditure. Initially, during the early reform and opening up period, foreign investment was relatively low, and government revenue depended mainly on state-owned enterprises, private enterprises, and township enterprises, with township enterprises becoming important sources of local tax revenue (Chen, 2010). Consequently, there was no investment surge in economic public goods such as infrastructure, which appeared only after the fiscal decentralization system was implemented.

2.2.2.2 Urban Public Goods Supply After Tax-Sharing System (1994 to Present)

The reform of the tax-sharing system implemented in 1994 shifted fiscal powers upwards while leaving administrative duties to local governments, creating challenges in meeting the rising demand for public goods. Local governments continued to favor economic over non-economic expenditures, resulting in a relative scarcity of non-economic public goods (Li & Zhang, 2017). This trend differed slightly before and after the 2008 global financial crisis.

As illustrated in Tables 2.5 and Fig. 2.6, prior to the crisis, the proportion of local government spending on economic construction as a measure of economic public goods expenditure continued to increase, from 146.645 billion yuan in 1994 to 912.836 billion yuan in 2006, with an annual growth rate of 16.46%. However, the proportion decreased from 36.31% in 1994 to 30.00% in 2006. The reduction was primarily due to the central government's measures aimed at preventing overheating of local economic investments, which required local governments to curtail their spending. Meanwhile, the supply of non-economic public goods lagged. The absolute amount of expenditure on science, education, culture, and health continued to

Table 2.3 1986 survey of urban residents' medical insurance

Medical insurance system	Large cities		Medium cities		Small cities		Total	
	Surveyed population	Proportion/%	Surveyed population	Proportion /%	Surveyed population	Proportion /%	Surveyed population	Proportion/%
Public medical care	9029	16.53	4956	15.53	1699	16.83	15,684	16.23
Labor protection medical care	26,367	48.28	14,206	44.51	3532	34.98	44,105	45.64
Partially Free medical care	13,445	24.62	7860	24.62	2065	20.45	23,370	24.15
Self-financed medical care	5775	10.57	4898	15.34	2801	27.74	13,474	13.94
Total	54,616	100.00	31,920	100.00	10,097	100.00	96,633	100.00

Data Source China Health Statistics Yearbook (1987)

Table 2.4 Major categories of local fiscal expenditure unit: 100 million yuan

Year	Total expenditure	Basic construction expenditure	Agricultural expenditure	Science, education, culture, and health expenditure	Administrative management expenditure
1979	629.05	187.73	85.13	116.46	51.77
1980	564.33	131.52	76.78	138.46	60.66
1981	516.42	83.86	68.39	150.12	65.18
1982	580.84	101.74	72.15	173.90	73.60
1983	654.36	115.27	69.40	196.53	87.14
1984	799.96	149.53	77.30	230.05	115.81
1985	1037.92	188.35	79.19	275.58	117.94
1986	1363.85	198.38	98.68	325.84	138.01
1987	1409.18	159.52	102.66	348.82	146.46
1988	1649.35	156.01	124.11	426.28	165.74
1989	1921.07	154.59	154.69	486.83	190.46
1990	2083.34	174.07	171.60	540.31	214.10
1991	2373.09	184.87	189.02	592.32	241.85
1992	2544.68	212.91	206.12	698.95	303.01
1993	3289.68	273.28	242.44	851.77	379.99

Data Source Compilation of Statistics for Fifty Years of New China

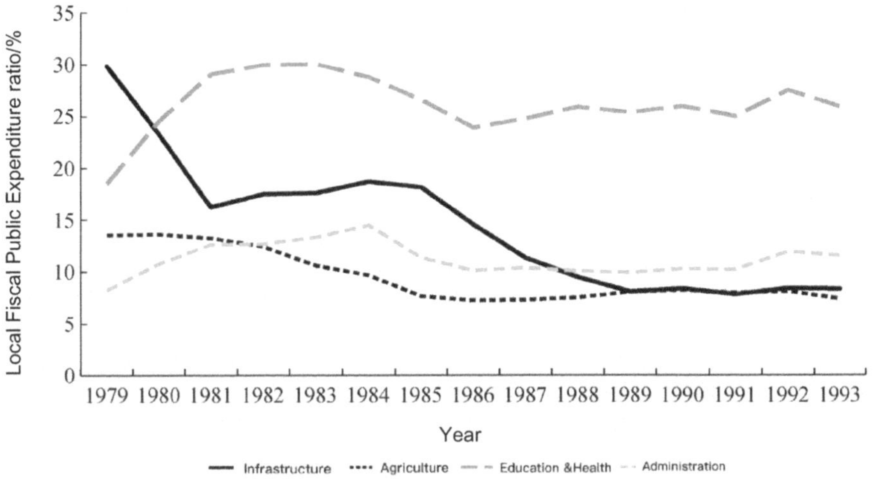

Fig. 2.5 Changes in the proportion of local fiscal public expenditure (1979 1993) (*Data Source Compilation of Statistics for Fifty Years of New China*)

increase from 116.748 billion yuan in 1994 to 706.777 billion yuan in 2006. Expenditure on science, education, culture, and health increased from 1,167.48 billion yuan in 1994 to 7,067.77 billion yuan in 2006, yet its annual growth rate of 16.19% was lower than that of economic construction, resulting in a considerable gap between the two until 2002. In 1994, expenditure on public services such as science, education, culture, and health was approximately 28.92%. But by 2006, it had diminished to 23.23%. Expenditure on social security remained below 5% for many years, but after 1998, it rose rapidly and stabilized at around 13%. This development was partly attributable to the central government's explicit goal in 1998 to establish a reform target for the public finance system, as well as the separate allocation of funds for retirement and social security subsidies for public institutions. Administrative expenses remained steady at around 16% during this time. In 1978, they were at 4.4%, rose to less than 10% by 1990, and reached 16.6% in 1994. This trend suggests that China's administrative management system reform has not kept pace with economic reforms.

During this period, local government fiscal expenditure showed a trend towards the provision of public services, yet economic development remained the primary function of local governments, with its expenditure still dominating. Under the economic decentralization and political centralization system, driven by the goal of economic growth and corresponding incentive mechanisms (Fu & Zhang, 2007; Qiao et al., 2005; Fu, 2010; Chen, 2010; Zhang, 2018), as well as the land finance model (Tang et al., 2016), local governments naturally adopted a concept of "prioritizing economic development over public services".

In 2007, reforms were implemented to fiscal revenue and expenditure items, especially in adjusting the statistical scope of fiscal expenditure items. To facilitate comparison with the analysis of the structure of public goods supply before the reform, the post-reform fiscal expenditure categories were adjusted accordingly compared to pre-reform categories. As shown in Table 2.6 and Fig. 2.7, especially from 2008 onwards, economic development expenditure entered a relatively high-speed growth phase, increasing from 842.387 billion yuan in 2007 to 7,727.876 billion yuan in 2018, with its proportion of public expenditure rising from 21.97% in 2007 to 41.06% in 2018. During this period, the average annual growth rate was 22.32%, with a slight decrease in proportion observed after 2017. Expenditure on science, education, culture, health, and social security expenditure began to slowly rise around 2012, while the proportion of administrative management expenditure demonstrated a clear downward trend.

Although there has been an increase in local economic and non-economic public goods supply, the driving factors differ between the two. Rapid growth in economic development expenditure is largely a response to the changing economic development environment following the 2008 global financial crisis. As the global financial crisis led to challenges, such as weak external demand, sluggish internal demand, and declining economic growth rates, the government implemented large-scale fiscal investment plans, spurring an increase in local fiscal expenditures, particularly in economic public goods such as infrastructure construction. In contrast, the increase

Table 2.5 Major public expenditure items of local finance (1992–2006) unit: 100 million yuan

Year	Total expenditure	Basic construction expenditure	Agricultural expenditure	Science, education, culture, and health expenditure	Administrative management expenditure
1994	4038.19	1466.45	1167.48	94.16	670.56
1995	4828.33	1772.38	1356.02	114.66	803.00
1996	5786.28	2143.04	1591.88	126.74	969.36
1997	6701.06	2426.11	1780.90	141.05	1060.63
1998	7672.58	2758.85	1985.83	570.55	1235.72
1999	9035.30	3214.82	2244.78	863.18	1410.33
2000	10,366.70	3512.08	2571.58	1129.47	1659.46
2001	13,134.60	4503.12	3143.41	1581.23	2054.92
2002	15,281.50	4912.49	3708.88	2037.28	2486.24
2003	17,229.90	5210.09	4187.95	2417.05	2898.18
2004	20,592.81	6368.01	4851.14	2817.04	3472.81
2005	25,154.31	7625.97	5803.88	3357.96	4195.64
2006	30,431.33	9128.16	7067.77	4005.57	4983.90

Data Source China Statistical Yearbook (2007)
Note The economic development expenditure mainly includes essential construction costs, agricultural support, funds for economically underdeveloped areas, urban maintenance fees, minimal construction expenses, geological exploration costs, land and sea development expenditures, enterprise transformation and upgrading funds, additional working capital for businesses, industry and commerce departmental expenses, vehicle purchase taxes, and policy subsidies. Scientific and technological expenses, aiming to support development in these areas, are often grouped with traditional livelihood expenditures, which include education, science, culture, and health. Retirement and social security expenditures for government agencies are now designated as separate budget items and may be combined with social welfare expenses into social security expenditures. Administrative management expenses encompass costs incurred by the state budget for administrative agencies, political parties, groups, and diplomatic affairs

in non-economic public goods supply reflects the shift in primary social priorities in the new era of socialism along with the strong public demand of residents. The notable decline in administrative management expenditure is closely tied to the comprehensive reform efforts proposed since the 18th National Congress of the Communist Party of China, including the strict implementation of "the Eight Rules", anti-corruption measures and the proposals set forth at the 19th National Congress to establish a service-oriented government that prioritizes public needs. Furthermore, reform measures promoting "streamlining administration and delegating powers, improving regulation, and upgrading services" (SAS) have made public services crucial assessment targets for local governments and key indicators of functional transformation.

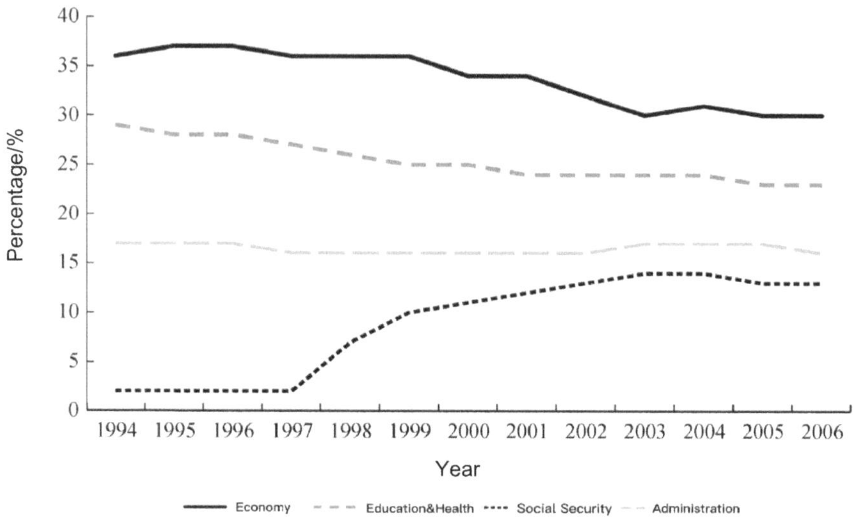

Fig. 2.6 Changes in major public expenditure items of local finance (1992–2006) (*Data Source China Statistical Yearbook*)

2.3 Urban Public Goods Supply System and Its Reform

The factors influencing the supply of urban public goods are manifold, and the supply system shapes the pattern and mechanisms of urban public goods provision. Influenced by the planned economic system, China's urban public goods supply system is characterized by a three-tiered supply system involving the central government, local governments, and institutional enterprises. At the core of this supply system is the funding for public goods, which has evolved over different periods in alignment with changes in the fiscal system. Moreover, in China's system for the supply and distribution of urban public goods, the "system of unit" has served a crucial supplemental or substitute role in the urban governments' supply of public goods. Given the fiscal system's direct impact on the public goods supply system, this section focuses on examining the changes in the fiscal system and their effects on the public goods supply system.

2.3.1 Public Goods Supply System Under the Centralized Financial System (1949–1978)

Before the reform and opening up, China predominantly operated a centralized planned fiscal system, characterized by unified leadership, delineated income and expenditure, and tiered management. During this time, two experiments in fiscal

Table 2.6 Major public expenditure items of local finance (2007–2018) Unit: 100 million yuan

Year	Total expenditure	Basic construction expenditure	Agricultural expenditure	Science, education, culture, and health expenditure	Administrative management expenditure
2007	38,339.29	8423.87	10,312.68	5104.53	6354.07
2008	49,248.49	11,989.26	13,235.83	6460.01	7451.37
2009	61,044.14	22,135.63	16,349.63	7851.85	8080.00
2010	73,884.43	29,760.48	19,541.13	8680.32	8499.74
2011	92,733.68	38,290.46	25,446.99	10,606.92	10,084.77
2012	107,188.30	43,147.16	31,628.45	11,999.85	11,702.14
2013	119,740.30	49,167.37	34,153.56	13,849.72	12,217.07
2014	129,215.50	54,052.20	37,220.92	15,268.94	12,492.49
2015	150,335.60	64,928.82	42,971.21	18,295.62	12,753.67
2016	160,351.40	68,264.17	46,485.66	20,700.87	13,581.37
2017	173,228.30	71,487.13	50,508.85	23,610.57	15,238.90
2018	188,196.30	77,278.76	54,314.25	25,827.54	16,871.01

Data Source China Statistical Yearbook (2009)
Note Expenditure on economic development encompasses urban and rural community affairs, agricultural and forestry water management, environmental protection, housing security, transportation, financial regulation, resource exploration, power, information, grain and oil reserves management, land and resources, meteorology, commercial services, and post-disaster reconstruction. Science, education, culture, and health expenditures pertain to technology, education, medical care, culture, and media. Social security expenditure covers only social security and employment. General public service expenditure primarily supports the operation of government institutions, the functioning of various government units, the project needs of different departments, and local implementation of voluntary retirement compensation for military personnel; this can be included in administrative management expenditure for consistency with analyses prior to 2007

decentralization were conducted: "fiscal decentralization" and "fiscal responsibility system". The first experiment occurred in 1958 with a fiscal reform that set expenditures based on revenues. As shown in Table 2.7, this reform led to a rapid decline in the central government's revenue share (from 80.41% in 1958 to 24.38% in 1959), a decrease of nearly 70%. Simultaneously, the expenditure share decreased by 37.62% within the same year (from 70.97% in 1957 to 44.27% in 1958). Conversely, the local government's revenue share increased by 2.86 times in the reform year (from 19.59% in 1958 to 75.62% in 1959), and the expenditure share increased by 0.92 times (from 29.03% in 1957 to 55.73% in 1958).

Figures 2.8 and 2.9 indicate that this fiscal reform experiment significantly enhanced the financial capabilities of local governments. The second decentralization experiment, starting in 1971, was the "all-round responsibility system", which continued the trend of increasing local fiscal revenue shares from the first attempt. This fiscal management reform allowed local governments to improve their fiscal funds through over-collection and savings, thereby stimulating their initiative.

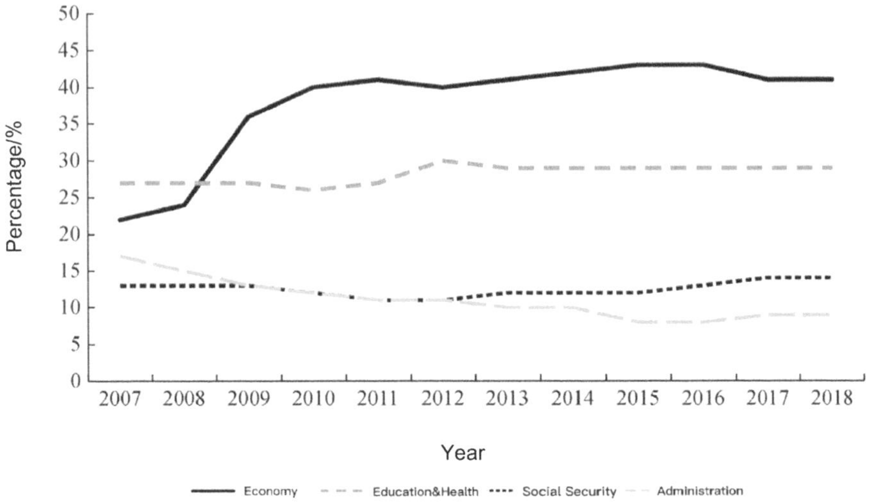

Fig. 2.7 Changes in major public expenditure items of local finance (2007–2018) (*Data Source China Statistical Yearbook*)

However, throughout the planned economy era, despite two brief periods of decentralization and several adjustments (as shown in Table 2.8), local fiscal powers remained limited. Whether through the "practice of five-year expenditure approval based on revenues" or the "revenue and expenditure contract system", the reform measures offered only restricted autonomy to local government, which often lacked depth and did not constitute a market-oriented fiscal decentralization model (Ding, 2008).

During the planned economy era, the central government markedly controlled the urban public goods supply system. However, constrained by the heavy industry development strategy, the central government often had an "absence" in the supply of non-productive public goods, typically provided by government-affiliated institutions. These institutions directly took on the role of raising funds and resources for public goods supply. This was determined by the scarcity of overall social resources and the limited capacity of the government to mobilize resources. Hindered by the political-economic system, China struggled to establish a public goods supply and tax system suited to a modern society. To reduce the burden of social public management, the government had to transfer the responsibility for providing public goods to institutional organizations, which took on the significant role of supplying public goods (Ye, 2003). Under the administrative planned system, social resources were controlled by the state and allocated to different institutions, which then distributed, possessed, and utilized these limited resources. Urban residents' livelihoods and social security were closely linked to these institutions, which provided various public goods at different levels and of different natures. The state used institutions as intermediaries to regulate social resources and achieve redistribution, making it a

Table 2.7 Proportion of central and local fiscal revenue and expenditure (1952–1978) unit: %

Year	Central		Local	
	Revenue proportion	Expenditure proportion	Revenue proportion	Expenditure proportion
1952	–	74.05	–	28.23
1953	83.01	73.92	16.99	26.08
1954	76.57	75.25	23.43	24.75
1955	77.60	76.52	22.40	23.48
1956	79.28	70.35	20.73	29.65
1957	73.53	70.97	26.47	29.03
1958	80.41	44.27	19.59	55.73
1959	24.38	45.90	75.62	54.10
1960	24.95	43.29	75.05	56.71
1961	21.53	45.02	78.47	54.98
1962	29.68	61.60	70.32	38.40
1963	23.06	57.92	76.94	42.08
1964	25.23	57.10	74.77	42.90
1965	32.97	61.78	67.03	38.22
1966	35.17	63.07	64.83	36.93
1967	31.58	61.37	68.42	38.63
1968	29.65	61.34	70.35	38.66
1969	32.48	60.69	67.52	39.31
1970	27.60	58.88	72.40	41.12
1971	16.03	59.50	83.97	40.50
1972	13.80	56.33	86.20	43.67
1973	14.80	55.56	85.20	44.44
1974	17.21	50.34	82.79	49.66
1975	11.85	49.87	88.15	50.13
1976	12.74	46.84	87.26	53.16
1977	13.02	46.67	86.98	53.33
1978	15.52	47.42	84.48	52.58

Data Source China Statistical Yearbook (1981)

sub-optimal choice under specific historical conditions and economic development circumstances. For the government, having institutions take on some of the responsibilities for providing urban public goods and handling public affairs was also an institutional design that balanced "cost–benefit" without increasing the tax burden.

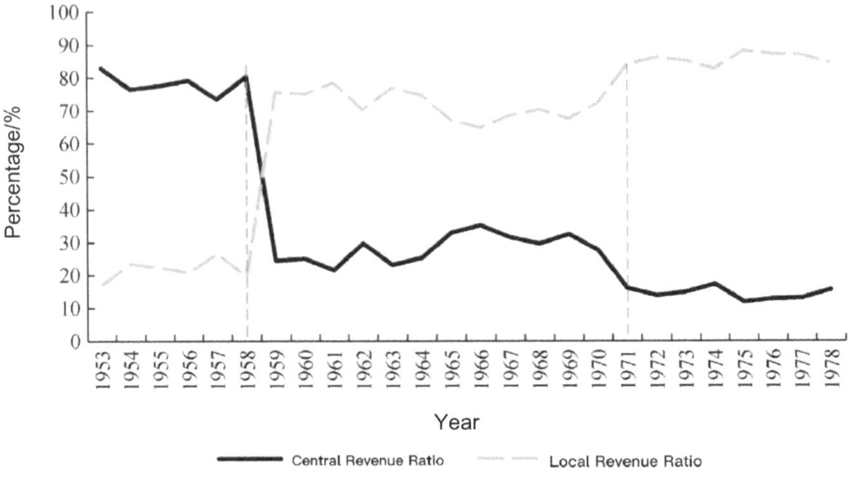

Fig. 2.8 Changes in the proportion of central and local fiscal revenue (1953–1978) (*Data Source China Statistical Yearbook*)

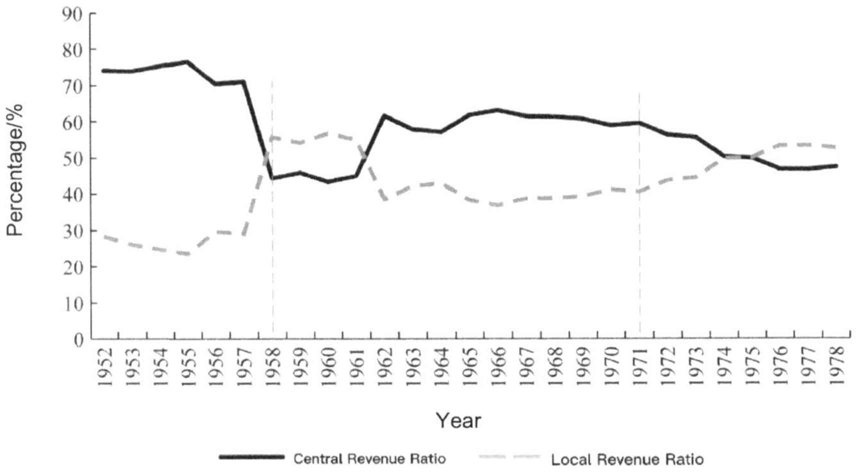

Fig. 2.9 Changes in the proportion of central and local fiscal expenditure (1952–1978) (*Data Source China Statistical Yearbook*)

2.3.2 *Public Goods Supply System Under the Fiscal Decentralization (1979—1993)*

Since the economic reforms began, China has undergone significant changes in its fiscal system, with constant adjustments in the economic relations between central

Table 2.8 Evolution of China's fiscal system (1950–1978)

Period	Overview of the fiscal system
1950	Highly centralized, unified collection and expenditure
1951–1957	Division of revenue and expenditure, hierarchical responsibility
1958	Expenditure is determined by revenue and is fixed for five years
1959–1970	Decentralization of revenue and expenditure, planned responsibility
1971–1973	Fixed revenue and expenditure, responsibility for revenue and expenditure
1974–1975	Revenue retention is based on fixed proportions, additional revenue divided by newly determined proportions
1976–1978	Fixed revenue and expenditure, revenue, and expenditure linked, total revenue sharing

Data Source 60 Years of China's Fiscal System: Evolution, Operation, and Optimization (Wang et al., 2009, Issue 10)

and local governments. From 1979 to 1993, China's fiscal management system experienced multiple adjustments centered on the "decentralization of power and transfer of profits", including "delineation of income and expenditure, and hierarchical fiscal responsibility". This fiscal decentralization gradually broke down the centralized fiscal management system, altering the fiscal interest patterns between the central and local governments, marking the beginning and turning point of fiscal decentralization reforms in China (Yu, 2010; Ding, 2008). In 1980, the State Council issued the *Interim Provisions on the Implementation of 'Delineation of Income and Expenditure, Hierarchical Fiscal Responsibility*', deciding to implement this fiscal management system, which some scholars summarized as "the central and local governments dividing revenue and expenditure" (Tsui & Wang, 2004). In practice, this fiscal management system was implemented differently based on different regions' fiscal foundations and realities. For instance, Jiangsu Province continued the fixed proportion contract model, and Guangdong and Fujian provinces implemented a "delineation of income and expenditure, fixed remittance or fixed subsidy" decentralization method. At the same time, Beijing, Tianjin, and Shanghai adopted the "sharing in the total revenue, annual determination" system. Since then, each province (autonomous region, municipality directly under the Central Government) has had the autonomy to adjust local fiscal revenues and expenditures (Ding, 2008). Compared to the decentralization reforms before 1978, the fiscal system clarified the scope of fiscal revenues and expenditures of central and local governments according to administrative affiliations, granted local governments more initiative, and institutionalized the fiscal relations between central and local governments, thoroughly motivating the local governments. However, before the implementation of the tax-sharing system, the central government still bore heavy fiscal expenditures, and public functions were not decentralized. Before 1985, the central government's fiscal expenditures always accounted for more than 50%, with fiscal revenue never exceeding

Table 2.9 Proportion of central and local fiscal revenue and expenditure (1979–1993) unit: %

Year	Central		Local	
	Revenue proportion	Expenditure proportion	Revenue proportion	Expenditure proportion
1979	20.18	51.11	79.82	48.89
1980	24.52	54.26	75.48	45.74
1981	26.46	54.96	73.54	45.04
1982	28.61	52.99	71.39	47.01
1983	35.85	53.89	64.15	46.11
1984	40.51	52.52	59.49	47.48
1985	38.39	39.68	61.61	60.32
1986	36.68	37.93	63.32	62.07
1987	33.48	37.38	66.52	62.62
1988	32.87	33.92	67.13	66.08
1989	30.86	31.47	69.14	68.53
1990	33.79	32.57	66.21	67.43
1991	29.79	32.21	70.21	67.79
1992	28.12	31.28	71.88	68.72
1993	22.02	28.26	77.98	71.74

Data Source China Statistical Yearbook (1979–1994)

40.51% and declining annually (see Table 2.9, Figs. 2.10, 2.11).[2] Fiscal decentralization weakened central financial power, leading to consecutive deficits in the central budget (Gao, 2018).

After 1986, new situations arose in the fiscal conditions of central and local governments. Their revenues declined in some regions with rapid economic development and high fiscal revenue remittance ratios. The central government's "total sharing" method was seen as "whipping the fast and hardworking—unfair punishment" (Deng & Tang, 2011). In practice, some local governments and their enterprises took advantage of the central government's insufficient grasp of local fiscal and tax information, reporting lower income bases and profit levels. Some local governments even adjusted budgeted revenues to off-budget or extra-budgetary revenues to reduce their sharing with the central government. These practices led to a statistical, fiscal revenue slide in economically fast-growing coastal areas. To stimulate local governments to increase fiscal revenue and to stop or even reverse this distorted situation,

[2] Central expenditures include central economic construction expenditures, defense expenditures, expenditures on foreign affairs and central-level scientific, educational, cultural, and health undertakings, and administrative management expenses. Local expenditures include local economic construction expenditures, local scientific, educational, cultural, and health undertakings, and administrative management expenses.

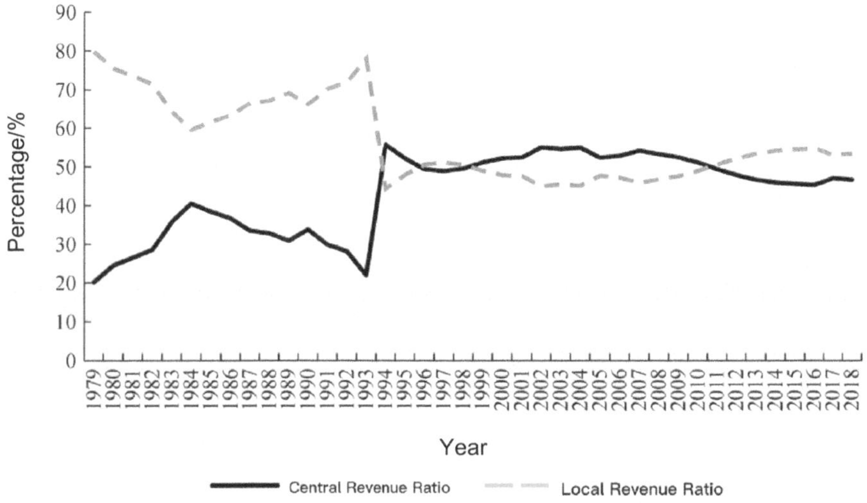

Fig. 2.10 Changes in the proportion of central and local fiscal revenue (1979–2018) (*Data Source China Statistical Yearbook*)

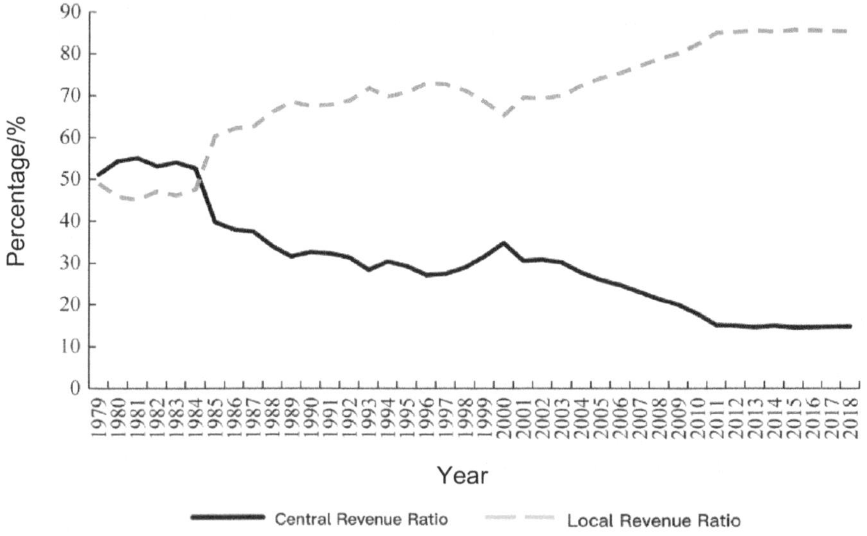

Fig. 2.11 Changes in the proportion of central and local fiscal expenditure (1979–2018) (*Data Source China Statistical Yearbook*)

in July 1988, the *State Council's Decision on Implementing the Fiscal Decentralization Locally* was issued, and the state began implementing different contract methods based on the specific conditions of different regions, as detailed in Table 2.10.

Implementing fiscal decentralization significantly inspired local governments and adjusted the pattern of economic surplus division between the central and local governments. However, we must also recognize that while decentralizing powers and transferring profits, the central government also shouldered significant costs of institutional changes, leading to negative consequences such as a decline in central financial power and inflated local interests. As shown in Fig. 2.12, from 1979 to 1993, the national fiscal revenue as a percentage of GDP continuously declined,

Table 2.10 1988 China's fiscal responsibility system

Responsibility form	Base	Responsibility method	Implementing regions
Increasing revenue responsibility	1987 final accounts revenue and local expenditure capacity	Local revenue within the growth rate is divided between central and local based on fixed retention and submission proportions; all revenue exceeding the growth rate is retained by the local; any shortfall in the growth rate affecting the central submission is covered by local funds	Beijing, Hebei, Harbin, Jiangsu, Zhejiang (excluding Ningbo), Ningbo, Henan, Chongqing, Liaoning (excluding Shenyang and Dalian), Shenyang
Total revenue sharing	1986, 1987 local revenue and expenditure	Local retention and central submission proportions are determined based on the ratio of total expenditure in the local budget to total revenue	Tianjin, Shanxi, Anhui
Total revenue sharing with growth sharing	The previous year's actual revenue	Base portion retained by total revenue sharing ratio; growth portion divided by a new ratio	Dalian, Qingdao, Wuhan
Increasing submission responsibility	1987 central submission revenue	Increase central submission by a fixed proportion	Guangdong, Hunan
Fixed amount submission	Original fixed revenue and expenditure base	Determine a fixed submission amount for revenue exceeding expenditure	Shanghai, Shandong, Heilongjiang
Fixed amount subsidy	Original fixed revenue and expenditure base	Fixed subsidy for expenditure exceeding revenue	Jilin, Jiangxi, Gansu, Shaanxi, Fujian, Inner Mongolia, Guangxi, Tibet, Ningxia, Xinjiang, Guizhou, Yunnan, Qinghai, Hainan, Wuhan, Chongqing

Data Source: *Illustrated Fiscal Relations between Governments in China* (Li Ping, China Financial and Economic Publishing House, 2006)

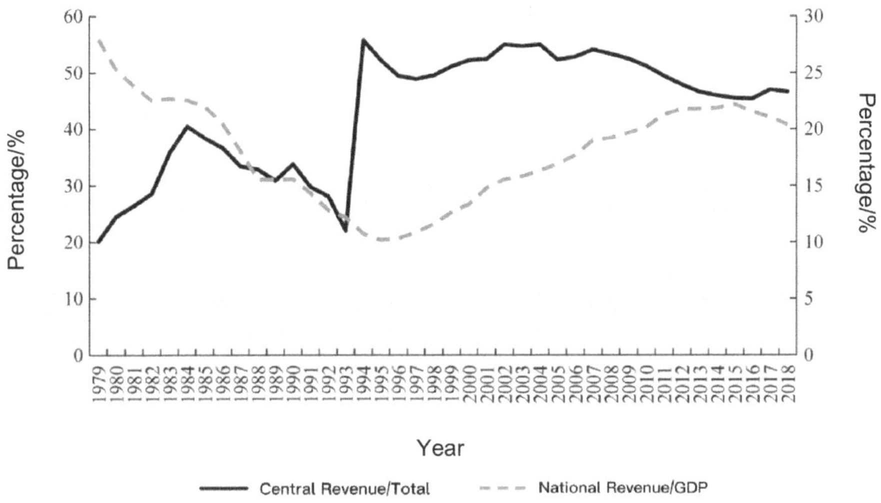

Fig. 2.12 Changes in the proportion of central fiscal revenue to national fiscal revenue and national fiscal revenue to GDP (*Data Source China Statistical Yearbook*)

from 27.96% in 1979 to 12.19% in 1993; central fiscal revenue as a percentage of national fiscal revenue briefly rose before rapidly declining, from 40.51% in 1984 to only 22.02% in 1993.

The adjustments in the fiscal system also significantly impacted the supply of urban public goods, breaking the central centralized system. As the central government's control over economic resources and financial power decreased, local governments' resource mobilization capacity and financial power continuously strengthened. This incentivized local governments to utilize resources for economic development fully and laid the economic foundation for local governments to assume the responsibility for supplying most public goods after that. In 1985, the state successively announced a series of decisions and opinions on public sector reforms, including the *CCP Central Committee's Decision on Educational System Reform* and the *CCP Central Committee's Decision on Science and Technology System Reform.* The reforms focused on the supply system, management model, and operational mechanisms of public services, heralding the comprehensive reform of the urban public goods sector. Initially, the government began to loosen its monopoly over public service departments, introducing market competition mechanisms and gradually breaking the management pattern where the government was responsible for all public affairs. Furthermore, the government increased its fiscal investment in public sectors, leading to the emergence of "outside the system" public service departments based on social needs.

Additionally, from the perspective of the supply and distribution systems of urban public goods, from 1978 to the mid-1990s, the function of various organizational units gradually shifted from management-oriented to economically oriented. As their autonomy expanded, enterprises and public institutions acquired relatively independent economic interests, and some units became independent and closely linked economic institutions. Consequently, disparities arose in the public goods available to members of different units, with members of units that controlled more resources and held significant social status often enjoying better social welfare and access to more public goods. Thus, during this period, urban residents' access to welfare, medical services, and pension security was closely related to their respective units. This led to significant variations in access to public services, which was more pronounced than during the planned economy period.

2.3.3 *Public Goods Supply System Under the Tax-Sharing Fiscal Management System (1994–2002)*

The fiscal contracting system boosted local governments' enthusiasm for industrial development, yet it also resulted in cases where local authorities under-reported corporate profits or transferred profits outside the system for personal gain (He et al., 2014). To enhance the central government's macro-control capabilities and reshape local government behavior patterns to meet the needs of the socialist market economy, China introduced the tax-sharing fiscal management system reform in 1994.

First, the tax-sharing system allocated fiscal revenues between the central and local governments according to tax types, primarily categorized into central taxes serving macroeconomic control and national interests, shared taxes directly tied to economic development and jointly managed, and local taxes suitable for local collection yet challenging to collect (as shown in Table 2.11).

Second, the tax-sharing system clarified the respective responsibilities of central and local governments and divided the scope of fiscal expenditures (as shown in Table 2.12). Central finance mainly provided expenses for national defense, foreign affairs, operation of central government bodies, and directly managed enterprises. At the same time, expenditures required to optimize the national economic structure, coordinate regional development, and control macroeconomics were also covered by central finance. Operational expenses for local administrative bodies and expenditures needed for local economic development and public utilities were primarily provided by local finance.

Lastly, the tax-sharing system transformed the tax collection system. After its implementation, China established separate central and local tax institutions, promoting an indirect tax system dominated by value-added and unified corporate income tax. In addition, to motivate local governments and protect their existing interests, China established a tax return system suitable for the tax-sharing system.

After the implementation of the tax-sharing system, the share of central fiscal revenue in the national fiscal revenue rapidly increased, reaching 55.7% in 1994, a 153% increase when compared with 1993. Meanwhile, as the intensity and transparency of tax collection improved, the share of fiscal revenue to GDP also gradually

Table 2.11 Division of central and local tax revenue

Central revenue	Local revenue	Shared revenue
Domestic consumption tax	Personal income tax	Domestic value-added tax
Customs duties	Urban land use tax	Corporate income tax
Consumption tax and VAT	Farmland occupation tax	Personal income tax
	Fixed asset investment regulation tax	Stamp duty
	Land VAT	Securities transaction tax
	Property tax	Resource tax
	Inheritance tax	Business tax
	Vehicle and vessel usage tax	Urban maintenance and construction tax
	Vehicle and vessel license plate tax	
	Deed tax	
	Slaughter tax	
	Banquet tax	
	Agricultural tax, animal husbandry tax, and local surcharges	

Data Source Reform of China's Fiscal System: Institutional Evolution and Optimization (Wang et al., 2009, Issue 45)

Table 2.12 Division of central and local fiscal expenditure

Central fiscal expenditure	Local fiscal expenditure
National defense	Local administrative management
Armed police	Public security, procuratorate, and court expenditure
Foreign affairs and foreign aid	Part of armed police expenditure
Central administrative management	Militia affairs
Central government basic construction investment	Local government basic construction investment
Technical transformation and new product trial production for central enterprises	Technical transformation and new product trial production for local enterprises
Geological exploration	Agricultural expenditure
Central government arranged agricultural expenditure	Urban maintenance and construction
Debt repayment and interest payments for domestic and foreign debts	Local culture, education, health, and other public services
Public security, procuratorate, and court expenditure	Price subsidies and other expenditures
Culture, education, health, and science expenditure	

Table 2.13 Providers of different types of public goods under the planned economy system

Provider institutions	Government departments	State-owned enterprises	Public institutions
Public goods	National defense	Postal service	Primary and secondary education
	Foreign affairs	Electric power	Sports facilities
	Judicial system	Railways	Libraries
	Public security	Municipal construction	Hospitals
	Fire services	Public transportation	Welfare housing

increased. By 1996, the national fiscal revenue as a percentage of GDP reversed the downward trend of the previous 17 years, exceeding 15% by 2002. Subsequently, the central and local governments formed a relatively independent and self-stabilizing fiscal budget system, continuously enhancing the central government's macroeconomic control capabilities. This alleviated the long-standing unstable budget revenue and expenditure conflicts between the central and local governments, deepening the "self-awareness of local (urban) governments" and strengthening the motivations for local government fiscal revenue growth (He et al., 2014).

However, under the tax-sharing system, since local governments took most public affairs responsibilities, local governments faced significant financial pressure, viewing the public sector economy as a financial burden (Zhu, 2004a, 2004b). Inter-regional economic competition led local governments to invest in economically oriented public products overly, causing a structural distortion in public goods supply (Qian & Roland, 1998), leading to a local fiscal expenditure bias towards "prioritizing infrastructure over public services" (Fu, 2007; Qiao et al., 2005; Fu, 2010). Top-down performance assessments further caused local government expenditure preferences to be heavily influenced by "promotion" incentives (Zhou, 2004; Zhang & Zhou, 2007; He, 2014). The land finance model derived from the tax-sharing system also prompted local governments to focus on urban infrastructure construction (Tang et al., 2016), struggling to provide other non-economic public goods and failing to reflect the government's public fiscal function.

Another significant change during this period was that, as economic reforms accelerated, many state-owned enterprises and public institutions were drawn into the tide of market competition. The monopoly rights and pricing rights of state-owned enterprises were gradually weakened, forcing internal reforms, and part of the social welfare of enterprise employees shifted from implicit to explicit costs. In reforming the national social security system, the unit benefits of state-owned enterprises and public institution employees continuously decreased, leading to the dissolution of the "system of unit". Public services such as social security for urban workers began to evolve from exclusively government-provided to diversely provided by both the government and the market.

2.3.4 Public Goods Supply System Under the Public Financial Function System (2003–2012)

As the economy developed and living standards improved, the demand for urban public goods significantly increased, highlighting the supply and demand contradictions. To alleviate social tensions and promote healthy urban development, the 16th National Congress of the Communist Party in 2002 recognized public services as a core government function. In 2003, the third plenary session of the 16th Central Committee of the Communist Party passed the *Decision on Several Major Issues Concerning the Improvement of the Socialist Market Economy System*, emphasizing the public nature of finance and setting the establishment of a public financial system as a goal for reform. This decision also explicitly called for accelerating government function transformation and enhancing the fiscal system.

During this period, fiscal system reforms focused on tax revenue as the primary source of government income. Reforms aimed at regularizing government revenue structure and reducing off-budget government income, such as abolishing the vehicle purchase surcharge and converting it into a vehicle purchase tax. Regarding the income division between central and local governments, the reforms continued to adjust and optimize the division of fiscal powers, scientifically allocating central and local income in taxes like securities transaction stamp duty, income tax, and export tax rebates. Adjustments were also made to divide public expenditures between governments to alleviate financial difficulties at the grassroots level and ensure essential public expenditures, preventing provincial and municipal governments from shifting expenditure responsibilities to county and township governments. When provincial and municipal governments delegate tasks to county and township governments, they must provide corresponding special funding; a reasonable division of responsibilities must be established for jointly undertaken tasks. Overall, the fiscal system reforms during this period centered on the theme of the public fiscal system, accelerating the transformation of government functions, playing a significant role in perfecting the socialist market economy, promoting the equalization of essential public services, improving people's livelihoods, and promoting sustainable economic and social development.

From the perspective of the providers and distribution system of urban public goods, as marketization increased, investment in urban public infrastructure construction and public services grew significantly, and the financial and debt pressures on local governments also increased. The successful transition of the government fiscal system to one that matches the market economy ensured that residents could equitably access public goods rather than dividing the benefits of public goods based on residents' "unit" status (Wang, 2007).

2.3.5 Public Goods Supply System Under the Modern Fiscal System (2013–Present)

In 2013, the third plenary session of the 18th Central Committee of the Communist Party passed the *Decision on Several Major Issues Concerning Comprehensively Deepening Reform*, outlining the goals for fiscal system reform. In June 2014, the Central Political Bureau reviewed and approved the *Overall Plan for Deepening Fiscal and Tax System Reform*, setting the goal of the fiscal system reform as "establishing a unified, complete, legally regulated, transparent, efficient, and sustainable modern fiscal system that is conducive to optimizing resource allocation, maintaining market unity, promoting social fairness, and ensuring long-term national stability". The plan also stated that by 2016, key tasks and objectives of the fiscal reform should be largely completed, with the goal of fundamentally establishing a modern fiscal system by 2020.

During this period of fiscal system reform, they have achieved breakthroughs in three main areas: (a) In budget management system reform, rather than being limited to developing reform plans based on the general public budget as in the past, the scope of the new fiscal and tax system reform extended to all of the government's "four budgets"[3] revenues and expenditures. It was specified that all fiscal budgets and final accounts should be standardized and transparent (except for confidential information), increase the proportion of central general transfer payments, and clean up, integrate, and standardize special transfer payments. The reform aimed to establish a "comprehensive, standardized, and transparent" budget management system covering all government revenues and expenditures; (b) In tax system reform, the focus shifted from merely increasing or decreasing the total amount of tax revenue to optimizing the tax revenue structure, improving the local tax system, stabilizing the macro tax burden, and legally regulating taxation. The reform aimed to clarify the establishment of taxes, increase the proportion of direct taxes, and gradually increase the share of property tax in local fiscal revenue. The goal of tax system reform was to establish a modern tax system that was stable and conducive to social fairness and market unity; (c) Regarding the financial relationship between the central and local governments, the reform went beyond simply adjusting the increase and decrease of financial powers between the central and local governments. A new round of reforms re-examined the issue of tax rights between the central and local governments. Based on the functions and attributes of various taxes, a reasonable division of central and local income was made, and after adjusting the income division, the financial gap formed by the localities was resolved by the attributes of different taxes. After adjusting income allocation, local financial gaps were resolved through tax refunds from central finance. A system was established to align responsibilities and expenditures, which enabled the central government to delegate partial authority expenditure responsibilities to local governments in regional public service areas. In general, the period's fiscal system reforms aimed to establish a system that aligns

[3] The "four budgets" refer to the general public budget, the government fund budget, the state-owned capital operation budget, and the social insurance fund budget.

fiscal responsibilities with authority while maintaining stable central and local fiscal powers.

Fiscal system reforms during this period played a key role in advancing the modernization of national governance, particularly in urban areas. By January 2018, China's urbanization rate had reached 59.85%, with coastal regions approaching or exceeding the average urbanization rates of developed countries, marking the initial transformation to "Urban China". Urban governments strengthened their role as primary providers of basic public services. In January 2018, the State Council issued the *Reform Plan for Central and Local Joint Fiscal Powers and Expenditure Responsibilities in the Field of Basic Public Services*, which defined the shared responsibility between the central and local governments for funding and delivering key public services. This plan prioritized basic public services, such as compulsory education, student assistance, basic employment services, basic pension insurance, basic medical care, basic health and family planning, basic livelihood assistance, and basic housing security, and also standardized lists, benchmarks, guidelines for fiscal responsibilities across government levels, with the goal of establishing a transparent and effective basic public service system. At the same time, social organizations began playing a vital role in supplying urban public goods, with urban governments gradually increasing their procurement of public services from these organizations. Based on regional reform practices in 2013, the State Council issued the *Guidance on Government Purchase of Services from Social Forces*, aiming to guide the government and social forces in jointly improving public service delivery. The Third Plenary Session of the 18th Central Committee of the Communist Party of China stated in its *Decision on Major Issues Concerning Comprehensively Deepening Reforms* that competition mechanisms should be introduced for service-oriented management, and services should be procured through contracts or delegation. In conclusion, during this period, the supply of urban public goods responded to societal and resident needs, focusing on investments in projects directly benefiting residents' welfare.

2.4 Urban Public Goods Supply Mechanisms and Their Reforms

After the founding of the People's Republic of China, rapid economic and social development has profoundly changed people's lifestyles and living conditions. With the development of the economy, society, and culture, the demand for public goods has evolved, necessitating ongoing adjustments in urban public goods supply mechanisms. For much of this period, the government played a predominant role in public goods supply. However, as China moved towards a socialist market economy, the urban planned economic system gradually receded. The development of market mechanisms and financial markets facilitated the formation of diversified supply systems involving collaboration between government, market, and multiple entities.

2.4.1 Administration Mechanism of Government-Controlled Urban Public Goods Supply (1949–1978)

During the planned economy period, under a centralized financial system, the government and state-owned enterprises were responsible for investing in urban public infrastructure and providing basic public services. Additional social welfare and public goods were provided based on the specific unit or enterprise involved. Consequently, the provisioning mechanism for public goods during this period was primarily managed by the government, with key roles played by central and local governments, public institutions, and state-owned companies in investing, producing, distributing, and operating these goods.

Urban public goods under this government administration mechanism exhibited several characteristics: (1) The supply level was low. Despite the government's efforts to transfer some economic surplus from rural to urban and industrial sectors through fiscal measures and the price scissors difference between industrial and agricultural products, building an industrial system, cumbersome industry, with concentrated economic resources aimed to catch up with developed nations, making it difficult to allocate a substantial portion of fiscal funds for public infrastructure or provide adequate social security; (2) The supply efficiency could have been higher. Government administrative departments dominated all processes related to the investment, production, distribution, and operation of public goods by state-owned enterprises, complicating the formulation of effective supply plans for private products and making it difficult to discern actual demand for public goods due to insufficient information and lack of adequate external supervision mechanisms. For instance, there was a severe shortage of medical resources in the healthcare sector, yet a significant wastage of doctor and pharmaceutical resources; (3) Although the provision of public goods pursued absolute equality institutionally, widespread disparities were prevalent due to supply shortages. Significant differences exist among units and enterprises providing employees with education, healthcare, housing, and social security projects, particularly relevant to economics and urban development.

2.4.2 Exploration of Market Supply Mechanism of Urban Public Goods Supply Under the Government Leadership (1979–1992)

In 1978, the Third Plenary Session of the 11th Central Committee of the Communist Party initiated a shift from an administrative planned economy to a market economy centered on economic construction. Although initial reforms occurred in the private products sector, by the early 1980s, reforms began to be experimented with and expanded in the public goods sector. These changes commenced with the establishment of a socialized public service system and a societal investment mechanism for public infrastructure.

During this period, the public health sector, which had frequently been subject to social criticism, became a focal point of reform efforts. While the state worked to improve the construction of urban state-owned and collective medical institutions, it also began encouraging and permitting private investment in the healthcare sector. In 1979, the Ministry of Health, the Ministry of Finance, and the National Labor Bureau jointly issued the *Opinions on Strengthening the Economic Management Pilot Work of Hospitals*. Furthermore, in 1981, the Ministry of Health issued the *Provisional Measures for Hospital Economic Management*, signifying the state's initiation of using economic instruments to manage the healthcare sector. These measures included pilot projects such as the "Five Fixed and One Prize" system, the "Quota-based Subsidy, Economic Accountability, Assessment, and Rewards" system, and attempts to improve medical institutions' accounting and operational management. Based on these efforts, the 1982 issuance of the *National Hospital Work Regulations* by the Ministry of Health explicitly stated that hospital economic management should "use economic means to ensure the rational utilization of human, material, and financial resources, improve the quality of healthcare and services, and gradually implement cost accounting". Additionally, enterprise management practices could be adopted in the general services sector. Concurrently, the 1980 State Council approval of the *Ministry of Health Request for Instructions on Permitting Individual Practices in Medicine* allowed for a shift away from the absolute dominance of state-owned and collective medical institutions, facilitating the formation of a diversified ownership healthcare service system. This broadened the supply channels for medical resources and further propelled the reform of state-owned medical institutions. Subsequently, various reform plans were implemented in the public health and medical sectors. Although the outcomes of these reforms were not notably significant and societal satisfaction was relatively low, they nonetheless broke the monopoly of government administrative control over the healthcare system, allowing social capital to enter the healthcare sector and laying the early groundwork for a multi-provider mechanism involving both government and society (Li, 2009). By 1985, the transformation of the public goods supply mechanism had extended to all public products and services areas. The intensive issuance of a series of documents, including the *Decision of the Central Committee of the Communist Party of China on the Reform of the Science and Technology System*, the *Decision of the Central Committee of the Communist Party of China on the Reform of the Education System, the Opinions on the Reform of Performing Arts Groups*, the *Draft Plan on the Reform of the Sports System*, and the *Report on Several Policy Issues Concerning Health Work Reform*, marked the comprehensive launch of market-oriented reforms in the urban public goods supply mechanism.

During this period, changes in the urban public goods supply mechanism had the following features:

(1) Diversified investment mechanisms existed. While the government continued to play a dominant role, it gradually abandoned its previous approach of handling everything and began experimenting with introducing domestic private capital, foreign investments, and other social capital into the investment and construction

of public infrastructure. This period also saw the allowance for private and social capital to invest and operate in public service sectors, forming a mechanism for diversified investments in public goods.

(2) Attempts were made to diversify public goods' production and supply mechanisms to fulfill urban residents' varied and multi-faceted needs. Moreover, the traditional administrative allocation and planned supply mechanism of public goods started to be replaced by market-driven supply mechanisms.

(3) In terms of operation and management mechanisms, the state began to grant managerial autonomy to urban public sectors, allowing cooperation with private sectors and integrating market operation mechanisms to adjust the types and quantities of public products according to market demands. Simultaneously, to deal with the inadequate funding for urban public sector operations, the state allowed public sectors to adopt flexible and diverse charging methods for some public utilities.

2.4.3 Urban Public Goods Supply Mechanism with Dual Leadership of Government and Market (1993–2002)

In 1992, the 14th National Congress of the Communist Party explicitly set the goal of establishing a socialist market economic system, recognizing the fundamental role of the market in resource allocation. This marked a new phase in the supply of urban public goods, focusing on transforming government functions to accelerate market-oriented reforms in public sectors.

In 1993, the State Council initiated significant institutional reforms, transforming 18 specialized economic departments, such as the Ministry of Aerospace Industry, Ministry of Light Industry, and Ministry of Textiles, into economic entities and industry associations and restructuring sectors like electricity, oil, and railways into corporations. These government department reforms and functional adjustments laid the institutional groundwork for introducing social capital and implementing market mechanisms in public infrastructure and other public goods sectors. In 1995, a national conference on the reform of institutions and personnel systems of public institutions was held in Zhengzhou, which initially formulated reform strategies for separating government functions from business operations, modern management, and diversified operations in public institutions. In 1996, the General Office of the CPC Central Committee and the General Office of the State Council issued opinions on several issues concerning the reform of institutions of public sectors, clarifying the goals and approaches to reforming China's public sectors. The central government focused on adjusting and optimizing government functions, using the reform of institutions and the opening up of public goods supply areas to accelerate the transition to a public goods market supply mechanism. In 1998, the State Council conducted its fourth institutional reform, abolishing 15 ministries and commissions, such as the Ministry of Electric Power Industry, Ministry of Coal Industry, and Ministry of Posts and Telecommunications. Some administrative functions from these ministries were delegated to enterprises or handed over to the State Economic and Trade Commission and the State Planning Commission. Management and operation of urban utilities like water, natural gas, and transportation were assigned to the Ministry of Construction. At the same time, the entry into the pharmaceutical industry, product pricing, and corporate behavior were overseen by the Ministry of Health and the State Drug Administration. Furthermore, some pricing authority for essential products was decentralized, granting enterprises the right to generate profits through increased charges (Zou, 2007). In 2001, the National Development and Reform Commission issued guidelines to promote and guide private investment, explicitly stating encouragement for private investment in operational infrastructure and public welfare projects through sole proprietorships, partnerships, joint ventures, and franchise operations. For example, in primary education and public infrastructure, the 1993 *Outline for Reform and Development of Education in China* issued by the CPC Central Committee and the State Council was the first to clearly articulate China's policy on promoting private education with the principle of "actively encourage, strongly support, correctly guide, and enhance management". By the end of 1996, there were 1,453 private primary schools and 1,467 private middle schools (Zhang, 2009). In May 1995, the National Planning Commission approved China's first BOT project—the B Power Plant Project in Laibin, Guangxi. In May 2002, half of the state-owned shares of the Shanghai Pudong New Area Water Company were sold at a premium to the foreign enterprise Vivendi (Pan, 2007).

The characteristics of urban public goods supply mechanisms during this period included: Firstly, with the backdrop of "optimizing government functions", the scope of government regulation over utilities and other areas was relaxed. Selected urban public infrastructure and social services areas were opened to societal participation, with some public sector management systems transitioning from approval to registration systems and incorporating market mechanisms. Secondly, in constructing urban public infrastructure, the introduction of bidding and other market competition mechanisms expanded the financing channels for infrastructure. Especially in sectors like urban roads and transportation, communications, healthcare, culture, education, and public health, trial market-based management methods were implemented to improve the efficiency of fiscal funds and public goods supply, better meeting the growing needs of urban development and residents. Lastly, there was an emphasis on strengthening governmental regulatory functions over public goods. While emphasizing the market supply mechanism for public goods, the government continued to improve supervision over public products involving public interest through the administrative power system and institutional norms. Nevertheless, it began to enhance professional management across different public sectors. The level of quality supervision over "intangible public goods" in the public service domain was also improved.

2.4.4 "Government + Market + Society" Multi-stakeholder Collaboration Mechanism for Urban Public Goods Supply (2003—Present)

In 2003, the Third Plenary Session of the 16th Central Committee of the CPC introduced policies to break monopolies and open markets, aiming to advance the marketization of municipal utilities and infrastructure construction. In February 2004, the Ministry of Construction issued the *Regulations on the Franchise Management of Municipal Public Utilities*. Subsequently, it developed accompanying *Model Texts for Urban Water Supply Franchise Agreements, Pipeline Gas Franchise Agreements*, and *Urban Household Garbage Disposal Franchise Agreements* in September. Following this, cities such as Beijing and Shenzhen formulated franchise operation methods. The *Several Opinions of the State Council on Encouraging, Supporting, and Guiding the Development of Non-public Economies* issued in February 2005 explicitly stated: "Support private capital to actively participate in the investment, construction, and operation of urban utilities and infrastructure such as water supply, gas supply, heating, public transportation, and sewage and garbage disposal". Under these policy measures, the traditional government-led model in the municipal sector was gradually replaced by a diversified investment structure encompassing foreign capital, private capital, and state-owned enterprises. Simultaneously, market supply mechanisms in urban public sectors like primary education, public health and basic medical care, and public cultural and sports facilities evolved. In July 2012, the State Council issued the *12th Five-Year Plan for the National Basic Public Services System*, clarifying the public service supply system and mechanism of "government leadership, societal participation, and both public and private provisioning". In November 2013, the Third Plenary Session of the 18th Central Committee of the CPC passed the *Decision of the CPC Central Committee on Major Issues Concerning Comprehensively Deepening Reforms*, proposing the reform method of government purchasing public services for public goods supply, stipulating "introducing competitive mechanisms in principle for all transactional services, and purchasing through contracts, commissions, and other means from society".

Continuing to deepen and refine the urban public goods market supply mechanism, the state also introduced a series of policies to encourage the development of social organizations (volunteer organizations, non-profit organizations, etc.). In September 2004, the Fourth Plenary Session of the 16th Central Committee of the CPC made a systematic and comprehensive elaboration on improving social organizations and enhancing their functions in serving society. In 2007, the 17th National Congress of the CPC further proposed establishing a "leadership by Party committees, government responsibility, societal collaboration, public participation" social management system. The *Twelfth Five-Year Plan for National Economic and Social Development of the People's Republic of China*, issued in March 2011, stated: "Insist on nurturing development and managing supervision simultaneously, promote the healthy development of social organizations, and utilize their roles in providing services, reflecting demands, and regulating behavior". The dense rollout of government policies spurred the vigorous development of social organizations in China. The *2018 Statistical Bulletin of Social Affairs Development* showed that by the end of 2018, there were approximately 817,000 social organizations nationwide, including about 366,000 social groups, 7,034 foundations, and about 444,000 private non-enterprise units. These social organizations employed up to 9.804 million people across various sectors, such as scientific research, education, health, social services, culture, and sports.

As the number and scale of social organizations continue to grow, and their layout, structure, and quality are constantly being optimized and strengthened, their role and impact in public service sectors have become increasingly prominent. To develop these organizations in an orderly manner, the government has issued a series of policies to guide and promote their participation in the supply of urban public goods. In February 2008, the Second Plenary Session of the 17th Central Committee of the Communist Party of China passed the *Opinions on Deepening the Reform of the Administrative Management System*, which highlights the need to better utilize the role of citizens and social organizations in the management of social public affairs, and to provide public goods more effectively through institutional arrangements and innovations. Additionally, the *Guiding Opinions of the State Council Office on Government Purchasing Services from Social Forces* and the *Guiding Opinions of the State Council on Promoting the Healthy Development of the Charity Sector* were also issued. In 2017, the report of the 19th National Congress of the CPC required improving the guarantee and level of people's livelihoods, strengthening and innovating social governance, pushing the focus of social governance downward to the grassroots, leveraging social organizations, and achieving healthy interaction between government governance and social regulation, as well as resident self-governance. Under a series of clear policy directions from the government, social organizations have initially formed a comprehensive management system characterized by "full categorization, different levels, complementary functions, wide coverage, and distinct features", jointly shaping a new cooperative supply mechanism for public goods together with the government and private(market) sector (Wang & Salamon, 2010).

Despite certain restrictions on the development of social organizations and their relatively slow increase in number and expansion in scope and scale, these organizations have played an irreplaceable role in providing public services and improving social governance. For instance, during the outbreak of Severe Acute Respiratory Syndrome (SARS) in 2003, the Wenchuan earthquake relief in 2008, and the COVID-19 pandemic in 2019, various social forces demonstrated their capabilities by offering volunteer services, earning wide recognition and attention from all sectors of society.

The changes in the urban public goods supply mechanism during this period exhibit several notable characteristics:

(1) Market-oriented reform: Under government leadership, market-oriented reforms of public goods provision were implemented, and the trading of public goods property rights became more standardized. Public bidding for public

goods projects became common and standardized, regardless of the investor type. Systems like Public–Private Partnerships (PPP) and franchising were gradually established and refined.

(2) Diversified supply mechanisms: To ensure public interest and meet diverse resident needs, the government integrated private enterprises, foreign enterprises, and social organizations into a diversified supply mechanism, while maintaining its primary position.

(3) Increased investment in public infrastructure: Rapid socioeconomic development led to expanded investment in urban public infrastructure, particularly after the 2008 global financial crisis, driving increased government investment in public goods to sustain economic growth. Central and local governments financed large-scale investments in public infrastructure such as railways, roads, airports, electricity, and environmental protection facilities through fiscal input and financing platforms while expanding social security systems and broadening the scope of social services and their benefits.

Despite these advancements, challenges arose with increased public goods investment, such as rising government debt, over-investment in some infrastructure projects, and poor investment returns.

2.5 Experience, Lessons and Prospects in China's Urban Public Goods Supply Practices

2.5.1 *Experience and Lessons*

The previous analysis of urban public goods evolution and supply mechanisms indicates that since the founding of the People's Republic of China, the supply of urban public goods can be divided into two stages: the planned economy period and the market economy period. During the planned economy, constrained by the strategies for national economic recovery and heavy industrial development strategies, both urban public goods were limited in both quantity and quality. Provision was largely restricted to basic production and living needs, falling short of the developmental demands of residents. Following the reform and opening up policy, rapid economic growth and urbanization led to rapid urban public economy development. Initially, urban economic work focused on economic construction for a long time, reflecting a typical feature of "production and construction finance" (Gao, 2018). The government often overlooked or undervalued the supply of urban public goods (Wong, 2004). This began to change after the establishment of the socialist market economy reform objectives and tax-sharing reform in the early 1990s. However, the supply of public goods remained skewed towards economic goods to support infrastructure demands for economic development and urbanization. In the early twenty-first century, with further market-oriented reforms and the government's emphasis on public service functions, the supply of urban public goods began to see significant changes, focusing more on non-economic public goods directly related to people's livelihoods. In recent years, both central and local governments have prioritized building a basic public service system, aiming to develop a service-oriented government to meet the diverse, multi-level needs of citizens. In urban public goods provision, the supply of goods directly related to residents' lives has been steadily increasing.

From the reform of the urban public goods supply system, it becomes clear that these reforms should be seen in the context of broader fiscal system reforms. The transformation in fiscal systems has been crucial for developing urban economies and providing public goods. Reflecting on the reforms of China's fiscal mechanisms, it can be noted that they were centered on activating both the central and local "initiatives", unifying the efficiency and equity of public goods provision and promoting the modernization of urban and national governance. These reforms underwent five stages: centralized revenue and expenditure, graded responsibility, tax-sharing reform, emphasizing public finance functions, and establishing a modern fiscal system. Correspondingly, the urban public goods supply system also underwent a series of transformations, transitioning from government-led to market-provided, eventually forming a collaborative supply system with multiple entities dominated by the government, market, and social organizations. Examining fiscal system and urban public goods supply mechanism reforms, the core lies in transforming government functions, fostering social forces, and leveraging market mechanisms to meet residents' diverse, differentiated public goods needs, enhancing their sense of public service satisfaction.

2.5.2 Prospects for Future Development

After a detailed examination of the historical evolution and systematic changes in urban public goods supply, the following insights on the future development of the public goods sector and the reform of supply mechanisms can be drawn:

(1) Accelerating the reform of the administrative management system can effectively transform government roles and establish a service-oriented government that meets public needs. The orientation and functional framework of the Chinese government are predominantly shaped by the party's and nation's developmental strategies and specific evaluation metrics (Yu, 2011). Under "a city built by and for the people", reasonably defining the roles of government, market, and society in urban public goods provision is crucial. Advancing the separation of government and enterprises, as well as government and public affairs, not only aids in transforming the core functions of the government towards basic public services but also facilitates private social capital's participation in the investment, production, and operation of public goods, thereby harmonizing efficiency, fairness, and quality in public goods delivery.

(2) It is necessary to proactively advance fiscal system reforms to standardize the financial relationships between central and local governments. Currently, local governments have approximately 50% of the financial power but bear 85% of responsibilities, resulting in a 30% expenditure gap that increases the burden of local government's public goods provision responsibilities. To address this revenue-expenditure mismatch, local governments often resort to enhancing non-tax revenues through land rentals and governmental charges. Therefore, it is crucial to clarify the powers and responsibilities between central and local authorities, leveraging the "dual initiatives" of the central and local governments, balancing efficiency and equity, and aligning short-term and long-term objectives (Lou, 2014; Liu, 2020), to match responsibilities with financial authority, and thereby enhance the efficiency of urban governance.
(3) It is necessary to improve the diverse supply model for urban public goods. While establishing the government's leading role is essential, it is equally important to fully leverage market mechanisms and a multi-stakeholder collaborative system in the supply of urban public goods. This includes continually refining various participants' roles and functional divisions in public goods provision. Government, market (private) sector, and social organizations will be the primary public goods supply entities. An optimal diversified supply structure should allow market-provided goods to be supplied by the market, socially provided goods by social organizations, and those that cannot be produced by the government.
(4) It is necessary to establish and improve mechanisms for demand expression and display in urban public goods supply, and public goods supply performance evaluation systems. Currently, China lacks adequate mechanisms for expressing and displaying demand for public goods. The insufficiency of formal channels for public interest expression reduces the effectiveness of public decision-making and can lead to non-institutionalized interest appeal actions (such as mass incidents). Moreover, the government's "top-down" public decision-making process can disconnect urban public goods supply from residents' preferences and needs. Advances in information technology offer solid guarantees for promoting scientific government decision-making, precise social governance, and efficient public goods provision. Therefore, China should accelerate the establishment and improvement of mechanisms for expressing and displaying urban public goods demand, steadily expand public participation in public goods supply decision-making and budget formulation, and refine public decision-making processes.
(5) It is vital to fully utilize social financing channels and the fund allocation functions of the capital market, as well as to innovate public infrastructure investment, financing mechanisms, and property rights trading mechanisms. Generally, public infrastructure involves significant investments, prolonged capital turnover periods, and slow capital returns. Given the current macro policy context and limited fiscal resources, addressing the growing demand for urban construction and residents' infrastructure needs is urgent for the government. Therefore, exploiting the financial market is necessary for multi-channel financing. For example, infrastructure real estate investment trusts (REITs), as an

emerging investment model, can increase direct financing and diversify investment tools in infrastructure construction. This diversified investment mechanism also benefits social investors by diversifying their asset allocation. In April 2020, the issuance of the *Notice on Implementing Pilot Work for Public Infrastructure Real Estate Investment Trust* by the China Securities Regulatory Commission and the National Development and Reform Commission marked the official initiation of the REITs pilot projects in infrastructure. In June 2021, the first batch of REITs was officially listed on the stock exchanges, indicating the formal application of this financial tool in infrastructure construction.

Another important task is to rectify issues from Public–Private Partnership (PPP) model in infrastructure construction and fully leverage social capital in public goods provision. In recent years, while the role of the PPP model in infrastructure construction has become increasingly prominent, the practice has revealed problems such as "debt investment with equity character" and "small equity with large debt", inconsistent with the intended objectives of the PPP model. Additionally, the excessively high proportion of state-owned capital in social capital does not align with the government's original intent for adopting the PPP model. Some local governments have faced heightened financial tensions, increasing the risk of systemic financial instability. This calls for government departments to strengthen the inspection and regulation of local hidden debts to prevent excessive borrowing while fostering a favorable market environment to attract social capital, particularly private (non-state-owned) capital to enhance its active role in infrastructure development.

References

Chen, S. (2010). Tax-sharing reform, local fiscal autonomy, and public goods provision. *China Economic Quarterly, 9*(4), 1427–1446.

Deng, Z., & Tang, W. (2011). Refining the fiscal management system of the tax-sharing system from the perspective of 60 years of fiscal system changes in New China. *Southeast Academic Research, 5*, 31–39.

Ding, J. (2008). Fiscal decentralization and public product provision incentives during China's transition [Doctoral dissertation]. Fudan University.

Fu, Y. (2007). China-style decentralization, local fiscal models, and public goods provision: Theory and empirical research [Doctoral dissertation]. Fudan University.

Fu, Y. (2010). Fiscal decentralization, government governance, and non-economic public goods provision. *Economic Research, 45*(8), 4–15.

Fu, Y., & Zhang, Y. (2007). Chinese-style decentralization and bias in fiscal expenditure structure: The cost of competing for growth. *Management World, 2007*(3), 4–12.

Gao, P. (2018). 40 years of China's fiscal reform: Basic trajectory, experiences, and principles. *Economic Research, 53*(3), 4–20.

He, Q. (2014). Research on government procurement of public services [Doctoral dissertation]. Fiscal Science Research Institute of the Ministry of Finance.

He, Y., Wang, G., & Chen, S. (2014). Political analysis of urban government expenditure in China. *Chinese Social Sciences, 7*, 87–106.

Jia, Z., & Lu, H. (2010). Fiscal decentralization and the effectiveness of public goods provision in education and livelihood: Empirical analysis based on provincial panel data in China. *Quantitative & Technical Economics, 27*(6), 139–150.
Li, W. (2009). Review and reflection on China's pharmaceutical and medical system reform: An interest group analysis [Doctoral dissertation]. Nankai University.
Li, Y., & Zhang, Z. (2017). Does transfer payment increase the incentive for government social public goods provision? *Economic Research, 52*(1), 119–133.
Liu, W. (2013). Research on the contemporary Chinese system of public goods supply and demand [Doctoral dissertation]. Jilin University.
Pan, S. (2007). Urban infrastructure construction financing management and performance evaluation [Doctoral dissertation]. Hunan University.
Qian, Y. Y., & Roland, G. (1998). Federalism and the soft budget constraint. *American Economic Review, 88*(5), 1143–1162.
Qiao, B., Fan, J., & Feng, X. (2005). China's fiscal decentralization and compulsory primary education. *Chinese Social Sciences, 2005*(6), 37–46.
Shu, C. (2010). Provision of local public goods under China's local fiscal decentralization system: Theory and empiricism [Master's thesis]. Jiangxi University of Finance and Economics.
Tang, Y., Chen, Q., & Man, L. (2016). Capitalization, fiscal incentives, and local public service provision: Empirical analysis based on 35 large and medium-sized cities in China. *China Economic Quarterly, 15*(1), 217–240.
Tsui, K. Y., & Wang, Y. Q. (2004). Between separate stoves and a single menu: Fiscal decentralization in China. *The China Quarterly, 177*, 71–90.
Wan, Y., & Wang, D. (2019). Toward balanced and sustainable development: 40 years of urban public services in China. *Urban Governance Research, 1*, 11–30, 12.
Wang, L., Chen, G., & Jing, Z. (2009). Innovation in financing methods for urban infrastructure construction in China. *Journal of Central University of Finance & Economics, 12*, 53–57.
Wang, P., & Salamon, L. M. (2010). *Research on government procurement of public services from social organizations: China and global experiences*. Peking University Press.
Wang, Y. (2007). Study on the structure of China's fiscal expenditure [Master's thesis]. Dongbei University of Finance and Economics.
Wei, X. (2002). Regional differences in the composition of infrastructure investment in China. *Shanghai Economic Review, 12*, 20–25.
Wong, J. (2004). The adaptive developmental state in East Asia. *Journal of East Asian Studies, 4*(3), 345–362.
Ye, W. (2003). Research on the provision of public goods in China [Doctoral dissertation]. Sichuan University.
Yu, C. (2010). *The evolution and innovation of China's fiscal decentralization*. Economic Science Press.
Yu, J. (2011). China's public service system: Development process, social policy, and institutional mechanism. *Academic Monthly, 43*(3), 5–17.
Zhang, H. (2018). *Research on the impact of foreign trade differences on coordinated regional economic development in China*. People's Publishing House.
Zhang, J., & Zhou, L. (2007). *Competing for growth: The political economy of China's growth*. Shanghai People's Publishing House.
Zhang, J., Gao, Y., Fu, Y., et al. (2007). Why does China have good infrastructure? *Economic Research, 3*, 4–19.
Zhang, X. (2009). Historical evolution and reflection on the development of private education in China over 60 years since the founding of New China. *Education & Vocation, 30*, 16–19.
Zheng, X. (2010a). Analysis of the impact of China's fiscal system on urban scale [Master's thesis]. Graduate School of Chinese Academy of Social Sciences.
Zheng, X. (2010b). Research on the diversified development of public service provision entities in China [Doctoral dissertation]. East China Normal University.

Zhu, H. (2004a). Decentralization reform, fiscal incentives, and the restructuring of state-owned enterprises. *World Economy, 12*, 14–24.
Zhu, H. (2004b). Inter-regional competition, fiscal self-sufficiency, and the privatization of state-owned enterprises. *Economic Research, 10*, 24–34.
Zou, X. (2007). From government monopoly of public services to diversified provision: Research on government regulation toward new public management [Doctoral dissertation]. Fudan University.

Chapter 3
Empirical Research on the Supply Mechanisms of Urban Public Goods

With the advancement of socioeconomic development, urban public goods have become increasingly diversified, forming a multifunctional and complex system. The public goods supply mechanism has also evolved, giving rise to various systems, including governmental supply mechanisms, market (private) supply mechanisms, societal (voluntary) supply mechanisms, and multi-stakeholder cooperative supply mechanisms. It's traditinally believed that, government supply mechanisms focus on pure public goods that are highly public, non-competitive, and non-exclusive. In contrast, market (private) supply mechanisms are suitable for quasi-public goods, including infrastructure and network carrier public goods. Societal (voluntary) supply mechanisms leverage societal forces and capital, often through third-party or non-profit organizations, to expand supply channels and diversify supply methods. Meanwhile, multi-stakeholder cooperative supply mechanisms involving collaboration between governments, enterprises, and social entities, are commonly applicable to the construction and management of various public goods. In practice, while some public goods clearly fall within the domain of either government or private investment, production, and distribution, their distinction often blurs. A hybrid economy has emerged where both market and government mechanisms play active roles in public goods provision. Following the 2008 global financial crisis, international collaboration between governments and societal forces strengthened while increased marketization attracted social capital, making the multi-stakeholder cooperative supply mechanism more prevalent.

This chapter analyzes the factors influencing the supply of urban public goods. With a focus on the current situation in China, we empirically examine government supply mechanisms, market (private) supply mechanisms, societal (voluntary) supply mechanisms, and multi-stakeholder cooperative supply mechanisms from the perspectives of institutional evolution and mechanism development.

B. Wu et al., *Effective Supply Mechanism of Urban Public Goods*, Public Economy and Urban Governance in China, https://doi.org/10.1007/978-981-96-2608-3_3

3.1 Mechanisms for Urban Public Goods Supply

3.1.1 Types of Supply Mechanisms for Urban Public Goods

The supply of urban public goods involves three primary dimensions: supply entities, supply content, and supply mechanisms. The supply entities include the government, enterprises, and social organizations; the supply content encompasses infrastructure such as transportation, telecommunication, energy, and the environment, as well as public services like education, healthcare, and social security; the supply mechanisms refer to how public goods are supplied, determining the relationships between various influencing factors and defining their inherent characteristics and operational mechanisms.

3.1.1.1 Government Supply Mechanism

Within the urban public goods supply system, many public goods and services exhibit substantial public welfare attributes, making their benefits non-excludable and their provision non-rivalrous. Due to market failures, market mechanisms alone are insufficient to operate effectively in this domain, as private firms are generally reluctant to invest in these sectors without governmental intervention to promote public interests.

Before China's reform and opening up, all public goods were government-invested, constructed, operated, and distributed under a planned economy system. With the reform, the public goods supply mechanisms have evolved continuously, but government investment remains the primary modality. Currently, urban infrastructure such as roads, underground pipelines, transport facilities, pollution control, and utilities are invested by governments or state-owned enterprises. Public services such as postal services, civil aviation, cultural and sports amenities, basic education, public healthcare, and social security are also supported by governments. With the development of the market economy, government investments in certain public infrastructures and services may adopt outsourcing or voucher systems for supply. Some public goods may also emerge as collaborative investments between the government and private enterprises, with the governments maintaining ownership and control to enhance the government supply mechanism. Government-supplied public goods include national defense, basic education, public health, science and technology, and broadcast media. Public services provided by state-owned enterprises mainly include telecommunication infrastructure, energy infrastructure, and other public utilities. Moreover, government subsidies are instrumental in achieving specific political, economic, and social targets, such as urban housing subsidies or medical facility subsidies. Vouchers, such as school fee waivers or medical cards, and support for specific groups further enhance the supply mechanisms (Zhang & Zheng, 2019).

Governments can provide public goods through direct investment or capital input. Traditionally, all public goods sectors were government-funded, but market mechanisms have shifted government investments towards non-market fields, such as public infrastructure, ecological protection, basic research, and national security. These investments are non-commercial and focus on public and foundational construction. The government offers financial support in priority areas that encourage social capital participation, incentivizing more social capital by prioritizing projects that include social capital, using tools like investment subsidies, fund injections, guarantees, and loan interest subsidies.

3.1.1.2 Market (Private) Supply Mechanism

Many urban products and services with public functions do not exhibit all public characteristics. Technologies and market transactions can define their property rights and eliminate exclusivity, thereby introducing market competition for investment, construction, and operation. These quasi-public goods typically encompass terminal infrastructure projects and elective services, such as urban transit, utility supplies, healthcare services, tertiary education, and broadcast media.

Under the market supply mechanism, public goods are not only directly invested in and operated by private firms, but also benefit from market competition mechanisms introduced by the government through innovative operating models such as contracting, franchise operation, and user fees. In the contracting system, governments set quantity and quality standards for public goods/services, invite tenders from enterprises and non-profits, with the selected bidders providing the goods/services per the contract. Under the contracting system, the government, as the investor, ensures the supply of public goods necessary for urban society and the public, while the contractors take on the responsibility of construction or operation and service provision. This system breaks away from the traditional patterns of the government solely investing in and operating all public goods, thereby improving supply efficiency through competition. Currently, in various urban sectors in China, including environmental protection, healthcare, social governance, road traffic, and communication, the contracting operating model has been implemented, with government procurement being an important form of contracting. For example, in community health services, the government contracts operational enterprises and institutions to provide medical care, healthcare, rehabilitation, and health education services.

Franchise operation is a system in which the government grants exclusive operating rights to private enterprises or social organizations, allowing them to invest in, construct, and manage public infrastructure and provide public services. This system involves the government delegating part of its public goods supply function to franchise operators (Zheng, 2015). Urban public infrastructure projects typically have significant social and public welfare aspects, large-scale constructions requiring considerable investment, and long service lives that yield relatively stable returns. Examples include electricity, gas, water supply, sewage treatment, and waste management systems that can utilize the franchise model. The government can establish franchise operation contracts with enterprises, outlining the franchise conditions and permitting them to build and manage these projects (Jiang, 2014). In April 2015, with the approval of the State Council, the National Development and Reform

Commission and five other ministries issued the *Regulations on the Management of Franchise Operation of Infrastructure and Public Utilities*. This framework aimed to promote franchise operations in energy, transportation, water conservation, environmental protection, and municipal utilities, offering guidance for social capital to enter the franchise sector. Currently, the majority of municipal infrastructure in China is managed by state-owned enterprises, effectively acting as franchise operators.

With technological advancements and improved market mechanisms, modern cities are increasingly providing public infrastructure and services as public goods through user fees. Individuals, families, and organizations pay these fees to government entities or operating companies based on their consumption levels. This fee-based approach is prevalent in sectors like cable television, healthcare, and highways. As market competition is introduced in public services, the supply methods for these goods are becoming more varied. In the fee-based model, consumers have the freedom of choice, and their preferences influence the quantity and structure of public service provision.

3.1.1.3 Social (Voluntary) Supply Mechanism

The government and the market mechanisms constitute the two most fundamental structures in the supply of public goods. However, both the government and market mechanisms are susceptible to failure. This susceptibility is mainly due to the indivisibility and non-exclusivity characteristics of public goods, which lead to the "free rider problem" problem when people consume public goods. Additionally, public goods often generate positive externalities, complicating optimal market provision and resource allocation. While government supply mechanisms can mitigate market failures, they frequently focus on the needs of the majority or the "meso-position selection", neglecting the specific or excess demands of smaller groups (Xi, 2006), thus leading to government failures as well.

Market and government failures open up opportunities for the social (voluntary) supply mechanism of public goods. The mechanism involves society members voluntarily establishing autonomous organizations and employing a reciprocal mechanism to meet their public needs (Zhou & Song, 2008). As a supplement to government and market supply mechanisms, the social (voluntary) supply mechanism can help address the deficiencies brought about by government and market failures, providing some public goods that the market is unwilling to offer and the government is unable to supply. Under this mechanism, social members create non-profit organizations, known as the third sector, to deliver public services that cannot be effectively managed by government departments and enterprises (Wang, 1999).

Social organizations supply public goods mainly through two mechanisms: (a) social organizations independently conduct public service activities. Guided by government policies, these organizations obtain funding from businesses or use their own resources to develop volunteer programs for specific populations (Yuan & Liu, 2014); (b) social organizations providing public goods on behalf of the government or corporate entities, acting as agents while the government or enterprises serve as principals. This arrangement facilitates a complementary relationship among the government, enterprises, and social organizations (Xi, 2006).

Just as government and market mechanisms can fail, social organizations also have their limitations, known as voluntary failures. A notable limitation is the limited resources that social organizations can mobilize, making it challenging to achieve their public service supply goals (Salamon & Anheier, 1997). Additional issues like dependence on government departments, the informal nature of third-sector activities, the "paternalism" of charitable organizations, and corruption in volunteer activities further contribute to voluntary failures (Wang, 1999; Xi, 2006). These challenges highlight the necessity for government oversight and guidance in the activities of social organizations. On one hand, the government encourages and protects social organizations through legislation; On the other, it strengthens the evaluation, auditing, and supervision of social organization's service processes.

3.1.1.4 Multi-stakeholder Cooperative Supply Mechanism

The multi-stakeholder cooperative supply mechanism for urban public goods involves the joint participation of the government, enterprises, social organizations, and residents in producing, supplying, and managing public goods. Within this framework, the government typically acts as the planner, organizer, and leader of public goods supply, establishing legally binding cooperative relationships with enterprises and social organizations through appropriate cooperative mechanisms and regulations, thereby leveraging the synergistic effects of multi-stakeholder cooperation (Leng, 2010). Furthermore, the government designs mechanisms to address the challenges of public preference display and convergence, developing mechanisms for expressing and identifying residents' demands for urban public goods, democratic decision-making, financial support, multi-governance, and supervisory feedback (Luo & Yao, 2012).

Multi-stakeholder cooperative supply mechanisms primarily encompass public-private partnerships (PPP) and collaborations between government and third-party organizations. This mechanism is widely applied across various public goods sectors such as energy, transportation, water resources, environmental protection, healthcare, elderly care, education, and culture. In recent years, especially in China's public infrastructure sector, promoting and adopting the PPP model to involve social capital in public goods supply have enhanced investment capabilities and improved the quality and efficiency of public goods provision. The PPP model effectively leverages market mechanisms and innovates the supply mechanisms and investment approaches for public goods, ultimately maximizing public interests.

3.1.2 Factors Influencing the Supply of Urban Public Goods

Since the reform and opening up, China's public goods sector has undergone constant institutional changes, resulting in a diversification of supply entities and mechanisms and a supply mechanism dominated by the government with the active participation of the market and social organizations. However, despite urban development needs and rising public demands, the supply level and quality of public goods remain relatively low, exhibiting structural imbalances. Various factors affect the adequate supply of urban public goods, including the level of urban economic development, industrial structure, fiscal system, income mechanism, public goods allocation and supply mechanisms, and decision-making mechanisms (Leng, 2010; Song, 2020).

3.1.2.1 Urban Economic Development Level

Economic development has a direct impact on government fiscal revenue, fiscal policies and macroeconomic adjustments, as well as the quantity and structure of public goods supply. In the early stages of China's economic development, the government's primary goal was to increase investment and promote economic growth, paying less attention to public goods supply, especially non-economic public goods supply. At this stage, the supply of public goods was mainly economic public goods, and the supply level was low. As the economy develops, increased fiscal revenue allows the government to shift its focus toward high-quality economic and social development, emphasizing the supply of non-economic public goods supply. Subsequently, the total supply of public goods increases, and the supply structure shifts towards non-economic public goods.

Figure 3.1 illustrates the relationship and trajectory between China's economic development and public goods supply from 1990 to 2018. Annual GDP reflects economic development, while fiscal budgetary expenditure indicates public goods supply, both showing a synchronous upward trend. However, the growth rate of public goods supply lags behind that of economic development.

3.1.2.2 Urban Industrial Structure

The influence of industrial structure on public goods supply is mainly reflected in changes in public goods demand. In traditional agricultural societies, demand for public goods is low, resulting in a simple public goods structure. As urban industries develop, the industrial structure adjusts with the level of urban development, prominently displaying shifts among industrial, commercial, and service sectors. Urban industries also show characteristics of labor and technology aggregation. Thus, cities at different development stages and economic types will possess distinct industrial structures, influencing public goods supply. In industrial-dominated urban areas, the growth of manufacturing and logistics increases the demand for infrastructure,

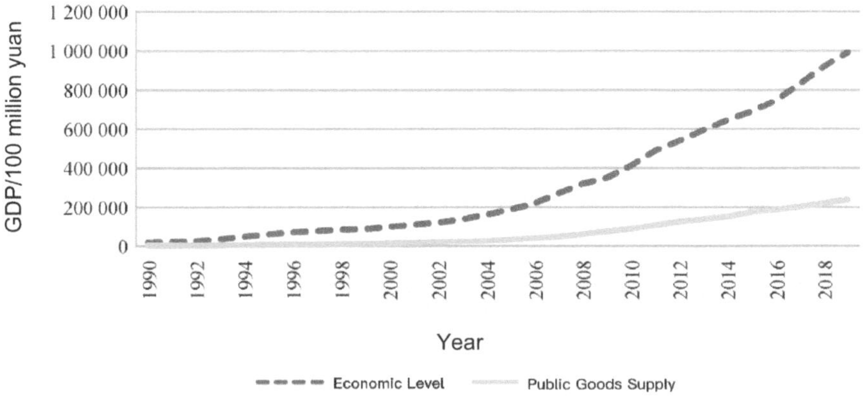

Fig. 3.1 The relationship and trends between economic development and public goods provision in China (1990–2018)

housing for workers, basic education, healthcare, and social security. In areas dominated by cultural tourism, education, and technology, the high mobility of the workforce heightens the need for transportation, communication, cultural education, and technology services (Min, 2011).

We conducted an empirical examination of the relationship between China's industrial structure and public goods supply from 1990 to 2018, using fiscal budgetary expenditure for public goods supply and the share of secondary and tertiary industry output in GDP as indicators of industrial structure. Our findings show that as industrial structure advances, public goods supply also increases, particularly after 2009, which suggests a mutually influential relationship between advanced industrial structure and public goods supply.

3.1.2.3 Urban Fiscal System and Income Mechanism

See Fig. 3.2.

The fiscal system establishes the fundamental framework for intergovernmental fiscal relationships, directly shaping local governments' fiscal authority and spending power. The varying fiscal responsibilities and revenue capacities of central and local governments influence the method of public goods supply. A well-designed fiscal system should encourage local governments to rationally determine the scale and structure of public goods supply, enhance quality and efficiency, and maximize social welfare within their jurisdictions.

The fiscal revenue mechanism involves the models' local governments use to fund and finance public goods supply. For local governments, developing a reasonable fiscal revenue mechanism is essential for creating an economically compatible and incentive-aligned decentralized fiscal system. Such mechanisms should be precise in

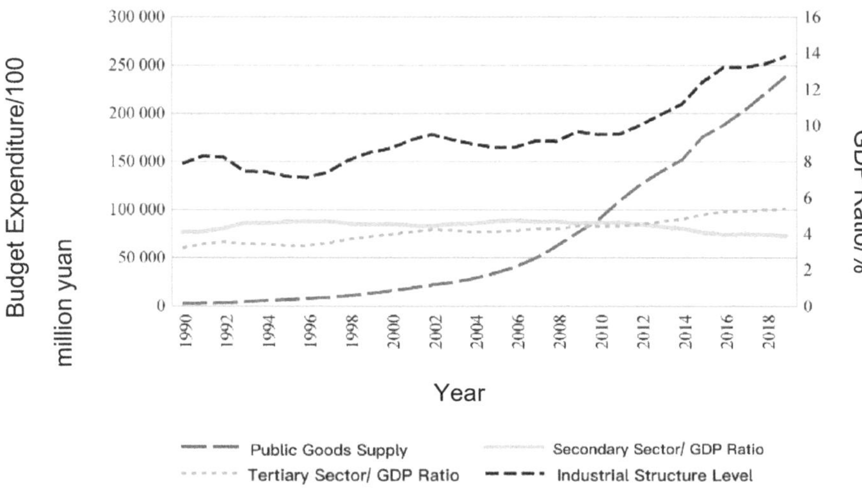

Fig. 3.2 The relationship and trends between national industrial structure and public goods provision (1990–2018)

authority, transparent in sources, responsible in usage, and well-defined in purpose to adequately plan and regulate the content and scale of public goods supply.

Before supplying public goods, the government needs to determine the appropriate quantity to produce, involving the scale and structure of public expenditure. The effectiveness of the fiscal system determines the maximum achievable public expenditure within limited resources. Furthermore, varying social preferences mean that, given constrained fiscal resources, forming a supply structure that accommodates diverse interests also depends on the fiscal system's effectiveness. Consequently, an effective fiscal system defines a rational framework for urban public goods supply. Moreover, the fiscal system influences the cost of public goods supply. All public goods require certain input, and an effective fiscal system enables the production of a set quantity of public goods with minimal input or the output of more public goods with a given input, thus lowering supply costs and improving efficiency (Southwestern University of Finance and Economics, School of Public Finance and Taxation Research, 2012).

A fiscal system also affects the funding method for public goods investment, determining revenue sources and financing methods. According to the "Wicksell-Lindahl equilibrium" in public finance theory, optimal public goods supply is achieved only when individuals contribute to public expenses in proportion to the benefits they receive. However, in reality, individuals do not always follow this principle when choosing public goods funding. This is often due to the fact that individuals may not always reveal their true preferences and significant disparities in payment capacities among the population, which means that less affluent groups, who frequently have the highest demands for public goods, cannot fully support them. Thus, beyond user fees, public goods funding needs fiscal support from the government and social capital under market mechanisms.

In China, the balance between fiscal centralization and decentralization plays a significant role in the supply of urban public goods. Fiscal decentralization can enhance supply efficiency and reduce production costs through the "yardstick competition" effect. After the tax-sharing reform, revenue constraints from interlocal tax competition assist in controlling government budgets and the scale of local public goods. Decentralized governments, with their informational advantages, can better align public goods supply with local residents' preferences, making the supply structure more reasonable (Zhang, 2006; Zhang and Gong, 2005). Conversely, centralized supply levels often fail to meet demand, thereby raising supply costs. Nevertheless, centralization is beneficial for the provision of nationwide and regional public goods, compensating for deficiencies in regional spillover effects.

3.1.2.4 Urban Public Goods Allocation and Supply Mechanism

The rational allocation structure, the flexibility of allocation mechanisms, and the diversity of supply mechanisms affect public goods supply efficiency. Urbanization, in particular, increases the demand for infrastructure and public services, raising the standard for supply quality. Consequently, it is essential that the allocation of public goods maintains a rational structure that accurately reflects the demands of residents. Urban public goods allocation should gradually shift from a top-down to a bottom-up mechanism, establishing robust frameworks for demand expression, participation, and feedback. This ensures the provision of appropriate public goods, leading to a more reasonable supply structure, cost reduction, and improved efficiency (Xia, 2013). Furthermore, there should be a transition from a "single" government supply model to a "diversified" supply approach involving the government, enterprises, social organizations, and residents. This would effectively leverage various mechanisms to enhance the supply of urban public goods.

3.1.2.5 Urban Public Goods Decision-Making Mechanism

Public goods decision-making mechanisms reflect how governments or societies respond to demand, selecting public goods projects and funding methods. These mechanisms vary depending on the political systems and levels of member participation in public goods demand and revenue choices.

From a public choice perspective, three decision-making mechanisms for expressing public goods demand are discussed: centralized decision-making, "voting by hand", and "voting by foot".

Centralized decision-making involves a single individual or a small group making collective choices, which is characterized by low costs and high efficiency but may replace collective preferences with those of the individual or small group. "Voting by hand" allows individuals to express preferences through voting, reflecting collective public goods preferences, and forming collective action decisions based on rules (Luo & Yao, 2012). "Voting by foot", based on the Tiebout model (Tiebout, 1956), suggests that individuals, aware of different public goods combinations and freely moving, choose to live in communities offering the most satisfactory arrangements. This mechanism shows preferences for public goods. The regionally optimal scale is achieved when the average cost of provided public goods is lowest (Liu, 2015; Southwestern University of Finance and Economics, School of Public Finance and Taxation Research, 2012). Despite practical restrictions limiting their theoretical effectiveness, these theories offer fundamental insights into public goods demand preference exploration and optimization decision-making mechanisms.

3.2 Government Supply Mechanism for Urban Public Goods

3.2.1 Evolution of the Government Supply Mechanism for Urban Public Goods in China

The government supply mechanism for urban public goods encompasses the direct provision or delegated production of public goods by government departments, state-owned enterprises, and public institutions. It is commonly understood that the government's role in public goods supply primarily aims to address market failures. The characteristics of urban public goods, particularly their non-excludability in usage, create externalities that impede the effectiveness of market competition mechanisms. The information asymmetry between supply and demand inevitably leads to market inefficiencies. Consequently, a profit-driven market mechanism struggles to balance public goods' supply and demand and often incurs efficiency losses. Only through government investment and operation can the public's demand for public goods be met during economic development. Moreover, during different periods, the government's provision of public goods also plays a crucial role in social resource allocation and social management.

When urban public goods are directly produced and supplied by the government, it means that government agencies and state-controlled enterprises are actively involved in providing urban public services and infrastructure. The leading providers of public goods are government-funded entities or those receiving construction and operational funding through budget appropriations, thus forming the integrated property rights characteristic of government and enterprise-unified systems. The government is responsible for formulating investment and production plans, issuing policies to promote their supply, allocating construction and operational funds, and appointing project leaders.

The systems and policies regarding the government provision of public goods in many countries have been criticized. Practices have shown that direct government or government-controlled entity investments, construction, and operations of urban public goods can lead to governmental administrative monopolies, inefficiency, and official corruption. Under government monopolies, since the government acts as a rule-maker, supervisor, and executor, it can use administrative measures to protect its public sectors and controlled enterprises. Government monopolies stifle the motivation for technological innovation in public enterprises and eliminate incentives to minimize costs, resulting in inefficiencies, cost inflation, and ultimately deviating from the goal of public interest maintenance (Jiang, 2014; Wu, 2008).

The entrusted production mode refers to the government directly commissioning for-profit enterprises or social organizations outside the public sector to construct and operate public goods. In this mode, the government remains the investor and owner of these goods, while the commissioned party takes on construction and management responsibilities, receiving investment or operational returns as per the agreement. Typically, the government selects these enterprises through a bidding process or direct authorization, signing entrustment agreements for its investment projects' construction or operational rights. Essentially, entrusted production represents a public-private partnership, separating the government's investment and management functions in the public products domain, allowing the government to focus resources on construction and regulatory oversight to enhance operational efficiency (Gao, 2004).

However, the government's entrusted production model has drawbacks. Asymmetric information and the difficulty in pricing public products, make it challenging to measure accurately comprehensive production, and operational costs. In practice, the bidding process often fails to resolve the accurate measurement of cost-benefit issues, especially for projects with operational difficulties and service quality concerns. Moreover, the government may find it difficult to accurately and promptly gauge public demand under this model, leading to a misalignment between constructed projects and public needs, reducing the social benefits of certain public products. There is also a risk of moral hazard that some commissioned enterprises might prioritize commercial interests over public benefits.

During the planned economy period, China's urban public infrastructure and service supply solely relied on a government provision mechanism. The government organized and realized the production and supply of public goods based on socioeconomic development and urban residents' needs. Given the shortcomings of this government supply mechanism, the government has continually introduced market mechanisms into urban public goods supply since the reform and opening up policy. On the one hand, the government has transferred some public good supply functions to enterprises and social organizations through open bidding, targeted entrustment, and invitations for bids. On the other hand, it has actively promoted the implementation of market supply mechanisms.

The evolution of urban public goods government supply mechanisms can be roughly divided into three stages:

3.2.1.1 Direct Government Provision Under Administrative Allocation of Public Goods

During the planned economy period, the government exclusively supplied urban public goods supply, including transportation infrastructure, communication facilities, water supply, power, and gas utilities within its administrative investment and management scope. Public services such as education, health, and sports were also considered government-provided welfare. During this time, the prices of most public goods remained unchanged by supply-demand dynamics and costs.

The basic model of urban public goods supply was characterized by a high degree of integration between government and enterprises, with public institutions and state-owned enterprises directly handling production and operations. The government made decisions regarding public goods provision, formulated construction plans, allocated resources, and directly invested in production and management. The government supervised construction and operational activities, determined distribution methods, principles, and standards, and set supply prices through administrative plans. Infrastructure project funding was entirely provided by the government, with construction and operating entities lacking market subject status, decision-making power in production and operations, and incentive mechanisms.

3.2.1.2 Gradually Introducing Market Mechanisms and Government Withdrawal from Comprehensive Public Goods Supply

After the reform and opening up, the government introduced a planned market economic system and a dual-track model to alleviate the limitations of planned economic competition. This shift led to the separation of urban public goods supply systems, with investment and production responsibilities shifting from government departments to enterprises. As the market economy developed, economic growth accelerated, and residents' incomes increased, resulting in a surge in demand for infrastructure and public services, which widened the funding gap. These supply-demand conflicts and fiscal pressures prompted the government to step back from certain production roles, inviting social capital to construct public facilities and utilizing market mechanisms for public goods supply structures.

The initial market mechanism involved the BOT (Build-Operate-Transfer) model, trialed in the mid-1980s, with the Shajiao B power plant being the first BOT project in urban infrastructure. In 1994, the State Council's 16th executive meeting reviewed and approved the *Outline of National Industrial Policy in the 1990s*, proposing to "strengthen infrastructure and fundamental industries", "expand foreign investment scope and encourage direct foreign investments in infrastructure and fundamental industries", fostering a policy environment for foreign and private domestic capital participation. Despite these efforts, domestic private investment in infrastructure projects remained minimal, with investments in transport, urban, and social infrastructure not exceeding 10% of total national investments by 2000.

After 2001, particularly the joining of the World Trade Organization, China's reform and opening up accelerated. The government relaxed restrictions on foreign and private domestic capital investments, with national and local authorities introducing a series of regulations to encourage private investments. In 2001, *Several Opinions on Promoting and Guiding Private Investment* and *Opinions on Accelerating the Development of the Service Industry During the Tenth Five-Year' Period* called for the gradual deregulation of investment fields. The 16th Central Committee's third plenary session report further emphasized: "clearing and revising laws and policies restricting the development of the non-public economy, removing systemic barriers; relaxing market access, allowing non-public capital into infrastructure, utilities, and other sectors not prohibited by laws and regulations; ensuring equal treatment for non-public enterprises in investment, financing, taxation, land use, and foreign trade". Consequently, public infrastructure sectors gradually opened up to foreign and private domestic capital, with non-state capital becoming one of the primary investment entities in urban public infrastructure.

3.2.1.3 Multi-stakeholder Cooperative Supply Led by the Government

Over the past decade, as the economic development model transformed, the government further decentralized power to stimulate the private economy. Its role in public goods supply has shifted from direct provider to policy maker, industry regulator, and performance overseer. The government now employs legal, economic, and administrative tools instead of direct intervention, retaining responsibility for essential public goods while increasingly acting as an investor. Construction and operational tasks are gradually transferred to commercial entities. The 2014 *Guiding Opinions on Government and Social Capital Cooperation* by the National Development and Reform Commission (NDRC) indicated that the government's primary role in public goods supply should be policy formulation, development planning, market regulation, and service guidance, with public institutions shifting from direct "providers" to indirect "partners" and "supervisors". The 2019 *Action Plan to Promote Strong Domestic Market Formation by Addressing Public Service Sector Shortcomings and Enhancing Quality* issued by several departments highlighted that the government should create policies, lead planning, foster environments, and provide regulatory services to encourage market and social organization involvement in public goods supply, promoting the marketization, diversification, and quality of non-essential public services. As regulations governing investment and construction by public departments improved, the past decade has seen significant engagement from foreign and domestic private capital in public infrastructure and service investments, making government-social capital cooperation a key approach to urban public goods supply.

3.2.2 Fiscal System and Government Provision of Urban Public Goods

The government's provision of public goods is closely linked to the fiscal system, which includes both the government's financial capacity and the fiscal relationship between central and local authorities. During the planned economy period, China had a centralized fiscal system, with the central government managing funds through a "unified revenue and expenditure" approach. Since the reform and opening up, the fiscal system has undergone continuous changes aimed at empowering local governments. In the 1980s, three major fiscal reforms were implemented: "delineation of income and expenditure, and hierarchical fiscal responsibility" fiscal system in 1980; "delineation of tax categories, determining revenues and expenditures, hierarchical fiscal responsibility" system in 1985; and the "multiple forms of contracting" system in 1988 (Zhao, 2009). These reforms partially decentralized fiscal authority and allowed local governments to retain tax revenues after remitting a fixed proportion to the central government. Additionally, local governments took on certain responsibilities for producing and supplying public goods. These fiscal reforms clarified the responsibilities of local governments, granting them the authority to raise and allocate fiscal revenues, thus incentivizing them to develop the economy, increase fiscal revenue, and provide public goods. However, this "contracting" fiscal system also led to market partitioning, redundant projects, and blind competition among local governments. The lag in off-budget fund management reforms allowed some local governments to transfer on-budget fiscal income to off-budget funds or "keep wealth with the people" through tax concessions, harming the central government's fiscal revenue (Huang, 2007; Tu, 2013; Xia, 2013).

To advance China's fiscal reforms and rectify issues arising from the "contracting" system, the fiscal system was shifted to the tax-sharing system in 1994. The tax-sharing system delineated the responsibilities and financial powers of the central and local governments, with the central government controlling tax revenue distribution decisions and concentrating on budget fiscal revenue centrally. Local governments gained the right to use budgeted revenues, with the central government making no explicit directives on the usage of local fiscal funds beyond earmarked transfers and statutory expenditures. Additionally, to bridge economic and fiscal disparities between regions, the central government provided subsidies to local governments that were insufficient to maintain basic public expenditures through transfer payments. The tax-sharing reform significantly impacted public goods sectors, leaving local governments responsible for providing public infrastructure, basic education, healthcare, social security, and other public goods within their jurisdictions, besides national security and nationwide public goods.

Overall, the tax-sharing reform safeguarded the central government's fiscal revenue, enhanced its financial capacity, and improved macroeconomic control while incentivizing local governments to develop the economy, raise fiscal revenues, and invest in public infrastructure. However, in practice, the new fiscal system encountered several challenges. Scholars have conducted in-depth research on the advantages and disadvantages of the tax-sharing system. Generally, the viewpoints are as follows: (a) The tax-sharing reform motivated local governments to increase fiscal revenues and raise construction funds. Some researchers found that China's fiscal decentralization provided effective incentives for local governments to pursue economic development. This incentive was particularly significant in urbanization and development zone construction, where land transfer revenues in economically developed regions increasingly outpaced general fiscal revenues, providing necessary funds for local government investments in public goods (Qian & Weingast, 1997); (b) Under the tax-sharing reform, public goods sectors' supply capacity and effectiveness are enhanced. Local governments have an advantage in obtaining demand information, lower supply agency costs, and possess incentives for yardstick competition and innovation in a competitive regional landscape (Boadway, 2006; Hayek, 1945). Tiebout (1956) argued that competition among local governments leads to Pareto-efficient public goods supply; (c) The fiscal decentralization system improves economic efficiency (Oates, 1972); (d) However, fiscal decentralization and local government competition can produce adverse effects. Some scholars point out that China's fiscal decentralization reform led to a unique situation of political centralization separating from economic decentralization, creating distortions under soft budget constraints (Qian & Roland, 1998). Ping and Bai (2006) revealed that local governments gained increased control over off-budget expenditures, a primary fiscal incentive source. Others noted that competition among local governments under fiscal decentralization could cause systematic distortions in public spending structures (Keen & Marchand, 1997). Li and Jiang (2010) empirically found that fiscal expenditure decentralization enlarged local government fiscal spending while revenue decentralization failed to impose practical constraints due to the lack of local government revenue autonomy. Some scholars also studied the impact of fiscal decentralization on public goods sectors, indicating that competition-oriented decentralization skewed local government fiscal spending structures. To attract investment, promote urbanization, and develop economic zones, local governments tended to invest heavily in productive public goods like infrastructure while severely neglecting social public goods like education and healthcare (Fu, 2007; Tu, 2013), leading to imbalanced public goods supply structures.

Given these drawbacks of fiscal decentralization, scholars have suggested further reforms. Some proposed balancing regional public goods supply through central fiscal transfers, emphasizing that the central government should address disparities caused by limited regional mobility and deficiencies in the guarantee system to promote equal access to basic public services (Ding & Deng, 2008; Fan & Zhang, 2013).

3.2.3 Empirical Analysis of the Government Supply Mechanism of Urban Public Goods in China

3.2.3.1 Urban Fiscal Expenditure and Public Goods Supply

Based on the evaluation methods of economic and non-economic public goods, we can calculate the supply indices of economic and non-economic public goods in Chinese cities from 2004 to 2017. The cities with the highest economic public goods supply indices are listed in Table 3.1, while those for non-economic public goods are in Table 3.2. The data show that the top cities for economic public goods supply are generally those with high or rapidly growing levels of economic development. Conversely, the top cities for non-economic public goods supply, while also economically developed, such as Dongguan, Chengdu, and Suzhou, are characterized by higher levels of social development.

Shenzhen stands out for its balanced supply of both economic and non-economic public goods, reflecting its relatively high socioeconomic development. To analyze the impact of Shenzhen's fiscal expenditure on public goods supply, we conducted a statistical analysis of local budgetary expenditures. Data from 2002 to 2006, presented in Tables 3.3 and 3.4 due to 2007 adjustments, revealed that capital construction expenditure comprised 19–31% of total budget expenditure, with combined capital and fund budget expenditures accounting for 21–32% of local fiscal outlays. In comparison, expenditures on non-economic public goods—covering

Table 3.1 Top 5 cities in economic public goods supply index

Year	City				
2004	Shanghai	Shenzhen	Beijing	Guangzhou	Tianjin
2005	Shanghai	Shenzhen	Beijing	Guangzhou	Dongguan
2006	Shanghai	Shenzhen	Beijing	Guangzhou	Tianjin
2007	Shanghai	Shenzhen	Beijing	Ordos	Guangzhou
2008	Shanghai	Shenzhen	Beijing	Tianjin	Kunming
2009	Shanghai	Shenzhen	Beijing	Kunming	Tianjin
2010	Shanghai	Shenzhen	Ordos	Chongqing	Fuzhou
2011	Chongqing	Shenzhen	Guangzhou	Beijing	Harbin
2012	Shenzhen	Shanghai	Guangzhou	Beijing	Nanning
2013	Shenzhen	Guangzhou	Beijing	Shanghai	Weifang
2014	Tianjin	Shenzhen	Qingdao	Guangzhou	Shanghai
2015	Tianjin	Shenzhen	Shanghai	Chongqing	Meishan
2016	Shenzhen	Chongqing	Chengdu	Suzhou	Shanghai
2017	Chongqing	Shenzhen	Suzhou	Chengdu	Shanghai

Source Rankings based on relevant data from the *China City Statistical Yearbook* (2005–2018)

Table 3.2 Top 5 cities in non-economic public goods supply index

Year	City				
2004	Shanghai	Beijing	Dongguan	Shenzhen	Chongqing
2005	Shanghai	Beijing	Shenzhen	Guangzhou	Chongqing
2006	Shenzhen	Dongguan	Shanghai	Beijing	Guangzhou
2007	Shenzhen	Dongguan	Shanghai	Beijing	Linfen
2008	Shenzhen	Shanghai	Beijing	Dongguan	Chongqing
2009	Shenzhen	Shanghai	Beijing	Dongguan	Linfen
2010	Shenzhen	Shanghai	Beijing	Chongqing	Guangzhou
2011	Shenzhen	Guangzhou	Wuhan	Shanghai	Beijing
2012	Wuhan	Shenzhen	Dongguan	Beijing	Chongqing
2013	Shenzhen	Dongguan	Shanghai	Beijing	Chongqing
2014	Shenzhen	Dongguan	Shanghai	Beijing	Zunyi
2015	Shenzhen	Dongguan	Shanghai	Beijing	Karamay
2016	Shenzhen	Dongguan	Ordos	Shanghai	Beijing
2017	Dongguan	Chongqing	Shenzhen	Guangzhou	Shanghai

Source Rankings based on relevant data from the *China City Statistical Yearbook* (2005–2018)

education, scientific research, healthcare, and urban maintenance—only constituted 18–19%. This suggests that Shenzhen primarily focused on economic public goods, with a smaller share allocated to non-economic public goods.

Table 3.3 Shenzhen local budgetary fiscal expenditure (2002–2006)

Category	2002	2003	2004	2005	2006
Local budgetary fiscal expenditure	3,121,929	3,591,471	3,862,873	6,131,996	5,844,526
General budget expenditure	3,077,761	3,489,526	3,775,720	5,991,560	5,714,231
Basic construction expenditure	975,608	967,480	1,030,730	1,163,851	1,294,500
Enterprise renovation fund	76,164	67,583	82,334	91,801	95,196
Science and technology expenses	168,543	148,567	188,451	274,750	285,699
Education expenditure	321,830	389,452	419,957	509,773	620,662
Scientific research expenditure	14,076	15,274	13,754	16,833	20,851
Medical and health expenditure	108,940	129,977	129,078	150,319	191,373
Retirement expenditure	32,856	41,733	39,081	59,397	68,832
Administrative expenses	184,477	266,062	295,003	360,788	460,825
Public security expenditure	244,007	329,012	370,732	467,631	508,305
Urban maintenance fee	116,713	132,964	165,308	214,855	247,733
Special expenditure	46,033	51,079	76,000	86,887	111,738

Source Shenzhen Statistical Yearbook (2003–2007)
Unit: ten thousand yuan

Table 3.4 Shenzhen local budgetary fiscal expenditure (2007–2017)

Year	General budget expenditure	Education expenditure	Scientific research expenditure	Cultural, sports, and media expenditure	Social security and employment expenditure	Medical and health expenditure	Fund budget expenditure
2007	7,279,677	905,646	500,263	91,236	251,242	254,677	1,988,478
2008	8,898,555	1,030,900	546,820	128,691	379,028	326,089	1,641,881
2009	10,008,394	1,366,266	791,591	345,197	414,619	549,917	1,532,373
2010	12,660,668	1,524,955	1,166,617	567,668	478,158	619,987	2,327,722
2011	15,905,599	1,967,928	704,863	460,504	518,856	786,926	1,920,221
2012	15,690,071	2,461,343	792,651	328,388	667,785	1,052,925	3,102,863
2013	16,908,280	2,877,280	1,329,814	329,433	784,985	1,069,185	3,613,114
2014	21,661,841	3,294,137	945,707	580,070	738,828	1,576,028	4,621,312
2015	35,216,708	2,885,520	2,143,182	527,260	845,801	1,505,974	3,427,517
2016	42,110,429	4,147,269	4,035,240	547,941	1,054,524	2,012,739	4,137,502
2017	45,938,003	5,090,971	3,518,252	571,218	2,397,159	2,442,264	5,370,357

Source Shenzhen Statistical Yearbook (2008–2018)
Unit: ten thousand yuan

After 2007, Shenzhen increasingly emphasized non-economic public goods. Calculations showed that non-economic public goods provision exceeded 30% and even reached over 60% in some years from 2007 to 2017.

3.2.3.2 Fiscal Decentralization, Local Government Competition, and Urban Public Goods Provision

Extensive empirical research has explored the impact of fiscal decentralization and local government competition on public goods provision, often based on provincial data without distinguishing between economic and non-economic public goods. This book examines 285 prefecture-level cities in China from 2004 to 2017 to empirically study the effects of fiscal decentralization and local government competition on economic and non-economic public goods provision. Fiscal decentralization is represented by local government budgetary autonomy (measured by the ratio of local budgetary revenue to local budgetary expenditure) (Gao, 2012). Competition among city governments is measured by the share of utilized foreign investment in GDP, following Zhu (2019) Additional control variables include per capita GDP, population density, employment figures, and industrial structure (measured by the share of secondary and tertiary industries in GDP). Data sources include *the China Urban Statistical Yearbook*. The empirical models established are as follows:

$$ecopub_{it} = \alpha_0 + \alpha_1 czfq_{it} + \beta X_u + u_i + v_t + \varepsilon_{it} \tag{3.1}$$

$$ecopub_{it} = \alpha_0 + \alpha_1 czfq_{it} + \alpha_2 zfjz_{it} + \beta X_{it} + u_i + v_t + \varepsilon_{it} \tag{3.2}$$

$$\begin{aligned} ecopub_{it} = {} & \alpha_0 + \alpha_1 czfq_{it} + \alpha_2 zfjz_{it} \\ & + \alpha_3 czfq_{it} \times zfjz_{it} + \beta X_{it} + u_i + v_t + \varepsilon_{it} \end{aligned} \tag{3.3}$$

$$\begin{aligned} ecopub_{it} = {} & \alpha_0 + ecopub_{i,t-1} + \alpha_1 czfq_{it} \\ & + \alpha_2 zfjz_{it} \times + \alpha_3 czfq_{it} \times zfjz_{it} + \beta X_{it} + u_i + v_t + \varepsilon_{it} \end{aligned} \tag{3.4}$$

$$necopub_{it} = \alpha_0 + \alpha_1 cz_{it} + \beta X_u + u_i + v_t + \varepsilon_{it} \tag{3.5}$$

$$necopub_{it} = \alpha_0 + \alpha_1 czfq_{it} + \alpha_2 zfjz_{it} + \beta X_{it} + u_i + v_t + \varepsilon_{it} \tag{3.6}$$

$$\begin{aligned} necopub_{it} = {} & \alpha_0 + \alpha_1 czfq_{it} + \alpha_2 zfjz_{it} \\ & + \alpha_3 czfq_{it} \times zfjz_{it} + \beta X_{it} + u_i + v_t + \varepsilon_{it} \end{aligned} \tag{3.7}$$

$$\begin{aligned} necopub_{it} = {} & \alpha_0 + necopub_{i,t-1} + \alpha_1 czfq_{it} \\ & + \alpha_2 zfjz_{it} \times + \alpha_3 czfq_{it} \times zfjz_{it} + \beta X_{it} + u_i + v_t + \varepsilon_{it} \end{aligned} \tag{3.8}$$

In these formulae, *ecopub* denotes economic public goods provision, *necopub* denotes non-economic public goods provision, *zfjz* denotes the degree of local government competition and X_{it} denotes control variables, including GDP per capita, population density, number of employees, and industrial structure; u_i and v_t denote individual fixed effects and time fixed effects respectively, and ε_{it} denotes the error term.

Based on the above model analysis, Table 3.5 presents empirical results on the relationship between local government fiscal autonomy, local government competition, and economic public goods provision. According to the results of Model 1 in Table 3.5, the impact of local government budgetary fiscal autonomy on the provision of economic public goods is negative. The results of Model 2 further indicate that, after adding the variable of local government competition, both local government fiscal autonomy and local government competition negatively affect the provision of economic public goods. The results of Model 3 show that after adding the interaction term between local government fiscal autonomy and local government competition, the impact of local government fiscal autonomy on the provision of economic public goods remains negative. In contrast, the effect of local government competition on the provision of economic public goods turns positive. The interaction term between local government fiscal autonomy and local government competition negatively affects the provision of economic public goods. The results of Model 4 indicate that after adding the lagged term of economic public goods provision to Model 2, both local government fiscal autonomy and local government competition negatively impact the provision of economic public goods, while the lagged term of economic public goods provision positively affects economic public goods provision. Based on the empirical results above, we provide the following explanation: On the one hand, in cities with higher fiscal autonomy, the government's flexibility in adjusting fiscal expenditure structures is higher (Jia & Guo, 2008). Moreover, local governments have more incentives to pursue economic development (Zhang & Gong, 2005; Zhou, 2007), which significantly boosts infrastructure levels and drives the provision of economic public goods. On the other hand, cities with lower fiscal autonomy need to obtain more central transfer payments. The transfer payment system plays a role in alleviating regional financial inequalities and promoting equalizing public services (Yu et al., 2020). These factors facilitate the provision of non-economic public goods. The effect of local government fiscal autonomy on the provision of economic public goods depends on these two mechanisms. Empirical results show that the impact of local government fiscal autonomy on the provision of economic public goods is consistently negative. This indicates that the provision effect of economic public goods in cities with higher fiscal autonomy is weaker than that of non-economic public goods in cities with lower fiscal autonomy.

Table 3.6 shows the empirical results of local government fiscal autonomy, local government competition, and non-economic public goods provision and the results of Model 5 in Table 3.6 indicate that local government budgetary fiscal autonomy positively impacts the provision of non-economic public goods. Model 6 further shows that after including the variable of local government competition, the impact of local

Table 3.5 Empirical results of local government fiscal autonomy, government competition, and supply of economic public goods

Variable	Model 1	Model 2	Model 3	Model 4
Lag of economic public goods supply				0.5516^{***} (0.000)
Local government fiscal autonomy	-0.0393^{***} (0.000)	-0.0356^{***} (0.000)	-0.0244^{***} (0.000)	-0.0221^{***} (0.000)
Government competition		1.2086^{***} (0.000)	0.5525 (0.460)	1.1282^{***} (0.000)
Fiscal autonomy × competition			-3.1499^{***} (0.011)	
GDP per capita	$3.89E08^{***}$	$3.82E08^{***}$	$3.84E08^{***}$	$1.84E08^{***}$
2013	(0.000)	(0.000)	(0.000)	(0.001)
Population density	$-8.78E08^{***}$ (0.000)	$-8.49E06^{***}$ (0.000)	$-8.35E06^{***}$ (0.000)	$-6.77E06^{***}$ (0.000)
Number of employee	$4.59E04^{***}$	$4.52E04^{***}$	$4.42E04^{***}$	$2.11E04^{***}$
2016	(0.000)	(0.000)	(0.000)	(0.000)
Industrial structure	0.0029^{***}	0.0028^{***}	0.0028^{***}	0.0021^{***}

Note *** denotes significance at the 1% level; the values in parentheses represent the p-values of the corresponding coefficients

government fiscal autonomy on the provision of non-economic public goods remains positive. In contrast, the impact of local government competition on the provision of non-economic public goods is negative. The results of Model 7 show that after adding the interaction term between local government fiscal autonomy and local government competition, both local government fiscal autonomy and local government competition positively affect the provision of non-economic public goods. In contrast, the interaction term negatively affects the provision of non-economic public goods. The results of Model 8 indicate that after adding the lagged term of non-economic public goods provision to Model 6, the impact of local government fiscal autonomy on the provision of non-economic public goods is positive. In contrast, the impact of local government competition on the provision of non-economic public goods remains negative, and the lagged term positively affects the provision of non-economic public goods. Referencing the interpretation of the results in Table 3.5, cities with lower fiscal autonomy receive more central transfer payments, which alleviates regional financial inequality and promotes the equalization of public services, thereby boosting the provision of local non-economic public goods.

This research indicates that increasing budgetary fiscal autonomy benefits non-economic public goods but negatively impacts the provision of economic public

Table 3.6 Empirical results of local government fiscal autonomy, government competition, and supply of non-economic public goods

Variable	Model 5	Model 6	Model 7	Model 8
Lag of non-economic public goods supply				0.4660*** (0.000)
Local government fiscal autonomy	0.0759*** (0.000)	0.0781*** (0.000)	0.0839*** (0.000)	0.0478*** (0.000)
Government competition		−0.7060** (0.022)	0.2112 (0.791)	−0.0471 (0.874)
Fiscal autonomy × competition			−1.6405 (0.212)	
GDP per capita	−1.17E08* (0.09)	−1.21E08* (0.081)	−1.20E08* (0.083)	−7.32E10 (0.905)
Population density	4.27E07 (0.778)	5.97E07 (0.694)	6.71E07 (0.658)	−1.90E06 (0.222)
Number of employees	−9.4E05*** (0.001)	−9.84E05*** (0.001)	−1.03E04*** (0.000)	3.85E06*** (0.885)
Industrial structure	−0.0009*** (0.002)	−8.975E04*** (0.002)	−8.99E04*** (0.002)	−4.11E05 (0.888)
Constant	0.1982*** (0.000)	0.2010*** (0.000)	0.1986*** (0.000)	0.0601** (0.028)
F-value	18.15***	16.01***	13.95***	149.66
Observations	3990	3990	3990	3705

Note *, **, and *** denote significance at the 10%, 5%, and 1% levels, respectively; the values in parentheses represent the p-values of the corresponding coefficients

goods. Additionally, local government competition intensifies this negative impact on economic public goods while diminishing the positive effect on non-economic public goods. As the economy shifts to a stage of high-quality development, the state should prioritize enhancing the quality and efficiency of non-economic public goods provision. Therefore, it is essential to boost local governments' budgetary fiscal autonomy by integrating prior off-budget revenues into the budgetary system and fostering collaboration among local governments in public goods provision.

3.2.4 Efficiency of Government Supply in Urban Public Goods

3.2.4.1 Measurement Method

The Data Envelopment Analysis (DEA), proposed by Charnes et al. (1978), is commonly used to measure urban public goods provision efficiency. This method evaluates public expenditure efficiency from the dimensions of input and output, considering whether it is possible to minimize inputs given outputs or maximize outputs given inputs. Suppose there are n decision-making units DMU_j $(1 < j < n)$, each with m inputs and s outputs. Let x_i and y_i be the input and output column vectors, respectively, and x and y be the $m \times n$ input matrix and $s \times n$ output matrix. Then, the comprehensive technical efficiency measurement for the i decision-making unit can be formulated as a linear programming problem, computed based on Eqs. (3.9) and (3.10).

$$\min \theta \tag{3.9}$$

$$\text{s.t}\begin{cases} \sum\limits_{j=1}^{n} X_j\lambda_j + s^- = \theta X_i \\ \sum\limits_{j=1}^{n} Y_k\lambda_k - s^+ = \theta Y_i \\ \sum\limits_{j=1}^{n} \lambda_k = 1 \\ \lambda_j \geq 0,\ s^- \geq 0,\ s^+ \geq 0 \end{cases} \tag{3.10}$$

In these equations, s^- and s^+ represent input redundancy and output deficiency slack variables, and $\sum_{j=1}^{n} \lambda_j$ represents the comprehensive efficiency score θ, with its value ranging from [0,1]. The closer the efficiency score is to 1, the higher the efficiency; otherwise, the lower the efficiency.

Table 3.7 Measurement indicators of government supply efficiency of urban public goods

Category	Indicator	Sub-indicator
Output indicators	Education	Student-teacher ratio in primary schools (number of full-time teachers in primary schools/number of enrolled students), student-teacher ratio in secondary schools (number of full-time teachers in secondary schools/ number of enrolled students)
	Healthcare	Number of hospital beds per 10,000 people, Number of healthcare personnel per 10,000 people
	Infrastructure	Urban road area per capita, Number of public buses per 10,000 people
Input indicators	Government public budget expenditure	Per capita public budget expenditure

3.2.4.2 Measurement Indicators

In measuring efficiency, the selection of input and output indicators is critical. Chen and Zhang (2008) assessed provincial fiscal expenditure efficiency in China using a single input-output framework, with per capita budgetary fiscal expenditure as the input and a weighted average of education, healthcare, and infrastructure indicators as the output. Wang and Zhang (2011) measured the public expenditure efficiency of Chinese prefecture-level cities in 2008, using budgetary fiscal expenditure as input and a comprehensive urban output indicator. Pang and Sun (2018) utilized a DEA model to analyze provincial fiscal expenditure efficiency, taking general public budget expenditure as the input and regional GDP and disposable income of urban and rural residents as the outputs. Zhang (2018) evaluated fiscal expenditure efficiency in 35 large and medium-sized cities in China, using public budget expenditure as input and constructing a comprehensive output indicator based on ten types of variables (e.g., education, healthcare, communication).

Considering the availability of urban-level public expenditure data and standard practices in literature, this study uses government public budget expenditure as the input variable for urban public goods provision. A comprehensive public expenditure output indicator is created using a simple weighted average of education, healthcare, and infrastructure indicators. Each category of output indicators is the simple average of normalized sub-indicators. Table 3.7 lists the selected indicators and their sub-indicators.

3.2.4.3 Measurement Results and Analysis

This study employs DEAP2.1 software to measure public goods provision efficiency in 267 prefecture-level cities in China. Tables 3.8 and 3.9 display the efficiency scores for these cities in 2005 and 2014, respectively. In 2005, the average efficiency score for public goods provision across the cities was 0.456. The top ten cities were Shenzhen, Huanggang, Zhoukou, Bozhou, Heihe, Heze, Suzhou, Xianyang, Fuyang, and Baoji, each scoring 1.000, except for Heze (0.986), Suzhou (0.958), Xianyang (0.881), Fuyang (0.843), and Baoji (0.835). The bottom ten cities included Fangchenggang, Guyuan, Yulin, Shantou, Longnan, Lvliang, Suzhou, Tongliao, Chizhou, and Chongqing, with scores of 0.232, 0.242, 0.246, 0.252, 0.253, 0.260, 0.261, 0.272, 0.274, and 0.274, respectively. This highlights significant disparities in public goods provision efficiency among cities.

Table 3.9 shows the efficiency of government supply of public goods in 267 prefecture-level cities in 2014. It can be observed that over time, the efficiency has improved to some extent. In 2014, the average efficiency value was 0.664. The top 10 cities were Shenzhen, Ordos, Kaifeng, Jieyang, Xingtai, Cangzhou, Yulin, Kunming, Baoding, and Guigang, with efficiency values of 1.000, 1.000, 1.000, 1.000, 0.977, 0.971, 0.970, 0.967, 0.967, and 0.930 respectively. The bottom ten cities were Zhaotong, Hezhou, Guang'an, Longnan, Chongzuo, Shantou, Fuzhou, Anshun, Yichun, and Lu'an, with efficiency values of 0.389, 0.406, 0.416, 0.421, 0.424, 0.441, 0.443, 0.446, 0.447, and 0.462 respectively. This indicates that the disparity in government supply efficiency of public goods among cities is gradually narrowing.

Overall, while urban public goods provision efficiency has improved in recent years, further enhancement is still needed. Nationally, provincial capitals, sub-provincial cities, and major central cities generally exhibit higher efficiency than other cities in their respective provinces. However, most prefecture-level cities still have relatively low efficiency in public goods provision.

Regionally, there are significant disparities in urban public goods provision efficiency. The central and western regions, in particular, lag far behind the eastern and northeastern regions. Table 3.10 reflects the efficiency of public goods provision across eastern, central, western, and northeastern cities from 2005 to 2014. Economic conditions and other factors contribute to substantial variations in efficiency across regions. Nevertheless, with the fiscal system's gradual improvement, average government provision efficiency has significantly increased. Notably, the eastern and western regions have seen marked improvements, with even more significant gains in the central and western regions.

3.3 Market (Private) Supply Mechanism of Urban Public Goods

3.3.1 Contents of Market (Private) Supply of Urban Public Goods

The market (private) supply of urban public goods primarily targets urban infrastructure and urban public services. Determining which public goods are suitable for market (private) supply mechanisms depends on the properties of the goods. Urban

Table 3.8 Government efficiency in the supply of public goods in 267 prefecture-level cities (2005)

City	Efficiency	City	Efficiency	City	Efficiency	City	Efficiency	City	Efficiency
Beijing	0.620	Yuncheng	0.516	Panjin	0.427	Mudanjiang	0.458	Huzhou	0.375
Tianjin	0.435	Xinzhou	0.297	Chaoyang	0.340	Heihe	1.000	Shaoxing	0.412
Shijiazhuang	0.404	Lvliang	0.260	Huludao	0.315	Suihua	0.443	Jinhua	0.356
Tangshan	0.372	Hohhot	0.403	Changchun	0.434	Shanghai	0.526	Quzhou	0.328
Qinhuangdao	0.433	Baotou	0.434	Jilin	0.397	Nanjing	0.453	Zhoushan	0.345
Handan	0.559	Wuhai	0.459	Siping	0.463	Wuxi	0.527	Taizhou	0.333
Xingtai	0.682	Chifeng	0.281	Liaoyuan	0.432	Xuzhou	0.469	Lishui	0.296
Baoding	0.638	Tongliao	0.272	Tonghua	0.378	Changzhou	0.447	Hefei	0.472
Zhangjiakou	0.367	Ordos	0.415	Baishan	0.446	Suzhou	0.455	Wuhu	0.411
Chengde	0.358	Hulunbuir	0.442	Songyuan	0.364	Nantong	0.449	Bengbu	0.609
Cangzhou	0.577	Bayannur	0.280	Baicheng	0.363	Lianyungang	0.432	Huainan	0.410
Langfang	0.320	Ulanqab	0.283	Harbin	0.454	Huaian	0.342	Ma'anshan	0.396
Hengshui	0.503	Dalian	0.464	Qiqihar	0.417	Yancheng	0.417	Huaibei	0.586
Taiyuan	0.548	Anshan	0.433	Jixi	0.576	Yangzhou	0.430	Tongling	0.415
Datong	0.347	Fushun	0.439	Hegang	0.400	Taizhou	0.357	Anqing	0.541
Yangquan	0.396	Benxi	0.495	Shuangyashan	0.435	Suqian	0.441	Huangshan	0.323
Changzhi	0.312	Jinzhou	0.386	Daqing	0.536	Hangzhou	0.462	Chuzhou	0.537
Jincheng	0.400	Yingkou	0.352	Yichun	0.432	Ningbo	0.365	Fuyang	0.843
Shuozhou	0.261	Fuxin	0.341	Jiamusi	0.351	Wenzhou	0.399	Suzhou	0.958
Jinzhong	0.345	Liaoyang	0.440	Qitaihe	0.391	Jiaxing	0.373	Lu'an	0.590
Bozhou	1.000	Yantai	0.407	Zhumadian	0.646	Shantou	0.252	Zigong	0.515
Chizhou	0.274	Weifang	0.484	Huangshi	0.649	Zhanjiang	0.401	Panzhihua	0.433

(continued)

Table 3.8 (continued)

City	Efficiency	City	Efficiency	City	Efficiency	City	Efficiency	City	Efficiency
Xuancheng	0.324	Jining	0.392	Shiyan	0.587	Zhaoqing	0.367	Luzhou	0.440
Fuzhou	0.396	Tai'an	0.417	Yichang	0.509	Huizhou	0.293	Deyang	0.404
Xiamen	0.451	Weihai	0.529	Xiangfan	0.534	Meizhou	0.448	Mianyang	0.442
Putian	0.577	Rizhao	0.604	Ezhou	0.402	Shanwei	0.438	Guangyuan	0.387
Sanming	0.509	Laiwu	0.407	Jingmen	0.575	Yangjiang	0.343	Suining	0.494
Quanzhou	0.297	Linyi	0.703	Xiaogan	0.807	Zhongshan	0.330	Neijiang	0.461
Zhangzhou	0.633	Dezhou	0.587	Jingzhou	0.690	Jieyang	0.544	Leshan	0.377
Nanping	0.562	Liaocheng	0.656	Huanggang	1.000	Yunfu	0.296	Nanchong	0.500
Longyan	0.421	Binzhou	0.278	Xianning	0.413	Nanning	0.407	Meishan	0.465
Ningde	0.465	Heze	0.986	Suizhou	0.781	Liuzhou	0.397	Yibin	0.321
Nanchang	0.370	Zhengzhou	0.453	Changsha	0.492	Guilin	0.427	Guang'an	0.447
Jingdezhen	0.393	Kaifeng	0.548	Zhuzhou	0.394	Wuzhou	0.366	Ya'an	0.287
Pingxiang	0.354	Luoyang	0.331	Xiangtan	0.485	Beihai	0.289	Ziyang	0.543
Jiujiang	0.434	Pingdingshan	0.424	Hengyang	0.694	Fangchenggang	0.232	Liupanshui	0.352
Xinyu	0.334	Anyang	0.445	Shaoyang	0.700	Qinzhou	0.501	Zunyi	0.437
Yingtan	0.327	Hebi	0.355	Yueyang	0.496	Guigang	0.717	Anshun	0.346
Ganzhou	0.496	Xinxiang	0.491	Changde	0.465	Yulin	0.617	Kunming	0.504
Jian	0.325	Jiaozuo	0.366	Zhangjiajie	0.512	Baise	0.335	Qujing	0.402
Yichun	0.387	Puyang	0.478	Yiyang	0.582	Hezhou	0.340	Yuxi	0.335
Fuzhou	0.395	Xuchang	0.802	Chenzhou	0.396	Hechi	0.396	Baoshan	0.328
Shangrao	0.444	Luohe	0.393	Yongzhou	0.629	Laibin	0.284	Zhaotong	0.352
Jinan	0.477	Sanmenxia	0.311	Huaihua	0.696	Chongzuo	0.295	Lijiang	0.313

(continued)

Table 3.8 (continued)

City	Efficiency	City	Efficiency	City	Efficiency	City	Efficiency	City	Efficiency
Qingdao	0.523	Nanyang	0.505	Loudi	0.676	Haikou	0.373	Lincang	0.290
Zibo	0.371	Shangqiu	0.558	Guangzhou	0.505	Sanya	0.319	Xi'an	0.397
Zaozhuang	0.349	Xinyang	0.449	Shaoguan	0.275	Chongqing	0.274	Tongchuan	0.535
Dongying	0.506	Zhoukou	1.000	Shenzhen	1.000	Chengdu	0.437	Baoji	0.835
Xianyang	0.881	Shangluo	0.527	Wuwei	0.374	Longnan	0.253	Zhongwei	0.290
Weinan	0.757	Lanzhou	0.468	Zhangye	0.320	Xining	0.451	Urumqi	0.700
Yan'an	0.315	Jiayuguan	0.477	Pingliang	0.391	Yinchuan	0.531	Karamay	0.591
Hanzhong	0.672	Jinchang	0.372	Jiuquan	0.387	Shizuishan	0.386		
Yulin	0.246	Baiyin	0.412	Qingyang	0.280	Wuzhong	0.318		
Ankang	0.595	Tianshui	0.449	Dingxi	0.409	Guyuan	0.242	Average	0.456

Table 3.9 Government supply efficiency of urban public goods in 267 prefecture-level cities in 2014

City	Efficiency	City	Efficiency	City	Efficiency	City	Efficiency	City	Efficiency
Beijing	0.568	Chengde	0.684	Shuozhou	0.512	Tongliao	0.608	Jinzhou	0.624
Tianjin	0.541	Cangzhou	0.971	Jinzhou	0.863	Ordos	1.000	Yingkou	0.619
Shijiazhuang	0.721	Langfang	0.611	Yuncheng	0.855	Hulunbuir	0.818	Fuxin	0.663
Tangshan	0.658	Hengshui	0.650	Xinzhou	0.586	Bayannur	0.721	Liaoyang	0.752
Qinhuangdao	0.839	Taiyuan	0.894	Lvliang	0.561	Ulanqab	0.712	Panjin	0.609
Handan	0.827	Datong	0.696	Hohhot	0.774	Dalian	0.725	Chaoyang	0.689
Xingtai	0.977	Yangquan	0.716	Baotou	0.655	Anshan	0.703	Huludao	0.666
Baoding	0.967	Changzhi	0.625	Wuhai	0.619	Fushun	0.690	Changchun	0.849
Zhangjiakou	0.763	Jincheng	0.745	Chifeng	0.642	Benxi	0.821	Jilin	0.736
Siping	0.817	Yangzhou	0.576	Chizhou	0.501	Weifang	0.748	Huangshi	0.755
Liaoyuan	0.728	Taizhou	0.633	Xuancheng	0.556	Jining	0.918	Shiyan	0.778
Tonghua	0.786	Suqian	0.551	Fuzhou	0.747	Tai'an	0.638	Yichang	0.710
Baishan	0.743	Hangzhou	0.757	Xiamen	0.594	Weihai	0.832	Xiangfan	0.557
Songyuan	0.678	Ningbo	0.646	Putian	0.521	Rizhao	0.609	Ezhou	0.622
Baicheng	0.602	Wenzhou	0.769	Sanming	0.730	Laiwu	0.648	Jingmen	0.727
Harbin	0.848	Jiaxing	0.728	Quanzhou	0.743	Linyi	0.639	Xiaogan	0.633
Qiqihar	0.644	Huzhou	0.657	Zhangzhou	0.693	Dezhou	0.674	Jingzhou	0.601
Jixi	0.788	Shaoxing	0.624	Nanping	0.622	Liaocheng	0.778	Huanggang	0.907
Hegang	0.789	Jinhua	0.640	Longyan	0.675	Binzhou	0.699	Xianning	0.549
Shuangyashan	0.785	Quzhou	0.563	Ningde	0.575	Heze	0.705	Suizhou	0.643
Daqing	0.906	Zhoushan	0.597	Nanchang	0.693	Zhengzhou	0.707	Changsha	0.833
Yichun	0.785	Taizhou	0.594	Jingdezhen	0.655	Kaifeng	1.000	Zhuzhou	0.831

(continued)

Table 3.9 (continued)

City	Efficiency	City	Efficiency	City	Efficiency	City	Efficiency	City	Efficiency
Jiamusi	0.701	Lishui	0.587	Pingxiang	0.546	Luoyang	0.693	Xiangtan	0.766
Qitaihe	0.639	Hefei	0.845	Jiujiang	0.642	Pingdingshan	0.632	Hengyang	0.766
Mudanjiang	0.735	Wuhu	0.778	Xinyu	0.488	Anyang	0.613	Shaoyang	0.614
Heihe	0.585	Bengbu	0.717	Yingtan	0.565	Hebi	0.575	Yueyang	0.643
Suihua	0.712	Huainan	0.593	Ganzhou	0.487	Xinxiang	0.611	Changde	0.650
Shanghai	0.492	Ma'anshan	0.603	Jian	0.553	Jiaozuo	0.640	Zhangjiajie	0.589
Nanjing	0.746	Huaibei	0.646	Yichun	0.447	Puyang	0.590	Yiyang	0.577
Wuxi	0.747	Tongling	0.705	Fuzhou	0.443	Xuchang	0.776	Chenzhou	0.818
Xuzhou	0.642	Anqing	0.639	Shangrao	0.616	Luohe	0.583	Yongzhou	0.548
Changzhou	0.697	Huangshan	0.630	Jinan	0.876	Sanmenxia	0.698	Huaihua	0.825
Suzhou	0.733	Chuzhou	0.767	Qingdao	0.770	Nanyang	0.563	Loudi	0.558
Nantong	0.693	Fuyang	0.662	Zibo	0.716	Shangqiu	0.609	Guangzhou	0.774
Lianyungang	0.502	Suzhou	0.494	Zaozhuang	0.581	Xinyang	0.495	Shaoguan	0.586
Huai'an	0.557	Lu'an	0.462	Dongying	0.798	Zhoukou	0.912	Shenzhen	1.000
Yancheng	0.639	Bozhou	0.535	Yantai	0.810	Zhumadian	0.676	Shantou	0.441
Zhanjiang	0.728	Yulin	0.676	Neijiang	0.582	Lincang	0.468	Zhangye	0.568
Zhaoqing	0.684	Baise	0.508	Leshan	0.592	Xi'an	0.699	Pingliang	0.660
Huizhou	0.713	Hezhou	0.406	Nanchong	0.554	Tongchuan	0.645	Jiuquan	0.624
Meizhou	0.650	Hechi	0.466	Meishan	0.673	Baoji	0.676	Qingyang	0.634
Shanwei	0.598	Laibin	0.475	Yibin	0.552	Xianyang	0.727	Dingxi	0.572
Yangjiang	0.529	Chongzuo	0.424	Guang'an	0.416	Weinan	0.641	Longnan	0.421
Zhongshan	0.658	Haikou	0.704	Ya'an	0.463	Yan'an	0.547	Xining	0.782

(continued)

Table 3.9 (continued)

City	Efficiency	City	Efficiency	City	Efficiency	City	Efficiency	City	Efficiency
Jieyang	1.000	Sanya	0.488	Ziyang	0.549	Hanzhong	0.674	Yinchuan	0.706
Yunfu	0.479	Chongqing	0.501	Liupanshui	0.643	Yulin	0.970	Shizuishan	0.792
Nanning	0.660	Chengdu	0.876	Zunyi	0.573	Ankang	0.493	Wuzhong	0.572
Liuzhou	0.691	Zigong	0.613	Anshun	0.446	Shangluo	0.465	Guyuan	0.507
Guilin	0.623	Panzhihua	0.757	Kunming	0.967	Lanzhou	0.740	Zhongwei	0.518
Wuzhou	0.556	Luzhou	0.549	Qujing	0.577	Jiayuguan	0.720	Urumqi	0.831
Beihai	0.568	Deyang	0.656	Yuxi	0.626	Jinchang	0.666	Karamay	0.617
Fangchenggang	0.473	Mianyang	0.771	Baoshan	0.466	Baiyin	0.699		
Qinzhou	0.672	Guangyuan	0.622	Zhaotong	0.389	Tianshui	0.502		
Guigang	0.930	Suining	0.636	Lijiang	0.668	Wuwei	0.541	Average	0.664

Table 3.10 Efficiency of government provision of urban public goods by region (2005–2014)

Region	2005	2006	2007	2008	2009
Northeast	0.439	0.631	0.656	0.692	0.598
East	0.446	0.621	0.653	0.685	0.608
Central	0.508	0.646	0.642	0.659	0.549
West	0.420	0.559	0.573	0.582	0.490
Region	**2010**	**2011**	**2012**	**2013**	**2014**
Northeast	0.647	0.681	0.611	0.543	0.723
East	0.643	0.672	0.661	0.574	0.682
Central	0.588	0.638	0.636	0.545	0.661
West	0.531	0.573	0.558	0.488	0.626

infrastructure can be categorized into networked and non-networked infrastructure based on the necessity of a delivery network. Networked infrastructure, such as urban water supply, piped gas, heating, and public transportation, requires a physical network to deliver services to residents. It exhibits the following characteristics: (a) substantial investment with long-term payback; (b) high asset specificity and sunk costs, rendering it non-repurposable after construction; (c) significant economies of scale and externalities, with unit costs decreasing as consumption rises. This prominent externality can optimize urban development conditions and drive urban economic growth. These characteristics render the sector naturally monopolistic (Wang, 2011).

Generally, the stronger the competitiveness and exclusivity of products and services and the lower the production sunk costs, the more effective and feasible it is to supply them through market mechanisms. Conversely, products with solid non-competitiveness and non-exclusivity are more suitable for government supply mechanisms (Kessides, 1993). Changes in technology and market conditions, however, can alter the competitiveness and exclusivity of products through institutional arrangements, thus providing greater flexibility and applicability to government or market supply mechanisms. As China's economy evolves and urbanization progresses, urban infrastructure products and services are exhibiting the following trends: (a) increasing competitiveness; (b) rising exclusivity as networked infrastructure access is limited to those connected; (c) diminishing natural monopoly as technological advancements allow for the vertical disintegration of infrastructure businesses, fragmenting networks into non-monopolistic components (Gao, 2004; Huang, 2009; Kunneke, 1999). However, with scientific and technological advancements, the vertical disintegration of urban infrastructure businesses allows network systems to be segmented into different technical components, making services non-monopolistic. For instance, urban water supply can be separated into networked and non-networked systems. The former retains natural monopoly characteristics, while the latter does not. This change significantly reduces the degree of natural monopoly. Thus, changes in urban infrastructure properties influence exclusivity and significantly impact production and supply methods (Gao, 2004; Yang, 2003).

Similarly, the mechanisms for urban public service supply have evolved. Initially, China's urban public service system was a centralized, government-controlled model, leading to low quality, inefficiency, and poor accountability from service providers. Following the reform and opening up policy, market mechanisms were introduced to the public service sector through outsourcing and service purchase, passing the supply responsibility from government departments to social organizations and private enterprises. This transformation accelerated public service marketization, improved quality and efficiency, and increased service provision projects (Xu & Zhao, 2013).

The marketization of public services means that projects previously undertaken by the government are now directly handled by market entities or by entities entrusted by the government (Chen & Hu, 2011). This market-based supply mechanism exhibits several new characteristics: (a) Separation of Decision-Making and Execution: Government roles shift from direct service provision to planning, decision-making, resource organization, and supervision; (b) Diversification of Supply Entities: Multiple entities—enterprises, social organizations, and individuals—contribute to public service provision, leading to various supply models like bidding, public-private partnerships (PPP), franchising, and voucher systems; (c) Citizen-Centric Services: Under the market mechanism, service provision more closely aligns with citizens' needs and preferences, allowing supply entities to gather public input more effectively and tailor services accordingly.

3.3.2 Evolution of Market (Private) Supply Mechanism for Urban Public Goods in China

The exploration of market supply mechanisms in urban infrastructure construction and operation in China began in the 1980s, although no corresponding policies and regulations were issued then. In the early 1990s, with the development of the market economy, the public products sector also began market-oriented reforms. The central government introduced a series of policies to promote market-oriented pilot projects for urban infrastructure construction. In 1995, the Ministry of Foreign Trade and Economic Cooperation issued a notice on absorbing foreign investment through the Build-Operate-Transfer (BOT) model, setting out several requirements for local governments. In August 1995, the State Planning Commission, Ministry of Electric Power, and Ministry of Communications jointly issued a notice on the approval and management of foreign-invested franchise projects, proposing the adoption of the BOT investment model to promote transportation and energy infrastructure construction. By 2002, various central ministries and commissions had issued multiple policy documents to promote public-private partnerships, including notifications on managing state-owned infrastructure asset transfers and opinions on promoting and guiding private investment.

Pilot projects for market-oriented mechanisms in infrastructure began in 1994. The State Planning Commission selected five projects: Guangxi Laibin B Power Plant, Guangdong Dianbai Highway, Chengdu Sixth Water Plant, Changsha Wangcheng Power Plant, and Wuhan Junshan Yangtze River Bridge, to implement the BOT model. Simultaneously, local governments also initiated BOT projects, such as the Beijing Tenth Water Plant, Beijing Fangshan University Town, Shanghai Huangpu River Bridge, Xinjiang Turpan Power Plant, Beijing Xiaojiahe Sewage Project, and Beijing Xihongmen Affordable Housing Project. These projects facilitated the application of market mechanisms in China's infrastructure sector, accumulating valuable experience for subsequent reforms (Liu, 2015).

Following China's accession to the World Trade Organization, foreign economic growth accelerated, and market-oriented reforms in the public products sector gained momentum. The 2003 Third Plenary Session of the 16th Central Committee of the Communist Party of China proposed actively developing and guiding the non-public economy, relaxing market entry restrictions, and allowing non-public capital into infrastructure, utilities, and other industries. Concurrently, the former Ministry of Construction issued opinions on accelerating the marketization of the municipal public sector. The implementation of these policies facilitated the entry of foreign capital into public infrastructure and eliminated barriers to private capital investment. Local governments began adopting market-oriented approaches for municipal public facility construction. In 2004, the Ministry of Construction introduced the *Municipal Utilities Franchise Management Measures*, formally incorporating the franchise model into municipal utility construction and operation. The 2005 *Opinions on Encouraging, Supporting, and Guiding the Development of Non-Public Economies* by the State Council further relaxed market entry restrictions for non-public economies, providing institutional support for private capital in urban public infrastructure and services. In 2010, *Opinions on Encouraging and Guiding Private Investment* encouraged private capital to participate in infrastructure, municipal engineering, and other public services, providing specific policy guidance for public-private partnerships (PPP) in infrastructure projects.

In line with national policies and driven by regional economic and urban development, China has undertaken large-scale urban public infrastructure construction over the past 20 years. Although most projects are still government and state-owned enterprise investments, many have adopted market mechanisms. Some projects are directly financed and constructed by private and foreign capital, utilizing market-oriented financing and operational methods. Notable projects include the Beijing Metro Line 4, Hefei Wangxiaoying Sewage Treatment Plant, Suzhou Wuzhong Waste-to-Energy Plant, Lanzhou Water Supply Equity Transfer, Tianjin Beishui Company Partial Equity Transfer, and the Beijing Yizhuang Gas BOT Project.

The 2008 global financial crisis severely impacted China's economic growth. In response, the Chinese government adopted an active fiscal policy to stabilize the economy, investing heavily in public infrastructure and thereby initiating large-scale infrastructure construction. During this period, private enterprises had limited direct investment in infrastructure projects that were primarily government-funded, mainly taking on engineering and contracting roles. However, the negative effects of excessive fiscal investment soon became apparent, leading the government to reevaluate the role of private capital in infrastructure development. Starting in 2010, policies such as the *Opinions of the State Council on Encouraging and Guiding the Healthy Development of Private Investment* and the *Notice of the General Office of the State Council on the Division of Key Tasks to Encourage and Guide Healthy Development of Private Investment*, were introduced to encourage and guide private enterprises to invest in public infrastructure and services. From 2013 onwards, the government provided more significant support for social capital, including private investment, in public infrastructure through several initiatives. A significant policy shift was to encourage private capital to participate in public facility construction through the Public-Private Partnership (PPP) model. The government's preference for the PPP model is mainly due to the substantial initial investments required for public infrastructure construction, which are generally difficult for private enterprises to bear alone. Additionally, private enterprises often lack sufficient support from financial markets. Only through cooperation with the government can they secure the necessary resources for project construction and operation. Under central government policies, local governments also introduced policies to encourage social capital investment in infrastructure. They actively explored new and innovative financing and investment models for urban infrastructure projects. In recent years, significant breakthroughs have been achieved in funding solutions and equity transactions for infrastructure projects. For example, the introduction of insurance fund investments has broadened capital sources for projects, while approaches like equity transfers, asset transactions, and asset securitization have been encouraged to activate existing assets, providing entry and exit opportunities for social capital.

The introduction of social capital and market mechanisms in urban infrastructure construction has also gradually established market mechanisms in the public service sector, forming a supply model led by the government with social participation, combining public and private provisions. The primary market supply methods in the public service field include government subsidies, concessions, government procurement of services, and voucher systems. Regarding concessions, details were discussed above and will not be reiterated here.

Currently, some public service projects are directly invested in and supplied by social organizations. To ensure regular operation, the government provides economic subsidies for projects with low profitability, relatively high risks, or unstable revenue expectations. These subsidies include financial support and tax incentives (Wu, 2008; Zheng, 2015).

The government procurement of services model is the primary market supply model for public services in China. In this model, the government publicly announces certain public service projects through open bidding, selecting qualified social forces to undertake these projects and paying them based on the quantity and quality of services provided. In September 2013, the *Guiding Opinions of the General Office of the State Council on Government Procurement of Services from Social Forces* was issued, clearly defining the purchasing entities, undertaking entities, procurement content, procurement mechanisms, and management methods, thus supporting local governments in promoting government procurement of services. Currently, this model has become the primary way for social forces to enter the public service field.

Additionally, the voucher system is another way of market-oriented supply of public services in China. Under this system, government departments issue consumption vouchers to eligible individuals for specific public goods or services. These vouchers represent a government commitment to cover the costs, allowing recipients to purchase the goods or services they need from the market. Providers of these goods or services can then redeem the vouchers from the government. By directly subsidizing consumers instead of producers, the voucher system introduces market mechanisms into public service provision, enhancing consumer purchasing power and choice and putting competitive pressure on service providers. This system can be widely applied in areas such as education, healthcare, food, housing, transportation, child care, elderly care, ambulance services, and vocational training.

The marketization reform of China's public product sector is government-led, with substantial government involvement and intervention in the market supply mechanisms. Purely private investment projects in public products are few and small in scale, not constituting the main mode of market (private) supply for public products.

3.3.3 Efficiency of Market (Private) Supply of Urban Public Goods

The degree of market development significantly affects the efficiency of the market (private) supply of urban public products. This analysis uses per capita GDP, population density, number of employees, and industrial structure as control variables, with a sample of panel data from 285 prefecture-level cities from 2004 to 2017, to empirically analyze the impact of market development on the supply of economic and non-economic public products in cities (see Table 3.11). The results indicate that market development positively affects the supply of both economic and non-economic public products. However, the impact is significant for economic public products and not significant for non-economic public products. Furthermore, the positive impact on economic public product supply is more significant than that on non-economic public products, suggesting that economic public products are more suitable for market (private) supply mechanisms.

To measure the efficiency of private supply in the urban public goods market, data from the 2017 national PPP management database was used, focusing on total investment amounts in city projects. The total investment in PPP projects is used as an input variable, while the output variables for economic public goods supply include per capita paved road area, the number of public buses (including electric buses) per 10,000 people, the number of international internet users, and the gas penetration rate. The output variables for non-economic public goods supply include the number of primary and secondary school teachers per 10,000 people, the number of primary and secondary schools, the number of hospital beds per 10,000 people, and the per capita

Table 3.11 Empirical analysis of the impact of market development on the supply of economic and non-economic public products

Variable	Economic public products	Non-economic public products
Marketization level	0.0022^{***} (0.009)	0.0009 (0.321)
Per capita GDP	$3.88E08^{***}$ (0.000)	$-1.19E08^{*}$ (0.088)
Population density	$-8.94E06^{***}$ (0.000)	5.53E07 (0.718)
Number of employees	$4.65E04^{***}$ (0.000)	$-1.00E04^{***}$ (0.001)
Industrial structure	0.0029^{***} (0.000)	-0.0009^{***} (0.001)
Constant term	-0.1711^{***} (0.000)	0.2283^{***} (0.000)
F-value	109.95^{***}	5.83^{***}
Observations	3990	3990

Note * and *** indicate significance at 10% and 1% levels, respectively; values in parentheses are corresponding p-values

volume of public library collections. The efficiency of private supply of economic and non-economic public goods in urban areas is measured using the Stochastic Frontier Analysis (SFA) method. The SFA model determines the frontier boundary through maximum likelihood estimation and features a composite error term. Since the frontier is stochastic, the conclusions are closer to reality. The results of the 2017 efficiency measurement for private supply in the urban public goods market are shown in Table 3.12. The results indicate that the cities with the highest efficiency in the private supply of economic public goods are Leshan, Beijing, Tianjin, Ankang, and Jiaozuo. For non-economic public goods, the top cities are Chongqing, Shanghai, Zhengzhou, Beijing, and Ordos. The efficiency of private supply of economic public goods is related to factors such as the scale of market investment, the degree of market maturity, and the incentive mechanisms for private supply. Similarly, the efficiency of private supply of non-economic public goods is also linked to the scale of market investment, the degree of market maturity, and the incentive mechanisms for private supply.

3.3.4 Limitations of the Private Supply Mechanism in Urban Public Goods

While the privatization of urban public goods supply can enhance efficiency and quality, it may also result in the loss of public benefits, the emergence of private monopolies, and an inappropriate shift in the government's role without effective

Table 3.12 Efficiency of private supply in the urban public goods market in 2017

Economic public goods				Non-economic public goods			
City	Supply efficiency	City	Supply efficiency	City	Supply efficiency	City	Supply efficiency
Leshan	0.241659	Ziyang	0.195747	Chongqing	0.999533	Shijiazhuang	0.999524
Beijing	0.231871	Taizhou	0.195452	Shanghai	0.999530	Jincheng	0.999524
Tianjin	0.210817	Guang'an	0.194643	Zhengzhou	0.999529	Anyang	0.999524
Ankang	0.207164	Shangluo	0.193913	Beijing	0.999528	Changzhi	0.999524
Jiaozuo	0.205809	Ordos	0.193818	Ordos	0.999527	Wenzhou	0.999524
Xianyang	0.205039	Weinan	0.193743	Cangzhou	0.999527	Zhangzhou	0.999524
Urumqi	0.204659	Nanping	0.193742	Xi'an	0.999527	Yulin	0.999524
Ya'an	0.204535	Shuangyashan	0.192869	Qingdao	0.999526	Baotou	0.999524
Xuchang	0.204265	Baoji	0.192495	Tianjin	0.999526	Handan	0.999524
Yulin	0.203504	Hengshui	0.192395	Xianyang	0.999526	Xingtai	0.999524
Xi'an	0.201847	Quanzhou	0.192213	Quzhou	0.999526	Ganzhou	0.999524
Anshan	0.201577	Lishui	0.192181	Wuhan	0.999526	Lishui	0.999523
Anyang	0.199960	Shangqiu	0.191731	Nanning	0.999526	Datong	0.999523
Panzhihua	0.199296	Hohhot	0.191715	Harbin	0.999525	Sanmenxia	0.999523
Tangshan	0.198615	Mudanjiang	0.191456	Xining	0.999525	Sanming	0.999523
Zigong	0.197849	Yichun	0.191407	Karamay	0.999525	Shiyan	0.999523
Wenzhou	0.197764	Yulin	0.191257	Dalian	0.999525	Panzhihua	0.999523
Bazhong	0.197507	Jiamusi	0.190807	Hohhot	0.999525	Hengshui	0.999523
Pingdingshan	0.197439	Chongqing	0.190712	Quanzhou	0.999525	Xinxiang	0.999523
Yibin	0.197273	Ganzhou	0.190413	Urumqi	0.999525	Guangyuan	0.999523
Xinxiang	0.196535	Hanzhong	0.190116	Yinchuan	0.999524	Longyan	0.999523

(continued)

Table 3.12 (continued)

Economic public goods				Non-economic public goods			
City	Supply efficiency	City	Supply efficiency	City	Supply efficiency	City	Supply efficiency
Zhoukou	0.190036	Ulanqab	0.187508	Ulanqab	0.999523	Yangquan	0.999522
Nanning	0.189962	Longyan	0.187461	Longyan	0.999523	Xinyang	0.999522
Ningde	0.189639	Jincheng	0.187223	Jincheng	0.999523	Nantong	0.999522
Qingdao	0.189567	Handan	0.187218	Handan	0.999523	Nanchong	0.999522
Luzhou	0.189518	Jinzhong	0.187206	Jinzhong	0.999523	Luzhou	0.999522
Yangzhou	0.189228	Changzhi	0.187193	Changzhi	0.999523	Anshan	0.999522
Tongliao	0.189160	Karamay	0.187136	Karamay	0.999523	Weinan	0.999521
Zhengzhou	0.188825	Quzhou	0.187135	Quzhou	0.999522	Ya'an	0.999521
Wuhan	0.188811	Jingzhou	0.187077	Jingzhou	0.999522	Ulanqab	0.999521
Nanchong	0.188635	Shiyan	0.187067	Shiyan	0.999522	Yangzhou	0.999521
Langfang	0.188435	Huludao	0.187051	Huludao	0.999522	Ningde	0.999521
Nantong	0.188434	Guangyuan	0.187039	Guangyuan	0.999522	Xuchang	0.999521
Zhangzhou	0.188352	Sanming	0.187013	Sanming	0.999522	Ankang	0.999521
Cangzhou	0.188083	Hulunbuir	0.186959	Hulunbuir	0.999522	Jinzhong	0.999521
Zunyi	0.188002	Xinzhou	0.186950	Xinzhou	0.999522	Yichun	0.999521
Harbin	0.188000	Shijiazhuang	0.186834	Shijiazhuang	0.999522	Nanping	0.999521
Meishan	0.188000	Yinchuan	0.186825	Yinchuan	0.999522	Shangluo	0.999521
Xingtai	0.187936	Sanmenxia	0.186735	Sanmenxia	0.999522	Ziyang	0.999521
Jingmen	0.187918	Xining	0.186725	Xining	0.999522	Xinyu	0.999520
Zhumadian	0.187887	Xiangyang	0.186713	Xiangyang	0.999522	Huludao	0.999520

(continued)

Table 3.12 (continued)

Economic public goods				Non-economic public goods			
City	Supply efficiency	City	Supply efficiency	City	Supply efficiency	City	Supply efficiency
Qinhuangdao	0.187877	Xinyu	0.186712	Xinyu	0.999522	Zigong	0.999520
Xinyang	0.187764	Hegang	0.186700	Hegang	0.999522	Meishan	0.999520
Jian	0.187716	Huangshan	0.186605	Huangshan	0.999522	Guang'an	0.999520
Kaifeng	0.187657	Chifeng	0.186597	Chifeng	0.999522	Bazhong	0.999520
Yangquan	0.187642	Baotou	0.186593	Baotou	0.999522	Tongliao	0.999520
Dalian	0.187604	Datong	0.186587	Datong	0.999522	Hanzhong	0.999520
Shanghai	0.187590	Mianyang	0.186583	Mianyang	0.999522	Leshan	0.999519
Yingkou	0.187543			Jingzhou	0.999522		

oversight. This can result in the inability to form fair, reasonable, and effective urban public goods pricing mechanisms. Moreover, due to insufficiently comprehensive and scientific performance evaluations by the government and imperfect supervision mechanisms, there are issues in both the efficiency and fairness of urban public goods supply. They are:

(1) Loss of Public Nature: Privatizing the supply mechanism breaks the administrative monopoly of the government over urban infrastructure, utilities, and public services, introducing competition to improve efficiency and service quality. However, some government departments equate marketization with privatization, handing over the supply of public utilities and services entirely to private capital, leading to private monopolies and the loss of the public nature of supply (Dong, 2011).
(2) Improper Role Transition of Government: In the market-oriented reform of urban public goods, the government's functions and roles should transition accordingly. For public goods supplied through market mechanisms, the government should transform from a direct producer and supplier to a planner, decision-maker, and regulator. However, some governments continue to oversee public goods projects through administrative orders, lacking effective regulatory frameworks (Jiang, 2014).
(3) Unformed Pricing Mechanism: A fair, reasonable, and effective urban public goods pricing mechanism has not yet been established. It is crucial for the government and private sectors to clearly define their responsibilities, obligations, and risks to ensure accountability. Enterprises must design reasonable income commitment mechanisms to ensure sustainable production and operation, reduce financing costs, and create effective incentive mechanisms.
(4) Incomplete Performance Evaluation and Supervision: The government's evaluation of enterprise performance in public goods production is not comprehensive or scientific enough, resulting in inadequate supervision mechanisms. The current oversight methods tend to be simplistic, relying heavily on administrative inspections that lack professionalism and a systematic regulatory framework. Additionally, the focus is on qualification and economic supervision, with insufficient social supervision and inadequate involvement of social forces in the regulatory process.

3.4 The Social (Voluntary) Supply Mechanism of Urban Public Goods

3.4.1 The Possibility of Achieving Social (Voluntary) Supply of Public Goods

In addition to government and market mechanisms, the social (voluntary) supply of public goods is an alternative approach. This model involves social organizations, enterprises, and individuals voluntarily providing public goods through social donations or public lotteries, often at no or minimal cost, and funds raised are allocated for cultural education, sports, poverty relief, and public welfare, thus supplementing government and market supply (Fan, 2005). The main categories of socially (voluntarily) supplied public goods include (a) Public Services for Special Groups: Non-profit organizations, often referred to as the so-called third sector, provide public services to socially disadvantaged or especially needy groups, including elderly care, unemployment training, charitable relief, and youth support; (b) Community Public Goods Supply: Social organizations frequently engage in community volunteer activities, including supporting people with disabilities, caring for the elderly and children, ensuring community safety, providing community cultural education, and offering legal assistance.

A functioning social (voluntary) supply mechanism for public goods requires a robust social foundation and cultural environment. It is necessary for a country to establish a corresponding legal framework to regulate and protect volunteer activities, and both society and government must create volunteer incentive mechanisms. The government could first implement a formal volunteer service system, fostering social integration, societal responsibility, and altruistic norms among participants. Also, multi-level incentive systems should be established, such as tax deductions and financial subsidies for individuals and enterprises. Social organizations should also enhance their organizational structures to improve professional service levels (Li, 2007).

The social (voluntary) supply mechanism of public goods can positively affect the overall supply of public goods through (a) Scale Effects: Voluntary supply can expand the overall supply scale of public goods to meet the growing demand; (b) Competitive Effects: Competing with government and market supply to potentially enhance the efficiency of public goods provision.

Factors influencing the social (voluntary) supply of public goods include group size, the marginal return of individual investment in public goods, initial endowment distribution, and social preferences. Inadequate institutional arrangements can lead to stronger "free rider problem" motivations and affect voluntary supply levels. Higher marginal returns from individual investments motivate more robust participation, thus positively correlating with voluntary supply levels (Buckley & Croson, 2006; Carpenter, 2007). More equitable initial endowment distribution also correlates with increased voluntary supply (Cherry et al., 2005; Sadrieh & Verbon, 2006). Social preferences, such as reciprocity or pure altruism, influence voluntary supply through altruistic preferences, warm-glow effects, and conditional cooperation, where certain types of social preferences lead individuals to invest in public goods regardless of others' actions (Goeree et al., 2002; Palfrey & Prisbrey, 1997; Fischbache & Gachter, 2006).

3.4.2 The Mechanism Design of Social (Voluntary) Supply of Public Goods

Theoretically, the existence of social (voluntary) supply behavior is evident, supported by numerous practical examples. It is essential to study the institutional arrangements and mechanism designs that can promote an adequate social (voluntary) supply of urban public goods.

The design of the social (voluntary) supply mechanism mainly includes information disclosure, communication and commitment, and voluntary punishment mechanisms (Zhang & Xia, 2009). Information disclosure encompasses decision information disclosure and identity information disclosure. If social organizations and individuals anticipate their actions being made public and socially recognized, their contribution to voluntarily supplying public goods can increase. The likelihood of decision information being disclosed can enhance members' cooperation levels. Disclosing participants' personal information can narrow the social distance between participants, enhance mutual recognition, and increase their concern for local welfare, thereby improving the level of voluntary public goods supply. In the social (voluntary) supply mechanism of public goods, signaling voluntary and cooperative behavior through identity information can promote coordination among participants or suppliers. Additionally, each social organization and individual, when deciding their contribution methods and supply quantities, usually refer to the behavior and contributions of similar participants, where identity information disclosure can influence the choice of reference standards for volunteers. Compared to disclosing the identity information of volunteers who supply public goods, the exchange of volunteer information among volunteers and within society can more effectively improve the level of voluntary public goods supply. Video communication, voice communication, and online communication can all increase the level of voluntary public goods supply. Furthermore, in long-term collaboration between volunteers and the government or relevant organizations, credible punishment threats can effectively maintain the effectiveness and cooperation of voluntary supply behavior. In mutual benefit preferences, adopting internal punishment mechanisms or third-party punishment mechanisms can effectively enhance cooperation levels, strengthen constraints, and achieve a more sustainable and effective public goods supply.

To sum up, to effectively achieve the social (voluntary) supply of public goods, it is essential to leverage advanced information technologies like the internet, big data, and artificial intelligence, and build information and interaction platforms for urban public goods supply. Government departments should support, guide, and regulate social organizations to play an active role in urban public goods supply. Social organizations oriented towards public welfare and altruism can expand the coverage of public goods to meet public demand. Social organizations and volunteers have direct contact with the public and have a better understanding of public needs, which enables them to identify public preferences for public goods more easily. Moreover, the participation of social organizations and volunteers in public goods supply can more effectively play a supervisory role (Wang, 2007).

3.4.3 Evolution and Case Studies of the Social (Voluntary) Supply Mechanism for Public Goods in China

3.4.3.1 Evolution of the Social (Voluntary) Supply Mechanism for Public Goods in China

For a long time, the public goods sector in China has been characterized by strong administrative control, and due to the limitations of social and economic development levels, the development of social service organizations, social fund organizations, and social volunteer teams has been slow and relatively small in scale. Over the past decade of social and economic development, the third sector has gradually developed. According to the *2019 Statistical Bulletin of Civil Affairs Development*, by the end of 2019, there were 866,000 social organizations, 643,000 grassroots autonomous organizations, 528,000 various community service institutions and facilities nationwide, with a comprehensive service facility coverage rate of 92.9% in urban communities. There were 13,000 regular social donation stations and charity supermarkets (including 3528 charity supermarkets), with 16.642 million person-times providing 43.269 million hours of volunteer service in the civil affairs field throughout 2019, and national social organization donation revenue reached 87.32 billion yuan. There were also 239 registered charitable trusts nationwide with a total asset scale of 2.76 billion yuan.

The development of social organizations in China has mainly experienced a process from a dual management system and social organization filing system to the establishment of a modern social governance system. In the 1980s and 1990s, China's management of social organizations primarily implemented a dual management system jointly responsible by the registration management agency and the business supervisory unit of social organizations. In 1988, the state promulgated the *Measures for the Administration of Foundations*. In 1989, the *Regulations on the Administration of Registration of Social Organizations* were promulgated, establishing a management system jointly responsible by the registration management agency (i.e., civil affairs departments) and the business supervisory unit. In 1998, the eighth executive meeting of the State Council passed the newly revised *Regulations on the Administration of Registration of Social Organizations* and the *Interim Regulations on the Administration of Registration of Private Non-Enterprise Units*, marking the formal formation of the dual management system for social organizations (Yuan & Liu, 2014). Numerous studies have shown that this system has many restrictive mechanisms, leading to social organizations showing characteristics of lacking vitality and strong dependence on the system (Huang, 2015; Wang, 2005; Wang & Jia, 2002; Yan, 2010). Entering the twenty-first century, the central government began actively exploring ideas to encourage the development of social organizations, continually releasing policy signals to promote the positive development of social organizations. In fact, local governments in cities like Beijing, Shanghai, Guangzhou, and Shenzhen have been exploring the social organization filing system at the grassroots community level since 2005 and exploring new systems for government purchasing social organization services such as "public welfare bidding" (Huang, 2015). Since the 18th National Congress of the Communist Party of China, the party and government have highly valued the role of social organizations in social governance, actively encouraging social organizations to participate in public services and social governance work, stimulating the vitality of social organizations, accelerating the formation of a social organization system, and innovating the social governance system. As China enters a new era, the central government has proposed establishing a social governance pattern of co-construction, co-governance, and sharing. To this end, the government can transfer some public undertakings to social organizations through purchasing services and bidding, fully leveraging social forces and public cooperation to enhance the socialization level of social governance (Dong, 2011).

3.4.3.2 Case Analysis: Social (Voluntary) Supply Mechanism of Shanghai's Community Public Welfare Venture Philanthropy Projects

Since 2009, the Shanghai Civil Affairs Bureau and its subordinate civil affairs departments have innovatively explored the funding methods of public welfare funds, drawing on charitable practices from the United States and Europe, and introduced the market-based public service operation mechanism of community public welfare venture philanthropy. Its purpose is to identify the needs of community residents, cultivate public welfare service projects welcomed by community residents, increase community residents' awareness and participation in charitable public welfare projects, mobilize social organizations to participate in community public welfare services, promote the professional and vocational development of community public welfare undertakings, and support the cultivation of a batch of capable and trustworthy social public welfare service organizations to continuously meet the diverse and personalized public service needs of community residents.

Formulating public welfare venture philanthropy project plans and carrying out community public welfare venture philanthropy activities are ways for the Shanghai civil affairs departments to support social organizations in engaging in voluntary service activities. The government selects social organizations through public welfare bidding and uses market-based operation models to apply venture capital tools to public welfare charitable undertakings, purchasing community public welfare service projects from social organizations and providing funds and social resources support for organizations engaged in social services (Song, 2020; Li & Tang, 2014; Liu & Qiu, 2014). The Shanghai Civil Affairs Bureau allocates a certain proportion of municipal public welfare funds from the annual lottery income, matches it with local government funds at the municipal and district (county) levels, entrusts non-profit organizations to manage public welfare venture philanthropy projects, and selects elderly services, disability assistance services, youth services, rescue assistance services, and other public welfare projects with investment and support value through community public welfare service project bidding. Those selected are officially established as projects (Jing & Gong, 2012). After several years of exploratory practice, the implementation of public welfare venture philanthropy plans has initially formed a new model of social voluntary service for innovative social management: (a) active guidance and support from the government; (b) wide participation of community residents, social organizations, and social workers; (c) selection of public welfare projects truly needed by community residents through open, fair, and just market competition; (d) introduction of social third parties for project auditing and performance evaluation. This model has benefited more community residents, promoted the professional and standardized development of community public welfare services, and supported a number of social organizations, especially grassroots livelihood service organizations.

The community public welfare venture philanthropy project in Shanghai has achieved collaboration between the government and social organizations, breaking the traditional public welfare fund funding mechanism and exploring a new mechanism for government and social organization cooperation in public goods supply. In the process of project implementation, social organizations play an important role: (a) they act as service producers, managing and operating specific services. Independent third-party organizations audit and evaluate these services, thus relieving the government from direct public goods supply duties; (b) social organizations serve as resource integrators, optimizing the allocation and utilization of resources. The government purchases services from these organizations and provides funding support, allowing them to deliver essential public services and enhance fund efficiency; (c) they function as key collaborators in government public services. By engaging in social governance and public service activities, these organizations become vital supplementary forces in government-led social governance, ensuring alignment between government objectives and community needs, and preventing both government and market failures in public service delivery.

However, problems exist in the promotion of Shanghai's community public welfare venture philanthropy project. They are:

(1) Funding instability: Funding primarily relies on government allocations, which are often not stable long-term. Community public welfare undertakings are generally long-term and fixed, so these service projects are greatly constrained

by funding, and their role in promoting the improvement of social organizations' operational capabilities and governance structure is limited.

(2) Too much Focus on administrative management: Many projects set up by government departments are for social administrative management purposes, not for establishing a community public service system and meeting residents' public service needs, leading to contradictions between supply and demand.
(3) Insufficient awareness among managers: The public welfare and charitable awareness of social organization managers and service personnel are insufficient. Many prioritize completing the government-assigned administrative management tasks to effectively serve community residents better.
(4) Limited participation: These projects are primarily government-led, with limited participation of social organizations and community residents in planning and decision-making processes, leading to a low alignment of some projects with social needs and limiting the initiative and innovation of social organizations (Li & Tang, 2014). Finally, there is a lack of scientific quantitative evaluation methods and systems for process supervision, quality control, and performance assessment of public welfare venture philanthropy projects (Jing & Gong, 2012; Li & Tang, 2014). Additionally, third-party organizations' evaluations overly consider whether they are conducive to the realization of government departments' management functions.

To address these challenges, community public welfare venture philanthropy should draw on the practical experiences of European and American countries while refining its operating mechanisms to align with China's national conditions and local community needs. This approach should emphasize the effective use of government and charitable funds, particularly by fostering collaboration with charitable foundations and commercial ventures. By strengthening the use of diverse investment tools, social organizations can improve their operational capabilities and governance structures, ultimately enhancing the quality and efficiency of their public services (Song, 2020; Li, 2018; Liu & Li, 2018; Liu & Qiu, 2014).

3.5 Multi-stakeholder Cooperative Supply Mechanism for Urban Public Goods

3.5.1 The Evolution of the Collaborative Supply Mechanism for Urban Public Goods in China

As previously noted, the multi-stakeholder collaborative supply mechanism for urban public goods involves the government, private sector, and societal organizations working together for the production, provision, and management of public goods. Generally, the government serves as the organizer and leader of this mechanism, responsible for planning and defining public goods supply projects while mobilizing private capital for the construction and operation of these projects.

Since the 1990s, China has been trying to incorporate private capital into public infrastructure projects through various policies. Traditionally, in the economic system, independent participation of private capital in the provision of public goods has been rare. The marketization of public goods supply in China is characterized by a multi-stakeholder collaboration between the government and social capital. In April 2014, the State Council initiated this shift by introducing social capital into infrastructure construction, launching the first batch of 80 public-private partnership (PPP) infrastructure projects. This marked a shift from policy guidance to practical implementation (Guo, 2014). In December 2014, the Ministry of Finance established the PPP Center and issued a list of 30 PPP demonstration projects along with operational guidelines. That same year, the National Development and Reform Commission (NDRC) released the *Guidance on Carrying Out Public-Private Partnership and the General Contract Guide for PPP Projects.* The State Council's *Guidance on Innovating Investment and Financing Mechanisms in Key Areas to Encourage Social Investment* encouraged active participation of social capital in municipal infrastructure construction and operation and urban water supply, heating, sewage, and waste treatment, resource utilization and treatment of construction waste, urban integrated utility tunnels, park supporting services, public transportation, and parking facilities by way of concession, investment subsidies, and government procurement of services. In April 2015, six ministries, including the NDRC, the Ministry of Finance, and the Ministry of Housing and Urban-Rural Development, jointly issued the *Administrative Measures for Concession of Infrastructure and Public Utilities* (hereinafter referred to as the *Administrative Measures*). The *Administrative Measures* have a significant impact on the government's use of concessions and PPP models to encourage and guide social capital in the provision of public goods, clarifying the principles of concession, the content of cooperation agreements, and management methods. *The Notice on Effectively Advancing Government and Social Capital Cooperation in Traditional Infrastructure*, issued by the NDRC in August 2016, outlined specific work arrangements for PPP projects in seven major infrastructure areas: energy, transportation, water conservancy, environmental protection, agriculture, forestry, and major municipal engineering, accelerating the progress of PPP projects in the infrastructure field. In March 2019, the Ministry of Finance issued the *Implementation Opinions on Promoting the Standardized Development of Government and Social Capital Cooperation*, emphasizing the importance of the PPP model in addressing the infrastructure gaps and promoting high-quality economic development. Local financial departments should, based on their financial capabilities, support standardized PPP projects through capital injections and operational subsidies (Fu et al., 2019).

The multi-stakeholder collaborative supply mechanism has gradually expanded into urban public services, education, healthcare, and elderly care, with numerous policy documents released. In October 2016, the Ministry of Finance released a notice to deepen the promotion of public-private partnerships in public service fields, requiring greater application of the PPP model and active guiding of various social capitals into investment and construction of projects in refuse disposal, sewage treatment, and other public services. In 2017, the PPP model was encouraged to support the elderly care industry, aiming to create a diverse, multi-tiered service market through government-social capital cooperation. In February 2020, the Ministry of Finance promulgated the *Administrative Measures for Government Purchasing Services*, clearly defining the purchasing entities, content, activity implementation, contracts, supervision, and legal responsibilities.

3.5.2 Methods of Multi-stakeholder Cooperative Supply of Urban Public Goods

The multi-stakeholder collaborative supply mechanism of public goods mainly involves addressing the issue of who provides the goods. There has always been significant theoretical and practical debate on this matter, with claims of government or market failure serving as the primary justifications for various stances. It is generally believed that governments must assume the responsibility of providing necessary, basic public goods, such as defense, public infrastructure, and public safety, establishing a fundamental platform for coordinated and sustainable economic and social development. For competitive and somewhat exclusive public goods, the private sector can supply them through market mechanisms. However, relying solely on either the government or the private sector often leads to efficiency and effectiveness problems for many public goods and services. Therefore, it is crucial to engage societal organizations and the private sector in a multi-stakeholder investment, production, and supply system. In a collaborative mechanism for public goods supply, the government holds a leading role, bearing the primary responsibility for public goods supply, yet functions as an equal partner in cooperation with both for-profit and non-profit organizations.

Effective multi-stakeholder collaboration in public goods supply requires appropriate institutional arrangements. Transitioning from a single-provider model to a multi-actor framework involves redefining relationships, including role separation, actor selection, role allocation, relationship dynamics, and the construction of functions and rights. Theoretically, employing competitive selection to choose, incentivize, and regulate actor behavior constitutes an effective institutional arrangement. Practically, successful cooperation relies on shared rights, transparent information, clear responsibilities, performance evaluations, willingness to cooperate, stability, and public participation and oversight. Key to establishing an effective multi-stakeholder collaborative supply mechanism is transforming government functions, clarifying the boundary between government and market, and enhancing governmental management capabilities. Only then can an adequate supply network be formed, harmonizing the objectives of all parties, integrating resources, leveraging comparative advantages, and eventually reconciling market efficiency with public interest.

Additionally, it is crucial to address the challenges of revealing and aggregating public preferences for public goods through mechanism design. This involves the development of mechanisms for expressing and identifying urban public goods demand, democratic decision-making, fiscal support, multi-stakeholder governance, and feedback supervision. Empowering the market mechanism and encouraging societal organizations and the public to participate in decision-making significantly enhance the effectiveness of public goods provision.

Currently, China's urban public goods collaborative supply methods mainly include government purchase of services and the PPP model. The government purchase of services model is predominantly applied in areas such as public services, education, elderly care, and healthcare, while the PPP model is primarily used in urban infrastructure construction. In recent years, rapid development has been seen in the government's purchase of services, achieving notable outcomes in urban non-economic public goods provision in various regions. For instance, Ningxia Hui Autonomous Region has expanded government procurement of preschool education services, guiding private kindergartens to offer preschool education services and forming a multi-tiered preschool education service supply system. In 2009, Chengguan District in Lanzhou, Gansu, created a virtual nursing home model based on government leadership, enterprise participation, market operation, and social engagement, meeting some elderly individuals' needs for professional, standardized home-based elderly care services (Wang, 2020). Suining district, Sichuan Province, explored market-oriented municipal services through government purchase mechanisms, providing citizen services and transforming municipal management from service provider to supplier and regulator, effectively saving fiscal funds and enhancing service quality.

China's multi-stakeholder collaborative supply mechanism has made significant contributions through years of development. It has introduced market competition mechanisms into urban public infrastructure construction and public service provision, standardizing project determination and collaborator selection while bolstering social organization participation in public goods provision, thereby compensating for government financial, operational, and professional skill deficits and enhancing public goods supply levels.

3.5.3 Methods and Scale of Government and Social Capital Collaboration

The previous discussion outlined the establishment and development of China's public-private partnership (PPP) from the perspective of market entities participating in the supply of public goods. Essentially, PPP is a typical method of government and social capital cooperation in providing public goods. It is an organizational and institutional arrangement for the public and private sectors to produce and supply public goods jointly. As defined by the United Nations Development Programme

(UNDP), PPP is a cooperative relationship among governments, enterprises, and social organizations centered around specific projects.

According to the *Guidance on Carrying Out Public-Private Partnership* issued in 2014, PPP projects mainly involve public services and infrastructure projects that the government is responsible for providing and are suitable for market operations. These include municipal facilities such as gas, electricity, water supply, heating, sewage, and waste treatment; transportation facilities like highways, railways, airports, and urban rail transit; Public services in healthcare, tourism, education, and elder care, along with water conservancy, environmental resources, and ecological protection projects, also fall under this umbrella. Operational PPP projects with transparent fees that fully cover investment costs can be carried out through government-granted concessions and models like build-operate-transfer (BOT) and build-own-operate-transfer (BOOT). Semi-operational projects, where operational fees do not cover investment costs and require government subsidies, can also use concessions alongside additional subsidies or direct government equity participation, usually based on models like BOT and build-own-operate (BOO). Non-operational projects, lacking a user fee structure and primarily reliant on government payments to recoup the investment, can be executed through government procurement of services using market models like BOO and entrusted operations.

PPP projects can employ various operational models depending on their nature and conditions, including concession, entrusted operation, management contract, BOT, BOO, transfer-operate-transfer (TOT), buy-build-operate (BBO), build-transfer-operate (BTO), build-lease-transfer (BLT), retrofit-operate-transfer (ROT), build-lease-operate-transfer (BLOT), build-lease-maintenance-transfer (BLMT), operation-maintenance (OM), and lease-operate-transfer (LOT). These models have different implementation scopes and conditions, each with unique characteristics and advantages. In China, the BOT model is the basic model for government and social capital cooperation and has been widely implemented in toll roads, power plants, wastewater treatment facilities, and other infrastructure projects (Wu, 2008; Zeng, 2018).

Statistics show that from 2014 to the end of May 2021, a total of 10,132 projects with an investment of 15.7 trillion yuan were included in the National PPP Comprehensive Information Platform Project Management Library. Of these, 7340 projects with an investment of 12 trillion yuan were signed and landed, with a landing rate of 72.4%. Additionally, 4444 projects, with an investment of 6.9 trillion yuan, had commenced construction, marking a 60.5% start rate. The distribution of cumulative investment in the National PPP Comprehensive Information Platform Project Management Library by industry is shown in Fig. 3.3. From the figure, it can be seen that the top five industries in terms of cumulative investment are transportation (5.2469 trillion yuan), municipal engineering (4.5355 trillion yuan), urban, comprehensive development (1.9681 trillion yuan), ecological construction and environmental protection (1.0709 trillion yuan), and tourism (410.3 billion yuan), accounting for 84.4% of the total investment in the management library. The implementation of PPP projects has effectively improved the supply level, quality, and efficiency of urban infrastructure.

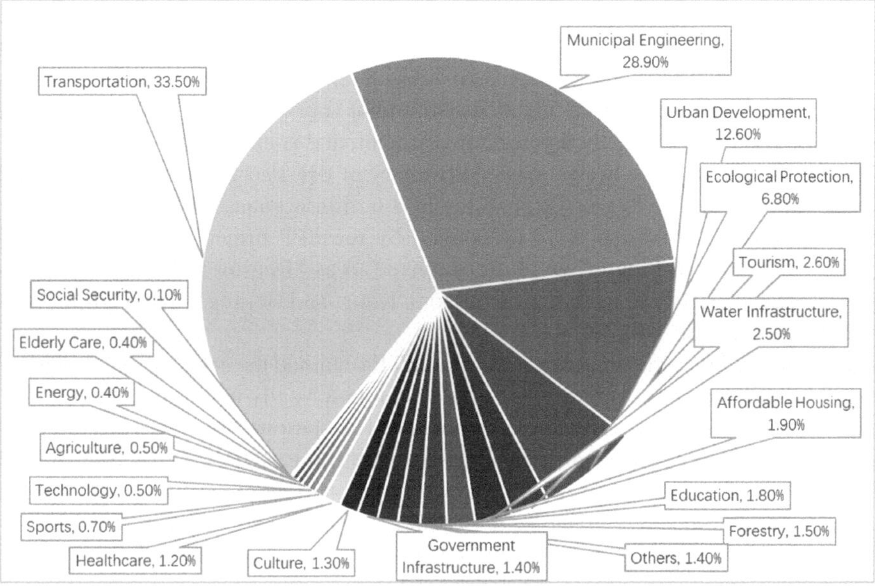

Fig. 3.3 Distribution of cumulative investment in the national PPP comprehensive information platform project management library by industry (unit: 100 million yuan). *Source* National PPP Comprehensive Information Platform Project Management Library May 2021 Report

3.5.4 Case Studies of Multi-stakeholder Cooperative Supply in Urban Public Goods

3.5.4.1 Public-Private Partnership Model of the Beijing Metro Line 4 Project[1]

The Beijing Metro Line 4 (hereinafter referred to as "Line 4") is one of the main lines in Beijing's urban rail network, spanning 50 km with a total of 35 stations. The total investment for the Line 4 project is 15.38 billion yuan. Construction began in August 2004, and the line commenced trial operation on September 28, 2009, with a current daily ridership exceeding 1 million passengers.

The first phase of the Line 4 project (from Gongyixiqiao Station to Anheqiao North Station) marked China's first large-scale PPP project in modern urban rail transit.

[1] The case study of the Beijing Subway Line 4 project is compiled based on the following sources: Anonymous. National Development and Reform Commission Releases Typical PPP Cases—Beijing Subway Line 4 Project [J]. *China Engineering Consulting*, 2015(9):23-26; Research Team of the Public-Private Partnership (PPP) Research Professional Committee of the Chinese Society for Fiscal Science, Jia Kang, Sun Jie. Case Study of the Beijing Subway Line 4 PPP Project [J]. *Economic Research Reference*, 2014(13):53-61; Wang Guanghong, Zhao Yongshan, Xu Xuecai. Study on the Application of the PPP Model in the Beijing Subway Line 4 Project [J]. *Cooperative Economy and Science*, 2015(23):44-46.

It was planned and implemented by the Beijing Infrastructure Investment Co., Ltd. (hereinafter referred to as "BII"). The project adopted a PPP financing cooperation model and is divided into two relatively independent components: Part A includes tunnel and station civil works with an investment of approximately 10.7 billion yuan, accounting for 70% of the total project investment, and is managed by Beijing MTR Corporation Limited, a wholly-owned subsidiary of BII. Part B includes vehicle and signal systems, with an investment of about 4.6 billion yuan, representing 30% of the total project investment, and is handled by the PPP project company Beijing MTR Corporation Limited (hereinafter referred to as "Beijing MTR"), which was established by BII, MTR Corporation of Hong Kong, and Beijing Capital Group with investment ratios of 2:49:49.

Upon completing the first phase, Beijing MTR obtained the usage rights for Part A assets through leasing. Beijing MTR is responsible for daily operation and management of Line 4, regular maintenance and upkeep of all station infrastructure (including Parts A and B), renewal of all public assets within the stations (excluding tunnel structures), and commercial operations within the stations. Investment and returns are recouped through ticket revenue and station commercial operations. The concession agreement spans 30 years, after which Part B facilities will be handed over to the Beijing municipal government at no cost, and Part A infrastructure will be returned to Beijing Metro Line 4 Investment Co., Ltd.

The first phase of Line 4 incorporates a reasonable fare compensation mechanism and passenger flow control mechanism, establishing a risk-sharing mechanism between the government and the market, providing investors with reasonable returns and effectively incentivizing participation. The fare compensation mechanism includes a fare difference compensation and revenue difference sharing mechanism, creating a long-term mechanism to share potential risks associated with metro fare adjustments. If the actual fare revenue is below the estimated fare revenue, the Beijing municipal government compensates the concession company for the shortfall; if the actual fare revenue exceeds the estimated fare revenue, the concession company returns 70% of the excess to the Beijing municipal government. Regarding passenger flow control, if actual passenger flow is below 80% of the forecast for three consecutive years, the concession company may apply for compensation or withdraw from the project. Conversely, if actual passenger flow exceeds the forecast, the Beijing municipal government shares 50% of the ticket revenue exceeding 10% of the forecasted passenger flow and 60% of revenue exceeding 20% of the forecast.

The Line 4 project has yielded significant social and economic benefits. The collaborative arrangement between the government and the concession company ensured fundamental interests, facilitating the smooth execution of project construction and operations.

3.5.4.2 Public-Private Partnership Model of the Shenzhen Universiade Center[2]

The Shenzhen Universiade Center (hereinafter referred to as the Universiade Center) is located on Longxiang Avenue in Longgang District, approximately 15 km from the city center. It served as the main venue for the 26th Summer Universiade in 2011 and is a central hub for Shenzhen's strategy to promote culture, sports, and public fitness. The Universiade Center includes a stadium, gymnasium, and swimming pool, with a total investment of approximately 4.1 billion yuan. The project covers a large area, extending 1050 m north to south and 990 m east to west, with a total land area of 520,500 square meters and a total building area of 290,000 square meters, equivalent to 132 standard football fields. The stadium was completed at the end of 2010 and became a landmark Shenzhen building.

After hosting the 26th Summer Universiade, the Universiade Center faced operational challenges, with annual maintenance costs reaching 60 million yuan, placing a heavy burden on the Shenzhen municipal government. To address the sustainable use and operation of the venues post-event, the Shenzhen municipal government adopted a public-private partnership model. Given the characteristics of the Universiade Center, its technical requirements, and social needs, the Shenzhen government chose the ROT (Retrofit-Operate-Transfer) model, entrusting the development and operation of one square kilometer of surrounding land to the Longgang District Government, in conjunction with the development of the Universiade Center. The Longgang District Government entrusted the operation and management of the venues to Kaisa Group Holdings Ltd. (hereinafter referred to as Kaisa Group), with an agreement that Kaisa Group would return all facilities to the Longgang District Government upon the expiration of the management term.

Kaisa Group, having secured the rights to operate all venues, became the general operator of the Universiade Center. Recognizing the nature of sports operations, it introduced professional operating teams to enhance the competitiveness of the Universiade Center and its venues through professional commercial operations. Specifically, Kaisa Group brought in teams such as Germany's AEG, Emperor Group, and Ti'Window, leveraging their resources in domestic and international sports events, performances, and venue operations. This collaboration formed an operational model involving the general operator and professional teams. By integrating sports with culture, exhibitions, and commerce, the operator built a commercial-venue-district interaction model, creating a business-sport linkage. Additionally, creating an operational reserve fund supported venue operations with commercial profits, further driving the development of the Universiade New Town.

---

[2] The case study of the Shenzhen Universiade Center project is compiled based on the following sources: Anonymous. National Development and Reform Commission Releases Typical PPP Cases—Shenzhen Universiade Center Project [J]. *China Engineering Consulting*, 2015(9):34–36; Zheng Fangyuan. Application of the PPP Model in Public Sports Venue Projects [J]. *Business Economics*, 2018(1):120–122, 155; Zeng Ke. Post-Event Renovation Strategies for Sports Centers Based on the ROT Operation Model: A Case Study of Shenzhen Universiade Center [D]. Harbin: Harbin Institute of Technology, 2015.

In this project, the government provided fiscal policy support for the operation. For the first five years, the government granted the general operator an annual subsidy of up to 30 million yuan for events and performances, encouraging the introduction of more and higher-quality events to enhance the venue's appeal. During the venue operation period, an operational reserve fund was established jointly by the Kaisa Group and the Longgang District Government. This fund, derived from operating profits, was used for daily maintenance and to increase event numbers and influence. An efficient operational performance evaluation mechanism was also established, with annual performance assessments and public satisfaction surveys conducted by management departments, as well as evaluations by third-party institutions with international venue operation experience. Additionally, a regulatory coordination service agency, comprising various relevant functional departments, was set up to assist the general operator in managing operations.

By integrating the ROT model into the operation of public sports venues, the government reduced costs and encouraged social capital investment, thereby enhancing operational efficiency and facilitating management reforms. The Universiade Center's public-private partnership for infrastructure projects provided valuable insights into responsibility allocation, rights and benefits distribution, commercial model selection, fiscal support policies, and performance evaluation mechanisms.

3.5.4.3 Evaluation of Implemented PPP Projects in China

Since 2014, with central policy encouragement and local government support, substantial social capital has participated in public infrastructure and services, easing fiscal pressure and enhancing urban infrastructure quality and efficiency. National PPP project review reveals that feasibility gap funding projects account for the majority of investment, comprising over 80% annually and up to 99% in some years. In terms of operational models, the BOT model predominates, accounting for over 85% of total projects according to data from the Ministry of Finance's PPP Center from 2009 to 2019. The BOO, ROT, and TOT models combined constitute only about 7% of total projects, with a small number of projects adopting the TOT + BOT model, accounting for about 3%.

Despite the PPP model allowance in most public sectors, practical application is primarily in transportation, municipal engineering, urban development, ecology, and environmental protection. The primary consideration for the government in adopting PPP models is funding, as it aims to attract social capital to address fiscal difficulties. This limited perspective, viewing PPPs as a temporary solution to fiscal crises rather than as a genuine reform of public goods supply mechanisms, is a fundamental reason for the contractual execution issues in some PPP projects. Furthermore, the standardization and clarity of power definition, revenue distribution, and risk sharing in PPP contracts need improvement, with some projects experiencing significant losses or excessive profits. While China has issued numerous policies on government and social capital cooperation, there is still a lack of comprehensive, systematic, and specialized laws and regulations. In response to the issues in PPP project implementation, the government has been rectifying, supervising, and guiding projects, to eliminate problematic ones. *The Implementation Opinions on Promoting the Standardized Development of Government and Social Capital Cooperation* issued by the Ministry of Finance in 2019, emphasizes the importance of "standardized operation, strict supervision, openness and transparency, and honest fulfillment of contracts" in advancing PPP projects. It particularly highlights the need to establish a complete system, strictly managing project entry, creating a dynamic adjustment mechanism, and managing PPP projects throughout their lifecycle. Fiscal investment is necessary and affordable and project decisions should be prudent and sufficiently informed, and partner selection should be fair and transparent. While PPP project standards have improved, further enhancements in social benefits and investment efficiency require ongoing legal system refinement, increased marketization, and reduced transaction costs.

References

Boadway, R. (2006). Intergovernmental redistributive transfers: Efficiency and equity. In E. Ahmad & G. Brosio (Eds.), *Handbook of fiscal federalism*. Edward Elgar Publishing.

Buckley, E., & Croson, R. (2006). Income and wealth heterogeneity in the voluntary provision of linear public goods. *Journal of Public Economics, 90*(4–5), 935–955.

Carpenter, J. P. (2007). Punishing free-riders: How group size affects mutual monitoring and the provision of public goods. *Games and Economic Behavior, 60*(1), 31–51.

Charnes, A., Cooper, W. W., & Rhodes, E. (1978). Measuring the efficiency of decision-making units. *European Journal of Operational Research, 2*(6), 429–444.

Chen, Q., & Hu, D. (2011). The diversification of government public service provision: Trends and strategies. *Journal of Shanghai Administration Institute, 12*(3), 31–39.

Chen, S., & Zhang, J. (2008). Research on the efficiency of fiscal expenditure in China's local governments: 1978–2005. *Chinese Social Sciences, 4*, 65–78.

Cherry, T. L., Kroll, S., & Shogren, J. F. (2005). The impact of endowment heterogeneity and origin on public good contributions: Evidence from the lab. *Journal of Economic Behavior & Organization, 57*(3), 357–365.

Ding, J., & Deng, K. (2008). Government preference, public goods provision, and fiscal decentralization in transition. *Economic Research, 7*, 78–89.

Dong, M. (2011). *Research on the innovation of the rural public product supply mechanism* [Doctoral dissertation]. Tianjin University.

Fan, L. (2005). *China's public goods market and voluntary provision analysis*. Shanghai, China: Shanghai People's Publishing House.

Fan, Z., & Zhang, J. (2013). Transfer payments, public goods provision, and the expansion of government scale. *World Economic Papers, 2*, 1–19.

Fischbacher, U., & Gachter, S. (2006). *Heterogeneous social preferences and the dynamics of free riding in public goods* [Working Paper]. Institute for Empirical Research in Economics.

Fu, J., Zhou, Y., & Liu, D. (2019). Normative promotion of high-quality development of PPP: A brief analysis of finance [2019] No. 10. *China Engineering Consulting, 4*, 32–35.

Fu, Y. (2007). *China-style decentralization, local fiscal models, and public goods provision: Theory and empirical research* [Doctoral dissertation]. Fudan University.

Gao, J. (2004). *Research on the market-oriented operation mechanism of urban infrastructure* [Doctoral dissertation]. Chongqing University.

Gao, L. (2012). Decentralization and livelihood: Empirical study on the impact of fiscal autonomy on public service satisfaction. *Economic Research, 47*(7), 86–98.

Goeree, J. K., Holt, C. A., & Laury, S. K. (2002). Private costs and public benefits: Unraveling the effects of altruism and noisy behavior. *Journal of Public Economics, 83*(2), 255–276.

Guo, W. (2014). An overview of the PPP model. *Economic Forum, 2014*(10), 88–91.

Hayek, F. A. (1945). The use of knowledge in society. *American Economic Review, 35*, 519–530.

Huang, G. (2009). *Research on the industrialization development of urban infrastructure in China* [Doctoral dissertation]. Harbin Institute of Technology.

Huang, J. (2007). Research on the realistic issues of China's fiscal decentralization. *Journal of Xiamen University (Philosophy and Social Sciences), 2007*(6), 97–104.

Huang, X. (2015). The institutional environment and development of contemporary Chinese social organizations. *Chinese Social Sciences, 9*, 146–164.

Jia, J., & Guo, Q. (2008). The regional economic growth effects of the fiscal responsibility arrangements between governments. *Economic Research, 6*, 37–49.

Jiang, M. (2014). *Research on the reform of local government public service provision mechanisms: Based on a public governance perspective* [Doctoral dissertation]. Wuhan University.

Jing, Y. J., & Gong, T. (2012). Managed social innovation: The case of government-sponsored venture philanthropy in Shanghai. *Australian Journal of Public Administration, 71*(2), 233–245.

Keen, M., & Marchand, M. (1997). Fiscal competition and the pattern of public spending. *Journal of Public Economics, 66*(1), 33–53.

Kessides, C. (1993). *The contributions of infrastructure to economic development*. The World Bank.

Kunneke, R. W. (1999). Electricity networks: How "natural" is the monopoly? *Utilities Policy, 8*(2), 99–108.

Leng, G. (2010). *Research on the provision of public goods by non-profit organizations in China* [Doctoral dissertation]. Southwestern University of Finance and Economics.

Li, J., & Tang, J. (2014). Government involvement in venture philanthropy: Models, mechanisms, and policies. *Public Administration and Policy Review, 3*(1), 60–68.

Li, W., & Jiang, N. (2010). China-style fiscal decentralization and the expansion of local government fiscal expenditure: An empirical test of the effectiveness of the "Leviathan" model in China. *Contemporary Finance & Economics, 6*, 26–31.

Li, X. (2007). *Research on urban community public goods provision* [Master's thesis]. Central China Normal University.

Li, Y. (2018). The experiential logic of China's social governance transformation. *Chinese Social Sciences, 11*, 58–73.

Liu, N. (2015). Local public goods: Empirical analysis of the efficiency of three demand expression mechanisms. *Local Finance Research, 2015*(3), 36–44.

Liu, Z., & Li, B. (2018). Research on the operational mechanism of venture philanthropy: With a discussion on the similarities and differences with commercial venture capital. *Comparative Economic & Social Systems, 3*, 181–191.

Liu, Z., & Qiu, S. (2014). The development and operation of venture philanthropy: European practices and implications for China. *Comparative Economic & Social Systems, 2*, 206–220.

Luo, L., & Yao, W. (2012). Theoretical research on the demand revelation mechanism for public goods. *Economic Dynamics, 11*, 45–48.

Min, Q. (2011). *From the demand for public goods to the balance of supply and demand: Theory and reality* [Doctoral dissertation]. Shandong University.

Oates, W. E. (1972). *Fiscal federalism*. Harcourt Brace Jovanovich.

Palfrey, T. R., & Prisbrey, J. E. (1997). Anomalous behavior in public goods experiments: How much and why. *American Economic Review, 87*, 829–846.

Pang, W., & Sun, Y. (2018). The spatial effects of fiscal decentralization and local government competition on fiscal expenditure efficiency. *Modern Economic Exploration, 10*, 42–49.

Ping, X., & Bai, J. (2006). China's fiscal decentralization and local public goods supply. *Finance & Trade Economics, 2006*(2), 49–55.

Qian, Y. Y., & Roland, G. (1998). Federalism and the soft budget constraint. *Journal of Economic Literature, 88*(5), 1143–1162.

Qian, Y. Y., & Weingast, B. R. (1997). Federalism as a commitment to preserving market incentives. *Journal of Economic Perspectives, 11*(4), 83–92.

Research team of the School of Finance and Taxation, Southwestern University of Finance and Economics. (2012). *Research on the effective provision of local public goods*. Beijing: Economic Science Press.

Sadrieh, A., & Verbon, H. A. A. (2006). Inequality, cooperation, and growth: An experimental study. *European Economic Review, 50*(5), 1197–1222.

Salamon, L. M., & Anheier, H. K. (1997). *Defining the nonprofit organization*. Walter de Gruyter.

Song, J. (2020). *Prediction of urban infrastructure investment and PPP financing mechanism under the new urbanization background* [Doctoral dissertation]. Beijing Jiaotong University.

Tiebout, C. M. (1956). A pure theory of local expenditures. *Journal of Political Economy, 64*(5), 416–424.

Tu, L. (2013). Empirical analysis of the impact of central transfer payments on regional financial balance. *Finance & Trade Economics, 2013*(3), 21–25.

Wang, C. (2007). Institutional innovation in the diversified governance model of public goods. *Management World, 3*, 160–161.

Wang, D., & Zhang, Q. (2011). Analysis of the efficiency of public expenditure by urban governments in China: An empirical study based on the four-stage DEA method. *Science of Finance and Economics, 3*, 41–48.

Wang, J. (2011). Classified privatization policy for deepening the reform of China's urban utilities. *Academic Monthly, 43*(9), 60–63.

Wang, M. (2020). Research on the "Internet+" smart health care service in Lanzhou. *Journal of Xi'an Petroleum University (Social Science Edition), 29*(4), 54–61.

Wang, M., & Jia, X. (2002). Analysis of the development of Chinese NGOs. *Management World, 8*, 30–43.

Wang, S. (1999). *Diversity and unity: Comparative study of the third sector*. Hangzhou: Zhejiang People's Publishing House.

Wu, M. (2008). *Research on the provision modes of public services* [Doctoral dissertation]. Xiamen University.

Xi, H. (2006). *Interests, power, and responsibility: Research on the mechanism of public goods provision*. Beijing: China Social Sciences Press.

Xia, C. (2013). Review of China's fiscal decentralization and public goods provision. *Finance & Trade Economics, 3*, 32–37.

Xu, J., & Zhao, T. (2013). The practical dilemmas and innovative paths of government procurement of public services: Practice from Shanghai. *China Administration, 8*, 26–30.

Yan, Z. (2010). Opportunities, challenges, and promotion ideas for the development of Chinese social organizations at the current stage. *Beijing Social Science, 2010*(1), 12–17.

Yang, J. (2003). *Research on infrastructure investment*. Beijing, China: China Economic Publishing House.

Yu, Y., Wang, Y., & Li, Q. (2020). Fiscal autonomy, fiscal expenditure structure, and total factor productivity: An examination of 230 prefecture-level cities. *Financial Research, 2020*(1), 28–46.

Yuan, H., & Liu, X. (2014). *Public policy research on the governance of social organizations*. Guilin, China: Guangxi Normal University Press.

Zeng, J. (2018). *Research on financial compensation issues for early termination in PPP sewage treatment contracts* [Master's thesis]. Hunan University.

Zhang, K., & Zheng, J. (2019). *Public administration* (2nd ed.). Beijing, China: Renmin University of China Press.

Zhang, Q. (2018). The mechanism and empirical identification of public expenditure efficiency promoting industrial structure upgrading. *Finance and Trade Economics, 39*(5), 146–159.

Zhang, X. B. (2006). Fiscal decentralization and political centralization in China: Implications for growth and inequality. *Journal of Comparative Economics, 34*(4), 713–726.

Zhang, Y., & Gong, L. (2005). Tax-sharing reform, fiscal decentralization, and economic growth in China. *Quarterly Journal of Economics, 2005*(4), 75–108.

Zhang, Y., & Xia, J. (2009). Research progress on voluntary public goods provision mechanisms. *Economic Dynamics, 2009*(1), 90–95.

Zhao, Y. (2009). Sixty years of China's fiscal system. *Economic Research Reference, 2009*(62), 2–16.

Zheng, D. (2015). *Analysis of the marketization of urban public services: A case study of the sanitation industry in Hedong District, Tianjin* [Master's thesis]. Tianjin University.

Zhou, L. (2007). Research on the tournament model for the promotion of Chinese local officials. *Economic Research, 2007*(7), 36–50.

Zhou, Y., & Song, Z. (2008). The voluntary provision mechanism of public goods: An experimental study. *Economic Research, 2008*(7), 90–104.

Zhu, Y. (2019). The impact of local government competition on consumption structure under the tournament model: A perspective from public goods provision competition. *China Economic Issues, 2019*(5), 76–93.

Chapter 4
Investment and Financing Mechanisms for Urban Public Goods

The level and structure of urban public goods provision are influenced by investment scale and direction, which are determined by economic development goals and strategies. Variations in national economic systems and mechanisms lead to differences in entities and methods involved in public good investment. This chapter summarizes the evolution of China's public goods investment system, analyzes the structure of urban public goods financing in China, and focuses on studying the government fiscal investment mechanism, market financing mechanism, and multi-stakeholder cooperative financing mechanism for public goods. It also outlines trends and models of various financing mechanisms, reveals existing problems through empirical analysis, and proposes corresponding solutions.

4.1 Overview of Urban Public Goods Investment Mechanisms

4.1.1 Contents and Entities of Urban Public Goods Investment

Cities consist of various resources and their products, with urban development representing an ongoing investment process with the aim of effectively utilizing natural and economic resources. This investment and development activity includes both direct production and daily living activities, along with efforts to provide infrastructure and public services that support these activities. The diverse nature and objectives of investment give rise to both urban private products and the public goods sector. Urban private product investment focuses on non-agricultural productivity, leading to varied industrial structures driven by technological advancements. In contrast, urban public goods investment reflects urban production patterns and lifestyle needs

B. Wu et al., *Effective Supply Mechanism of Urban Public Goods*, Public Economy and Urban Governance in China, https://doi.org/10.1007/978-981-96-2608-3_4

of residents, significantly influenced by urban production demands and community needs. Generally, urban public goods investment can be categorized into:

(1) Economic Public Infrastructure such as Water, energy, transportation, telecommunications, environmental, and safety facilities;
(2) Social Public Infrastructure including educational, health, sports, cultural, welfare, and public management facilities;
(3) Public Service Systems, which are essential for effective use of economic and social public infrastructure, including infrastructure operation systems and public service institution establishment and operation.

Investing in urban public goods aims to enhance city functions, maximize social and economic benefits, and achieve sustainability. In urban competition, the goal is also to boost urban economic growth and market competitiveness, achieving coordination between urban socioeconomic development and the ecological environment. Given the public and social nature of public goods, the government serves as the primary investor. Nevertheless, historically, the investment entities for public goods have varied significantly. Initially, investments were largely private, but after World War II, government-led investments became predominant, leading to the emergence of public–private partnerships in the 1990s. Currently, governments, enterprises, social organizations, and other entities all contribute to urban public goods, with the government remaining the primary and most significant investor. Since reform and opening up, China's urban public goods sector has evolved from exclusive government financing to an inclusive model involving various stakeholders, including the government, market participants (such as enterprises and private investors), and social organizations.

4.1.2 Investment Mechanisms for Urban Public Goods

Urban public goods investment mechanisms are mainly influenced by the functions of public goods, operational performance, and government fiscal conditions. To ensure the proper operation of urban production and support the daily lives of residents, maintain orderly urban socioeconomic activities, enhance urban comprehensive competitiveness, and improve the quality of life and well-being of urban residents, cities employ different investment mechanisms, aiming at maximizing the mobilization of funds for public goods investment. These mechanisms vary based on resource allocation methods and ownership.

4.1.2.1 Government Investment and Construction Mechanism

The government investment and construction mechanism involves direct investment in public infrastructure or service projects. This mechanism allows the city government to control resource usage and operational modes, allocate resources according to social needs, and meet public demands with no need to negotiate with private investors regarding the public functions of investment projects. However, the mechanism has its drawbacks. The government bears the entirety of investment, construction, and operation, resulting in a heavy fiscal burden. Furthermore, the government assumes all investment risks and ongoing costs, requiring continuous public service expenditure. Additionally, government entities may lack the necessary expertise in project construction and operation, which can lead to inefficient project execution due to complex decision-making processes.

4.1.2.2 Market Investment and Construction Mechanism

In the market-based investment mechanism, non-government entities, including enterprises and private investors, finance public goods projects. The government does not participate directly in funding but facilitates through financial guarantees, project authorizations, and bidding processes, entrusting implementation to contractors and operators. This mechanism can manifest in several forms, such as private (enterprise) investment in line with government project requirements or allowing investors to operate the project for a specified period after construction. Given the long-term investment horizon and low profitability of public goods projects, the government may grant concession rights and tax incentives to ensure profitability. For projects that require public resources like land, the government may also contribute through allocations. Although public goods projects are predominantly funded by private and social capital, the planning and functional aspects are typically government-decided, with investors required to meet governmental objectives.

The market-based investment mechanism involves the delegation of public goods investment, construction, and operation, which requires a mature market economy and a well-regulated society. International examples demonstrate that this mechanism can alleviate governmental financial pressures, facilitating the mobilization of resources to construct public infrastructure despite funding limitations and enabling urban economic development without incurring construction and operational risks. Additionally, this mechanism fosters competition in investment and operation, enhancing the performance of the public sector. However, potential issues may arise when profit-driven investors cut costs at the expense of project quality or service standards, potentially compromising the functionality of public goods projects. Therefore, the market-based investment mechanism represents not just a contractual relationship but a joint responsibility for public goods provision between the government and investors.

4.1.2.3 Public-Private Partnership (PPP) Investment Mechanisms

The PPP (Public-Private Partnership) investment mechanism involves collaboration between the government and social capital, comprising enterprises and social organizations. This mechanism occupies a position between purely governmental and market-based investment mechanisms. The PPP approach to public goods projects offers several advantages: (a) Optimal Utilization of Social Funds: By leveraging social funds for public infrastructure, PPPs alleviate fiscal pressure and reduce government debt; (b) Complementary Strengths: Different investment entities, guided by distinct principles, support and supervise one another throughout project construction and operation, leveraging their respective advantages and social functions. The government focuses on comprehensive planning aligned with public interests, while enterprises and social organizations, benefiting from their flexibility and proximity to the public, are better equipped to address public needs and enhance the reach of public goods; (c) Market-Oriented Investment: This approach enhances the operational efficiency of urban public goods through market mechanisms. Compared to purely private market investment mechanisms, PPPs are more effective in achieving construction goals and mitigating project risks.

However, PPP mechanisms also involve the challenges:

(1) Commercial Interests vs. Public Goals: Investors and operators tend to prioritize commercial interests, which can conflict with public interests once they acquire control over urban public goods. This divergence requires thorough communication and coordination between the government and its partners, requiring clear articulation of project objectives in cooperation agreements;
(2) Project Longevity and Stability: Public goods projects often involve long construction and operation cycles. The financial and operational stability of partners is crucial to project success. Any operational issues can disrupt projects, and high costs combined with regulated prices can lead to low returns, highlighting the need for financially robust investors and operators with sufficient cash flow to manage risks.

In PPP projects, governments attract investors through bidding, operating authorizations, and equity participation. Both developed and developing countries adopt PPP mechanisms for public goods projects, particularly in energy (electricity, gas), water supply, sewage, telecommunications, education, healthcare, and, most commonly, transportation infrastructure (airports, ports, roads, bridges, etc.).

4.1.3 Evolution of China's Public Goods Investment System

Within an economic framework, the public goods investment system refers to how government departments organize and manage public goods investment activities. It encompasses the composition of investment entities, the selection of investment tools, the integration of investment channels and networks, the establishment of investment incentives and constraints, and the construction of investment evaluation systems. Collectively, these elements constitute the complete organizational forms and methodologies for these activities.

During the planned economy period, the government was the sole investor in national economic activities across all sectors. With the advent of the reform and opening up and the establishment of a socialist market economy system, China recognized the need to reconcile the contradictions between the administrative planning investment system and the actual economic operation, leading to corresponding reforms in the investment system, which can be categorized into two developmental stages:

(1) The pre-reform era (before 1978), characterized by government administrative planning and investment entirely through fiscal revenue;
(2) The post-reform era (after 1978) was marked by a gradual shift toward market-oriented and diversified approaches to public goods investment.

From 1978 until the early 1990s, the government continued to be the primary investor in public goods, relying heavily on fiscal taxation. However, some public goods projects began experiencing social charges as a funding source. During this period, the government sought to boost fiscal revenue through higher tax rates and new taxes, specifically allocating funds for urban infrastructure construction. Some cities also started charging for infrastructure usage to raise construction funds (Lv & Tai, 2018). Major tax and fee projects for urban infrastructure construction and maintenance included:

(1) Urban maintenance and construction tax;
(2) Land use fees;
(3) Municipal public facility support fees and urban public facility capacity expansion fees;
(4) Revenue from the transfer of land use rights (Han, 2006).

From the mid-1990s to 2003, the government continued to play primary investment roles while experimenting with market mechanisms in urban public facilities. The reform of urban infrastructure investment and financing system reform accelerated in the mid-1990s through several key developments:

(1) Relaxation of investment policies: These changes allow foreign and private capital to participate in public infrastructure investment through sole proprietorship, cooperation, joint ventures, equity participation, and franchising;
(2) Market-oriented reforms: These include the establishment of franchise systems and reforms in usage fees and utility prices in municipal utilities;
(3) Implementation of the project legal person responsibility system: This also includes piloting capital systems and adopting bidding and engineering supervision practices (Guo & Mao, 2019; Zhang, 2006).

From 2003 to 2012, the urban public goods investment mechanism transitioned into the land finance phase, building on tax sharing and reforms in state-owned land use rights transactions. This period can be further divided into:

(1) 2003–2008: During this time, land transfer fees and related land income became the main funding source for public infrastructure construction. With

the rapid development of the urban real estate market, land finance and land financing gradually dominated public infrastructure construction. This mechanism enabled local governments to overcome funding constraints, making the government the primary investor in public goods;

(2) 2008–2012: After the 2008 global financial crisis, the "land mortgage + financing platform (urban investment bonds)" model emerged as the primary approach. Local governments established financing platforms to raise funds for urban infrastructure projects, issuing corporate bonds and medium-term notes, using land pledges or disguised guarantees to enhance financing credibility (Qi & Xu, 2017; Yang et al., 2018).

Since 2012, the central government has increased fiscal budget allocations for public infrastructure and expanded the issuance of special bonds for municipal construction, leading to a gradual increase in urban public goods investment. This period has also witnessed a marked acceleration of public goods construction marketization, with a strong push towards developing PPP (Public–Private Partnership) models, thereby forming a multi-stakeholder cooperative investment mechanism. The *Guiding Opinions of the State Council on Innovating Key Areas Investment and Financing Mechanisms and Encouraging Social Investment* issued by the State Council encouraged private and social funds to participate in infrastructure and public service investment, outlining the scope and methods for such participation. Consequently, various PPP models were widely implemented in public infrastructure projects, integrating state-owned and private capital to alleviate local government debt pressure (Qi & Xu, 2017).

To further economic development and enhance public infrastructure construction, the government expanded bond issuance after 2015, elevating central and local special bonds as key funding sources for urban public goods. Functionally, local government bonds are akin to municipal bonds. However, in terms of issuance mechanisms, local bonds in China exhibit lower administrative and normative standards, lower market transparency, and an underdeveloped self-discipline mechanism. Since 2009, local bond issuance methods have included "issuance and repayment by the central government", "self-issuance and central repayment", and "self-issuance and self-repayment". To standardize government bond issuance, the revised *Budget Law of the People's Republic of China* (2014) and the *Interim Measures for the Administration of General Bond Issuance by Local Governments* (2015) stipulated that local governments must issue bonds within budget constraints, repaying general public budget income for non-revenue public welfare projects (Li & Ren, 2013; Zhang, 2020; Zhang & Min, 2020). Currently, local bonds and land transfer income are vital for urban public goods investment.

According to the National Bureau of Statistics and the Ministry of Finance, the land transfer fee revenue in 2020 amounted to 8.4 trillion yuan. By the end of 2020, the central government debt balance stood at 20.890587 trillion yuan. In December 2020, the national local government debt balance was 25.6615 trillion yuan, within the limit approved by the National People's Congress, including 12.7395 trillion yuan of general debt and 12.9220 trillion yuan of special debt. Government bonds totaled 25.4864 trillion yuan, with 175.1 billion yuan of non-government bond forms of government debt. By the end of 2020, the combined central and local government debt totaled 46.6 trillion yuan. According to the 2020 fiscal expenditure report by the Ministry of Finance, approximately 80% of local government special bond expenditures were allocated to transportation, municipal and industrial park infrastructure, and livelihood services like vocational education, childcare, healthcare, and elderly care. Based on the data, it is estimated that about 23 trillion yuan of local government debt was directly invested in the public goods sector.

4.2 Investment Levels and Structures of Urban Public Goods in China

4.2.1 Analysis of Urban Public Goods Investment Levels

Since the reform and opening up, China has invested heavily in urban municipal public facilities. As shown in Table 4.1, the fixed asset investment in these facilities grew dramatically from 1.2 billion yuan in 1978 to 2012.32 billion yuan in 2018. In years of rapid growth, the proportion of the investment scale to the overall investment in fixed assets in the same period is 1.7% to 8.1%, and the proportion to the GDP in the same period is 0.3% to 3.3%.

The increasing investment has greatly enhanced the level of urban municipal public facilities, as illustrated in Table 4.2. From 1981 to 2018, the urban water supply coverage rate rose from 53.70% to 98.36%, gas supply rate from 11.60% to 96.70%, per capita road area from 1.80 to 16.70 square meters, and per capita park green space from 1.50 to 14.11 square meters. Additionally, the sewage treatment rate increased from 14.86% in 1991 to 95.49% in 2018. Despite these improvements, there remains substantial room for enhancement to meet the rising quality of life demanded by residents.

Since the mid-1990s, China has increased investment in municipal public facilities and also in non-economic public goods such as education, healthcare, and social security, as shown in Table 4.3. The national education expenditure rose from 86.705 billion yuan in 1992 to 4.613.5 billion yuan in 2018, significantly boosting the supply of educational public goods and enhancing China's human capital (An, 2008). From 1985 to 2016, depending on various technical substitution elasticities, the broad human capital of the country grew by 4.6–8.2 times, with an average annual growth rate of 3.6%–5.3%[1] over the past decade. Healthcare expenditure increased from 109.686 billion yuan in 1992 to 5912.19 billion yuan in 2018, accelerating hospital construction and the improvement of medical facilities. By the end of 2019, China had 6.30 hospital beds per 1000 people, 3.18 registered nurses per 1000 people, 2.61

[1] Central University of Finance and Economics, China Human Capital and Labor Research Center: *China Human Capital Report 2019*, December 2019.

Table 4.1 Fixed asset investment in urban municipal public facilities

Year	Completed investment/ 100 million yuan	Growth rate/%	Proportion of total social fixed asset investment/%	Proportion of GDP/%
1978	12.00	–	1.79	0.33
1979	14.20	18.02	2.02	0.35
1980	14.40	1.77	1.58	0.31
1981	19.50	43.81	2.03	0.40
1982	27.20	39.07	2.21	0.51
1983	28.20	3.72	1.97	0.47
1984	41.70	47.89	2.27	0.57
1985	64.00	53.60	2.52	0.70
1986	80.10	25.13	2.57	0.77
1987	90.30	12.79	2.38	0.74
1988	113.20	25.39	2.38	0.75
1989	107.00	−5.54	2.43	0.62
1990	121.20	13.30	2.68	0.64
1991	170.90	40.99	3.05	0.78
1992	283.20	65.71	3.50	1.04
1993	521.80	84.28	3.99	1.46
1994	666.00	27.64	3.91	1.37
1995	807.60	21.26	4.03	1.32
1996	948.60	17.46	4.14	1.32
1997	1142.70	20.45	4.58	1.43
1998	1477.60	29.31	5.20	1.73
1999	1590.80	7.66	5.33	1.76
2000	1890.70	18.85	5.74	1.89
2001	2351.90	24.40	6.32	2.12
2002	3123.20	32.79	7.18	2.57
2003	4462.40	42.88	8.03	3.25
2004	4762.20	6.72	6.76	2.94
2005	5602.20	17.64	6.31	2.99
2006	5765.10	2.91	5.24	2.63
2007	6418.90	11.34	4.67	2.38
2008	7368.20	14.79	4.26	2.31
2009	10,641.50	44.42	4.74	3.05
2010	13,363.90	25.58	4.81	3.24
2011	13,934.20	4.27	4.47	2.85
2012	15,296.40	9.78	4.08	2.83

(continued)

Table 4.1 (continued)

Year	Completed investment/ 100 million yuan	Growth rate/%	Proportion of total social fixed asset investment/%	Proportion of GDP/%
2013	16,349.80	6.89	3.66	2.75
2014	16,245.00	−0.63	3.17	2.52
2015	16,204.40	−0.25	2.88	2.35
2016	17,460.00	7.75	2.88	2.35
2017	19,327.60	10.70	3.01	2.34
2018	20,123.20	4.12	3.12	2.24

Data Source China Urban Construction Statistical Yearbook (2018)

general practitioners per 10,000 people, and 6.41 specialized public health personnel per 10,000 people; per capita healthcare total expenditure was 4656.7 yuan, with healthcare expenses accounting for 6.6%[2] of the GDP.

Since the reform and opening up, China's social security system has gradually improved, transitioning from being a basic livelihood guarantee tool to a wealth distribution mechanism that ensures citizens' development and equitable sharing (Zheng, 2010). Social insurance fund expenditures grew from 87.71 billion yuan in 1995 to 6779.27 billion yuan in 2018. This substantial increase in social insurance fund expenditures has led to a continuous rise in the number of participants in pension, medical, work injury, unemployment, and maternity insurance. By the end of 2019, 434.82 million people participated in the basic pension insurance for urban employees, 532.66 million in the basic pension insurance for urban and rural residents, 1354.36 million in basic medical insurance, 205.43 million in unemployment insurance, 254.74 million in work injury insurance, and 214.32 million in maternity insurance (Ma, 2020). The increase in insured individuals has positively contributed to maintaining social stability, fairness, and justice.

4.2.2 Analysis of the Structure of Urban Public Goods Investment

During the industrialization stages of economic development, public sector investments represent a large share of total social investments, laying foundational conditions for economic growth through social infrastructure, social services, and human

[2] National Health Commission: *2019 Statistical Bulletin on the Development of Health Services in China*, June 2020.

Table 4.2 Levels of urban municipal public facilities

Year	Water supply coverage/%	Gas supply coverage/%	Per capita road area/m^2	Sewage treatment rate/%	Per capita park green space area/m^2
1981	53.70	11.60	1.80		1.50
1982	56.70	12.60	2.00		1.65
1983	52.50	12.30	1.90		1.71
1984	49.50	13.00	1.80		1.62
1985	45.10	13.00	1.70		1.57
1986	51.30	15.20	3.10		1.84
1987	50.40	16.70	3.10		1.90
1988	47.60	16.50	3.10		1.76
1989	47.40	17.80	3.20		1.69
1990	48.00	19.10	3.10		1.78
1991	54.80	23.70	3.40	14.86	2.07
1992	56.20	26.30	3.60	17.29	2.13
1993	55.20	27.90	3.70	20.02	2.16
1994	56.00	30.40	3.80	17.10	2.29
1995	58.70	34.30	4.40	19.69	2.49
1996	60.70	38.20	5.00	23.62	2.76
1997	61.20	40.00	5.20	25.84	2.93
1998	61.90	41.80	5.50	29.56	3.22
1999	63.50	43.80	5.90	31.93	3.51
2000	63.90	45.40	6.10	34.25	3.69
2001	72.26	60.42	6.98	36.43	4.56
2002	77.85	67.17	7.87	39.97	5.36
2003	86.15	76.74	9.34	42.39	6.49
2004	88.85	81.53	10.34	45.67	7.39
2005	91.09	82.08	10.92	51.95	7.89
2006	97.04	88.58	12.36	55.67	9.30
2007	93.83	87.40	11.43	62.87	8.98
2008	94.73	89.55	12.21	70.16	9.71
2009	96.12	91.41	12.79	75.25	10.66
2010	96.68	92.04	13.21	82.31	11.18
2011	97.04	92.41	13.75	83.63	11.80
2012	97.16	93.15	14.39	87.30	12.26
2013	97.56	94.25	14.87	89.34	12.64
2014	97.64	94.57	15.34	90.18	13.08
2015	98.07	95.30	15.60	91.90	13.35

(continued)

Table 4.2 (continued)

Year	Water supply coverage/%	Gas supply coverage/%	Per capita road area/m^2	Sewage treatment rate/%	Per capita park green space area/m^2
2016	98.42	95.75	15.80	93.44	13.70
2017	98.30	96.26	16.05	94.54	14.01
2018	98.36	96.70	16.70	95.49	14.11

Data Source China Urban Construction Statistical Yearbook (2018)
Notes (1) Since 2006, per capita indicators and prevalence rate indicators have been calculated with the total population of urban areas and temporarily residing populations in urban areas as the denominator, based on household registration statistics and temporary population statistics from public security authorities
(2) The "per capita park green space" indicator was referred to as "per capita public green space" before 2005

Table 4.3 National education, health, and social insurance fund expenditures

Year	Total education expenditure	Total health expenditure	Social insurance fund expenditure
1992	867.05	1096.86	
1995	1877.95	2155.13	877.10
2000	3849.08	4586.63	2385.60
2001	4637.66	5025.93	2748.00
2002	5480.03	5790.03	3471.50
2003	6208.27	6584.10	4016.40
2004	7242.60	7590.29	4627.40
2005	8418.84	8659.91	5400.80
2006	9815.31	9843.34	6477.40
2007	12,148.07	11,573.97	7887.80
2008	14,500.74	14,535.40	9925.10
2009	16,502.71	17,541.92	12,302.60
2010	19,561.85	19,980.39	15,018.90
2011	23,869.29	24,345.91	18,652.90
2012	28,655.31	28,119.00	23,331.30
2013	30,364.72	31,668.95	27,916.30
2014	32,806.46	35,312.40	33,002.70
2015	36,129.19	40,974.64	38,988.10
2016	38,888.39	46,344.88	46,888.40
2017	42,562.01	52,598.28	57,145.60
2018	46,135.00	59,121.90	67,792.70

Data Source China Statistical Yearbook (2019)
Unit: 100 million yuan

capital. As economic development enters the post-industrialization stage and urbanization rises, there will be adjustments in public sector investments and expenditures, with a gradual decrease in public infrastructure investments and a progressive increase in expenditures on education, health, medical care, and social welfare. Table 4.4 shows the structure of urban public goods investment in China from 2007 to 2018.

It is shown from the investment structure of urban public goods from 2007 to 2018 that, except for the period after the 2008 global financial crisis when a robust fiscal stimulus plan led to an increase in the proportion of economic public goods supply, this trend slowed down since 2010, whereas the proportion of non-economic public goods supply has been rising (as seen in Fig. 4.1).

The structure of educational expenditure has also changed, as shown in Table 4.5, which includes total education expenditure, national fiscal education expenditure, private school education expenditure, social donations, and institutional income. The proportion of national fiscal education expenditure in total education expenditure decreased from 2000 to 2005 but has been increasing annually since 2006, reaching over 80% by 2017 (as seen in Fig. 4.2). However, the proportion of private education expenditure and social donations in total education expenditure remains low, not exceeding 1% by 2017.

Healthcare expenses in China are primarily borne by individuals and society. As shown in Table 4.6, before 2006, especially from 1995 to 2005, personal healthcare expenditures accounted for more than half of total healthcare expenses. Over the past decade, the proportion of government healthcare expenditure has increased, with

Table 4.4 Structure of urban public goods investment in China (2004–2018)

Year	Fiscal expenditure/ 100 million yuan	Non-economic public goods investment/100 million yuan	Economic public goods investment/ 100 million yuan	Non-economic public goods supply proportion/%	Economic public goods supply proportion/%
2007	49,781.35	27,217.01	22,564.34	54.67	45.33
2008	62,592.66	33,669.34	28,923.32	53.79	46.21
2009	76,299.93	37,703.35	38,596.58	49.41	50.59
2010	89,874.16	43,352.06	46,522.10	48.24	51.76
2011	109,247.79	54,537.93	54,709.86	49.92	50.08
2012	125,952.97	65,120.66	60,832.31	51.70	48.30
2013	139,744.26	72,237.29	67,506.97	51.69	48.31
2014	151,785.56	78,105.84	73,679.72	51.46	48.54
2015	175,877.77	89,754.54	86,123.23	51.03	48.97
2016	187,755.21	99,171.22	88,583.99	52.82	47.18
2017	203,085.49	109,702.78	93,382.71	54.02	45.98
2018	220,904.13	148,842.39	72,061.74	67.38	32.62

Data Source China Statistical Yearbook (2004–2018)

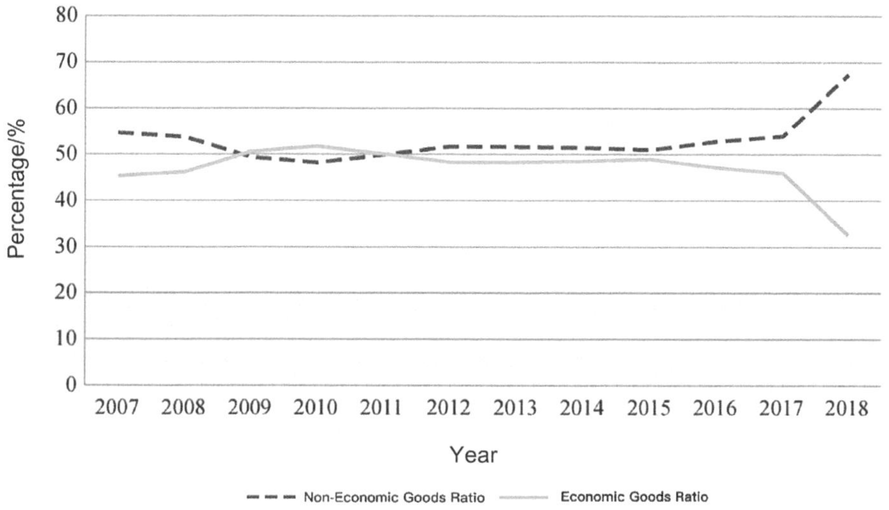

Fig. 4.1 Proportion of economic and non-economic public goods supply

social healthcare expenditure accounting for 43.66% of total healthcare expenses in 2018, followed by government (27.74%) and personal (28.61%) spending. However, compared to developed nations, the proportion of government expenditure on healthcare in China is relatively small. Thus, there is a need to boost fiscal investment in the health and medical sectors, especially to improve healthcare services in rural areas and the medical insurance system for rural residents.

Enterprises and individuals shoulder various social insurance funds, with government subsidies accounting for around 20%. According to data on national social insurance fund revenues, including contributions and fiscal subsidies for employee basic pension insurance, urban and rural residents' basic pension insurance, and basic medical insurance funds from 2013 to 2019, the proportions of fiscal subsidy revenues are as shown in Tables 4.7, 4.8, 4.9, and 4.10.

Tables 4.7, 4.8, 4.9, and 4.10 indicate that the proportion of fiscal subsidy revenues in total social insurance fund revenues has been rising, from 21.90% in 2013 to 24.00% in 2019. The fiscal subsidy proportion in employee basic pension insurance revenues remained above 14% and around 70% in urban and rural residents' basic pension insurance revenues. The absolute values of fiscal subsidies in these areas have been increasing rapidly, with compound annual growth rates of 16% and 13%, respectively. Although the proportion of fiscal subsidy revenues in total basic medical insurance fund revenues has shown a declining trend, its absolute value has risen rapidly from 301.2 billion yuan in 2013 to 579.624 billion yuan in 2019, with a compound annual growth rate of 14%. The rigid increase in fiscal subsidy proportions is due to the aging population trend and the declining social insurance contribution rates. This analysis indicates that the operation of pension insurance and medical

Table 4.5 Education expenditure

Year	Total education expenditure	National fiscal education expenditure	Private school education expenditure	Social donation expenditure	Operating income	Other education expenditure
1992	8,670,491	7,287,506		696,285		
1995	18,779,501	14,115,233	203,672	1,628,414		
2000	38,490,806	25,626,056	858,537	1,139,557	9,382,717	1,483,939
2001	46,376,626	30,570,100	1,280,895	1,128,852	11,575,137	1,821,643
2002	54,800,278	34,914,048	1,725,549	1,272,791	14,609,169	2,278,722
2003	62,082,653	38,506,237	2,590,148	1,045,927	17,218,399	2,721,943
2004	72,425,989	44,658,575	3,478,529	934,204	20,114,268	3,240,414
2005	84,188,391	51,610,759	4,522,185	931,613	23,399,991	3,723,842
2006	98,153,087	63,483,648	5,490,583	899,078	24,073,042	4,206,736
2007	121,480,663	82,802,142	809,337	930,584	31,772,357	5,166,242
2008	145,007,374	104,496,296	698,479	1,026,663	33,670,711	5,115,225
2009	165,027,065	122,310,935	749,829	1,254,991	35,275,939	5,435,371
2010	195,618,471	146,700,670	1,054,254	1,078,839	41,060,664	5,724,045
2011	238,692,936	185,867,009	1,119,320	1,118,675	44,246,927	6,341,005
2012	286,553,052	231,475,698	1,281,753	956,919	46,198,404	6,640,278
2013	303,647,182	244,882,177	1,474,089	855,445	49,262,087	7,173,384
2014	328,064,609	264,205,820	1,313,476	796,700	54,271,581	7,477,031
2015	361,291,927	292,214,511	1,876,620	869,960	58,097,239	8,233,597
2016	388,883,850	313,962,519	2,032,733	810,447	62,768,292	9,309,860
2017	425,620,069	342,077,546	2,250,061	849,974	69,575,734	10,866,754

Data Source China Statistical Yearbook (2018)
Unit: ten thousand yuan

insurance systems in China still heavily depends on fiscal subsidies, and the self-sustaining operation of social insurance funds is challenging.

Government subsidies exist in all insurance funds, such as pension, medical, work injury, and unemployment insurance funds, resulting in year-end surpluses that help balance fund revenues and expenditures (as seen in Table 4.11). As one of the fundamental institutional arrangements in countries worldwide, social security is transitioning from a tool for maintaining social stability and safeguarding livelihoods to a wealth distribution mechanism that ensures fairness, justice, and equitable sharing. Fiscal subsidies exceed contribution revenues in urban and rural residents' basic pension insurance and basic medical insurance, indicating that social security expenditures are primarily met through fiscal subsidies, thereby positively contributing to social stability.

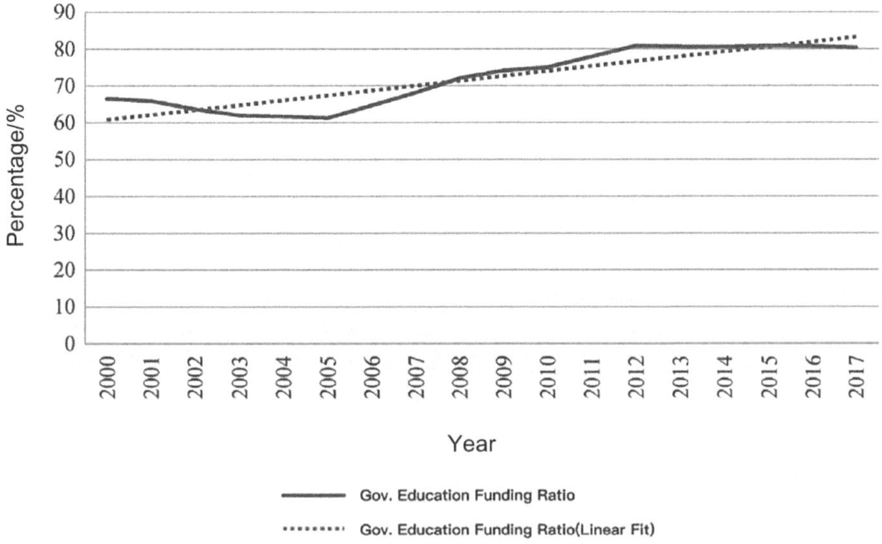

Fig. 4.2 Proportion of national fiscal education expenditure in total education expenditure

4.3 Government Fiscal Investment Mechanism for Public Goods

4.3.1 Government Fiscal Budget System Mechanism for Public Goods in China

4.3.1.1 Current Fiscal Budget Management System in China

Investment in public goods is directly related to the government's budgetary system. China's budget management system divides revenue and expenditure scopes and management authorities among local governments based on their responsibilities. In fiscal budget management, China implements a hierarchy of budgets—central budgets prepared by the State Council and local budgets prepared by local governments at their respective levels. These budgets are executed upon approval by the corresponding level of the People's Congress. Central and local budgets are referred to as central fiscal revenue and expenditure, and local fiscal revenue and expenditure, respectively.

The current budget system in China includes the general public budget, government fund budget, state-owned capital operation budget, and social security fund budget. The revised *Budget Law* in 2018 stipulates that all government revenues and expenditures must be included in the annual budget. The general public budget mainly covers fiscal revenues from taxes, arranged to ensure and improve people's livelihood, promote economic and social development, maintain national security,

Table 4.6 Health expenditure

Year	Total health expenditure/ 100 million yuan	Government health expenditure		Social health expenditure		Individual health expenditure	
		Absolute amount/ 100 million yuan	Proportion of total health expenditure/ %	Absolute amount/ 100 million yuan	Proportion of total health expenditure/ %	Absolute amount/ 100 million yuan	Proportion of total health expenditure/ %
1978	110.21	35.44	32.16	52.25	47.41	22.52	20.43
1979	126.19	40.64	32.21	59.88	47.45	25.67	20.34
1980	143.23	51.91	36.24	60.97	42.57	30.35	21.19
1981	160.12	59.67	37.27	62.43	38.99	38.02	23.74
1982	177.53	68.99	38.86	70.11	39.49	38.43	21.65
1983	207.42	77.63	37.43	64.55	31.12	65.24	31.45
1984	242.07	89.46	36.96	73.61	30.41	79.00	32.64
1985	279.00	107.65	38.58	91.96	32.96	79.39	28.46
1986	315.90	122.23	38.69	110.35	34.93	83.32	26.38
1987	379.58	127.28	33.53	137.25	36.16	115.05	30.31
1988	488.04	145.39	29.79	189.99	38.93	152.66	31.28
1989	615.50	167.83	27.27	237.84	38.64	209.83	34.09
1990	747.39	187.28	25.06	293.10	39.22	267.01	35.73
1991	893.49	204.05	22.84	354.41	39.67	335.03	37.50
1992	1096.86	228.61	20.84	431.55	39.34	436.70	39.81
1993	1377.78	272.06	19.75	524.75	38.09	580.97	42.17
1994	1761.24	342.28	19.43	644.91	36.62	774.05	43.95
1995	2155.13	387.34	17.97	767.81	35.63	999.98	46.40
1996	2709.42	461.61	17.04	875.66	32.32	1372.15	50.64
1997	3196.71	523.56	16.38	984.06	30.78	1689.09	52.84
1998	3678.72	590.06	16.04	1071.03	29.11	2017.63	54.85
1999	4047.50	640.96	15.84	1145.99	28.31	2260.55	55.85
2000	4586.63	709.52	15.47	1171.94	25.55	2705.17	58.98
2001	5025.93	800.61	15.93	1211.43	24.10	3013.88	59.97
2002	5790.03	908.51	15.69	1539.38	26.59	3342.14	57.72
2003	6584.10	1116.94	16.96	1788.50	27.16	3678.67	55.87
2004	7590.29	1293.58	17.04	2225.35	29.32	4071.35	53.64
2005	8659.91	1552.53	17.93	2586.40	29.87	4520.98	52.21
2006	9843.34	1778.86	18.07	3210.92	32.62	4853.56	49.31

Data Source China Statistical Yearbook (2019)

Table 4.7 Sources of national social insurance fund income (2013–2019)

Year	National insurance fund			
	Total income/ 100 million yuan	Social insurance fee income/100 million yuan	Fiscal subsidy income/100 million yuan	Fiscal subsidy income as a proportion of total income/ %
2013	32,829.00	24,664.00	7180.00	21.90
2014	37,667.00	28,088.00	8212.00	21.80
2015	44,660.34	32,518.48	10,198.15	22.80
2016	50,112.00	36,479.00	11,089.00	22.10
2017	58,437.57	42,417.66	12,351.76	21.10
2018	72,649.22	52,543.20	16,776.83	23.10
2019	80,844.09	57,849.05	19,392.61	24.00

Data Source 2013 and 2014 data from reports on the national social insurance fund budget by the Ministry of Finance; 2015, 2016, and 2017 data from explanations on the national social insurance fund final accounts by the Ministry of Finance; 2018 and 2019 data from the *China Fiscal Yearbook* (2019–2020)

Table 4.8 Sources of enterprise employee basic pension insurance income

Year	Enterprise employee basic pension insurance			
	Total income/ 100 million yuan	Insurance fee income/100 million yuan	Fiscal subsidy income/100 million yuan	Fiscal subsidy income as a proportion of total income/%
2013	18,791.00	15,501.00	2669.00	14.20
2014	21,489.00	17,554.00	3038.00	14.10
2015	26,554.00	21,096.00	3893.00	14.70
2016	28,519.00	22,407.00	4291.00	15.00
2017	33,542.04	26,228.39	4955.13	14.80
2018	37,520.97	29,507.15	5355.43	14.30
2019	38,174.79	30,008.75	5587.76	14.60

Data Source Data for 2013 and 2014 are cited from the *2013 National Social Insurance Fund Budget* and the *2014 National Social Insurance Fund Budget* published by the Ministry of Finance; data for 2015, 2016, and 2017 are cited from the *Explanations on the 2015 National Social Insurance Fund Final Accounts*, *Explanations on the 2016 National Social Insurance Fund Final Accounts*, and *Explanations on the 2017 National Social Insurance Fund Final Accounts* published by the Ministry of Finance; data for 2018 and 2019 are cited from the *China Fiscal Yearbook* (2019–2020)

and support the regular operation of state institutions. Due to differences in economic development levels and financial capacities among regions, the central general public budget includes tax refunds and transfer payments to lower-level local governments. The government fund budget deals with funds collected from specific objects over a stipulated period, dedicated to specific public projects. These revenues primarily

Table 4.9 Sources of urban and rural residents' basic pension insurance income (2013–2019)

Year	Urban and rural residents' basic pension insurance			
	Total income/ 100 million yuan	Insurance fee income/100 million yuan	Fiscal subsidy income/100 million yuan	Fiscal subsidy income as a proportion of total income/%
2013	2098.00	617.00	1414.00	67.40
2014	2296.00	648.00	1569.00	68.00
2015	2879.00	708.00	2044.00	71.00
2016	2956.00	737.00	2092.00	70.80
2017	3339.30	829.62	2319.19	69.50
2018	3870.12	881.10	2775.74	71.70
2019	4149.44	1000.17	2880.51	69.40

Data Source Data for 2013 and 2014 are cited from the *2013 National Social Insurance Fund Budget* and the *2014 National Social Insurance Fund Budget* published by the Ministry of Finance; data for 2015, 2016, and 2017 are cited from the *Explanations on the 2015 National Social Insurance Fund Final Accounts*, *Explanations on the 2016 National Social Insurance Fund Final Accounts*, and *Explanations on the 2017 National Social Insurance Fund Final Accounts* published by the Ministry of Finance; data for 2018 and 2019 are cited from the *China Fiscal Yearbook* (2019–2020).

Table 4.10 Sources of basic medical insurance fund income for residents (2013–2019)

Year	Basic medical insurance fund			
	Total income/ 100 million yuan	Insurance fee income/100 million yuan	Fiscal subsidy income/100 million yuan	Fiscal subsidy income as a proportion of total income/%
2013	3763.00	716.00	3012.00	80.00
2014	4399.00	816.00	3523.00	80.10
2015	5405.00	1114.00	4212.00	77.90
2016	6095.00	1406.00	4612.00	75.70
2017	6838.33	1812.72	4918.68	71.90
2018	7967.64	2487.07	5374.10	67.40
2019	8679.84	2773.31	5796.24	66.80

Data Source Data for 2013 and 2014 are cited from the *2013 National Social Insurance Fund Budget* and the *2014 National Social Insurance Fund Budget* published by the Ministry of Finance; data for 2015, 2016, and 2017 are cited from the *Explanations on the 2015 National Social Insurance Fund Final Accounts*, *Explanations on the 2016 National Social Insurance Fund Final Accounts*, and *Explanations on the 2017 National Social Insurance Fund Final Accounts* published by the Ministry of Finance; data for 2018 and 2019 are cited from the *China Fiscal Yearbook* (2019–2020).Data Source: Data for 2013 and 2014 are cited from the *2013 National Social Insurance Fund Budget* and the *2014 National Social Insurance Fund Budget* published by the Ministry of Finance; data for 2015, 2016, and 2017 are cited from the *Explanations on the 2015 National Social Insurance Fund Final Accounts*, *Explanations on the 2016 National Social Insurance Fund Final Accounts*, and *Explanations on the 2017 National Social Insurance Fund Final Accounts* published by the Ministry of Finance; data for 2018 and 2019 are cited from the *China Fiscal Yearbook* (2019–2020)

Table 4.11 Total social insurance fund revenue and expenditure in 2019

Item	Total	Enterprise employee basic pension insurance fund	Urban and rural residents' basic pension insurance fund	Employee basic medical insurance fund	Resident basic medical insurance fund	Work injury insurance fund	Unemployment insurance fund
1. Revenue	83,152.13	38,174.79	4149.44	15,638.36	8679.84	804.68	1248.77
1.1 Insurance fee income	59,991.47	30,008.75	1000.17	14,898.45	2773.31	744.73	1059.88
1.2 Fiscal subsidy income	19,103.12	5587.76	2880.51	92.88	5796.24	14.46	0.17
2. Expenditure	74,740.78	34,719.77	3148.31	12,489.78	8271.05	800.66	1284.32
social insurance benefit expenditure	72,914.48						
3. Current year surplus	8411.35	3455.02	1001.13	3148.58	408.79	4.02	−35.55
4. Year-end cumulative surplus	96,545.31	51,482.67	8283.60	22,315.66	5212.87	1774.58	4510.16

Data Source China Fiscal Yearbook (2020)
Unit: 100 million yuan

come from land sales, lottery issuance, etc., and are explicitly used for infrastructure construction and social development projects. The scope of the government fund budget is determined by funds revenue and actual expenditure needs, with a particular emphasis on the exclusive use of funds. The state-owned capital operation budget covers revenues from state-owned capital, with an increasing focus on allocating funds to the general public budget to expand revenue sources. The social insurance fund budget is designated for incomes from social security payments, general public budget arrangements, and other designated funds for social insurance expenditures. These budgets are compiled separately for different social insurance projects and aggregation levels to reflect each fund's income and expenditure.

4.3.1.2 Central and Local Government Financial Budget System Under the Mechanism of Division of Taxes

Since January 1, 1994, China has implemented a tax-sharing fiscal management system, which determines budgetary revenues based on the division of responsibilities among government levels, dividing various income categories, including taxes. While the specifics of the tax-sharing system and income distribution ratios have evolved over the years, its core principles have remained consistent. The key components of the tax-sharing system include the central-local division of fiscal revenue and expenditure and the central government's transfer payment system to local governments. These components directly determine the supply responsibilities and structures for public goods between central and local governments.

The central government is primarily responsible for nationwide expenditures on general public services, foreign affairs, public security, national defense, centrally managed agricultural and environmental protection expenses, and social development expenditures such as education, science, culture, health, sports, social security, and employment expenditures. Additionally, the central government supports macroeconomic regulation, economic structural adjustments, balanced regional development, and centrally managed social development expenditures. Local governments primarily bear regional expenditures on general public services and economic and social development needs.

The revenue division follows financial authority with responsibilities. Taxes significantly influence national interests and the macroeconomic structure, which fall under the central government, such as consumption tax, customs duties, headquarters business taxes of banks and insurance companies, and resource taxes. Taxes closely related to local economies and suitable for local administration fall under local governments, such as business taxes, local enterprise income taxes, personal income taxes, property taxes, land value-added taxes, deed taxes, etc. Some taxes directly related to economic development, such as value-added tax, enterprise income tax, and personal income tax, are shared between central and local governments.

Despite the clear division of powers and responsibilities between central and local governments under the tax-sharing system, differences in economic development levels have led to substantial disparities in financial capacities among local governments. To balance basic financial capacity across regions, China implements a fiscal transfer system from the central to local governments and from higher-level local governments to lower-level ones. Transfer payments cover general budget transfers and special transfers for urgent needs, major projects, etc. Data from the National Bureau of Statistics show that the total amount and proportion of general transfer payments in central fiscal expenditure have increased annually over the past five years (refer to Table 4.12).

4.3.1.3 Soft Budget Constraints and Fiscal Budget Management System Reform

Generally, the execution of government fiscal budgets is compulsory. However, under the decentralized tax system, the alignment of central and local government's responsibilities and financial powers with actual demands often falls short. This mismatch leaves local governments unable to guarantee basic public and construction expenditures based on budgetary revenues alone, making the constitutional prohibition of budget deficits challenging to enforce. Consequently, soft budget constraints have become the norm. In the current system, government fiscal operations lack effective democratic oversight, preventing taxpayers from controlling the flow and usage of fiscal resources, and soft budget constraints are increasingly prevalent at the local level (Fang & Zhang, 2009; Zhao & Yang, 2012). Additionally, research by Ping and Bai (2006) reveals that some local governments face "soft constraints within the budget" and "unconstraint outside the budget", causing irrational excessive borrowing behaviors and severely affecting local economic security and sustainable development (Chen et al., 2002; Fu et al., 2008).

Several factors contribute to the soft budget constraints (Fromaget, 2008; Wildasin, 2004), primarily including (a) Inadequate fiscal decentralization: Under the tax-sharing system, asymmetries between the responsibilities and financial powers of central and local governments mean some local governments lack the financial capacity to support public affairs and construction projects, forcing them to seek alternative financing sources (Cao et al., 2020); (b) Growing responsibilities: As economic and social development progresses, governments undertake more public affairs and social services, while fiscal decentralization lacks transparency and legal norms, leading to contention over financial powers and evasion of responsibilities between central and local governments, causing imbalances and excessive local fiscal pressure (Yao & Yang, 2003); (c) Excessive resource exploitation: Some local governments, long focused on economic development, have over-exploited resources, resulting in severe financial shortages. The lack of constraints in securing and allocating resources, including exploiting land and mineral resources and establishing financial platforms, further breaches fiscal budget constraints.

To address these issues, the central government has continually reformed the budget management system, enacting various laws, regulations, and policies aimed at integrating all government revenues and expenditures into the budget, establishing

Table 4.12 Status of central transfers to local governments

Year	National fiscal expenditure/100 million yuan	Total transfer expenditure		General transfer payments		Specific transfer payments		Tax rebates	
		Amount/100 million yuan	Percentage/%	Amount/100 million yuan	Percentage/%	Amount/100 million yuan	Percentage/%	Amount/100 million yuan	Percentage/%
2015	175,878	55,098	31	28,455	16	21,624	12	5019	3
2016	187,755	59,401	32	31,865	17	20,709	11	6827	4
2017	203,085	65,052	32	35,146	17	21,883	11	8023	4
2018	220,904	69,681	32	38,722	18	22,927	10	8032	4
2019	238,858	74,360	31	66,798	28	7562	3	–	–
2020	245,588	83,218	34	69,460	28	13,758	6		

Source China Statistical Yearbook (2015–2020)

Notes (1) The total transfer expenditure excludes the previous year's carryover

(2) Tax rebates were not published after 2018

(3) After 2018, part of the specific transfer payments was reclassified as shared responsibilities under general transfer payments, resulting in a sharp decline in specific transfer payments

(4) In 2020, a third category of special transfer payments amounting to 599.2 billion yuan was established, included in the specific transfer payments

a "complete, standardized, and transparent" modern budget management system, and controlling the scale of local government projects and debt. To control budget deficits strictly and prevent inter-annual debt transfers, China has established an inter-year budget balance mechanism and improved debt management and risk warning systems for central and local governments. Additionally, the central government allows local governments to issue bonds to finance investments under certain conditions (Hua & Wang, 2016; Wang et al., 2016). To address funding shortages in local public infrastructure development, the Ministry of Finance issued the *Interim Measures for Local Government Special Bond Issuance* in 2015, integrating special bonds into fiscal budget management to alleviate pressure on local government fiscal deficits and enhance transparency (Diao & Wang, 2017).

4.3.2 Investment Levels in Public Goods by Central and Local Governments

Based on the investment level of government expenditures on public goods and the ratio of central to local government expenditures, the level of investment can be assessed through fiscal expenditure statistics and land revenue and government funds, particularly focusing on public infrastructure investment levels.

Data on national, central, and local government expenditures, including the proportion of local fiscal expenditures and incomes, are presented in Table 4.13.

After the 1994 tax-sharing reform, the central government gained financial power, leaving significant expenditure responsibilities to local governments and creating fiscal difficulties for them (Xie, 2009; Yang & Yin, 2015). Table 4.13 shows that the proportion of local fiscal expenditures increased, fluctuating around 70% from 1994 to 2004, then rising from 74.14% in 2005 to 85.19% in 2018. Meanwhile, the proportion of local fiscal revenues has consistently stayed at 45–55%, highlighting the mismatch between local government financial powers and responsibilities. Despite raising resource allocation efficiency and stimulating productivity, fiscal expenditure decentralization has skewed fiscal expenditure structures towards economic projects, hindering the equalization of basic public services to some extent (Chen & Gao, 2012; Fu & Zhang, 2007; Zhang et al., 2007). Consequently, central fiscal transfer payments bear greater burdens for regional fiscal balance and non-economic social expenditures. State-specific infrastructure investment from central and local fiscal budgets will be discussed in Chapter Six. In practice, local government infrastructure and public service investments primarily rely on national fund revenues, with land revenues constituting a significant portion. Other income sources include urban infrastructure supporting fees, public welfare lottery funds, and vehicle tolls, among others.

To estimate the specific amount of government investment from land revenues, it is essential to measure land fiscal revenue first. The narrow scope of land fiscal income in recent years is shown in Table 4.14.

Table 4.13 Government investment expenditure on public products by national, central, and local governments

Year	National fiscal expenditure/100 million yuan	Central fiscal expenditure/100 million yuan	Local fiscal expenditure/100 million yuan	Local fiscal expenditure ratio/%	Local fiscal revenue ratio/%
1990	3083.59	1004.47	2079.12	67.43	66.21
1991	3386.62	1090.81	2295.81	67.79	70.21
1992	3742.20	1170.44	2571.76	68.72	71.88
1993	4642.30	1312.06	3330.24	71.74	77.98
1994	5792.62	1754.43	4038.19	69.71	44.30
1995	6823.72	1995.39	4828.33	70.76	47.83
1996	7937.55	2151.27	5786.28	72.90	50.58
1997	9233.56	2532.50	6701.06	72.57	51.14
1998	10,798.18	3125.60	7672.58	71.05	50.47
1999	13,187.67	4152.33	9035.34	68.51	48.89
2000	15,886.50	5519.85	10,366.65	65.25	47.82
2001	18,902.58	5768.02	13,134.56	69.49	47.62
2002	22,053.15	6771.70	15,281.45	69.29	45.04
2003	24,649.95	7420.10	17,229.85	69.90	45.36
2004	28,486.89	7894.08	20,592.81	72.29	45.06
2005	33,930.28	8775.97	25,154.31	74.14	47.71
2006	40,422.73	9991.40	30,431.33	75.28	47.22
2007	49,781.35	11,442.06	38,339.29	77.02	45.93
2008	62,592.66	13,344.17	49,248.49	78.68	46.71
2009	76,299.93	15,255.79	61,044.14	80.01	47.58
2010	89,874.16	15,989.73	73,884.43	82.21	48.87
2011	109,247.79	16,514.11	92,733.68	84.88	50.59
2012	125,952.97	18,764.63	107,188.34	85.10	52.09
2013	139,744.26	20,471.75	119,272.51	85.35	53.41
2014	151,785.56	22,570.07	129,215.49	85.13	54.05
2015	175,877.77	25,542.15	150,335.62	85.48	54.51
2016	187,755.21	27,403.85	160,351.36	85.40	54.66
2017	203,085.49	29,857.15	173,228.34	85.30	53.00
2018	220,904.13	32,707.81	188,196.31	85.19	53.39

Source China Fiscal Yearbook (2019)

Table 4.14 Revenue from state-owned land use rights transfer in China

Year	2013	2014	2015	2016	2017	2018	2019	2020
Revenue from state-owned land use rights transfer/trillion yuan	3.9	4.0	3.1	3.6	5.0	6.5	7.1	8.4
The proportion of land transfer revenue to local government fiscal revenue/%	57.0	53.0	37.0	41	55.0	66.0	72.0	84.0

Source Calculated based on data from the China Land Resources Statistical Yearbook (2014–2021) and the China Fiscal Yearbook (2014–2021)

Table 4.14 indicates that the proportion of national land use rights sales revenue relative to local government fiscal income increased dramatically after a slight drop in 2013–2015, reaching 84.0% in 2020, with national local government fiscal income at 10 trillion yuan and land use rights sales revenue at 8.4 trillion yuan. Analysis by Yang Liangsong et al. shows a high general dependence on land sales revenue across eastern, central, and western China. In 2019, land sales revenue accounted for 38.0% of general public budget revenue nationwide, 0.1% for the central government, and 72.0% for local governments; for the four major municipalities, municipal-level 32.0% and other non-municipal provincial levels, only 2.4%; municipal districts 56.0%, and other provincial cities 91.0%. According to the *Notice on Regulating the Management of State-owned Land Use Rights Sales Revenue and Expenditure* and other documents, the revenue and expenditure from land sales are included in the local government fund budget and subjected to strict usage restrictions. After deducting costs such as land acquisition and demolition compensation, net revenue from land sales is roughly 20% of total land sales revenue.

In terms of sources of investment in public infrastructure, besides government budget allocations, local governments also obtain funds through financing platforms. Financing platforms are wholly state-owned economic entities established by local governments with registered capital, including fiscal allocations, infrastructure operating rights, land, equity, fees, national bonds, and other state-owned assets or property rights. Their primary function is to serve as financing entities providing funding for local government investment projects. Before the implementation of the revised *Budget Law* in 2014, local governments did not have the right to issue government bonds, making borrowing through financing platforms the most critical financing method for local governments (Mao & Xu, 2021). Local governments use three main financing methods through these platforms: bank loans, issuance of municipal bonds, and project equity financing (He & Man, 2012; Zhang et al., 2019). Among these, bank loans account for the highest proportion due to the quality of land resources as collateral and the influence of local government officials on bank lending decisions (He et al., 2008; Lu & Yao, 2004; Sun et al., 2005). This lenient lending policy has led to the rapid accumulation of debt for local government financing platforms and a corresponding increase in the total amount and area of land mortgages.

Until June 30, 2018, there were 11,736 local government financing platforms, with 2629 of them stopping, leaving 9107 in operation. Data by Liu and Chen (2020) and Cao et al. (2019) at the prefecture-level show that since 2008, due to the economic stimulus plan, urban financing platforms and the total issuance of municipal bonds have increased rapidly, reaching nearly 3 trillion yuan and 3500 bonds in 2016, respectively. The scale of local government financing is shown in Table 4.15.

The income for local government financing platforms largely comes from land mortgage revenue and municipal bond income. According to Wind Information's statistics on 7936 local government financing platforms in 2014, 70% were construction financing platforms, with 15.4% explicitly for urban construction. The main financing methods for these platforms are bank loans and the issuance of municipal bonds. Therefore, land finance, local government debt, and urban infrastructure investment and financing are logically consistent. Especially after 2008, the central government's fiscal stimulus policy strengthened the dominant role of land financing in the economy, making land-based financing a primary means of urban construction and infrastructure financing as land transfer costs increased (Liu et al., 2017).

To limit the scale of local government financing, the central government required banks in 2009 to strictly control the credit scale of local financing platforms, prohibiting loans to platforms without operating income. Correspondingly, the policy relaxed local governments' issuance of municipal bonds (Qi & Xu, 2017). Overall, since 2008, local governments have mainly formed a financing model centered on "land + local financing platforms". Although this model has played an essential role in urban public infrastructure construction, it has also distorted local government economic behavior to some extent and triggered government debt risks. Consequently, the central government has repeatedly issued documents to regulate local

Table 4.15 Scale of local government financing

Year	Total land mortgage loans/ 100 million yuan	Land mortgage area/thousand hectares	Municipal bonds/100 million yuan	Interest rate/%	Financing platform debt/ 100 million yuan
2007	25,100.00	50.31	235.80	5.27	40,917.00
2008	19,000.00	54.48	495.00	6.04	57,925.00
2009	25,900.00	21.7	2602.38	6.00	92,714.00
2010	35,300.00	25.82	2725.00	5.94	119,394.00
2011	48,000.00	30.08	4394.00	6.51	143,643.00
2012	59,500.00	34.87	11,443.38	6.87	167,762.00
2013	77,600.00	40.39	13,603.48	6.47	200,904.00
2014	95,100.00	45.10	19,215.91	7.04	236,515.00
2015	113,300.00	49.08	18,315.36	5.60	259,667.00

Source The data on total land mortgage loans and land mortgage area are from the *China Land and Resources Statistical Bulletin* and *China Land and Resources Yearbook* (2004–2015); the data on municipal bonds, interest rates, and financing platform debt are from *Land-Based Finance, Infrastructure Construction, and Regional Economic Growth* (Ren et al., *Shanghai Economy*, 2019, Issue 6)

government financing platforms and control the scale of local government financing, gradually curbing local governments' land-based financing behavior.

4.3.3 *Public Goods Investment Structure by Central and Local Governments*

After the analysis of investment levels, it is necessary to examine the investment structure of central and local governments in public goods, including general public services, education, social security and employment, healthcare and family planning, transportation, and environmental protection. Tables 4.16, 4.17, and 4.18 provide comprehensive statistical data on expenditures in these areas at national, central, and local levels.

Tables 4.16, 4.17, and 4.18 reveal that in 2007, the central government's general public service expenditure accounted for about 25% of the national total, while local governments accounted for roughly 75%, increasing to nearly 90% by 2019. In 2019, education spending comprised about 15% of the national general public budget, with the central government contributing 5% and local governments 95%. Social security and employment expenditure comprised about 12%, with the central government bearing 4% and local governments 96%. Healthcare and family planning accounted for 7% of the national total, with the central government contributing 1% and local governments 99%. Transportation expenditure comprised 5%, with the

Table 4.16 Expenditure on general public services and education

Year	General public services expenditure			Education expenditure		
	National	Central	Local	National	Central	Local
2007	8514.24	2160.17	6354.07	7122.32	395.26	6727.06
2008	9795.92	2344.55	7451.37	9010.21	491.63	8518.58
2009	9164.21	1084.21	8080.00	10,437.54	567.62	9869.92
2010	9337.16	837.42	8499.74	12,550.02	720.96	11,829.06
2011	10,987.78	903.01	10,084.77	16,497.33	999.05	15,498.28
2012	12,700.46	998.32	11,702.14	21,242.10	1101.46	20,140.64
2013	13,755.13	1001.46	12,753.67	22,001.76	1106.65	20,895.11
2014	13,267.50	1050.43	12,217.07	23,041.71	1253.62	21,788.09
2015	13,547.79	1055.30	12,492.49	26,271.88	1358.17	24,913.71
2016	14,790.52	1209.15	13,581.37	28,072.78	1447.72	26,625.06
2017	16,510.36	1271.46	15,238.90	30,153.18	1548.39	28,604.79
2018	18,374.69	1503.68	16,871.01	32,169.47	1731.23	30,438.24
2019	20,344.66	1985.16	18,359.50	34,796.94	1835.88	32,961.06

Source China Fiscal Yearbook (2008–2020)
Unit: 100 million yuan

Table 4.17 Social security, employment expenditure, and medical, health, and family planning expenditure

Year	Social security and employment expenditure			Medical, health, and family planning expenditure		
	National	Central	Local	National	Central	Local
2007	5447.16	342.63	5104.53	1989.96	34.21	1955.75
2008	6804.29	344.28	6460.01	2757.04	46.78	2710.26
2009	7606.68	454.37	7152.31	3994.19	63.50	3930.69
2010	9130.62	450.30	8680.32	4804.18	73.56	4730.62
2011	11,109.40	502.48	10,606.92	6429.51	71.32	6358.19
2012	12,585.52	585.67	11,999.85	7245.11	74.29	7170.82
2013	14,490.54	640.82	13,849.72	8279.90	76.70	8203.20
2014	15,968.85	699.91	15,268.94	10,176.81	90.25	10,086.56
2015	19,018.69	723.07	18,295.62	11,953.18	84.51	11,868.67
2016	21,591.45	890.58	20,700.87	13,158.77	91.16	13,067.61
2017	24,611.68	1001.11	23,610.57	14,450.63	107.60	14,343.03
2018	27,012.69	1184.55	25,827.54	15,623.55	210.65	15,412.90
2019	29,379.08	1231.53	28,147.55	16,665.34	247.72	16,417.62

Source China Fiscal Yearbook (2008–2020)
Unit: 100 million yuan

Table 4.18 Transportation and energy conservation, environmental protection expenditure

Year	Transportation expenditure			Energy conservation and environmental protection expenditure		
	National	Central	Local	National	Central	Local
2007	1915.38	782.25	1133.13	995.82	34.59	961.23
2008	2354.00	913.20	1440.80	1451.36	66.21	1385.15
2009	4647.59	1069.22	3578.37	1934.04	37.91	1896.13
2010	5488.47	1489.58	3998.89	2441.98	69.48	2372.50
2011	7497.80	331.11	7166.69	2640.98	74.19	2566.79
2012	8196.16	863.59	7332.57	2963.46	63.65	2899.81
2013	9348.82	722.99	8625.83	3435.15	100.26	3334.89
2014	10,400.42	731.16	9669.26	3815.64	344.74	3470.90
2015	12,356.27	853.00	11,503.27	4802.89	400.41	4402.48
2016	10,498.71	812.12	9686.59	4734.82	295.49	4439.33
2017	10,673.98	1156.42	9517.56	5617.33	350.56	5266.77
2018	11,282.76	1313.71	9969.05	6297.61	427.56	5870.05
2019	11,817.55	1422.32	10,395.23	7390.20	421.19	6969.01

Source China Fiscal Yearbook (2008–2020)
Unit: 100 million yuan

central government at 12% and local governments at 88%. Environmental protection accounted for 3%, with the central government at 6% and local governments at 94%.

4.3.4 Issues and Recommendations for Government Investment in Public Goods

After the implementation of the tax-sharing system, China's government fiscal system has been continuously adjusted according to the actual situation, and the government budget management system for public products has also been modified. However, there are still some problems in practice. The imbalance between administrative and financial powers, soft budget constraints, low transparency of fiscal information, and poor openness in the government budget decision-making process constrain the establishment of an effective public product supply mechanism.

4.3.4.1 Existing Problems

(1) Soft Budget Constraints in Government Fiscal Budgets

Under the centrally managed administrative system, the central government is responsible for balancing local governments' final fiscal revenue and expenditure. Even after the implementation of the tax-sharing system, where the administrative and financial powers of the central and local governments are clearly divided, local governments still have the responsibility to balance their fiscal budgets. However, some local governments' budgetary investments in infrastructure construction exceed their capabilities, leading to insufficient funds and budget imbalances in public product projects. Consequently, the central government has to "rescue" these situations through transfer payments. This has led some local governments to arrange economic construction projects that habitually exceed their financial capacity. In particular, for some large-scale infrastructure projects, when there is a budget shortfall, local governments are unable to sustain the projects and have to seek help from the central government. If the central government does not "bail out" these projects, the budget funds already invested in the early stages will be wasted. This behavior weakens the budget constraints on construction projects and the overall government budget. Additionally, the budget imbalances of some projects affect the arrangement and supply of other public product projects, especially delaying or reducing the supply of urgently needed social service projects for residents.

(2) Insufficient Scientific Justification in Government Fiscal Budget Decision-Making, Limited Transparency and Openness of Budget Information and Decision Processes

The effectiveness of urban public product supply depends on whether the public products meet social and the public's needs. Therefore, in the decision-making process of public product projects, decision-makers need a scientific and open mechanism to obtain public demand information, allowing the public to choose public product projects. On the other hand, public participation in the supply process of public products is necessary to ensure that they fully understand and grasp the detailed and reliable public financial information provided by the government and exercise their supervisory rights (Deng & Liu, 2019; Guo et al., 2016). Increasing fiscal information transparency can reduce the information asymmetry between local governments and residents, enabling residents to understand the actual costs of public products and the tax burden they bear. This can better reflect residents' preferences for public products, thereby improving the supply mechanism and efficiency (Chu & Zuo, 2019). However, in current practice in China, the scientificity and feasibility of the planning on which public product project decisions are based are weak. Government departments' administrative goals and subjective will play a major role, and public opinion solicitation often becomes a formality. Under the administrative system that is accountable to higher authorities, local government public product supply budgets are often influenced by the incentive mechanisms of higher-level governments and rarely by local residents. Additionally, under the current economic and fiscal systems, the planning and decision-making departments for public product projects are separate from the fiscal budget departments, which compile and execute budgets, resulting in non-transparent information. Local people's congresses lack practical budget review, approval, and supervisory functions, and audit departments lack mandatory punitive measures, leading to incomplete handling and rectification of issues found during audits. These reasons cause discrepancies between urban public product project decisions and actual needs, insufficient rationality in fiscal budgets, weak enforceability, and low completeness and transparency of public product project fiscal information, ultimately affecting the establishment of an effective public product supply mechanism.

(3) Incomplete Budget Supervision Mechanism for Public Product Supply

Although China has introduced a supervisory mechanism through the People's Congress in the construction and budget execution of public products projects, the People's Congress examines the overall annual construction funds or particularly significant construction projects. The submitted fiscal budget lacks detailed project information, making it difficult to evaluate effectively. Especially in specific public expenditure budget management, some local governments, in pursuit of swift administrative power operations, often achieve "centralized power" by simplifying administrative procedures, avoiding or excluding the supervision and constraints of the People's Congress on public budgets. Many scholars have found through surveys of provincial and municipal People's Congresses and their standing committees with local legislative power that, although the basic system for budget supervision by local People's Congresses has been established with relatively clear regulations, its actual operation is influenced by the degree of cooperation from the supervisees and other administrative forces. In some regions, public product supply budget adjustments do not even require prior approval from the standing committee of the People's

Congress (Lin & Ma, 2012). Over the past decade, the central government has established and strengthened the audit system, but the focus of audits has been on the compliance of project construction, making it difficult to evaluate the scientificity of project decisions, the rationality of project budgets, and the performance of projects. Moreover, audits are retrospective, making correcting already occurred investment issues hard. Most critically, China has not yet established a valid and effective feedback mechanism from the public on government public decision-making matters, which affects the effectiveness of investment and the rationality of budgets in public product supply.

(4) Inconsistent Standards in Budget Management for Public Product Supply

The standardization of government fiscal budget management is crucial for the effective use of fiscal funds and risk prevention. However, in China's current government fiscal fund management, only the transparency of general public fiscal budgets is relatively high, with budget content requiring review and approval by various levels of the People's Congress, and management is relatively strict. Government fund budgets, earmarked for specific purposes, are managed by the collecting departments without needing approval from the People's Congress, making daily supervision by government departments challenging. Only some state-owned enterprises are included in the budget management of state-owned capital operations budgets, making it difficult for government departments and the public to exercise supervision. For social insurance fund budgets, policies and regulations strictly define their income and expenditure content, standards, and scope, with earmarked funds for specific purposes, but supervision is exercised by various levels of the People's Congress and government departments through filing. Since the elimination of off-budget items, the normativity of all revenue and expenditure budgets of local governments has improved but still has significant room for enhancement.

4.3.4.2 Reform Recommendations

To address the fiscal budget issues in government public product investments, this book incorporates insights of scholars, suggesting deeper fiscal system and mechanism reforms, and the enhancement of fiscal budget management:

(1) Strengthening Fiscal Budget Management: The effectiveness of public budget execution depends on the clarity of its purpose. Therefore, the government needs to develop long-term investment plans for public infrastructure construction, integrating annual budgets with medium-term budgets to enhance the planning of fiscal budget purposes;
(2) Improving Budget Supervision Systems: It is necessary to fully leverage the review and supervision roles of the People's Congress and audit departments to enhance the timeliness and constraints of fiscal budget use while increasing the transparency of fiscal budgets and their execution at all levels of local governments (Liu & Shen, 2011; Zeng, 2019);

(3) Promoting Local Government Investment Systems: It is vital to gradually shift the fiscal model of local governments from being based on land finance and financing platforms to a diversified financing model based on the municipal bond market;
(4) Improving Socioeconomic Benefits of Budgets: It is necessary to implement comprehensive budget performance management, integrate fiscal budgets with performance management, and establish a practical budget performance management system (Wang et al., 2020);
(5) Enhancing Fiscal Management System Below the Provincial Level: To equalize basic public services, local governments should define fiscal reform goals clearly, ensuring responsibility for service equalization within their regions. The central government should track and promote best practices from local governments, correcting deviations to maintain national consistency in fiscal goals;
(6) Incorporating Social Forces in Budgeting: It is important to engage with public opinions on public product supply and establish mechanisms for public selection and supervision. When preparing public projects, the government should seek input from social institutions and the public for more scientific decision-making. Based on an open and transparent fiscal budget information disclosure system, implement participatory budgeting, allowing the public to participate in the decision-making process of budget projects. Implementing participatory budgeting can enable the public to express their preferences for public products fully, thereby establishing a mechanism for public choice of public products and also playing a role in public supervision, ultimately forming a modern public finance system and mechanism.

4.4 Investment and Financing Mechanisms for Public Product Markets

4.4.1 Development Trends in Investment and Financing of China's Public Goods Markets

Before the 1990s, urban public products in China were mainly funded by government fiscal resources. However, due to the increasing demand for public products, inefficiencies in the use of fiscal funds, and limited fiscal capacities, China began to explore market-based investment and financing mechanisms for public products. Following the 1994 implementation of the tax-sharing reform, local governments were granted a lot more authority to raise fiscal funds. Mechanisms such as land leasing, government bond issuance, and state-owned enterprise financing platforms provided multiple avenues for government financing and collaboration with social funds for public product construction. These mechanisms laid a foundation for integrating market financing strategies into public product provision.

The introduction of market-based financing mechanisms in public infrastructure projects began with the 1984 Shajiao Power Plant project, which utilized a franchise model to attract commercial capital. Over the past three decades, private and social capital have increasingly participated in urban municipal and other public infrastructure projects, establishing a series of regulatory frameworks for market operations. The franchise model has expanded investment channels, addressing past fiscal funding shortages and enhancing the efficiency and quality of public product provision (Xiao, 2016).

Since 2003, China's infrastructure market-oriented investment and financing have entered a deep reform stage, with various market-oriented investment and financing practices emerging across different regions and rapidly increasing the number of such projects. In 2004, the Ministry of Construction issued the *Administrative Measures for Concession of Municipal Public Utilities*, providing a legal basis for market-oriented investment and financing projects. The government adopted the concession approach to introduce social capital, accelerating the market-oriented operation of municipal infrastructure construction and public utilities. The concession system not only guaranteed investors' investment and returns but also constrained the government's contractual compliance and regulatory behaviors. If social investors fulfill their responsibilities according to the concession agreement and accept government supervision, reasonable returns and relatively low-risk levels can be expected. For non-purely public welfare infrastructure projects, the government can attract social capital by setting reasonable project conditions and appropriate risk allocation. In practice, considering the particularity and safety of infrastructure, the government often selects investors through market competition methods such as bidding and competitive negotiation. The operational modes of market-oriented investment and financing projects are diverse, including project financing, equity transfer, project mergers and acquisitions, transfer of operating rights, and financial leasing, all of which have been widely used.

In 2013, the Third Plenary Session of the 18th CPC Central Committee proposed that the market should play a decisive role in resource allocation, accelerating the pace of market-oriented reforms in the public product sector. The model of government-social capital cooperation in providing public products began to emerge, gradually forming a diversified investment and financing mechanism for public products in China. In September 2014, the *Guidelines by the State Council on Strengthening the Management of Local Government Debt* encouraged social capital to participate in the investment and operation of public infrastructure through PPP and other means. In November 2014, the *Guidelines by the State Council on Innovating Key Areas of Investment and Financing Mechanisms to Encourage Social Investment* further required the acceleration of market-oriented reforms in public infrastructure and critical construction areas, improving the investment mechanisms for government-social capital cooperation to enhance the adequate supply capacity of public products. Following the promulgation of these policies, due to some issues in the implementation of the PPP model, the central government issued a series of policy documents to regulate the cooperation between local governments and social capital and to control the approval and scale of PPP projects. However, to date, the PPP model remains an effective method for implementing market-oriented mechanisms in China's public product sector. To deepen market-oriented reforms in the public product sector and activate the market transaction of existing public infrastructure assets, in April 2020, the China Securities Regulatory Commission and the National Development and Reform Commission jointly issued the *Guidelines on Promoting the Pilot Work of Real Estate Investment Trusts (REITs) in the Infrastructure Field*, allowing the listing and trading of existing infrastructure assets as trusts. This provided financial market conditions for revitalizing fixed assets and promoting high-quality infrastructure development.

4.4.2 *Methods of Investment and Financing in Public Goods Markets*

Investment and financing approaches for public product supply include both indirect financing (such as bank loans) and direct financing (such as equity securitization). A comprehensive financial market system consisting of various tools like credit financing, equity financing, bonds, and insurance broadens the financing channels for urban infrastructure and public product projects. Establishing an effective market financing mechanism requires setting up government-guided, market-operated infrastructure and public service development funds, alongside attracting private and social capital participation. Additionally, enhancing the relevant legal and regulatory framework is necessary to standardize local government borrowing, financing, and cooperation with social capital.

The primary market-based investment and financing methods for public products in China include.

4.4.2.1 "Government Investment + Fund" Mechanism

Under the "Government Investment + Fund" mechanism, the government specifies a fiscal investment budget based on the nature and construction needs of public infrastructure projects. Funds, such as the Infrastructure Construction Fund, Public Service Development Fund, and Housing Security Fund, are established according to different project funding needs. Additionally, the government can create equity investment and venture capital funds for certain infrastructure projects, setting investment and return conditions to attract social capital. In this mechanism, both the government and social capital investors participate in project construction and operation according to their investment amounts or equity shares without imposing discriminatory conditions on social capital. The "Government Investment + Fund" mechanism ensures government guidance over public product project goals while fully leveraging social capital to expedite infrastructure development.

4.4.2.2 Bond Financing Mechanism

Bond financing is one of the funding methods for public products, characterized by low financing costs. After the revision and implementation of the *Budget Law*, bond financing for local government public infrastructure projects has gained legal guarantees, becoming the main financing channel for local governments. Currently, the scale of local government bonds has exceeded national bonds, with the bond structure shifting from predominantly general bonds to primarily special bonds (Yang et al., 2018).

However, the issuance quota of local government bonds remains insufficient for the construction needs of public product projects, and the pressure on local government construction funding has not been alleviated. Critically, the actual guarantee and debt repayment capacity of some local government bonds are relatively weak, posing significant repayment risks. Therefore, it is urgent to improve the management of local government bond issuance quotas, establish differentiated local government pricing mechanisms, and enhance the market-based pricing level of bonds. At the same time, the current fiscal and debt information disclosure mechanisms of local governments need improvement, credit ratings need to be more impartial and reasonable, and the legal regulations on local government bond management need to be refined to build stricter bond supervision and repayment guarantee mechanism, reduce bond default risks, enhance the market tradability of local government bonds, and increase their creditworthiness (Yang et al., 2018).

4.4.2.3 Trust Financing Mechanism

Urban public product trusts involve the entrustment of funds by trustees to trust companies, which then invest the trust funds in urban public product projects to generate returns for the trustees or achieve specific purposes. These trusts can be categorized into equity trusts, loan trusts, financing lease trusts, and real estate trusts based on their investment or rights realization methods. The funds from urban public product trusts are used to construct public utility projects, with the assets typically belonging to the government, giving these trust products certain particularities. The repayment guarantees for urban public product trusts include government fiscal funds and expected returns from public projects, making these trust products relatively secure (Wang, 2012).

To develop and regulate China's trust industry, the 21st meeting of the Standing Committee of the Ninth National People's Congress passed the T*rust Law of the People's Republic of China* (hereinafter referred to as the *Trust Law*), which regulates the establishment of trusts, trust products, and the relationships between trust parties.

The trust products in the urban public product sector mainly include loan trusts, equity investment trusts, property rights trusts, and industrial fund trusts.

(1) Loan Trust

It refers to trust companies absorbing funds through trusts and lending these funds to urban public product projects, recovering the principal and interest of trust loans upon maturity. Loan trust products have distinct characteristics, with relatively simple trust and loan processes and relatively specific product yields referencing bank interest rates. Generally, loan trust products have strong risk controllability, making them easily understood and accepted by the public.

(2) Equity Investment Trusts

It refers to trust companies absorbing funds through trusts and using these funds to acquire equity stakes in project companies jointly initiated by public product project sponsors or to increase capital and shares in already established project companies, thereby obtaining equity returns. Equity investment trust funds can increase the capital of project companies and their owners' equity, introducing social capital into government-sponsored public product projects and transforming the equity structure of project companies. Trust companies often appoint directors or shareholder representatives to participate in project company management, optimizing the governance structure of project companies.

(3) Property Rights Trusts

This involves government departments or public utility legal persons entrusting specific properties or property rights as trust properties to trust companies. Trust properties can include movable property trusts, real estate trusts, securities trusts, and other property rights trusts. The properties in urban public product property rights trusts mainly comprise operational and financializable infrastructure. Government departments or public utility legal persons gain trust benefits from establishing trusts, while trust companies, after being entrusted, transfer their held trust benefits to investors for financing. Investors who subscribe to trust products become trust beneficiaries.

(4) Industrial Fund Trusts

This involves trust companies absorbing trust funds through collective trust plans to establish industrial fund trusts. Urban public product industrial fund trusts primarily invest in urban public infrastructure projects through equity, debt, or rights investments. One of the characteristics of industrial fund trusts is that trust companies typically participate in the management of investment projects or entrust professional consultants to manage trust assets (Wang, 2012).

It should be noted that the *Trust Law* also makes detailed provisions for public welfare trusts, clarifying that trusts can be established for purposes such as poverty alleviation, disaster relief, assisting disabled persons, and promoting education, science, culture, art, sports, healthcare, environmental protection, and other social welfare causes, as well as maintaining the ecological environment. The law also stipulates the disposal of trust property and income for public welfare trusts.

4.4.2.4 Securitization of Infrastructure Assets

Asset securitization, known as asset-backed securities (ABS), is a financing method where tradable securities are issued based on a designated asset portfolio. This method typically relies on the future cash flows of these assets for repayment, bolstered by structural credit enhancements, to issue the securities. This approach serves to mobilize social funds for infrastructure development and operations, enhance asset liquidity, revitalize existing assets, and elevate capital efficiency (Wang, 2015). According to the *Guideline on the Negative List of Underlying Assets for Asset Securitization Business* formulated by the Asset Management Association, there are two primary methods for securitizing infrastructure assets: (a) securitizing the future revenue streams of completed infrastructure projects, and (b) securitizing the fiscal subsidies owed by debtors (such as local governments) in PPP projects. Currently, China's infrastructure-linked asset securitization offerings can be broadly grouped into energy, rail transit, and municipal development products.

Asset-backed notes (ABN) are another form of debt financing in asset securitization. These notes are supported by the future cash flows generated by specific assets, with a commitment to repay principal and interest within a specified period. Typically, enterprises and financial institutions sell cash-flow-generating assets to trustees, who then issue commercial papers backed by these assets to obtain the required funds from the market.

The securitization of infrastructure assets is significant for the development of the urban public product sector. It addresses the issue of poor liquidity in public infrastructure assets, allowing for financing at lower costs compared to bank loans or capital markets. Moreover, securitization helps reduce risk assets and improve the quality of public sector assets.

4.4.3 Empirical Analysis of Market Investment and Financing in China's Urban Public Goods

4.4.3.1 Local Bonds, Urban Investment Bonds, and Infrastructure Investment Benefits

To empirically analyze the impact of local bonds and urban investment bonds on the benefits of urban infrastructure investment, we collected and calculated the outstanding local debts from 30 provinces (autonomous regions and municipalities) from 2012 to 2017, and the outstanding urban investment bonds and infrastructure investment benefit data from 2010 to 2017.[3]

[3] Due to the difficulty of data collection, this analysis does not include the regions of Hong Kong, Macau, and Taiwan. Additionally, due to incomplete data, the Tibet Autonomous Region is also excluded from the research sample. The data on local debt balances for 2012 and 2013 are sourced from the debt audit results of the audit offices of each province (autonomous region and directly administered municipality). The data for local debt balances from 2015 to 2017 are sourced from

The measurement of infrastructure investment benefits in each province (autonomous region and municipality) uses the BCC (Banker Charnes Cooper) model in the DEA method based on input–output indicators. According to the indicators of the *China Statistical Yearbook*, input indicators include:

(1) Investment in the production and supply of water, electricity, coal, and gas;
(2) Investment in transportation, storage, and postal services;
(3) Investment in water conservancy, environment, and public facility management;
(4) Investment in information transmission, computer services, and software;
(5) Investment in health, culture, sports, and entertainment;
(6) Investment in education. For output indicators, this study selects each province's per capita GDP and urbanization rate (autonomous region and municipality).

Using a panel model with fixed individual and time effects, the empirical analysis of the impact of local bonds and urban investment bonds on infrastructure investment yields the results shown in Table 4.19.

Empirical results indicate that local bonds and urban investment bonds significantly negatively impact infrastructure investment. In fact, besides bridging the fiscal gap in local government public investments, local bonds can be an essential model for the intertemporal optimization of public investments. Government debt financing can promote the optimal allocation of production factors and improve

Table 4.19 Empirical results of local bonds, urban investment bonds, and infrastructure investment efficiency

Variable	Dependent variable: infrastructure investment efficiency	
	Model 1	Model 2
Local bonds	-0.0000479^{***} (0.000)	
Urban inv. bonds		-0.0000421^{***} (0.004)
Constant	0.735^{***} (0.000)	0.521^{***} (0.000)
Individual FE	Yes	Yes
Time PE	Yes	Yes
F-value	38.44	8.28
Sample Size	166	240

Note *** indicates significance at the 1% level; values in parentheses are the p-values of corresponding coefficients

the Ministry of Finance's publication on the local government debt balances for various regions nationwide. The 2014 local debt balance data are calculated based on the estimation method provided by Xiang Houjun and Wu Jiao (2017). The outstanding balance of urban investment bonds is obtained from the Wind database and is calculated based on the issuance and maturity dates of urban investment bonds in the Wind database. The balance for each year is computed using the bond issuance dates and maturity terms for each province (autonomous region and directly administered municipality).

investment benefits (World Bank, 2004; Yakita, 2008). However, this requires a standardized local debt management system and reasonable debt scale (Jia & Guo, 2011). Whether debt financing can promote the optimal allocation of production factors and enhance investment efficiency is closely related to the effectiveness of government debt management systems (Miao & Zhao, 2019). The empirical results reflect that increasing the scale of local bonds and urban investment bonds currently does not favor the improvement of infrastructure investment efficiency in China. This is partly related to the effectiveness of China's government debt management system and partly to excessive competition among local governments. Driven by the goal of maximizing short-term economic output, the scale of local bonds and urban investment bonds in various regions exceeds the optimal range that can improve factor allocation efficiency and investment efficiency. Further expansion of local bonds and urban investment bonds will negatively affect investment efficiency. Currently, China should reform and improve the local government debt management system further.

4.4.3.2 Market-Based Financing and Infrastructure Sector Output, Infrastructure Investment Efficiency

Our analysis indicates that local bonds and urban investment bond financing models hinder improvements in urban infrastructure investment efficiency. The next section examines the influence of market-based financing models on infrastructure output and investment efficiency, using data from 2007 to 2016 across the same 30 provinces. Due to limitations in data collection and measurement indicators, the infrastructure output is represented by the transportation sector's output value, drawn from the transportation, storage, and postal industry figures in the *China Statistical Yearbook*. The input–output indicators and measurement models for infrastructure investment efficiency are consistent with the abovementioned empirical analysis.

The macroeconomic environment, local government investment decisions, population growth, education, and health factors also affect infrastructure investment efficiency.

(1) Infrastructure investment, economic development levels, and urbanization rates influence each other, affecting investment scale and efficiency.
(2) Urban population size impacts infrastructure demand levels; larger populations generally require higher quality, investment levels, and efficiency.
(3) Local government fiscal revenue and investment decisions significantly impact infrastructure investment.
(4) Education development levels affect human capital, influencing infrastructure investment efficiency.

The empirical analysis thus selects per capita GDP, population, urbanization rate, average years of education per capita, and fiscal self-sufficiency rate as control variables. Urbanization rate is measured by the proportion of the urban population to the total population. The calculation method for average years of education per capita is as follows: six years for primary education, nine years for junior high education, twelve years for senior high and vocational education, fifteen years for associate degrees, sixteen years for bachelor's degrees, and nineteen years for graduate education. Based on the national population change sampling survey data, multiplying the number of people with different education levels in each province (autonomous region and municipality) by corresponding average years of education, summing the results, and dividing by the total surveyed population yields the average years of education per capita data.

Empirical results indicate that the scale of market-based financing significantly positively impacts the output value of the transportation infrastructure sector.

The empirical results indicate that the scale of market-oriented investment and financing has a significantly negative impact on the efficiency of infrastructure investment. At the current stage in China, although the market-oriented investment and financing model can increase the output value of the infrastructure industry, it still cannot improve the efficiency of infrastructure investment. This may be related to the low degree of marketization, imperfect market mechanisms, and high market transaction costs in China.

Table 4.20 Empirical results of market-based financing and infrastructure sector output

Variable	Transportation infrastructure sector output
Market-based financing	0.0330*** (0.000)
Per capita GDP	0.0068*** (0.001)
Population	0.0896*** (0.000)
Urbanization rate	0.1771 (0.958)
Fiscal self-sufficiency	252.4759 (0.181)
Constant	−373.4837*** (0.001)
Individual FE	Yes
Time FE	Yes
F-value	287.83*** (0.000)
Sample Size	300

Note *** indicates significance at the 1% level; values in parentheses are the p-values of corresponding coefficients

Table 4.21 Empirical results of market-oriented financing and infrastructure investment efficiency

Variable	Infrastructure investment efficiency
Market-oriented investment and financing	−6.68E06*** (0.003)
Per capita GDP	3.53E06*** (0.015)
Population	−4.45E05*** (0.000)
Urbanization rate	0.0117*** (0.000)
Average years of education per capita	−0.0423* (0.079)
Fiscal self-sufficiency rate	−0.4348*** (0.001)
Constant	0.5524*** (0.000)
Individual fixed effects	Yes
Time fixed effects	Yes
F-value	94.28*** (0.000)
Sample size	300

Note *, *** denote significance at 5% and 1% levels, respectively; values in parentheses are p-values

4.4.3.3 Market-Oriented Investment and Financing and Municipal Facilities Investment Efficiency

To empirically analyze the impact of market-oriented investment and financing models on the efficiency of municipal facilities investment, the efficiency of urban municipal infrastructure investment is used as the dependent variable, with the scale of market-oriented investment and financing in urban municipal facilities as the core independent variable. Per capita GDP, population, urbanization rate, average years of education per capita, and fiscal self-sufficiency rate are selected as control variables. A panel model controlling for individual and time effects is used for empirical analysis. The research sample and calculation period comprise panel data from 30 provinces (autonomous regions and municipalities) in China from 2009 to 2017.[4] Data from the *China Urban Construction Statistical Yearbook* are used to measure the scale of market-oriented investment and financing for urban municipal facilities using "domestic loans + bonds" (Market-Oriented Investment and Financing Model 1) and "current year's funding sources subtotal - central government appropriations - local government appropriations" (Market-Oriented Investment and Financing Model 2).

[4] Due to the difficulty of data collection, this analysis excludes the regions of Hong Kong, Macau, and Taiwan. Additionally, due to incomplete data, the Tibet Autonomous Region is also excluded from the research sample.

According to the *China Statistical Yearbook* (2010–2018), input indicators such as the urban water supply rate, urban gas supply rate, number of public transportation vehicles per ten thousand people, per capita urban road area, per capita park green area, and number of public toilets per ten thousand people are selected. Per capita regional GDP and urbanization rate are selected as output indicators. The CCR (Charnes Cooper Rhodes) model and Malmquist productivity index model are used to measure the investment efficiency of urban municipal facilities in 30 provinces (autonomous regions and municipalities) in China from 2009 to 2017. The selection, measurement, and data sources of the control variables are similar to those in the analysis of market-oriented investment and financing and infrastructure investment efficiency.

The empirical results show that before adding control variables, Market-Oriented Investment and Financing Model 1 positively impact the efficiency of urban municipal facilities investment. After adding control variables, the impact of Model 1 becomes negative but not significant. Before adding control variables, Market-Oriented Investment and Financing Model 2 positively impacted the efficiency of

Table 4.22 Empirical results of market-oriented investment and financing and urban municipal facilities investment efficiency

Variable	Model 1	Model 2	Model 3	Model 4
Market-oriented investment and financing model 1	1.07E08** (0.041)	−1.92E09 (0.543)		
Market-oriented investment and financing model 2			9.35E09*** (0.004)	1.11E11 (0.996)
Per capita GDP		−1.36E06** (0.029)		−1.39E06** (0.028)
Population		−4.95E06* (0.061)		−5.15E06** (0.057)
Urbanization rate		0.0104*** (0.000)		0.0104*** (0.000)
Average years of education per capita		0.0021 (0.853)		0.0023 (0.838)
Fiscal self-sufficiency rate		0.0632 (0.357)		0.0583 (0.395)
Constant	0.7134*** (0.000)	0.1936*** (0.010)	0.6977*** (0.000)	0.1920*** (0.010)
Individual Fixed Effects	Yes	Yes	Yes	Yes
Time Fixed Effects	Yes	Yes	Yes	Yes
F-Value	4.23** (0.041)	97.22*** (0.000)	8.21*** (0.005)	97.39*** (0.000)
Sample Size	270	270	270	270

Note *, **, *** denote significance at 10%, 5%, and 1% levels, respectively; values in parentheses are p-values

urban municipal facilities' investment. After adding control variables, the impact of Model 2 remains positive but not significant. This indicates that Market-Oriented Investment and Financing Model 1 generally has a negative impact on the efficiency of urban municipal facilities investment, while Model 2 generally has a positive impact. It also suggests that the current "domestic loans + bonds" market-oriented investment and financing model is still insufficient to improve the investment efficiency of municipal infrastructure. Only relying on social capital and private capital financing models outside of these methods may improve the efficiency of municipal facilities investment.

4.4.4 Problems and Solutions in Public Goods Market Investment and Financing

In the reform of investment and financing mechanisms for urban public goods in China, the development of market-based investment and financing mechanisms has undergone a transition from a single mechanism to a diversified one. Overall, the direction of urban public goods investment and financing reform is to cultivate and improve market investment and financing mechanisms and develop mechanisms for cooperation between the government and social capital. However, in practice, the role of market-based and diversified investment and financing mechanisms in the field of public goods supply in China has not been fully realized and cannot yet fully meet the market's requirements for resource allocation. The main issues are as follows:

4.4.4.1 Over-Reliance on Land Finance for Urban Public Infrastructure Construction

Currently, China's urban construction investment and financing model fundamentally relies on land finance as an expansion engine. Local governments use land transfer revenues as a basis to leverage land financing and expand urban construction investment. Before the implementation of the amended *Budget Law* in 2014, urban construction investment and financing mainly relied on financing platform companies, with financing typically guaranteed by land transfer revenues. The land transfer revenues of local governments affected the debt repayment capacity of these financing platforms (Yang et al., 2018; Zhang et al., 2018). After the implementation of the amended *Budget Law* in 2014, the financing of government financing platform companies was restricted, and issuing local bonds became an important financing model for urban construction. Under the local government bond financing model, special bonds, as the main instrument, are repaid through government fund income and particular income corresponding to the projects, which still heavily rely on land transfer revenues (Liu & Long, 2021). Similarly, under the PPP (Public–Private Partnership) model, a large portion of government-paid or gap-funded PPP projects are also primarily funded by government fund budgets based on land transfer revenues (Wu, 2020).

4.4.4.2 Accumulation of Implicit Debt Risks of Local Governments

Implicit debt of local governments refers to debts incurred beyond the statutory government debt limit, whether through direct obligations or promises to repay with fiscal funds or illegally guaranteed (Mao et al., 2019). This includes debts incurred by local state-owned enterprises and institutions on behalf of the government with local government guarantees or financial support, as well as medium- to long-term debts generated through mechanisms like government investment funds, PPPs, and government purchase of services, which involve agreements to repurchase investment principal or guarantee minimum returns (Xu et al., 2020). The trend of implicit debt is notable, with various forms, including obligations of state-owned enterprises, unpaid project payments, and trust financing debts, making their regulation more challenging due to their large scale (Liu et al., 2017). Implicit debt exacerbates the government's overall debt risk. Though it is not directly classified as government debt following the 2014 amended *Budget Law*, implicit debt remains a substantial fiscal risk.

4.4.4.3 Difficulties in Realizing the Market-Oriented Transformation of Local Financing Platform Companies

Under the hierarchical fiscal system based on tax-sharing, fiscal decentralization creates primary conditions for financing platforms to borrow funds (Mao et al., 2019). In a decentralized fiscal system, soft budget constraints and implicit guarantees from the central government to local governments are inevitable (Guo et al., 2016; Ma & Ma, 2018; Wang et al., 2016). This provides institutional insurance for the borrowing of local financing platform companies, which often use local government land transfer revenues as collateral (Liu & Chen, 2020; Yang et al., 2018; Zhang et al., 2018). Under the current system and government investment and financing system, local financing platform companies inherently possess the function of raising funds for the government, making it difficult for them to achieve genuine market-oriented transformation.

To address the above issues in the market investment and financing mechanisms of urban public product sectors, the following policy recommendations are proposed:

(1) Establishing a Scientific Public Product Value Compensation Mechanism and Innovate Subsidy Methods. To promote the development of market-oriented investment and financing models for public products, the government should establish a public product value compensation mechanism and innovate subsidy methods. This includes implementing user-pay and beneficiary-pay mechanisms

for public products, especially urban public infrastructure. Additionally, the government should deepen price mechanism reforms in the public infrastructure sector, establish a rational pricing, adjustment, and compensation mechanism for public products, and develop an investment return mechanism for projects. The government should also actively perform regulatory duties to internalize the positive externalities of public product supply.

(2) Reforming Government Investment and Financing Systems and Promoting the Transition from Government Credit-Driven Models to Enterprise and Market Credit-Driven Models. For sustainable development of market-oriented investment and financing models for urban public products, it is essential to construct an investment and financing system that aligns with both government and market investments, enhancing market constraints and regulating government investment behavior (Mao & Xu, 2021). It is also important to reconstruct the credit structure, transitioning from government credit-driven models to models driven by government, enterprise, and market credit. Efforts should be made to transition land finance from land-based revenue to land and tax revenue, promote property taxes, and use land-related special taxes as relatively stable primary sources of local government revenue (Wu, 2020).

(3) Optimizing the Financing Structure of Market-Oriented Financing Projects for Public Products. For market-oriented financing projects for urban public products, China should optimize the financing structure by increasing the proportion of direct financing and broadening channels for long-term funds. In promoting urban economic development and adequate public product supply, the financing model should shift from being primarily indirect to a combination of indirect and direct financing, steadily increasing the proportion of direct financing, expanding the scale of bond financing, and clarifying the relationship between the government and the market. Efforts should also be made to make local government debt explicit and transparent through legislation, constraining market-based debt financing by local governments. Additionally, channels for long-term funds to participate in public product supply should be expanded to match better project financing terms, such as involving insurance funds, which are currently the central long-term funds domestically, in market-oriented public product investment projects to address the mismatch between project terms and investment return cycles.

(4) Promoting the Market-Oriented Transformation of Local Government Financing Platform Companies. The issues faced by financing platforms cannot be resolved quickly. Various scholars have proposed suggestions for the market-oriented transformation of financing platforms (Mao & Xu, 2021; Xu et al., 2020). These include adjusting fiscal relations between the central and local governments, balancing local governments' public affairs and financial resources, objectively assessing and analyzing the matching relationship between authority and financial resources, and dynamically adjusting the proportion of fiscal revenue distribution based on regional conditions to address vertical fiscal imbalances. A balancing mechanism between fiscal revenue,

public product supply, and government debt should be established, and comprehensive budget management and performance management should be improved, abandoning soft budget constraints and central government implicit guarantees. It is also crucial to construct a market-oriented system and mechanism that aligns government investment with social capital investment; for financing platform companies, a market-oriented credit enhancement mechanism should be cultivated to replace reliance on government credit and guarantees. Given the specific nature of the public product sector, financial market innovation tools should be used to meet investment needs. Furthermore, modern corporate governance structures should be established for financing platform companies, promoting the separation of government and enterprise, clear property rights, simple hierarchical structures, and adequate capital. Local governments, financing platforms, and other stakeholders should clarify their respective responsibilities and work collaboratively to advance market-oriented transformation. To effectively mitigate the implicit debt risk of local governments and realize the market-oriented transformation of local financing platform companies, China should adopt a step-by-step implementation principle (Mao & Xu, 2021) to gradually strip away government financing functions and properly resolve the implicit debt of local financing platforms. New market contractual relationships should be established between the government and financing platforms, allowing financing platform companies to become market entities that operate independently and bear their own profits and losses, growing into modernized local state-owned enterprises under market constraints.

(5) Forming a Diversified Pattern of Public Product Investment and Financing Main Bodies with Joint Efforts from the Government and Market. To achieve this, China should prioritize the following strategies:

*Reinforcing the rigid constraints of government investment and limiting government investment priorities to functions that compensate for market failures;

*Promoting market-oriented reforms in public product investment and financing, opening up the public product investment market, broadening financing channels, reducing financing costs, and improving investment returns;

*Broadening financing channels by granting social capital a leading role in competitive public product investment, encouraging social capital to participate in the entire process of urban infrastructure construction and public service provision, and leveraging the professional capabilities and advantages of social capital.

4.5 Multi-stakeholder Cooperative Financing and Investment Mechanism for Public Goods

4.5.1 Development Trends of Multi-stakeholder Cooperative Financing and Investment for Public Goods

The multi-stakeholder cooperative financing and investment model for public goods refers to partnerships between governments and enterprises or other social capital to jointly invest in and construct public goods projects. In this model, parties sign cooperation agreements that define their rights and obligations and jointly fund projects while sharing benefits and risks. This model combines the strengths of government fiscal investment mechanisms and market financing and investment mechanisms, making it more conducive to the fair and adequate supply of urban public goods. The establishment of a multi-stakeholder cooperative financing and investment mechanism is also a process of reforming government investment methods and cultivating market investment mechanisms.

In the construction of urban public infrastructure in China, the government has accumulated significant experience in cooperating with social capital through concessionary operations, leading to the gradual development of institutional norms. After extensive exploration, the concession model has evolved from the initial BOT (Build-Operate-Transfer) model to include BOOT (Build-Own-Operate-Transfer), TOT (Transfer-Operate-Transfer), and other variations. To encourage and guide social capital to participate in the construction and operation of infrastructure and public utilities, improve the quality and efficiency of public services, protect the legal rights of concessionaires, and ensure public interest and safety, in March 2015, the National Development and Reform Commission (NDRC) and the National Development Bank jointly issued a notice on promoting developmental financial support for government and social capital cooperation. This notice explicitly proposed the flexible use of financial instruments such as fund investments, bank loans, and bond issuances to establish a diversified PPP (Public–Private Partnership) project funding mechanism. In April 2015, the NDRC and five other ministries jointly issued the *Management Measures for Concession Operations of Infrastructure and Public Utilities*, which provided detailed regulations on the scope, principles, signing and performance, amendments and termination of concession agreements, supervision, public interest protection, and legal responsibilities. These regulations clarified the various methods that concession operations of infrastructure and public utilities could adopt and specified the terms of these concessions. Government authorities also issued various policy documents encouraging and standardizing the cooperation between government and social capital for public infrastructure construction. Notably, in May 2015, the Ministry of Finance and other departments released the *Guiding Opinions on Promoting Government and Social Capital Cooperation Models in Public Service Areas* to transform government functions, stimulate market vitality, increase the supply of public goods and services, and innovate public service supply mechanisms through the significant promotion of government and social capital cooperation models. The guidelines recommended adopting such models extensively in areas like energy, transportation, water conservation, environmental protection, agriculture, forestry, technology, affordable housing projects, healthcare, elderly care, education, and culture. In October 2016, the NDRC issued the *Guidelines for Implementing Government and Social Capital Cooperation Projects in Traditional Infrastructure Fields*. These guidelines addressed challenges in collaboration and the standardization of the procedures for traditional infrastructure PPP projects.

Practical experience has proven that in the realm of public goods and services, government and social capital cooperation fosters urban public goods financing mechanism innovation, broadens social capital investment channels, promotes a diversified supply of urban public goods, speeds up the transformation of government functions, and fully leverages the advantages of both government and market investment mechanisms.

4.5.2 Major Financing and Investment Models for Multi-stakeholder Cooperation in Public Goods

The main models for multi-stakeholder cooperative financing and investment in public goods include Concession, PPP, and PFI (Private Finance Initiative). Concession models mainly encompass BOT and its derivatives such as BOOT and TOT; PPP models have been widely employed in urban infrastructure construction, characteristic town development, public utilities, and the elderly care industry; PFI models focus on integrating private investment in urban infrastructure, public utilities, and services. Below are descriptions of these three models.

4.5.2.1 Concession Model

The Concession model includes different forms, primarily detailed as follows:

(1) BOT Model

The BOT (Build-Operate-Transfer) model refers to a contractual agreement between the government and a private enterprise, where the government grants a concession to a project company established by the enterprise to take on the responsibilities of investment, financing, construction, and operation of urban infrastructure projects. Within the concession period, the project company has the right to charge fees or sell products to infrastructure users to recover investments, repay loans, and earn a certain profit. The government retains the authority to supervise and regulate the project. Upon the expiration of the concession period, the project company transfers the infrastructure to the government according to the agreement, either free of charge or for a fee. The BOT model not only improves efficiency by adopting a market-oriented approach to constructing and operating infrastructure but also focuses on market-based financing for the projects. Companies involved in BOT projects have specific legal characteristics: first, the limited nature of the project rights transfer period, meaning the project company only holds operational rights during the agreement's validity; second, the transfer of responsibility, where the government transfers the responsibility for construction and operation to the project company during the agreement period; and third, the project's required funds are primarily the responsibility of the contracted investor, with the government not providing guarantees but potentially participating in the investment through equity. The government's adoption of the BOT model for infrastructure construction can alleviate fiscal burdens, avoid risks associated with project construction and operation, and enhance management levels to strengthen the project's market competitiveness. The World Bank has summarized various forms of BOT models worldwide, including the basic BOT form and two other variations: BOO (Build-Own-Operate) and BOOT (Build-Own-Operate-Transfer). In the BOO model, the government grants a concession to the project company's investors, allowing them to invest, finance, construct, and operate the project during the agreement period. The project company retains the operational rights and revenue rights after completion, without the need to transfer the project to the government at a later date. In the BOOT model, the government grants a concession to the project company's investors, allowing them to invest, finance, construct, own, and operate the project. The project company holds the ownership of the assets for a specified period after completion but must transfer the property rights to the government according to the agreement upon its expiration.

(2) TOT Mode

The TOT (Transfer-Operate-Transfer) model refers to a financing mechanism where the government or state-owned enterprises transfer the operational rights of already operational infrastructure projects to investors for a specified period in return for a fee. Investors exercise these operational rights, recoup their entire investment, and earn a reasonable profit over the agreed period. Upon the expiry of the concession, the operational rights revert to the government or state-owned enterprises. This model typically involves transferring operational rights rather than equity, except in specific circumstances.

Utilizing the TOT model helps monetize existing urban infrastructure, allowing funds obtained from transferring operational rights to be used for constructing new projects, thereby accelerating urban development. It also facilitates the transition of government roles from directly managing public infrastructure to supervising and ensuring that these infrastructures serve the public interest. The introduction of market mechanisms effectively allocates social resources and enhances the efficiency of public infrastructure operations (Liu, 2004; Qiao, 2008).

4.5.2.2 PPP Model

The PPP (Public–Private Partnership) model involves the government public sector signing concession agreements with private enterprises to collaboratively build and operate public infrastructure projects, forming a partnership of shared benefits, risk-sharing, and full lifecycle collaboration. Compared with BOT (Build-Operate-Transfer) and other government concession models, the PPP model sees more government involvement in construction and subsequent operations, while private enterprises play a significant role in early-stage project planning. In the PPP model, the government grants the private enterprise the concession to build, operate, and generate returns from the project, effectively making it a financing model for public infrastructure. The partnership involves not only cooperation in operational rights but also in property and revenue rights. Private enterprises use their own funds or loans for investment and achieve reasonable returns through user fees or partial government payments and subsidies.

The Public–Private Partnership (PPP) model offers several advantages in urban public infrastructure projects: (a) Mobilizing Social Capital: PPP can widely mobilize social capital to participate in project construction, thereby alleviating government financial pressure and enhancing the supply capacity of public goods; (b) Improving Quality and Efficiency: Private sector partners are involved in the entire project lifecycle, effectively improving project construction quality and efficiency. In the PPP model, companies participate in planning and design phases, facilitating the introduction of advanced technologies and management expertise and leveraging their professional strengths; (c) Enhancing Project Credibility: The strategic alliance formed between the government and enterprises in PPP projects enhances project credibility, making it easier to secure funding from financial markets and improve financial stability; (d) Shared Control and Risk Mitigation: For the government, PPP reduces investment requirements while retaining certain control over project construction and operation. For enterprises, PPP helps mitigate institutional risks associated with the early and operational stages of the project.

During PPP implementation, managing the relationship between the government and social capital is critical. Key points include balancing public interest (represented by the government) with capital interest (pursued by enterprises), reconciling the normative administrative processes of public sectors with the operational flexibility of the market, and managing the relative monopoly of PPP projects against the competitive market of private projects. The core solution lies in implementing PPP models strictly according to relevant laws and ensuring all parties fulfill their contractual duties.

4.5.2.3 PFI Model

The Private Finance Initiative (PFI) model involves private enterprises investing in, constructing, and operating infrastructure projects. The government proposes infrastructure projects based on social needs. These projects are then constructed and operated by private enterprises that win open bidding competitions. Typically, after the concession period ends, enterprises transfer the projects to the government public sector. There are differences between PFI and BOT Models: (a) In BOT, the government defines specific project plans and requirements, while in PFI, the government outlines basic needs, allowing enterprises to develop detailed plans; (b) BOT projects specify land supply and subsidies; in PFI, the government offers a minimum revenue guarantee, with flexible negotiations on revenue, subsidies, land, and pricing; (c) PFI concession holders may lack construction and operational capabilities and may subcontract these tasks; (d) Under BOT, project assets are typically transferred to the government without charge upon expiration, whereas PFI arrangements can vary based on project characteristics and cost recovery.

In urban infrastructure construction, the most significant advantage of the Private Finance Initiative (PFI) model is its flexibility due to fewer constraints from government policies and regulations. This flexibility allows for adjustments in business strategies based on market demand changes during construction and operation. The PFI model is more attractive for social capital involvement in urban public infrastructure projects. With more rights in the PFI model, private enterprises can better leverage market mechanisms during project construction and operation, improving efficiency and transferring project risks (Yao, 2009).

4.5.3 Empirical Analysis of Multi-stakeholder Cooperative Financing and Investment for Public Goods in Urban China

Since China's reform and opening up, the rapid development of urbanization and industrialization has significantly increased the demand for urban public infrastructure construction, creating substantial financial pressure on the government and driving reforms in public sector mechanisms. As Table 4.23 indicates, from 2014 to 2018, there was more than a tenfold increase in local government bonds, market-oriented infrastructure investment projects, PPP projects, and PPP scales. Infrastructure investment projects are gradually becoming market-oriented, and utilizing private capital to meet infrastructure project funding needs is becoming a significant trend and method.

According to Table 4.24, nearly half of the social capital in PPP projects is provided by private enterprises, with local state-owned enterprises contributing around 30%. These two types of enterprises constitute the primary sources of social capital for PPP projects. Additionally, the proportion of social capital provided by local state-owned enterprises is gradually increasing, showing a trend of crowding out private social capital.

From 2016 to 2019, the data of PPP projects in various provinces (autonomous regions, municipalities) showed an overall increasing trend. Provinces with a higher number of PPP projects include Zhejiang, Shandong, Henan, Sichuan, and Guizhou.

Table 4.23 Dynamics of market-oriented development of infrastructure investment projects table

Project	2014	2015	2016	2017	2018
Local government bonds/100 million yuan	4000	38,351	60,458	43,581	41,652
Market-oriented infrastructure investment projects/100 million yuan	3591	12,964	43,286	58,747	32,149
Number of PPP projects	115	846	2527	3381	2275
Number of PPP-like projects	182	601	858	907	784
PPP scale/100 million yuan	2072	7477	33,386	51,673	27,489
PPP-like scale/100 million yuan	1519	5487	9900	7073	4660

Data Source 2018 Infrastructure Investment Development Report

Table 4.24 Ownership structure of completed PPP projects

Ownership	2015	2016	2017	2018
Central enterprises	18.20	24.00	25.10	19.60
Local state-owned enterprises	20.50	25.40	30.10	33.10
Private enterprises	60.60	49.60	43.90	46.20
Others	0.80	1.00	0.90	1.10

Data Source 2018 Infrastructure Investment Development Report
Unit: %

From 2016 to 2019, the investment amount in PPP projects across 31 provinces (autonomous regions, municipalities) also showed an overall increasing trend (Table 4.26). Provinces with higher PPP project investments include provinces Jiangsu, Zhejiang, Shandong, Henan, Sichuan, Guizhou, and Yunnan. Dividing the total PPP project investment by the number of PPP projects, we can find that cities and provinces (autonomous regions, municipalities) with higher average investment per project include Beijing, Tianjin, Jilin, Jiangsu, Chongqing, Tibet, Gansu, and Ningxia.

As shown in Table 4.27, PPP projects cover a wide range of areas, such as transportation, ecological construction and environmental protection, municipal engineering, area development, tourism, affordable housing projects, and public services. In public services, PPP projects focus on healthcare, education, and cultural industries, with relatively fewer projects in elderly care and social security.

As shown in Table 4.28, transportation, ecological construction and environmental protection, municipal engineering, area development, tourism, affordable housing projects, and public services enjoy higher PPP project investments. In public services, PPP project investments are also mainly in healthcare, education, and cultural industries, with relatively lower investments in elderly care and social security, with the lowest in social security.

Table 4.25 Number of PPP projects in 31 provinces[5] (autonomous regions, municipalities) 2016–2019

Province (autonomous region, municipality)	2016	2017	2018	2019
Beijing	98	87	104	111
Tianjin	17	36	54	68
Hebei	450	574	461	464
Shanxi	41	189	371	404
Inner Mongolia	828	680	392	382
Liaoning	487	383	250	294
Jilin	61	107	165	173
Heilongjiang	144	226	135	139
Shanghai	1	4	6	8
Jiangsu	346	470	501	453
Zhejiang	317	421	565	589
Anhui	180	258	448	474
Fujian	280	353	424	431
Jiangxi	311	411	415	455
Shandong	1087	1141	1036	1036
Henan	795	1339	1046	1063
Hubei	132	569	714	730
Hunan	316	578	437	429
Guangdong	118	229	454	524
Guangxi	183	181	235	247
Hainan	155	171	164	142
Chongqing	66	78	48	56
Sichuan	848	1293	1245	750
Guizhou	1788	1829	1251	1199
Yunnan	417	387	450	477
Tibet	–	4	2	2
Shaanxi	316	478	464	476
Gansu	470	239	106	124
Qinghai	72	116	71	52
Ningxia	72	140	51	51
Xinjiang	852	1420	528	508

Data Source National Development and Reform Commission PPP Project Database

With the data from Table 4.26 on the PPP project investment amounts in 31 provinces (autonomous regions, municipalities) from 2016 to 2019, together with the urban municipal facility levels from the *China Urban Construction Statistical*

[5] Due to the difficulty of data collection, the statistics here do not include the regions of Hong Kong, Macau, and Taiwan.

Table 4.26 PPP project investment in 31 provinces (autonomous regions, municipalities) 2016–2019

Province (autonomous region, municipality)	2016	2017	2018	2019
Beijing	2317.00	2610.44	2459.50	2511.35
Tianjin	150.00	1360.82	1782.52	2927.06
Hebei	6788.00	7607.07	7400.66	7897.75
Shanxi	551.00	1580.33	2847.58	3734.17
Inner Mongolia	7096.00	7214.62	3876.67	3479.53
Liaoning	5619.00	4567.01	3180.79	3300.13
Jilin	1309.00	2894.06	3099.81	2955.41
Heilongjiang	2023.00	2285.59	1539.14	1485.90
Shanghai	14.00	30.25	43.03	46.69
Jiangsu	6798.00	10,104.15	10,287.04	9101.75
Zhejiang	5432.00	8120.99	10,953.54	11,186.14
Anhui	2118.00	2700.84	5003.21	5157.51
Fujian	3983.00	4386.65	4582.05	4396.63
Jiangxi	1806.00	2525.47	3523.76	3972.70
Shandong	12,229.00	11,927.22	11,406.59	11,117.64
Henan	9538.00	15,712.87	13,473.41	13,337.96
Hubei	2391.00	7189.88	9520.79	9863.63
Hunan	5109.00	9023.08	6229.85	5706.27
Guangdong	1902.00	3447.12	6042.10	6393.45
Guangxi	2137.00	1819.25	3065.43	3512.68
Hainan	1653.00	1575.41	1333.22	1199.19
Chongqing	2141.00	2414.19	1254.41	2128.03
Sichuan	9180.00	15,747.65	18,569.87	13,210.93
Guizhou	16,034.00	17,836.14	16,808.54	17,934.98
Yunnan	10,302.00	10,455.37	11,152.34	11,302.27
Tibet	–	119.92	97.44	97.44
Shaanxi	3310.00	5118.96	5313.24	5453.67
Gansu	5732.00	4373.82	2623.84	3045.57
Qinghai	1126.00	1252.00	1291.09	1299.68
Ningxia	1736.00	2317.03	528.11	807.84
Xinjiang	4393.00	13,070.61	7014.60	7197.26

Data Source National Development and Reform Commission PPP Project Database
Unit: 100 million yuan

Table 4.27 Number of PPP projects by industry 2016–2019

Industry	2016	2017	2018	2019
Energy	195	212	150	155
Transportation	1375	1941	1771	1707
Water conservancy construction	518	678	566	543
Ecological construction and environmental protection	633	958	1076	1114
Municipal engineering	3998	5049	4704	4699
Area development	688	841	803	794
Agriculture	111	154	119	114
Forestry	17	35	56	97
Science and technology	127	180	163	164
Affordable housing projects	515	530	303	243
Tourism	659	865	626	583
Healthcare	494	561	405	382
Elderly care	283	295	190	169
Education	553	714	603	559
Culture	317	416	325	310
Sports	208	242	183	173
Social security	103	112	68	61
Government infrastructure	175	324	271	257
Others	936	317	242	217

Data Source National Development and Reform Commission PPP Project Database

Yearbook, we selected five indicators to reflect the levels of urban municipal facilities: water supply coverage rate, gas supply coverage rate, per capita road area, sewage treatment rate, and greening coverage rate of built-up areas. We used a panel data model at the provincial (autonomous region, municipality) level for econometric analysis. The effects of PPP investment models on the levels of urban municipal facilities are shown in Table 4.29.

The results show that the PPP investment model has a significantly negative impact on the water supply coverage rate and gas supply coverage rate; the impact on per capita road area and greening coverage rate of built-up areas is positive but not significant; the impact on the sewage treatment rate is significantly positive. Therefore, it can be seen that the PPP investment model is more suitable for projects that can generate stable cash flow and require a long post-operation period, such as sewage treatment plants. These projects utilize the operational management capabilities of social capital to improve their operational efficiency. Conversely, for purely public municipal facility projects, such as municipal roads, the PPP investment model is not as effective in improving operational efficiency. However, collaboration with social capital can alleviate the government's financial pressure for such projects.

Table 4.28 Investment in PPP projects by industry 2016–2019 (Table 4.28)

Industry	2016	2017	2018	2019
Energy	1220.00	1416.49	807.68	845.48
Transportation	39,573.00	53,885.06	52,812.18	54,702.61
Water conservancy construction	3874.00	5626.06	4938.19	4697.59
Ecological construction and environmental protection	6534.00	10,502.81	11,311.67	11,603.99
Municipal engineering	37,801.00	49,207.79	49,565.76	48,953.46
Area development	13,984.00	18,720.88	23,452.41	23,124.62
Agriculture	747.00	1189.38	1044.35	1267.90
Forestry	80.00	543.48	977.75	1805.58
Science and technology	1087.00	1421.53	1186.61	1115.33
Affordable housing projects	7560.00	7916.39	4749.76	3742.93
Tourism	7154.00	11,108.80	8293.99	7325.87
Healthcare	2333.00	2770.91	2620.14	2522.60
Elderly care	1659.00	1886.16	1178.28	1048.72
Education	2189.00	3330.24	3342.67	3056.54
Culture	2141.00	2920.04	2765.81	2779.99
Sports	1405.00	1913.00	1591.51	1658.93
Social security	252.00	289.27	219.59	217.29
Government infrastructure	2000.00	3103.73	2668.91	2608.85
Others	3405.00	3858.05	3100.83	2950.51

Data Source National Development and Reform Commission PPP Project Database
Unit: 100 million yuan

Using data from Table 4.26 on PPP project investment amounts in 31 provinces (autonomous regions, municipalities) from 2016 to 2019, the supply of non-economic public products in cities is measured by average years of education, the number of hospital beds per thousand people, and per capita social security expenditure. Empirical analysis using panel data from 31 provinces (autonomous regions, municipalities) from 2016 to 2019 shows the effects of PPP investment models on non-economic public product supply, as shown in Table 4.30.

The results show that the PPP investment model has a significantly positive impact on the number of hospital beds per thousand people and per capita social security expenditure, while the impact on the average years of education is significantly negative. This indicates that the PPP investment model can increase the supply of social undertakings such as healthcare and social security. However, the PPP investment model is currently facing challenges in promoting the increase in the supply of social undertakings such as education.

Table 4.29 Effects of PPP investment models on levels of urban municipal facilities

Variable	Water supply coverage rate	Gas supply coverage rate	Per capita road area	Sewage treatment rate	Greening coverage rate of built-up areas
PPP project investment amount	−0.000101** (0.015)	−0.000340*** (0.003)	0.000167 (0.127)	0.000215** (0.013)	0.000037 (0.636)
Constant	98.632*** (0.000)	97.112*** (0.000)	15.415*** (0.000)	92.363*** (0.000)	39.682*** (0.000)
Individual fixed effects	Yes	Yes	Yes	Yes	Yes
Time fixed effects	Yes	Yes	Yes	Yes	Yes
F-value	6.22	9.13	2.38	6.50	0.23
Sample size	90	90	90	90	90

Note **, *** represent significance at the 5% and 1% levels, respectively; values in parentheses indicate the p-values of the corresponding coefficients

Table 4.30 Effects of PPP investment models on non-economic public product supply

Variable	Average years of education per capita	The number of hospital beds per thousand people	Per capita social security expenditure
PPP project investment amount	−0.000084*** (0.000)	0.000059*** (0.000)	0.0299*** (0.000)
Constant	9.743*** (0.000)	5.395*** (0.000)	610.347*** (0.000)
Individual fixed effects	Yes	Yes	Yes
Time fixed effects	Yes	Yes	Yes
F-value	17.00	13.30	16.05
Sample size	90	90	90

Note *** represents significance at the 1% level; values in parentheses indicate the p-values of the corresponding coefficients

4.5.4 Issues and Solutions in Multi-stakeholder Cooperative Financing and Investment for Public Goods

In public product financing mechanisms, multi-stakeholder cooperative financing is an ideal investment mechanism that can achieve multi-party cooperation, complementary advantages, shared risks, and profit sharing. However, the investment and operation of social capital in public welfare projects in China are still in an exploratory phase, with numerous issues emerging during project advancement that require urgent resolution.

4.5.4.1 Inefficient Government-Business Communication Mechanisms

In cases of disputes in multi-stakeholder cooperative projects, most enterprises and the government fail to resolve their disputes after communication and negotiation, due to ineffective communication and cooperation mechanisms between the government and enterprises. This communication mechanism has hindered the smooth development of multi-stakeholder cooperative financing projects. In multi-stakeholder cooperation, some local governments often act with administrative power and are unable to serve and care for enterprises and listen carefully to their opinions and suggestions. Conversely, some enterprises tend to emphasize private gains, neglecting social responsibility and even harming public interests. These factors hinder the establishment of a collaborative partnership between the government and enterprises. Moreover, in the context of information asymmetry between the government and enterprises, if enterprises find it difficult to obtain timely and accurate financing information, an efficient communication mechanism cannot be established, and the quality and efficiency of multi-stakeholder cooperation will decline.

4.5.4.2 Incomplete Legal Framework

A sound legal environment and a favorable business environment are crucial for establishing an efficient multi-stakeholder cooperation financing mechanism for public goods. Although there are many policy documents regarding multi-stakeholder cooperation in China, they lack systematization and legal-level regulations. Despite the legislative work on multi-stakeholder cooperation starting in 2014, no related laws have been enacted to date. Ineffective legal frameworks and an unfavorable business environment increase the institutional transaction costs for social capital involvement in multi-stakeholder cooperation, reducing their confidence in local governments (Shen et al., 2020).

4.5.4.3 Excessive Burden on Social Capital

Due to the long construction and operation cycles of multi-stakeholder cooperation projects, which usually last for 10–30 years, unforeseeable changes in laws, market conditions, public product demand, and project leadership will occur over such long periods. This makes it impossible for the government and social capital parties to anticipate and specify all potential contract changes (Yang & Nie, 2006; Hart, 2003). Consequently, there has always been the "public goods burden" in China's multi-stakeholder cooperation market. Local governments often impose excessive public goods responsibilities on social capital, significantly increasing the risks associated with their participation in multi-stakeholder cooperation projects (Ke et al., 2009; Qi et al., 2009).

4.5.4.4 High Transaction Costs

Numerous empirical studies indicate that the current government regulations and policies are complex. Compliance imposes significant taxes and fees on enterprises. Furthermore, the contract negotiations and implementations of government-social capital cooperation projects involve high transaction costs. This is particularly challenging for investments with asset-specificity, as enterprises lack the flexibility to adjust their operations in response to market changes and social demands (He & Liu, 2016). When sunk costs are high, strategic behaviors and transactional threats exist between government and enterprises, and entry and exit barriers are significant, the transaction costs for multi-stakeholder cooperation projects increase substantially, leading to reduced financing performance (He & Liu, 2016). Additionally, issues such as poor communication mechanisms between government and enterprises, insufficient legal frameworks for multi-stakeholder cooperation, and the excessive burden of public goods on social capital further escalate transaction costs.

To address these issues within multi-stakeholder cooperation, this book proposes the following recommendations:

(1) Improving the Business Environment for Multi-Stakeholder Cooperation: A favorable business environment is crucial for reducing institutional transaction costs for social capital involvement, enhancing confidence in local governments, and promoting participation in projects. To attract social capital into PPP projects, local governments should simplify administrative approval processes, optimize property rights protection, and deregulate controls. These steps will reduce institutional and informational transaction costs for social capital (Shen et al., 2020).

(2) Establishing Efficient Government-Enterprise Communication Mechanism: Good communication between government and enterprises is essential for improving their relationship. Governments should set up efficient communication systems and create regular communication mechanisms. Dialogue and communication with enterprises and providing them with services should be integral parts of government work. Governments should promptly collect and address feedback and suggestions from enterprises, explain relevant laws and regulations, provide business consultation, and offer procedural guidance. Additionally, leveraging information technology to build communication platforms can establish standardized and systematic communication channels. Governments should also consider rational suggestions and effectively address enterprises' legitimate concerns.

(3) Optimizing Risk Sharing and Benefit Compensation Mechanisms in Government-Enterprise Cooperation: As social capital increasingly participates in infrastructure projects, the supply of multi-stakeholder cooperation projects

increases. However, the market risks for social capital involvement in public infrastructure are higher due to the improved infrastructure environment and reduced economic latecomer advantages. Thus, instead of high government holdings to attract social capital, local governments should enable social capital to form clear expectations of future returns. This can motivate social capital to participate actively in public infrastructure development. Specific actions include Enhancing professionalism in public product pricing to alleviate the burden on social capital caused by market price fluctuations. Governments could pilot third-party pricing, using specialized third-party agencies to provide pricing decisions, considering the interests and risks of social capital, local governments, and the public to ensure fairness and credibility in public product pricing, Establishing credible mechanisms for benefit and risk compensation. Authorities should improve the top-level design of risk-sharing mechanisms and provide supplementary explanations based on sector and regional development levels. They should analyze the risk-bearing capacity, control costs, and match risks with rewards to determine reasonable risk-sharing proportions, clearly defining the responsibility boundaries for social capital in project participation. Because public product construction has externalities, builders must bear certain social responsibilities. Without legal constraints, local governments might impose excessive public reasonable burdens on social capital under the guise of social responsibility. Governments should set relevant norms to delineate social capital's social responsibilities, boosting their confidence and ensuring better provision of public goods (Gong et al., 2019).

(4) Reducing Institutional Transaction Costs: This requires improving laws and regulations and optimizing approval processes during multi-stakeholder cooperation. Authorities should swiftly research and formulate relevant laws and regulations for multi-stakeholder cooperation, drawing from both international experiences and national contexts. Legal provisions should clearly define project planning, financing, asset ownership, operations, fee structures, and property transfers to mitigate institutional and market risks (Zhuang & Zeng, 2019). Additionally, governments should streamline approval processes for project planning, decision-making, contract signing, construction, and operations. Since public infrastructure projects involve various stakeholders, long construction periods, and significant operational uncertainties and risks, optimizing approval procedures can enhance efficiency and reduce institutional costs. Lastly, authorities should improve supporting mechanisms for infrastructure projects, design rational governance structures within multi-stakeholder cooperation models, and establish penalty mechanisms for breaches to ensure the effective functioning of multi-stakeholder financing mechanisms.

References

An, T. (2008). The historic turning point of fiscal expenditure structure adjustment in China. *Local Finance Research, 2008*(5), 4–8.

Cao, G., Liu, C., Zhou, L., et al. (2020). Fiscal pressure and the rise of local government financing platforms. *Financial Research, 2020*(5), 59–76.

Cao, J., Mao, J., & Xue, Y. (2019). Why urban investment bonds continue to grow: An empirical analysis based on new data. *Finance & Trade Economics, 40*(5), 5–22.

Chen, K., Hillman, A. L., & Gu, Q. (2002). Fiscal centralization and changes in local government behavior: From helping hands to grabbing hands. *Economics Quarterly, 2002*(4), 111–130.

Chen, S., & Gao, L. (2012). Central-local relations: A reassessment of the measurement and role mechanism of fiscal decentralization. *Management World, 2012*(6), 43–59.

Chu, D., & Zuo, X. (2019). New progress in research on the economic and social effects of fiscal transparency. *Economics Dynamics, 2019*(5), 135–148.

Deng, S., & Liu, L. (2019). Research on the impact of fiscal transparency on local government debt risk: A perspective based on intergovernmental games. *Financial Research, 45*(12), 4–17.

Diao, W., & Wang, N. (2017). Spatial pattern and dynamic evolution of local governments' debt repayment capacity in China: A classified assessment of general and special debts. *Financial Discussions, 2017*(4), 26–36.

Fang, H., & Zhang, J. (2009). The fiscal behavior of local government expansion in China: Observations and explanations. *Economics Quarterly, 8*(3), 1065–1082.

Fromaget, X. (2008). *The soft budget constraint problem in transition and developing countries* [Doctoral dissertation]. University of Tampere.

Fu, R., Wang, W., & Miao, X. (2008). Exploration of local government debt risk and sustainable scale in China. *Finance & Trade Economics, 2008*(10), 82–87.

Fu, Y., & Zhang, Y. (2007). Chinese-style decentralization and bias in fiscal expenditure structure: The cost of competing for growth. *Management World, 2007*(3), 4–12, 22.

Gong, Q., Zhang, Y., & Lei, L. (2019). Public-private partnerships (PPP): The burden theory of public goods from the perspective of incomplete contracts. *Economic Research, 54*(4), 133–148.

Guo, Y., & Mao, J. (2019). 70 years of local government debt governance in China: Retrospective and outlook. *Finance & Trade Economics, 40*(9), 51–64.

Guo, Y., He, Y., & Li, L. (2016). Bailout expectations, public pool incentives, and local government borrowing in major countries. *Economic Research, 51*(3), 81–95.

Han, J. (2006). *Research on the innovation of the financing system for urban infrastructure construction in China* [Doctoral dissertation]. Nankai University.

Hart, O. (2003). Incomplete contracts and public ownership: Remarks, and an application to public-private partnerships. *The Economic Journal, 113*(486), C69–C76.

He, J., & Liu, F. (2016). Transaction costs, sunk costs, natural monopolies, and governance mechanisms in public-private partnerships. *East China Economic Management, 30*(11), 150–156.

He, X., Zhu, H., & Chen, X. (2008). The multiple interests of government and the lending behavior of banks. *Financial Research, 2008*(6), 1–20.

He, Y., & Man, Y. (2012). Local financing platform debt: Scale, risks, and governance. *Fiscal Research, 2012*(2), 34–37.

Hua, G., & Wang, Y. (2016). On the legalization of central-local fiscal relations in China: The perspective of local debt issuance. *Journal of Anhui University (Philosophy & Social Sciences Edition), 40*(5), 134–141.

Jia, J., & Guo, Q. (2011). Fiscal rules, economic growth, and the scale of government debt. *World Economy, 34*(1), 73–92.

Ke, Y., Wang, S., & Chen, B. (2009). Government incentives for private capital participation in infrastructure PPP projects. *Tsinghua University Journal (Natural Science Edition), 49*(9), 1480–1483.

Li, H., & Ren, L. (2013). Fiscal decentralization, budget constraints, and the efficiency of local public goods supply. *Contemporary Finance & Economics, 3*, 35–43.

Lin, M., & Ma, J. (2012). Research on the budget supervision of local people's congresses in China. *China Social Sciences, 6*, 73–90, 207.
Liu, R., & Long, X. (2021). Local government bond banks: Theoretical logic, practical basis, and implementation paths. *Central University of Finance and Economics Journal, 4*, 14–23.
Liu, S., Shi, Y., & Wu, J. (2017). Failure of the institutional public debt management model: Reflections from a public risk perspective. *Management World, 1*, 5–16.
Liu, Y. (2004). *Construction project management* (2nd ed.). Tsinghua University Press.
Liu, Y., & Chen, J. (2020). Land system, financing model, and China's unique industrialization. *China Industrial Economy, 3*, 5–23.
Liu, Y., & Shen, K. (2011). Public capital financing by local governments in China: Problems, challenges, and countermeasures. *Financial Review, 3*(3), 1–18.
Lu, F., & Yao, Y. (2004). Legalization, financial development, and economic growth under financial repression. *China Social Sciences, 1*, 42–55.
Lv, B., & Tai, H. (2018). From fiscal contracting to the tax-sharing system: Unleashing two positive forces. *Finance & Trade Economics, 39*(10), 17–29.
Ma, J. (2020). High-quality economic development: Vivid practice of Xi Jinping's new socialist economic thought with Chinese characteristics. *Theory Journal, 7*, 37–40.
Ma, W., & Ma, C. (2018). Government guarantees, growth constraints, and the debt inflation trap of local governments. *Economic Research, 53*(5), 72–87.
Mao, J., & Xu, J. (2021). The market-oriented transformation of local financing platform companies: Institutional origins, characteristics, and paths to realization. *Finance & Trade Economics, 42*(3), 28–43.
Mao, J., Liu, P., & Lv, B. (2019). The institutional foundation of local public debt growth: Perspectives on both fiscal and financial aspects. *China Social Sciences, 9*, 45–67.
Miao, X., & Zhao, Y. (2019). The impact of local debt on regional total factor productivity growth: Group analysis based on different levels of fiscal independence. *Finance & Trade Economics, 40*(12), 50–64.
Ping, X., & Bai, J. (2006). China's fiscal decentralization and local public goods supply. *Finance & Trade Economics, 2006*(2), 49–55.
Qi, L., & Xu, L. (2017). Reforming public goods financing models to address shortcomings. *Economic Research References, 26*, 44–61.
Qi, X., Ke, Y., & Wang, S. (2009). Main risk factors in China's PPP projects: A case-based analysis. *China Soft Science, 5*, 107–113.
Qiao, H. (2008). The relationship between the nature of infrastructure and the financing model of infrastructure projects. *East China Economic Management, 3*, 74–78.
Shen, Y., Guo, F., & Li, Z. (2020). Local government's own fiscal capacity, business environment, and PPP project investment. *Finance & Trade Economics, 41*(12), 68–84.
Sun, Z., Liu, F., & Li, Z. (2005). Marketization degree, government intervention, and corporate debt structure: Evidence from listed companies in China. *Economic Research, 5*, 52–63.
Wang, H., Liu, M., & Cheng, W. (2020). Key and difficult points in the comprehensive implementation of public finance budget performance management. *China Collective Economy, 21*, 43–44.
Wang, W. (2015). *Research on the risks and prevention of local government financing platforms in China* [Master's thesis]. Capital University of Economics and Business.
Wang, Y. (2012). Trust mechanism, trust financing, and urban public goods supply model research. *Modern Management Science, 7*, 53–55.
Wang, Y., Chen, Y., & Du, J. (2016). Soft budget constraints and local government debt default risks in China: Evidence from financial markets. *Economic Research, 51*(11), 96–109.
Wildasin, D. E. (2004). The institutions of federalism: Toward an analytical framework. *National Tax Journal, 57*(2), 247–272.
World Bank. (2004). *Should borrowing by the public sector be decentralized?* [Decentralization Thematic Team Report].

Wu, Y. (2020). Building a sustainable financing mechanism for urban construction. *China Development Watch, 22*, 47–49.

Xiao, L. (2016). Market-oriented reform of public goods financing: From franchising to PPP models. *Science Development, 2*, 45–55.

Xie, X. (2009). Improve the system that matches central and local financial powers and responsibilities, and promote scientific development and social harmony. *Fiscal Research, 2*, 2–4.

Xu, J., Mao, J., & Guan, X. (2020). A reassessment of implicit local government debt: Precise definition of financing platform companies and financial potential. *Management World, 36*(9), 37–59.

Yakita, A. (2008). Sustainability of public debt, public capital formation, and endogenous growth in an overlapping generations setting. *Journal of Public Economics, 92*(3/4), 897–914.

Yang, J., Yang, Q., & Liu, K. (2018). Land-based financing and debt growth: Empirical research based on panel data from prefecture-level cities. *Finance & Trade Economics, 39*(2), 52–68.

Yang, L., & Yin, H. (2015). Fiscal capacity and expenditure responsibilities of county-level governments: From a fiscal hierarchy perspective. *Financial Research, 4*, 82–98.

Yang, R., & Nie, H. (2006). Incomplete contract theory: A review. *Economic Research, 2*, 104–115.

Yao, J. (2009). Application of PFI in public project financing. *Contemporary Economics, 2*, 100–101.

Yao, Y., & Yang, L. (2003). Institutional supply imbalance and the consequences of China's fiscal decentralization. *Strategy & Management, 3*, 27–33.

Zeng, B. (2019). Strengthening fiscal budget management and reforming the fiscal budget supervision system. *Fiscal & Accounting Learning, 36*, 99–101.

Zhang, C. (2006). *Research on financing for urban construction in China* [Doctoral dissertation]. Dongbei University of Finance and Economics.

Zhang, J., Gao, Y., Fu, Y., et al. (2007). Why does China have good infrastructure? *Economic Research, 3*, 4–19.

Zhang, L. (2020). Local government debt expansion strategy: Evidence from the issuance of urban investment bonds. *China Industrial Economy, 2*, 44–62.

Zhang, L., Nian, Y., & Liu, J. (2018). Land market fluctuations and local debt: The case of urban investment bonds. *Economics Quarterly, 17*(3), 1103–1126.

Zhang, L., Wei, H., & Ou, D. (2019). Land-based financing, local debt, and leverage: Land mortgage analysis of local financing platforms. *Financial Research, 3*, 92–110.

Zhang, Q., & Min, X. (2020). Institutional change, scale structure, and resolving local government debt risks. *Jianghan Forum, 1*, 24–30.

Zhao, Y., & Yang, Z. (2012). Examining the impact of democratic participation on public goods expenditure bias. *Management World, 6*, 74–85.

Zheng, G. (2010). China's social security reform and future development. *Journal of Renmin University of China, 24*(5), 2–14.

Zhuang, X., & Zeng, F. (2019). Research on PPP risk-sharing based on transaction cost theory. *Construction Economics, 40*(9), 39–45.

Chapter 5
The Supply Mechanism of Urban Public Infrastructure

Urban public infrastructure plays a crucial role as a physical foundation that connects various facets of socioeconomic activities within the city. Its quality directly impacts the living standards of urban residents, the productivity level of the city, and urban development. As urbanization and informatization progress, cities are expanding in size and the range of urban economic activities is diversifying, and urban management practices are becoming more scientific and varied, leading to continuous advancement in the scale, types, forms, and operational models of urban public infrastructure and the forming of a complex system. Effectively supplying public infrastructure to meet urban development demands and ensuring its efficient functionality presents a significant challenge in urban operations. This chapter provides an in-depth analysis of the current state of urban public infrastructure in China, detailing its characteristics, functions, and supply mechanisms, while exploring methods to evaluate its performance.

5.1 Urban Public Infrastructure and Its Functions

5.1.1 Urban Public Infrastructure and Its Composition

Urban public infrastructure is the essential material foundation for urban residents' lives and the city's production and operation, evolving with changes in urban socioeconomic activities. According to the *1994 World Development Report* by the World Bank, infrastructure is defined as permanent, complex engineering structures, equipment, facilities, and the services they provide, necessary for both enterprise production and residents' living (World Bank, 1994). The primary role of urban public infrastructure is to provide basic facilities that support urban economic activities and enhance the quality of residents' lives. In recent years, with the development of new energy technology, the internet, and big data, new public infrastructures

B. Wu et al., *Effective Supply Mechanism of Urban Public Goods*, Public Economy and Urban Governance in China, https://doi.org/10.1007/978-981-96-2608-3_5

such as public credit platforms, public information platforms, and logistics centers have also become important components of urban public infrastructure. These new public infrastructures offer platform-based, intermediary services to governments, enterprises, and consumers, constituting social public facilities within production and circulation fields, exhibiting characteristics of the public or quasi-public goods (Zhou, 2019).

To facilitate scientific research, many scholars have classified public infrastructure according to their research objectives. Functionally, urban public infrastructure typically includes water supply and drainage, energy, transportation, postal and telecommunication, environmental, and defense and disaster prevention facilities. Some scholars conceptualize urban public infrastructure as a system comprising six subsystems: energy systems, transportation systems, postal and telecommunications systems, water resources and supply drainage systems, environmental systems, and disaster prevention systems (Cheng et al., 2012). The World Bank (1994) categorizes urban public infrastructure based on its comprehensive functions into economic public infrastructure and social public infrastructure. Economic public infrastructure, which directly supports economic activities, includes transportation, postal and telecommunications, and energy supply, and is further subdivided into productive public infrastructure and living public infrastructure, depending on the nature of the services provided. In contrast, social public infrastructure refers to facilities that enhance people's quality of life, including educational, healthcare, cultural, social welfare, and public management services. This classification enriches the understanding of public infrastructure and its roles within urban settings.

Public infrastructure can be categorized into network and central types based on their functional forms (Biehl, 1991). Network public infrastructure includes transport networks, energy networks, and information networks, characterized by extensive spatial and fluid functionality. In Contrast, central public infrastructure, such as schools, hospitals, and museums, is characterized by spatial aggregation and fixed functionality. Based on the compensatory operational characteristics of urban public infrastructure investment projects, they can be classified into operational, quasi-operational, and non-operational categories. Operational infrastructure, including toll roads and bridges, generates revenues sufficient to recoup investments and yield profits. Quasi-operational infrastructure, such as rail transit and wastewater treatment plants, typically fails to fully recoup investments or achieve social average profitability. Non-operational infrastructure, including public education and health services, cannot generate income through operation (Chen et al., 2017).

Moreover, some scholars classify urban public infrastructure by technical performance into equipment-oriented hardware public infrastructure (including roads, railways, metros, airports, ports, power, communications, water supply, heating, and underground pipe networks) and technical public infrastructure (including software and high-tech equipment and materials used in information and hardware public infrastructure). Classified by the nature of demand, urban public infrastructure can be divided into basic security public infrastructure (mainly including water supply, power supply, gas supply, heating, and sewage and stormwater treatment systems) and economic and social development public infrastructure (including transport systems, communication systems, energy power systems, housing reserve, and cultural, health, and educational institutions and facilities) (Guo, 2008).

5.1.2 Basic Characteristics of Urban Public Infrastructure

Urban public infrastructure has distinctive features as the spatial carrier of urban socioeconomic activities and the operational system of urban production and life. In the following paragraphs, urban public infrastructure from the perspectives of its function, service scope, and differentiation from private products will be analyzed.

5.1.2.1 Public Nature

Urban public infrastructure is designed to serve all enterprises, organizations, families, and individuals. Unlike typical private products, public infrastructure is inherently indivisible, allowing it to support a wide array of production and living sectors, and because of high construction costs and economies of scale, it tends to be used in a broad range of areas. Despite differences in competitiveness and exclusivity, the basic physical characteristics and functional purposes of public infrastructure define their public or quasi-public nature.

In modern urban economies, advancements in ownership structures, technological methods, and market transaction methods enable certain urban public infrastructures, particularly those related to economic activities such as transport, communications, and energy, to be constructed and operated with private or social investment on a market basis. Despite similar investment and operational mechanisms with private goods, this infrastructure maintains a public nature. While most urban public infrastructure is state-owned or operated by state enterprises due to its public nature, investment, and operation reforms allow some public infrastructure to transition to private investment and operation while retaining its public function.

5.1.2.2 Externality

As a common resource of the city, the function of urban public infrastructure bears various externalities. First, it enhances the efficiency of factor mobility in urban economic activities and creates fundamental external production conditions for urban economic sectors, thus boosting production efficiency and unlocking urban manufacturing potential. Second, alongside producing positive external effects, it can also generate negative ones, such as urban noise, emissions, and restrictions on residents' freedom. The presence of externalities in public infrastructure, coupled with limitations in local government fiscal mechanisms, leads to unique phenomena in urban operations. For instance, governments in adjacent administrative regions may be reluctant to invest in environmental or transportation infrastructure (Tang, 2019).

Furthermore, urban public infrastructures tend to be larger in scale than private facilities, amplifying their externalities. However, advancements of technology and management practices are increasingly effective in internalizing these externalities.

5.1.2.3 Low (Non-) Profitability and Stable Benefits

As basic utility facilities, urban public infrastructure serves all city organizations and residents. It promotes orderly urban operations and distinguishes them from general goods by not aiming at profit maximization, and adhering to low (non-) profitability principles. When the government provides urban public infrastructure, the construction funds come directly from fiscal budgets, with tax revenue from infrastructure users financing the projects, thus imposing a non-profit nature on government-provided public infrastructure. In modern cities, with the marketization of public product supply, most public infrastructures are operated by commercial enterprises. Despite profit motives, these enterprises' operational rights stem from government authorizations and are usually conditional, hence limiting charges and profits, aligning them with low profitability objectives. While direct economic benefits for suppliers may be limited, the stable and large-scale nature of infrastructure services typically ensures a steady social revenue for operators, highlighting a key aspect of urban public infrastructure operations.

5.1.2.4 Systematic and Supporting Nature

Urban public infrastructure encompasses an extensive system, including underground, surface, and aerial subsystems. Different types of urban public infrastructures play a specific role in economic development, and the absence of any component can reduce the efficiency of urban economic activities. A thriving and livable city requires comprehensive public infrastructure that provides essential survival resources such as roads, water supply, and power, as well as foundational development elements like communication networks and educational facilities. Thus, high-quality urban development relies on an integrated public infrastructure system. These interdependent components form a comprehensive network that collectively drives urban economic growth (Tao et al., 2018).

As technology advances and lifestyles evolve, urban public infrastructure increasingly expands from physical to network information forms. The Internet and its applications usher in new urban public infrastructure, with the Internet of Things altering the content and breadth of urban public infrastructure, forming a large-scale system with new functionalities on existing material bases.

Additionally, rapid technological progress has raised the expectations of urban stakeholders on the quality of urban public infrastructure, leading to the integration of high-tech solutions that enhance the intelligence and user-friendliness of infrastructure, resulting in the emergence of modern public infrastructures. A notable example is Shanghai's bus station, which exemplified the "smart city" initiative by providing users with real-time information and route inquiries through an intuitive user-friendly interface (Zhong et al., 2019).

5.1.2.5 Social Welfare Nature

Most urban public infrastructures have public qualities, providing residents with easier access to educational, medical, cultural, and sports services. In modern urban socioeconomics, the increasing proportion of public product supply enhances the living standards of urban inhabitants and eliminates class disparities from unequal private wealth and income. Consequently, the availability and public nature of these infrastructures enhance overall social welfare, raising the individual welfare of urban residents across all socioeconomic strata.

5.1.3 Functions of Urban Public Infrastructure

During urban development, public infrastructure stands as one of the essential elements shaping development, production, and living standards. Especially under modern economic conditions, the economic agglomeration effect of cities relies on the regular operation of public infrastructures. The World Bank's surveys across various countries have shown that public infrastructure can promote economic growth, alleviate poverty, and improve the environment.

5.1.3.1 Investment Spillover Effect and Economic Growth Effect

As a key driver of social capital, urban public infrastructure has a substantial investment spillover effect. First, favorable public infrastructure can create optimal operating conditions for urban enterprises, stimulating corporate investments. For example, improved transportation infrastructure lowers logistics costs and boosts production and circulation efficiency, attracting more corporate investments. Empirical studies show that China's rapid infrastructure development since its reform and opening up has significantly improved the investment environment, thus attracting substantial foreign investments (Zhao, 2012). Quantitative research reveals that transportation infrastructure improvements accounted for 56.42% of foreign direct investment attraction in the Chengdu-Chongqing urban agglomeration (Yang et al., 2018). Ans also investing in urban public infrastructure generates significant forward and backward linkages, promoting growth in related industries.

Both domestic and international research has shown that urban public infrastructure investments contribute to economic growth through spillover effects. In the United States, between 1949 and 1985, the output elasticity of public investment toward economic growth was 0.39 (Aschauer, 1989). Analysis of U.S. manufacturing data from 1970 to 1987 found that public capital contributed 20%-30% to production growth (Schwartz, 1996). Subsequent studies revealed output elasticities for core public infrastructures (roads, highways, airports, water systems) between 0.055 and 0.110 from 1965 to 1983 across 50 U.S. states (Aschauer, 1990). Munnell (1990) analyzed data from 48 U.S. states between 1970 and 1986, using a Cobb–Douglas production function method, finding output elasticities of 0.06 for highways, 0.12 for water facilities, and 0.01 for other public infrastructure investments. A translog production function analysis revealed direct output elasticities of 0.04, 0.15, and -0.02 for highways, water facilities, and other public capital, respectively. Chinese researchers have also examined public infrastructure's impact on economic growth. Lou Hong's (2003) empirical research concluded that China's output elasticity of public infrastructure capital was 0.2347. Fan and Bai (2004) suggested an output elasticity as high as 0.695 for China's public infrastructure capital. Guo et al. (2021) noted a U-shaped trend in public infrastructure capital returns across different infrastructure types and regions, with social public infrastructures showing higher returns than economic ones, and the eastern region outpacing central and long-running low returns in the western region.

5.1.3.2 Social Welfare Enhancement Effect

Urban public infrastructure, whether pure public or quasi-public, inherently serves all urban organizations and individuals, enhancing social welfare, thus differing fundamentally from private products. The provision and service process of public infrastructure manifests its welfare effect, which varies with the type of the public infrastructure, and through coordination among various infrastructures, it generates external and ancillary welfare effects. For instance, improved transportation and public infrastructure efficiency boost consumption (Su et al., 2005; Wang, 2017). Educational infrastructure promotes education levels and human capital. Economic public infrastructure primarily boosts users' external efficiency, while social public infrastructure enhances the users' internal experiences to achieve its welfare benefits.

5.1.3.3 Spatial Scale Effect and System Effect

Generally, urban public infrastructure investments are large-scale, with extensive spatial distributions and service scopes that affect all aspects of urban socioeconomics. For effective functioning, systematic planning, construction, and operation within the entire city are essential. This integrated approach can reshape urban production and living patterns, thus increasing efficiency in economic transactions and social activities. Moreover, urban public infrastructure manifests strong system effects; the absence of any component hinders overall functioning. Interdependencies among various infrastructures, such as transport, environmental management, and communications, form a comprehensive urban public infrastructure system. Thus, it is crucial to consider both individual and inter-connected infrastructures for optimal systemic effects.

The spatial scale and system effects of urban public infrastructure underpin its functionalities in attracting enterprises and residents, thus promoting urban aggregation. Production-necessitated public infrastructure and associated services in urban settings mitigate economic activity costs. Empirical studies confirm that public infrastructure construction and service supply significantly drive industrial and enterprise aggregation in China (Ren et al., 2010; Tang et al., 2018; Yang et al., 2018).

5.1.3.4 Economic Efficiency Enhancement Effect

High-quality, comprehensive public infrastructure significantly boosts enterprise economic efficiency. First, a robust transportation infrastructure facilitates inter-regional product marketing, accelerating inventory clearance and thus increasing sales efficiency (Li et al., 2009; Liu et al., 2011). Second, improved public infrastructure aids resource mobility across regions, achieving Pareto improvements in resource allocation, thus mitigating resource misallocation and enhancing utilization efficiency (Zhang et al., 2019). Third, new urban infrastructures can fully leverage economic factors and create conducive conditions for technological innovations and technological advancements. Thus, urban public infrastructure functions as the socioeconomic "booster" and "lubricant", facilitating operations for energy supplies, supply chain security, and operational optimizations in cities. Consequently, a robust public infrastructure fosters cities' resource allocation capabilities, ultimately enhancing multifactor productivity (Xie, 2018). Fourth, networked public infrastructures tightly interlink neighboring regions, and positively impact neighboring regions' economic efficiency (Pereira et al., 2003; Cohen & Paul, 2004; Wei, 2010; Liu, 2010; Jin et al., 2012).

5.1.3.5 Urbanization and Population Mobility Effect

The diverse impacts of urban public infrastructure enhance convenience in urban life, improve social welfare, and attract rural populations, thus promoting urbanization and demographic change. In many countries, urbanization is closely linked to the expansion and enhancement of public infrastructure. Since the reform and opening up in China, urban public infrastructure construction has addressed both rural migration and economic growth demands. To achieve development and attract investments in development zones, cities require efficient public infrastructure—which is essential for land financial models. In this context, local governments accelerate economic infrastructure investments to spur land development, promote city land urbanization, and expand urban areas (Huang et al., 2014). Furthermore, urban public infrastructures surpass rural ones in scale, structure, and efficiency, especially in social services. This ensures residents' survival and development needs, underscoring urban advantages and attracting rural populations, thus driving urbanization.

5.2 The Scale and Structure of Urban Public Infrastructure Supply in China

5.2.1 Estimation of the Asset Value of China's Urban Public Infrastructure

Urban public infrastructure is extensive in scope, rich in content, and varied in forms, making the choice of measurement units directly critical for assessing its development. Currently, capitalizing public infrastructure is an effective measurement approach, commonly using flow and stock measurement methods. Capital flow refers to the investment amount at a specific point, while capital stock represents the total capital accumulated over a period, reflecting the scale of existing infrastructure and its overall service capacity.

Currently, China's statistical departments have not provided readily available statistics on urban public infrastructure capital, making it crucial to calculate capital stock for a true understanding of public infrastructure construction. Various methods can be used for this calculation:

(1) Investment substitution method: This approach adds the sectoral investment data of economic and social public infrastructure to determine the nominal total investment;
(2) Exclusion method: This method measures economic public infrastructure investment by subtracting real estate and household fixed asset investment from total fixed asset investment;
(3) Ratio method: It calculates capital stock by dividing capital formation or fixed asset investment by 10%;
(4) Fixed asset investment calculation: Here, fixed asset investment is used for urban public infrastructure investment;
(5) Perpetual inventory method: Similar to capital stock assessment methods, it offers an ongoing measure of accumulated investment.

Among these methods, the perpetual inventory method stands out as providing an objective measure of China's urban public infrastructure construction. Therefore, this book adopts this method to calculate urban public infrastructure capital stock (Jinge, 2016; Wang, 2016).

Based on the World Bank's definition of public infrastructure and the statistical classification in the *China Fixed Asset Investment Statistical Yearbook*, this book defines the statistical range of fixed asset investment in economic public infrastructure as "production and supply of electricity, gas, and water", "geological exploration and water management", "transportation, storage, and postal industries" for the period before 2002; From 2003 onwards, it includes "production and supply of electricity, gas, and water", "transportation, storage, and postal services", "information transmission, computer services, and software", and "water conservancy, environment, and public facility management". Social public infrastructure, which directly or indirectly improves human living quality, typically includes cultural, educational, social welfare, and healthcare facilities. Therefore, this book defines the statistical range of fixed asset investment in social public infrastructure as "healthcare, sports, and social welfare", "education, culture, and broadcasting arts", "scientific research and comprehensive technical services", and "government agencies, party agencies, and social organizations" before 2002; and from 2003 onwards, it includes "healthcare, social security, and social welfare", "education", "culture, sports, and entertainment", "scientific research, technical services, and geological exploration", and "public administration and social organizations". The depreciation rate for economic public infrastructure is set at 9.21%, for social public infrastructure at 8.51%, and the comprehensive depreciation rate at 8.85%. To eliminate inflation factors, the calculation of public infrastructure capital flow and stock uses the 1997 fixed asset investment price index as the base period, with results shown in Table 5.1.

Table 5.1 Statistics on China's public infrastructure capital flow and stock (Unit: 100 million yuan)

Year	Public infrastructure capital flow	Public infrastructure capital stock	Economic public infrastructure capital flow	Economic public infrastructure capital stock	Social public infrastructure capital flow	Social public infrastructure capital stock
1997	–	22,517.60	–	16,168.10	–	6349.50
1998	6820.38	27,423.77	5057.78	19,739.66	1762.60	7568.68
1999	6652.87	31,784.93	4937.08	22,892.40	1715.79	8646.00
2000	6485.35	35,516.46	4816.37	25,566.18	1668.98	9561.31
2001	8436.75	40,796.62	6089.04	29,201.36	2347.71	11,056.87
2002	9485.06	46,612.64	6609.75	32,981.50	2875.31	12,930.08
2003	15,372.52	57,309.55	11,431.36	40,849.27	3941.16	15,583.35
2004	25,247.80	75,087.54	19,380.50	54,487.08	5867.30	19,506.47
2005	30,818.73	95,810.83	23,965.38	70,567.44	6853.35	23,853.59
2006	36,680.70	119,384.64	29,420.10	89,549.71	7260.60	28,059.85
2007	41,711.80	143,882.10	33,662.30	109,316.28	8049.50	32,303.00
2008	50,262.40	169,934.71	40,592.30	130,220.22	9670.10	36,864.65
2009	70,307.77	210,006.09	56,625.30	162,225.77	13,682.47	44,244.46
2010	83,031.30	254,119.27	67,023.30	197,390.10	16,008.00	52,337.64
2011	81,461.53	289,615.87	64,992.59	224,827.90	16,468.95	59,363.01
2012	95,174.84	331,140.21	75,467.23	256,643.68	19,707.61	67,930.48
2013	115,188.70	382,494.64	92,514.80	296,913.45	22,673.90	77,744.29
2014	139,205.34	445,222.39	111,672.32	346,031.73	27,533.02	89,904.04
2015	164,282.08	521,428.95	132,648.41	406,335.25	31,633.67	104,130.63
2016	190,916.62	609,594.62	154,387.18	476,101.65	36,529.44	120,566.36
2017	216,775.86	699,614.24	175,744.96	547,345.22	41,030.90	137,048.80

Source Public infrastructure capital flow data derived from the *China Fixed Asset Investment Statistical Yearbook*, and the capital stock data is calculated based on this yearbook

As shown in Table 5.1, the overall public infrastructure investment in China has proliferated, with investment flow reaching approximately 21.68 trillion yuan in 2017, including 17.57 trillion yuan in economic public infrastructure and 4.10 trillion yuan in social public infrastructure. From 1949 to 1978, China's public infrastructure investment was minimal, with a significant lag in urban and rural infrastructure construction. After the reform and opening up, the construction speed accelerated, mainly due to increased infrastructure investment in central, western, and northeastern regions. In total, the national public infrastructure stock was approximately 69.96 trillion yuan in 2017, with economic and social public infrastructure stocks at 54.73 trillion yuan and 13.70 trillion yuan, respectively.

Given the disparities in social statuses and economic development levels across China's provinces (autonomous regions, municipalities), there must be significant differences in public infrastructure investment. Hence, the capital stock of public infrastructure across 31 provinces[1] (autonomous regions, municipalities) is further statistically analyzed, as shown in Table 5.2.

As observed in Table 5.2, the public infrastructure capital stock across various provinces (autonomous regions, municipalities) has shown a year-over-year increase. There is a notable regional disparity, with more extensive stocks in the developed eastern regions and smaller stocks in the underdeveloped western areas. However, with the implementation of national strategies for regional balance, such as the Western Development Strategy, the growth rate of capital stock in the central and western regions has been greater post-2005, narrowing the gap in public infrastructure capital flow between regions.

In terms of the capital stock of public infrastructure, Xue Guizhi (2018) measured the investment stock of ten types of municipal public infrastructure, including road transport, water supply, drainage, heating, gas, landscaping, sanitation facilities, environmental protection, flood control, and civil air defense, to reflect the stock level of urban municipal public infrastructure nationwide. The results are shown in Table 5.3.

The data in Table 5.3 show that since China's reform and opening up, the level of urban municipal public infrastructure stock has continuously risen, growing from 3.560 billion yuan in 1978 to 1,317.284 billion yuan in 2014. This significant increase correlates closely with China's rapid urbanization and industrialization processes.

5.2.2 Statistics on Physical Stock of Urban Public Infrastructure in China

The capital stock of public infrastructure can be estimated on the basis of the fixed asset investment of urban public infrastructure. However, fixed asset investment is a complex combination of various data, including historical construction worker wages and material costs, which cannot accurately reflect the actual construction conditions

[1] Due to the difficulty of data collection, this analysis excludes the regions of Hong Kong, Macau, and Taiwan.

Table 5.2 Public infrastructure capital stock across provinces (Autonomous Regions, Municipalities) (Unit: 100 million yuan)

Province (Autonomous Region, Municipality)	1997	2001	2005	2009	2013	2017
Beijing	1084	1750	3129	6405	9453	13,448
Tianjin	361	660	1718	4594	9329	15,338
Hebei	1524	2327	4483	9828	19,043	34,641
Liaoning	539	1248	2972	8543	18,077	21,737
Shanghai	781	1667	3611	8108	9693	12,288
Jiangsu	1750	2952	7653	13,367	23,197	43,635
Zhejiang	1469	2770	7266	13,164	20,425	38,173
Fujian	1192	1518	3120	7995	16,250	34,152
Shandong	1504	2599	6236	13,349	25,195	47,540
Guangdong	2648	3746	8009	15,900	26,120	40,042
Hainan	107	298	568	1296	2195	4099
Shanxi	349	910	2122	5145	10,176	16,243
Jilin	372	735	1707	4608	8506	14,910
Heilongjiang	729	1239	2358	5411	9762	14,842
Anhui	533	1042	2632	6753	12,585	25,408
Jiangxi	436	785	2566	5310	8884	17,000
Henan	1094	1895	4521	9326	15,431	30,298
Hubei	936	1938	3968	8388	15,526	29,621
Hunan	670	1218	2881	6866	13,744	28,718
Inner Mongolia	418	714	2998	7757	14,512	24,714
Guangxi	602	1181	2544	5940	12,595	24,779
Chongqing	416	721	2250	5359	9925	19,361
Sichuan	747	1959	4637	10,799	21,476	40,272
Guizhou	354	670	1834	3671	8129	19,897
Yunnan	493	1055	2649	6379	11,897	24,045
Tibet	50	156	457	765	1089	1274
Shaanxi	350	943	2420	6356	11,931	25,020
Gansu	318	610	1360	2888	6175	11,933
Qinghai	167	295	629	1197	2378	5422
Ningxia	189	309	653	1247	2234	4843
Xinjiang	336	889	1861	3290	6561	15,923

Source Calculated based on relevant data from the *China Fixed Asset Investment Statistical Yearbook*

Table 5.3 Urban municipal public infrastructure stock nationwide (1978 as a base year) (Unit: 100 million yuan)

Year	Amount	Year	Amount	Year	Amount	Year	Amount
1978	35.60	1988	203.66	1998	1093.78	2008	5376.76
1979	41.60	1989	227.08	1999	1336.76	2009	6331.52
1980	47.09	1990	251.70	2000	1584.29	2010	7825.60
1981	54.78	1991	286.43	2001	1858.96	2011	9149.68
1982	65.85	1992	341.06	2002	2214.69	2012	10,444.52
1983	76.39	1993	425.42	2003	2758.33	2013	11,811.00
1984	92.46	1994	520.99	2004	3185.09	2014	13,172.84
1985	116.53	1995	628.27	2005	3763.17		
1986	144.37	1996	746.95	2006	4251.98		
1987	172.95	1997	887.37	2007	4775.53		

Source Measurement of the capital stock and output elasticity of china's urban public infrastructure (Xue, *Economic Review*, 2018, No. 4)

and service capacity of public infrastructure. A more direct measure is to evaluate public infrastructure's physical stock statistically. According to the National Bureau of Statistics, the physical stock of urban public infrastructure in China is shown in Table 5.4.

It is evident in Table 5.4 that the physical stock of urban public infrastructure in China shows a noticeable trend: the physical stock of public infrastructure related to people's livelihood changes relatively minor, whereas the physical stock of economic public infrastructure changes significantly.

5.2.3 *Structure of Urban Public Infrastructure Supply in China*

As previously noted, in recent years, the supply of economic public products in urban areas of China has been much greater than that of social public products. This disparity is also evident in urban public infrastructure construction, where the stock of economic public infrastructure significantly surpasses that of social public infrastructure (see Table 5.5).

Table 5.5 shows that the structural ratio of economic to social public infrastructure nationwide has always been greater than two, showing an upward trend from 2.55 in 1997 to 3.99 in 2017. A significant turning point occurred in 2009 when the ratio exceeded 3, primarily due to China's economic stimulus plan implemented in response to the 2008 financial crisis, which allocated substantial funds towards economic public infrastructure construction. This structural imbalance is directly

Table 5.4 Statistics on urban public infrastructure physical stock

Project	2015	2016	2017	2018	2019
Length of water supply pipes/km	710,206	756,623	797,355	866,820	920,082
Length of drainage pipes/10,000 km	54	58	63	68	74
Length of gas pipelines/km	528,388	578,260	641,170	716,008	783,313
Length of heating pipelines/km	204,413	213,569	276,288	371,120	392,917
Length of roads/10,000 km	37	38	40	43	46
Railway operating mileage/10,000 km	12	12	13	13	14
Highway mileage/10,000 km	458	470	477	485	501
Expressway mileage/10,000 km	12	13	14	14	15
Number of public buses and trams	482,975	515,051	554,820	565,933	584,026
Number of sanitation vehicles	165,725	193,942	228,019	252,484	281,558
Number of waste treatment plants	890	940	1013	1091	–
Number of public toilets	126,344	129,818	136,084	147,466	153,426
Number of parks	13,834	15,370	15,633	16,735	18,038
Number of public libraries	3139	3153	3166	3176	3196
Number of hospital beds/10,000 beds	702	741	794	840	881
Number of research and development institutions	3650	3611	3547	3306	3217
Number of primary and secondary schools	242,930	229,751	218,903	212,739	210,784

Source China statistical yearbook (2016–2020)
Note The number of public libraries, hospital beds, research and development institutions, and primary and secondary schools data are national data from the *China Statistical Yearbook*, while other data are urban data. The length of gas pipelines includes artificial gas pipelines, liquefied petroleum gas pipelines, and natural gas pipelines. The length of the heating pipelines provides steam and hot water pipelines. The number of primary and secondary schools includes regular junior high schools and regular primary schools

related to China's economic growth goals and the competitive model of local governments. Regionally, all areas exhibit a high level of public infrastructure supply, indicating that provinces, autonomous regions, and municipalities have long prioritized economic public infrastructure construction over social public infrastructure.

Table 5.5 Structure of public infrastructure supply in China (1997–2017)

	1997	2001	2005	2009	2013	2017
Nationwide	2.55	2.64	2.96	3.67	3.82	3.99
Beijing	1.79	1.22	1.45	2.62	2.93	3.63
Tianjin	2.32	3.12	3.42	5.46	5.37	4.54
Hebei	2.02	2.62	2.16	3.40	4.19	4.21
Liaoning	1.98	2.78	2.41	3.69	3.82	4.11
Shanghai	2.19	2.48	3.41	6.51	5.77	5.66
Jiangsu	2.45	2.44	3.24	3.81	3.58	3.29
Zhejiang	2.76	2.88	3.88	5.30	4.94	5.08
Fujian	5.97	4.41	3.82	4.54	4.81	5.13
Shandong	2.95	2.64	1.63	1.64	1.61	1.85
Guangdong	3.47	2.74	3.15	4.29	4.96	5.14
Hainan	0.98	2.26	2.63	2.61	3.11	3.54
Shanxi	3.42	4.80	5.86	6.89	6.38	6.13
Jilin	3.23	1.99	1.99	3.45	3.91	3.94
Heilongjiang	4.17	2.65	2.43	3.06	3.25	3.22
Anhui	1.94	2.30	2.19	3.16	2.93	3.24
Jiangxi	4.74	4.05	3.26	3.19	3.32	3.30
Henan	1.77	2.33	3.36	3.38	3.61	3.70
Hubei	1.70	2.33	3.20	3.24	3.17	4.07
Hunan	1.57	2.06	2.15	3.05	3.26	3.15
Inner Mongolia	2.41	2.64	5.22	5.11	5.41	5.86
Guangxi	4.15	4.56	4.89	4.74	4.58	3.98
Chongqing	2.04	1.86	2.94	4.43	4.88	6.31
Sichuan	1.86	2.73	3.71	4.87	5.59	5.84
Guizhou	7.85	6.32	5.88	6.55	8.58	7.09
Yunnan	1.38	2.09	3.87	4.73	4.87	4.27
Tibet	0.72	1.98	2.49	2.33	2.47	2.77
Shaanxi	1.73	2.83	2.47	2.26	2.50	3.54
Gansu	4.05	2.90	2.52	2.21	2.59	2.85
Qinghai	6.95	4.80	4.65	4.90	3.73	4.35
Ningxia	10.81	6.82	5.87	4.85	5.23	5.75
Xinjiang	1.87	3.09	3.36	3.70	4.78	4.92

Source Derived by dividing the stock of economic public infrastructure by the stock of social public infrastructure for each province (autonomous region, municipality)

5.3 Analysis of the Investment and Financing of Urban Public Infrastructure in China

5.3.1 Investment Scale and Growth Trends in Urban Public Infrastructure in China

For decades, public infrastructure investment in Chinese cities has primarily relied on government fiscal expenditure. Since the late 1980s, capital markets have also been utilized for investment and financing, with some projects allowing participation from private and foreign capital. During the planned economy period, due to economic development constraints, urban public infrastructure investments mainly aimed at providing water, electricity, coal, and roads for industrial development. It wasn't until the 1990s, with the acceleration of urbanization and the rise of urban real estate, that comprehensive urban public infrastructure was developed. After the 1990s, especially following the financial crisis in 2008, economic public infrastructure construction became a driving engine for economic growth, and investment in social public infrastructure also increased steadily with urban social development (see Table 5.6).

As shown in Table 5.6, urban fixed asset and public infrastructure investments have been growing in recent years, with 2017 investment amounting to approximately 63,168.4 billion yuan and 14,000.5 billion yuan, respectively. As a significant component of urban fixed asset investment, public infrastructure investment increased its share from 17% in 2014 to 22% in 2017, with investment speeds accelerating. In recent years, urban public infrastructure construction projects have increased, expanding from energy facilities and transportation facilities to safety management and underground utility corridors, with the investment proportion relative to fixed asset investment constantly increasing.

Table 5.7 shows that the transportation sector has the highest investment in urban municipal utilities. For example, in 2019, the investment in rail transit was 585.560 billion yuan, and 765.530 billion yuan in roads and bridges. Gas and central heating had a respective investment of 24.27 billion yuan and 33.3 billion yuan in 2019.

Table 5.6 Urban public infrastructure investment and fixed asset investment (Excluding Households) (2014–2017)

Project	2014	2015	2016	2017
Public infrastructure investment/100 million yuan	86,669	101,271	118,878	140,005
Fixed asset investment/100 million yuan	502,005	551,590	596,501	631,684
Public infrastructure as a percentage of fixed asset invest/%	17	18	20	22

Source 2018 Urban public infrastructure construction market situation analysis report
Note Public infrastructure investment does not include the production and supply of electricity, heat, gas, and water

Table 5.7 Fixed asset investment in national urban municipal utilities by industry (2015–2019) (Unit: 100 million yuan)

Project	2015	2016	2017	2018	2019
Total fixed asset investment	16,204.44	17,459.97	19,327.61	20,123.20	20,126.30
Water supply	619.93	545.85	580.14	543.00	560.10
Gas	350.47	408.91	445.68	295.10	242.70
Central heating	516.83	481.87	584.20	420.00	333.00
Rail transit	3707.15	4079.48	5045.22	6046.90	5855.60
Roads and bridges	7414.00	7564.33	6996.65	6922.40	7655.30
Underground utility corridors		294.71	240.83	619.20	558.10
Drainage	982.68	1222.51	673.37	1529.90	1562.40
Flood control			421.05		
Landscaping	1594.65	1670.15		1854.70	1844.80
Sanitation	398.04	445.21	1759.64	470.50	557.40
Others	620.70	746.97	1390.95	1421.40	956.90

Source China urban construction statistical yearbook

Generally, economic public infrastructure investment significantly outweighs social public infrastructure investment within urban municipal utilities.

5.3.2 *Analysis of Investment Sources and Structure in Urban Public Infrastructure*

5.3.2.1 Government Budget Investment and Financing Investment

Government fiscal budget expenditures and various forms of financing investments account for a considerable proportion of urban public infrastructure investment in China. According to the *China Urban Construction Statistical Yearbook*, the fixed asset investment amounts for projects such as water supply, gas, central heating, rail transit, roads and bridges, drainage, flood control, landscaping, sanitation, and underground utility corridors can be calculated based on funding sources. Due to the difficulty in obtaining accurate data on government municipal project investments, this book roughly classifies central and local fiscal appropriations as direct government investments (Yan Chengliang, Gong Liutang, 2014), as shown in Table 5.8.

From Table 5.8, it can be seen that from 2015 to 2019, the proportion of government budgetary investment in urban municipal utility investment remained around 30%. Local governments are the major investors, with relatively small central government investment. In 2019, central government investment was only 41.3 billion yuan, while local government investment amounted to 545.7 billion yuan. From 2015 to

Table 5.8 Government direct investment in national urban municipal utilities construction (2015–2019) (Unit: 100 million yuan)

Project	2015	2016	2017	2018	2019
Total investment/100 million yuan	1527	16,377	18,245	17,839	18,871
Central fiscal appropriations/100 million yuan	202	119	290	255	413
Local fiscal appropriations/100 million yuan	4406	5184	5466	4552	5457
Government investment (Budgetary Investment) /100 million yuan	4609	5303	5756	4808	5870
Government budgetary investment as a % of total investment	30	32	32	27	31

Source China urban construction statistical yearbook

2019, central government investments fluctuated, whereas local government investments generally maintained a growth trend. This is primarily because following the 1994 tax-sharing reform, the central government transferred significant responsibilities to local governments and entrusted the construction funds to local governments through transfer payments, making local governments the leading force in urban public infrastructure investment.

The increase in government budgetary public infrastructure investment depends on the rise in government revenue, particularly the increase in land use rights transfer fees, which has been previously discussed in this book and will not be repeated here. In addition to investing in public infrastructure through budgetary expenditures, local governments also raise funds through financing platforms for public infrastructure investment. The primary function of local government financing platforms is to provide financing services for local government investment projects. Further analysis of financing platforms raising funds for urban public infrastructure is provided in other chapters of this book.

5.3.2.2 Private and Social Investment

The reform of urban public product investment and financing mechanisms in China mainly involves the integration of market mechanisms into public infrastructure projects, enabling private and social capital to participate directly. To estimate the proportion of social funds in urban municipal utilities investment, this book considers sources of funds other than central and local fiscal appropriations as social capital investment in public infrastructure. Given the limitations in data availability, the following section selectively reflects social capital investment through municipal utilities construction funds (see Table 5.9).

From Table 5.9, it can be seen that construction funds for urban public infrastructure are mainly raised through government-controlled companies directly borrowing loans, various investment platforms raising funds, PPP, and other methods, which also include a portion of social funds. The proportion of foreign and private direct

Table 5.9 Social investment in fixed assets of national urban municipal utilities construction (2015–2019) (Unit: 100 million yuan)

Project	2015	2016	2017	2018	2019
Domestic loans	3986	4339	4988	4509	5039
Bonds	189	133	163	117	392
Foreign capital utilization	47	35	29	47	50
Self-raised funds	4258	3963	4998	5105	4707
Other funds	2187	2603	2312	3254	2813
Social investment (Off-Budget Investment)	10,667	11,073	12,489	13,032	13,001

Source China urban construction statistical yearbook

investment has always been minimal. Infrastructure and other municipal special bonds approved or directly issued by the central government have increased in recent years but remain a small overall proportion. Although most social funds come from financial markets, they essentially still represent government investments or liabilities.

5.3.2.3 Public–Private Partnership (PPP) Investment

To diversify investment channels and reform mechanisms for urban public infrastructure, China has promoted the PPP model since 2014. According to the Ministry of Finance's Government and Social Capital Cooperation Center website, by February 2021, the national PPP project management database had accumulated 9,965 projects with an investment amount of 15.35 trillion yuan. PPP projects showed a growth trend until 2018, peaking in 2017 with 3,381 projects amounting to 5,167.3 billion yuan. However, affected by the Ministry of Finance's document No. 92 in 2017, which regulated the operation of PPP projects, the number and funding of PPP projects sharply declined from 2018 onward.

According to the data from the National Development and Reform Commission's PPP project library, most PPP projects in China are urban public infrastructure investment projects (refer to Tables 4.27 and 4.28 in Chapter Four).

5.3.3 Factors Influencing Urban Public Infrastructure Investment and Financing in China

5.3.3.1 Rate of Return

In a market economy system, the marginal rate of return on capital determines the direction of capital movement, a rule that also applies to public infrastructure investment and financing. With the advancement of market mechanisms in the construction and operation of public infrastructure, the market role in capital allocation has become increasingly prominent, and the marginal rate of return on capital has increasingly significant impacts. Theoretically, suppose the marginal rate of return on capital is greater than or not less than that in non-public infrastructure fields. In that case, private capital will enter the public infrastructure field, thereby increasing investment in urban public infrastructure. Conversely, if the former is lower than the latter, private capital will be reluctant to enter the public infrastructure field. Additionally, as urban public infrastructure belongs to public goods, the government often sets high service or operational prices, requiring construction and operating enterprises to have low profitability or even no profitability. This significantly impacts private enterprises motivated by maximizing capital returns. Therefore, the government often serves as the prominent investor in urban public infrastructure. Also, given the long-term nature of urban public infrastructure investment, particularly under capital market conditions where public infrastructure capital has a certain degree of transaction liquidity, some enterprises participate in public infrastructure investment to gain long-term stable returns despite lower project investment returns.

5.3.3.2 Political System and Institutional Factors

Economic activities are closely influenced by a country's basic economic system, especially economic activities in public product sectors related to public welfare and national development. Public infrastructure is a complex system characterized by diverse types, large scale, significant investment, and high construction technology requirements. It directly affects the vital interests of urban residents and the economic activities of urban enterprises, making its construction and operation highly influenced by the national political system and social governance mechanisms. Typically, due to the public nature of these goods, the government is responsible for their construction. In the absence of particular institutional arrangements, private capital generally shows little interest in entering the public infrastructure field for public welfare. Historically, with economic development and urban prosperity, public infrastructure has been predominantly government-funded. However, issues such as administrative corruption, inefficiency, and fiscal strain arise in the government-led construction and operation of public facilities. Consequently, since the late 1970s, economically developed Western countries have reformed the economic institutions of the public sector, implementing privatization of public infrastructure projects. Although this reform process is ongoing and influenced by the mixed economic system, public infrastructure investment and construction mechanisms show a trend toward public–private cooperation.

In China, since reform and opening up, the establishment of a socialist market economy has brought significant changes to the institutional mechanisms of the public product sector. As discussed in previous sections, China's public goods supply mechanism has transformed from a government supply mechanism to a pluralistic supply mechanism involving the government, market, and society. This transformation has occurred alongside changes in China's economic system, with public infrastructure construction and operation being among the earliest and most thoroughly reformed areas introducing market mechanisms.

Furthermore, the nature of the socialist market economy in China necessitates that the government plays a leading role in supplying public goods and representing public interests. Consequently, although private and social capital investment is on the rise in urban public infrastructure investment, central and local governments remain the primary investors. Additionally, some scholars assert that the investment behavior of local government officials in China is influenced by the central government's evaluation mechanisms, thereby affecting the proportion of public infrastructure construction expenditure in local government public spending. In the competition for regional economic growth, local governments increase public infrastructure investment to promote local economic development (Tang & Chen, 2012; Chu & Wang, 2019; Estache & Sinha, 1999; Kappeler & Vaelilae, 2008; Ding et al., 2015).

5.3.3.3 Government Financial Factors

The level of economic development and government financial resources influences the scale of urban public infrastructure investment and construction. Government budget revenue and public expenditure structure determine the level and structure of public infrastructure investment. A financially strong government has a more significant public expenditure budget, leading to larger-scale urban public infrastructure construction. In national fiscal relations, if the central government possesses more substantial financial resources, there will be more investment in national public infrastructure construction. Conversely, financially robust local governments, with more funding channels, will focus on constructing public infrastructure within their administrative regions. If local government finances are insufficient, they will be unable to provide infrastructure effectively.

5.3.3.4 Financial Market Development Factors

Urban public infrastructure projects usually involve large-scale construction and investment. Relying solely on government financial resources can be insufficient, especially during rapid economic development and significant urbanization. Therefore, both government-led initiatives and social capital-led urban public infrastructure construction significantly depend on the development and openness of the financial market. On the one hand, for less competitive and more public infrastructure, financial market arrangements can facilitate institutional innovation and diversify ownership structures. On the other hand, a well-developed financial market can mobilize societal funds towards urban public sectors and reduce financing costs.

5.4 Urban Public Infrastructure Supply Mechanisms

5.4.1 Evolution of Urban Public Infrastructure Supply Mechanisms

5.4.1.1 Theories of Urban Public Infrastructure Supply

The theoretical discourse on public infrastructure supply mechanisms has evolved from a binary debate between government and market supply to an advocacy for diversified supply mechanisms. Supporters of the government supply mechanism argue that urban public infrastructure is a public good characterized by externalities, non-exclusivity, and non-competitiveness, which can lead to market failures. Thus, government investment in public infrastructure is essential for public welfare, as highlighted by economists like Adam Smith, Keynes, and Samuelson.

However, government supply mechanisms can also experience failure. According to public choice theory, the government is also a microeconomic entity and does not always prioritize public interest in economic activities. Additionally, government behavior is not always rational, leading to mistakes, especially in the absence of adequate information. Scholars like Wolf and Stiglitz identify externalities as a primary contributor to government failure. For example, while public expenditure projects may benefit the majority, they may also impose external costs on a minority. Other causes include imperfect competition, where public services are monopolistic (a natural monopoly), information asymmetry, and distributional inequities. Clearly, public infrastructure provided by a "failing" government is not the best institutional arrangement. Therefore, a market supply mechanism based on private property theory may provide a more efficient means of supplying public infrastructure (Yue, 2009).

With the development of theories such as the property rights theory of the New Institutional Economics School, Tiebout's "voting by foot" mechanisms, and Hurwicz's practical incentive theory, the core issue of public infrastructure supply mechanisms is no longer about choosing between market and government mechanisms. Instead, the focus has shifted to how to innovate supply institutions and supply methods to leverage the advantages of different supply mechanisms. Oates (1972) proposed that the selection of public service projects should be based on the needs of local residents, giving decision-making power over public goods to the lowest administrative level. This approach can obtain accurate information about residents' consumption preferences for public goods at a lower cost, thereby better addressing the benefits and costs of residents enjoying public goods. Ostrom (1990) analyzed the possibility of solving public affairs using non-state (decentralized) and non-market (privatized) solutions. She argued that problems do not exclusively require state or market interventions but can be addressed through social self-organization and autonomy (the third sector). These theories provide significant insights for studying urban public infrastructure supply mechanisms. As our understanding deepens, the trend toward diversification of supply mechanisms becomes increasingly evident. Adequate urban public infrastructure relies on various components, including funding, construction, management, consumption, and maintenance. The construction and operation of urban public infrastructure can be segmented, allowing for different entities and mechanisms to be selected for each phase. Particularly with technological innovation and capital market development, this segmentation facilitates the establishment of diverse supply mechanisms for urban public infrastructure.

5.4.1.2 Evolution of Urban Public Infrastructure Supply Mechanisms in China

During the planned economy period, urban public infrastructure in China was invested and managed by the government and state-owned enterprises. After the reform and opening up, China gradually allowed private capital to participate in the investment and construction of urban public infrastructure. However, due to the public goods nature of public infrastructure and institutional path dependence, the government has not carried out thorough reforms in the public infrastructure field. Therefore, the supply of urban public infrastructure in China still follows a pattern dominated by the government supply mechanism, supplemented by market and third-sector supply mechanisms such as social organizations. The evolution of urban public infrastructure supply mechanisms in China can be divided into the following stages:

(1) Government Supply Mechanism Stage During the Planned Economy Period

In this period, the planning, construction, and operation of urban public infrastructure in China were entirely controlled by central and local governments. The administrative level determined the scale and facilities of urban construction, with funds allocated by higher-level finance. Notably, the use and services of urban public infrastructure were also allocated by government plans. Prices of municipal public infrastructure products and services such as water, electricity, coal, and transportation were determined by government plans, and some public infrastructure was supplied based on unit nature and administrative level. Due to the backward technology and lack of investment funds, cities generally face issues such as outdated public infrastructure, poor systems, and insufficient scale. This also led to high operating costs for infrastructure, with municipal enterprises operating at a loss. Meanwhile, the demand for infrastructure such as transportation, telecommunications, and energy by urban residents could not be met.

(2) Government-Dominated Supply Mechanism with Moderate Introduction of Market Mechanism Stage

In this stage, the government introduced a market supply mechanism, with state-owned enterprises as investment and operation entities. As industrialization and urbanization accelerated, the demand for public infrastructure in urban economic activities increased, requiring infrastructure such as transportation. However, due to insufficient construction funds, the government found it difficult to raise financial funds to expand the infrastructure construction scale. Starting in the 1990s, government public goods departments were forced to reform, attempting to introduce foreign and domestic private capital investment in fields such as transportation, water, and electricity. Examples include introducing foreign investment to build water plants, power plants, and bridges through BOT (Build-Operate-Transfer) methods. One such project was the Laibin B Power Plant in Guangxi, arranged by the former State Planning Commission as a BOT pilot project. On the other hand, reforms separated government functions from enterprise management, reorganizing government departments responsible for urban public infrastructure into state-owned enterprises to carry out construction and operation activities. The reliance on financial allocations for infrastructure construction funds gradually changed, beginning to absorb private and social funds, particularly through the financial market. Consequently, the government began establishing state-owned infrastructure investment enterprises, whose main business was investing in and operating urban public infrastructure. Although these enterprises were government-controlled state-owned enterprises, they primarily financed, constructed, and operated through market mechanisms. This created a supply mechanism where the investment entity and property owner were government enterprises, but construction and operation were carried out in market-oriented ways. Especially after the tax-sharing reform, China clarified the financial and administrative powers between the central and local governments. Under the dual development goals of economic growth and urbanization, the pressure on urban and development zone infrastructure construction demand increased, and funding became tighter. However, with the development of the land transaction market, local governments obtained significant revenue by selling land use rights, raising most of the urban infrastructure construction funds, which promoted the development of market supply mechanisms for urban public infrastructure.

(3) Coexistence Stage of Government Supply Mechanism, Market Supply Mechanism, and Multisubject Cooperation Mechanism

China's economy was hard hit in the 2008 global financial crisis. To combat external economic shocks, public product investment, primarily in public infrastructure construction, became a crucial force supporting China's economic growth. Subsequently, the investment and financing mechanisms, operation mechanisms, and service mechanisms of public infrastructure underwent considerable changes. In the investment field, under a government-led framework, resources were allocated through the market, with private investment, public–private partnerships, and government-social organization cooperation increasingly entering the public infrastructure construction field. Meanwhile, many public infrastructure enterprises were restructured and listed to become public companies. The market-oriented operation of urban public infrastructure gradually expanded, forming a diversified supply mechanism pattern in the urban public infrastructure field. A recent example is the construction of the Hangzhou-Shaoxing-Taizhou high-speed railway, a PPP (Public–Private Partnership) project jointly funded by private capital, China Railway Group Limited, Zhejiang Provincial Transportation Investment Group Co., Ltd., and local governments, with private capital holding the controlling stake. This project, with a total investment of approximately 52 billion yuan, is operated and managed by commercial enterprises with autonomous ticket pricing rights.

5.4.2 Investment Mechanisms for Urban Public Infrastructure in China

5.4.2.1 Investors in Urban Public Infrastructure

The main investors in urban public infrastructure include the government and various enterprises. Through financial market instruments, individuals and other social institutions can also be involved in the investment. The government primarily invests in infrastructure with strong public characteristics and low profitability, while different market entities invest in infrastructure with potential economic returns. The third sector, driven by public welfare purposes, fills the gaps left by government and market supplies.

So far, the government remains the largest investor in urban public infrastructure construction and operations in China, involving both central and local governments. These entities differ significantly in their investment priorities due to their varying functions and goals. The central government focuses on projects with cross-regional impact, whereas local governments concentrate on improving local infrastructure to enhance service capacity. In terms of financing tools, the central government relies mainly on fiscal budgets and debt financing, while local governments use a mix of tax-based fiscal budgets, central government transfers, government bonds, land revenues, and loans from financing platforms.

Market investors in urban public infrastructure primarily include enterprises, individuals, and foreign investments. Enterprises use their funds and loans for infrastructure projects, while individuals participate by purchasing government bonds and stocks. With increased openness, foreign capital also engages in infrastructure projects through direct investments and joint ventures. These investors seek capital performance returns. In the past decade, innovations in capital markets and financing systems have seen private capital extensively invest in urban infrastructure through PPPs and equity participation, deeply integrating into infrastructure operations and services.

The third sector involves various social organizations and philanthropic foundations. Funded mainly through social donations and non-profit funds established by corporations and social groups, these organizations face small and unstable funding and are vulnerable to external interference. However, their targeted services can enhance the supply quality of service-oriented urban infrastructure.

5.4.2.2 Investment Mechanisms for Urban Public Infrastructure

Investment mechanisms vary among different public infrastructure projects. Some infrastructure integral to national and public welfare, such as municipal pipelines, urban roads, urban ecological environments, and public information networks, are non-profit and primarily funded by the government. Other infrastructure, providing urban production and living services, can be profitably operated and marketed, including water treatment plants, sewage treatment plants, gas plants, heating stations, toll roads, bridges, and public transportation. These are typically funded and operated by commercial enterprises through policy-making or market tools (Wang, 2002).

The degree of publicness of urban public infrastructure is typically determined by its exclusivity and competitiveness. This categorization splits urban infrastructure into private product nature, quasi-public product nature, and pure public product nature, as shown in Table 5.10.

Advancements in technology and capital markets enable some traditionally exclusive public goods projects to achieve cost recovery through fees, enhancing investment competitiveness. Changes in institutional, technological, and market conditions in public goods economic activities also spur significant shifts in infrastructure investment and operation modes. These now consider the identification and fee-collection feasibility rather than project nature and function, enabling privatized or collaborative government-enterprise operations under particular institutional arrangements.

Furthermore, infrastructure projects can be classified by their cash flow and economic returns during operation. This method divides urban infrastructure into market-operable, quasi-market-operable, and non-market-operable projects (Cui et al., 2009). Market-operable projects, akin to private products, include electricity, highways, and water supply, which, though public, allow for fee-for-service through

Table 5.10 Attributes and investment modes of urban public infrastructure

Classification	Project attributes	Infrastructure projects	Investment mechanisms & investors
Private product nature	Exclusive, competitive	Electricity, tap water, telecom, taxi platforms, sports venues	Market mechanism: private enterprises, state-owned enterprises
Quasi-public product nature	Private exclusive, partially competitive	Primary education, information networks, public transportation	Government and market mechanisms: government, state-owned enterprises, private enterprises
Pure public product nature	Non-exclusive, non-competitive	Public safety, public health, parks, roads	Government mechanism: government

technology, attracting private investment and market operation. Given the multi-stage, long-term, high-cost nature of infrastructure investment, government policy support is essential to attract private and social capital.

Quasi-market-operable projects, like quasi-public product infrastructure, primarily provide public services to urban production and life. These projects, subject to societal and political constraints, innovate through technical and operational models for market operation. As their pricing impacts wider society, they are strictly regulated, resulting in lower investment returns requiring government subsidies and protection. However, given high social demand, significant investor interest, and operational scale, there is ample competitive space.

Public product infrastructure, fundamental to urban operation and development, remains challenging to market operation due to non-fee collection or difficulty in fee collection. Taxes paid by urban enterprises and residents primarily fund this infrastructure's construction and operation, making the government the key investor and operator for such projects.

5.4.2.3 Transformation of Urban Public Infrastructure Investment and Financing Systems

The systems for urban public infrastructure investment and financing are designed to meet public interest needs and oversee the fundraising, utilization, supervision, and management of construction funds. Investment involves gathering financial resources to construct infrastructure projects. Regarding supply, funding sources come from multiple economic sectors and actors, particularly taxes collected from urban enterprises and residents. Demand is based on the public needs of urban socioeconomic units and residents. Given the nature of public infrastructure, investment decisions require stringent institutional regulation across project selection, investor identification, and fund management.

A typical decision process for large-scale public infrastructure projects in China involves government or relevant organization proposals, expert and public consultations, legislative discussions, and final approval. Projects, based on their nature, select investors through competitive consultations, inviting bids, or competitive negotiations, ensuring compliance with government regulations.

Before the reform and opening up, under the planned economy system, the central government had all financial and administrative powers. With financial powers, the revenues of state-owned enterprises were primarily owned by the state and used according to national policies. With administrative powers, to ensure the smooth operation of the planned economy system, the government implemented a comprehensive policy in both social welfare and economic construction. Additionally, the government provided full financial guarantees throughout the urban life. Consequently, for highly public urban infrastructure, the government fully funded construction projects, which were built by relevant government departments or state-owned enterprises. After the reform and opening up, the urban public sector introduced a market economy system, gradually adjusting the relationship and roles of the government and market in resource allocation. Private capital is progressively invested in urban public infrastructure. Particularly after the tax-sharing reform, the financial and administrative responsibilities between the central and local governments became more apparent, with local governments beginning to take primary responsibility for investing in urban public infrastructure. Due to financial constraints, local governments began to explore market mechanisms for public infrastructure construction and introduce private and social capital.

With ongoing economic reforms, foreign investment was also allowed in China's urban public infrastructure construction. The *Foreign Investment Industrial Guidance Catalogue*, published in 1995, included urban public infrastructure construction projects. Currently, projects open to direct foreign investment include urban sewage and waste treatment, urban transportation infrastructure construction and operation, and the production and supply of water, electricity, and gas, among others (Yuan et al., 2017). With the promotion of the free trade zone system, some cities started implementing a negative list for foreign investment, allowing foreign investors to invest in almost all areas of urban public infrastructure.

Urban public infrastructure financing involves raising funds for investments in urban infrastructure, serving as the initial phase of such projects. Before the reform and opening up, funds for urban public infrastructure construction were primarily raised through government fiscal appropriations, with the government supporting investments through unified planning and allocation. After the reform and opening up, China began introducing market economic mechanisms, diversifying public infrastructure financing channels and methods. (a) Besides taxes, revenue from land sales became a significant source of funds for public infrastructure construction, significantly enhancing government fiscal investment capacity; (b) In addition to investment from government fiscal budgets, financing from various platforms and state-owned construction companies became a significant source of public infrastructure construction funds; (c) China gradually relaxed restrictions on domestic and foreign private capital and social funds, allowing them to enter the urban public infrastructure investment field through various means; (d) Government-enterprise cooperation introduced large amounts of social capital into urban public infrastructure through project financing methods like BOT (Build-Operate-Transfer), TOT (Transfer-Operate-Transfer), and equity financing methods like PPP (Public–Private Partnership). These initiatives yielded positive outcomes in projects like urban water supply, sewage treatment, and waste management.

It can be expected that with the deepening of market-oriented reforms in China, the market-based methods of urban public infrastructure financing will continue to diversify. In April 2020, the China Securities Regulatory Commission and the National Development and Reform Commission jointly issued a notice on advancing the pilot work of Real Estate Investment Trusts (REITs) in the infrastructure sector, marking the official start of the pilot work of public REITs in China's public infrastructure sector. In August 2020, the China Securities Regulatory Commission issued the *Guidelines for Public Offering of Public Infrastructure Securities Investment Funds*, marking the launch of public infrastructure REITs. Real Estate Investment

Trusts (REITs) are essential for securitizing real estate and some public infrastructure. Infrastructure or real estate securitization involves converting relatively illiquid, non-securitized infrastructure or real estate directly into securities assets in the capital market, enabling property rights transfer transactions through financial markets. Real estate securitization includes two primary forms: project financing securitization and mortgage securitization. This financial tool effectively revitalizes existing assets, creating a virtuous investment cycle, increasing the proportion of direct financing, and reducing corporate leverage ratios. Moreover, REITs offer high liquidity, stable returns, and robust security, enriching investment varieties in the capital market and expanding social capital investment channels (Xie Song, 2020). REITs provide small and medium-sized investors with opportunities to invest in real estate and public infrastructure with stable returns, enabling public participation in urban real estate and public infrastructure investment, embodying the principles of inclusive finance.

5.4.3 Issues and Reform Measures in the Investment and Financing System for Urban Public Infrastructure

5.4.3.1 Existing Issues

After over 40 years of reforms, significant changes have taken place in China's investment and financing systems for urban public infrastructure. Notably, there has been a steady increase in marketization and investment efficiency. However, with the deepening of reforms and the growing demands, problems have emerged in the investment and financing mechanisms for urban public infrastructure, which include:

(1) Frozen Investment System

Traditionally, the government has played a dominant role as the leading investor and operator of urban public infrastructure. Though reforms since the opening up have shifted some responsibilities away from the government, the process remains incomplete. In recent years, the government's dominance as the largest investor in public infrastructure has become more pronounced, with private capital showing tendencies to exit the field. This situation is likely to cause a shortage of funds for urban public infrastructure construction (Wang et al., 2011) and hinder improvements in operational efficiency.

(2) Low Investment Efficiency

Although the marketization of urban public infrastructure supply has improved in recent years, administrative control remains significant. Excessive administrative intervention in constructing and operating some public infrastructure projects results in high costs and low efficiency. Due to the widespread impact on residents, service providers often ignore costs and operational efficiency to ensure service continuity, leading to inefficiencies. Additionally, local governments often lack the professional expertise to regulate companies involved in public infrastructure, usually resorting to simplistic administrative management, resulting in inadequate regulation which further lowers operating efficiency and effectiveness.

(3) Slow Growth in Government Revenue and Inefficient Financing Channels

Currently, fiscal revenue is a critical and stable funding source for public infrastructure. However, with the slowing economic growth in China, fiscal revenue is also slowing down or even declining. Furthermore, consistent efforts to reduce the tax burden on enterprises make it difficult for the government to increase fiscal revenue by levying higher taxes. Therefore, over a certain period, fiscal revenue as a funding source for public infrastructure exhibits some uncertainty. Declining land sale revenues and stricter central government controls on local government financing platforms and debts further restrict local government budget and extra-budgetary funds, hindering the sustainable growth of urban public infrastructure investment.

(4) Blurred Boundaries between Government and Financing Platform Companies

Under the current investment and financing mechanism for urban public infrastructure, solely state-owned investment (construction) companies serve as the financing entities, with their registered capital originating from government fiscal allocations. Thus, the government is essentially the factual investor, directly taking on the primary responsibility for public infrastructure construction (Shi, 2010). This leads to a dependency of financing platform companies on the government, resulting in unclear boundaries between the two.

5.4.3.2 Reform Measures

In response to the issues above, the government has been implementing reforms in recent years through institutional arrangements and leveraging the role of financial market mechanisms to encourage social capital investment in public infrastructure, thereby enhancing investment and financing capabilities. Measures can include:

(1) Innovating Investment and Financing Models and Methods

Currently, government investment remains a large proportion of urban public infrastructure financing, leading to significant debt pressures. It is imperative to reduce the government's investment share through marketization reforms and investment mechanism innovations. Drawing from international experience and domestic practices, involving social capital in the investment and operation of urban public infrastructure is effective. Urban public infrastructure supply consists of multiple interconnected segments, necessitating a comprehensive approach to address supply challenges: (a) Broaden channels for social capital involvement in public infrastructure supply beyond traditional BOT models; (b) Establish standardized urban public infrastructure investment funds, allowing private and social capital to participate in fund creation and operation; (c) Utilize financial credit and capital markets, innovate financial instruments, and issue public infrastructure lotteries and bonds to finance urban public infrastructure; (d) Separate auxiliary project operations in public infrastructure from core business activities for market-oriented operations, thereby reducing the burden on state-owned sectors and enhancing efficiency and the competitiveness of core businesses.

(2) Improving Legal Frameworks for Investment and Financing in Public Infrastructure to Protect Social Capital Rights

While PPPs have been initiated in some public infrastructure projects to address funding issues, many problems have arisen due to the lack of genuine mechanism reforms. The absence of a comprehensive legal framework and standardized operational procedures has been a primary reason for such issues. When construction projects encounter problems, ineffective coordination jeopardizes social capital rights and increases project risks. Thus, the government needs to expedite the formulation of laws based on practical experiences to govern the involvement of social capital in public product projects and improve related investment and financing regulations. This includes ensuring equal status and fair treatment of social capital vis-à-vis government capital and urging social capital to adhere to relevant laws and regulations during project construction and operations to enhance legal awareness and protection.

(3) Enhancing Social Capital's Capacity to Participate in Urban Public Infrastructure Projects

Social capital in China has had limited involvement in urban public infrastructure projects, often lacking comprehensive understanding due to the long investment cycle and significant public interest in these projects. They tend to manage these projects with a commercial focus, often neglecting essential environmental assessments or lifecycle planning, which leads to increased risks. Financial institutions treat these projects like commercial endeavors, resulting in high financing costs and shorter loan terms. Thus, to address these challenges, the government should:

(1) Enhance the overall capability of social capital in infrastructure projects by improving creditworthiness and providing policy support to bolster resilience against risks;
(2) Create an information transparency platform for public infrastructure projects, ensuring investors are well-informed about project requirements;
(3) Increase supervision of social capital and offer credit services to financial institutions;
(4) Develop appropriate financial tools for long-term investment projects and leverage capital market functions to innovate equity trading systems, boosting long-term investment capacity.

5.5 Operational Mechanism of Urban Public Infrastructure

5.5.1 Analysis of Urban Public Infrastructure Operation in China

With rapid urbanization and infrastructure development, China now boasts one of the largest scales of urban public infrastructures in the world, but the per capita level remains relatively low, insufficient to meet the increasing demand brought by urbanization (see Table 5.11).

Table 5.11 indicates that while the quantity of various urban public infrastructures in China demonstrates an overall growth trend, there is an apparent characteristic: the growth rate of social public infrastructure is slow, whereas the number of economic public infrastructures shows significant changes.

Decades of investments and construction have gradually improved operational efficiency and international competitiveness of urban public infrastructure.

Table 5.11 Statistics on urban public infrastructure operations (2015–2019)

Project	2015	2016	2017	2018	2019
Water supply pipeline length/km	710,206	756,623	797,355	866,820	920,082
Drainage pipeline length/10,000 km	54	58	63	68	74
Gas pipeline length/km	528,388	578,260	641,170	716,008	783,313
Heating pipeline length/km	204,413	213,569	276,288	371,120	392,917
Road length/10,000 km	37	38	40	43	46
Railway operating mileage/10,000 km	12	12	13	13	14
Highway mileage/10,000 km	458	470	477	485	501
High-grade highway mileage/10,000 km	12	13	14	14	15
Number of operating public buses and trolleys	482,975	515,051	554,820	565,933	584,026
Number of sanitation vehicles	165,725	193,942	228,019	252,484	281,558
Number of waste treatment plants	890	940	1013	1091	–
Number of public toilets	126,344	129,818	136,084	147,466	153,426
Number of parks	13,834	15,370	15,633	16,735	18,038
Number of public libraries	3139	3153	3166	3176	3196
Number of hospital beds/10,000 beds	702	741	794	840	881
Number of research institutions	3650	3611	3547	3306	3217
Number of primary and secondary schools	242,930	229,751	218,903	212,739	210,784

Source China statistical ycarbook

Note Data regarding public libraries, hospital beds, research institutions, and schools' data are derived from national statistics in the *China Statistical Yearbook*, while other data are drawn from urban overview statistics. Gas pipeline length combines artificial coal gas pipelines, liquefied petroleum gas pipelines, and natural gas pipelines; heating pipeline length combines steam and hot water pipelines; The schools include primary and junior high schools

According to the *Global Competitiveness Report* by the World Economic Forum, the overall quality of China's public infrastructure ranks in the mid-to-high range globally (see Table 5.12).

The subitem comparison in Table 5.12 reveals that the operational efficiency of economic public infrastructure in China has improved considerably, while the efficiency and service quality of social public infrastructure have not shown significant improvement. China's power and communication public infrastructures operate with relative efficiency, and traditional transport infrastructures are operationally at a medium level, which shows very low operational efficiency when in comparison with China's extensive road infrastructure network. Beyond technical factors, outdated management systems are a crucial factor in this disparity. China's transportation system has long been constrained by traditional administrative management, resulting in high transportation and maintenance costs and severely limiting the effectiveness of the road infrastructure.

Table 5.12 International comparison of China's public infrastructure operational efficiency

Project	2015–2016	2016–2017	2017–2018	2018–2019	2019–2020
Number of countries	140	138	137	140	141
Overall public infrastructure quality	/51	/42	/46	78.1/29	77.9/36
Transport infrastructure efficiency (quality)		/43	/47		68.9/24
Road infrastructure	/42	/39	/42	59.7/42	59.7/45
Railway service efficiency (quality)	/16	/14	/17	59.0/25	59.0/24
Air service efficiency (quality)	/51	/43	/45	60.7/63	60.7/66
Port service efficiency (quality)	/50	/49	/49	58.6/48	58.6/52
Utility public infrastructure					86.9/65
Power supply quality	/53	/56	/65		99.0/18
Power transmission and distribution losses				98.8/21	
Water reliability				64.9/68	64.9/68
Information and communication technology				71.5/26	78.5/18
Broadband internet usage				53.7/36	57.1/32

Source Global competitiveness report

Note The number before the slash indicates the score, and the number after the slash indicates the international ranking. Due to the varying statistical subjects and scope each year, some data are missing. Utility public infrastructure includes large categories such as power and water supply

5.5.2 Urban Public Infrastructure Operational Models

With societal development and technological advancements, operational and managerial approaches to urban public infrastructure are continually evolving. A significant change is the increasing involvement of private and social capital in urban public infrastructure construction and operational management.

As previously noted, aside from a few urban public infrastructures crucial to national security that require direct government management, many urban public infrastructures can be operated by commercial enterprises or other economic organizations, or provided to society through government procurement from enterprises. Urban public infrastructure forms an integrated system composed of various business segments that need inter-departmental coordination and cooperation for orderly and efficient operations. The competitive and exclusive nature of different subsystems and segments varies greatly, providing opportunities for diverse operational models for each subsystem and segment. In practice, urban public infrastructure systems and segments can be separated, and operational models can be chosen based on their competitiveness and exclusivity (see Table 5.13).

During operations, if any segment of urban public infrastructure, such as detection, maintenance, or management, shows high competitiveness and exclusivity, a market operational model can be implemented. Such involvement not only improves the supply efficiency of urban public infrastructure but also alleviates fiscal pressures on the government.

For segments with high exclusivity and low competitiveness or low exclusivity and high competitiveness, a quasi-market operational model can be implemented, balancing market mechanisms and government administrative mechanisms. In cases of high exclusivity and low competitiveness, market mechanisms should primarily operate with government support. Conversely, when exclusivity is low and competitiveness is high, government mechanisms should take precedence, supported by market forces. The government can encourage social capital participation through subsidies.

If there is low exclusivity and competitiveness, administrative mechanisms or non-market operational models can be adopted and operated by government-controlled companies with fiscal subsidies to cover operational losses. This approach ensures the social benefits for those who do not achieve direct economic gains. To maintain normal operations of urban public infrastructure, the government can also guide non-profit organizations and other social groups (Cui et al., 2009).

5.5.3 Problems and Reform Measures in Urban Public Infrastructure Operation

Urban public infrastructure operational levels reflect the city's management capacities and service provision for enterprises and the public. Since the reform and

Table 5.13 Operational models for urban public infrastructure

Operational activities	Exclusivity and competitiveness	Operational entities	Operational models
Testing	Strong exclusivity, strong competitiveness	Enterprises	Operate in the market
	Strong exclusivity, weak competitiveness	Primarily enterprises, with government support	Operate mainly in the market
	Weak exclusivity, strong competitiveness	Primarily government, with enterprise support	Operate mainly administratively
	Weak exclusivity, weak competitiveness	Government-led multi-stakeholder management	Under administrative control
Maintenance	Strong exclusivity, strong competitiveness	Enterprises	Operate in the market
	Strong exclusivity, weak competitiveness	Primarily enterprises, with government support	Operate mainly in the market
	Weak exclusivity, strong competitiveness	Primarily government, with enterprise support	Operate mainly administratively
	Weak exclusivity, weak competitiveness	Government-led multi-stakeholder management	Under administrative control
Upkeep	Strong exclusivity, strong competitiveness	Enterprises	Operate in the market
	Strong exclusivity, weak competitiveness	Primarily enterprises, with government support	Operate mainly in the market
	Weak exclusivity, strong competitiveness	Primarily government, with enterprise support	Operate mainly administratively
	Weak exclusivity, weak competitiveness	Government-led multi-stakeholder management	Under administrative control
Management	Strong exclusivity, strong competitiveness	Enterprises	Operate in the market
	Strong exclusivity, weak competitiveness	Primarily enterprises, with government support	Operate mainly in the market
	Weak exclusivity, strong competitiveness	Primarily government, with enterprise support	Operate mainly administratively
	Weak exclusivity, weak competitiveness	Government-led multi-stakeholder management	Under administrative control

opening up, China has emphasized urban development, proposing "city management", focusing on urban industry development and expanding the city scale through land resources reallocation, development zones, and real estate development. Significant achievements have been made in urban public infrastructure construction with substantial improvements in operational management quality. However, deficiencies remain in ensuring efficient management, safe operation, and convenient services.

5.5.3.1 Existing Problems

Existing Problems include:

(1) Prioritization of Construction Over Operation in Urban Development and Management Concepts. In urban development and management, there is a prevailing tendency to prioritize construction over operation. New projects can generate immediate urban economic growth through investment, allowing governments to showcase their achievements. In contrast, the operation, management, and maintenance of public infrastructure are time-consuming and labor-intensive, yielding neither immediate economic growth nor direct economic benefits. This has led to a general preference for construction over operation among urban public infrastructure developers and managers (Wang et al., 2009), resulting in low efficiency of urban public infrastructure supply. Compared to advanced international cities, China lags in road traffic flow, communication capacity, and energy utilization efficiency. Notably, common issues include low utilization rates of sports and cultural infrastructure, single service modes, and poor operational efficiency. Even cities with relatively high operation levels fall short of their international counterparts. For instance, while New York has 214 public libraries and Shanghai has 245, the service effectiveness differs markedly: 64.7% of New York's population holds library cards compared to just 4.6% in Shanghai (Qi, 2013).

(2) Lack of Scientific Planning and Coordination in Urban Public Infrastructure. There is a lack of scientific planning for urban public infrastructure, along with insufficient coordination between planning, construction, and operation. During the investment and construction of urban infrastructure projects, planning and feasibility studies are often inadequate. A prominent issue is the lack of scientific justification for the optimal selection of construction projects within a certain period, with insufficient consideration of their relationship to related infrastructure. As a result, despite continuous investment, it is challenging to form integrated networks. Projects frequently suffer from a lack of coordination with supporting infrastructure upon completion or even remain ineffective due to the absence of complementary facilities. Additionally, planning often lacks scientific foresight, underestimating changes in economic and social demand growth and technological development, leading to resource wastage in urban public infrastructure construction.

(3) Unreasonable Pricing and Charges. In the provision of urban public infrastructure, the pricing and charging issues arise mainly in two areas: determining the fee standards and methods of charging. Urban public infrastructure serves the broader public, yet citizens' varying payment capacities make pricing difficult. Low fees can lead to undersupply and wasteful behavior, while high fees can exclude some citizens from services, contradicting the principles of public infrastructure provision. Charging issues arise from the difficulty of strictly excluding non-payers to ensure the rights of payers, making it challenging to decide who should pay and how. Essential facilities related to urban development and basic living standards, such as roads, public safety, and public health, cannot rely on user fees. Consequently, many urban public infrastructure users expect to be "free riders", unwilling to pay for services, which undermines the effectiveness of the pricing mechanism in these areas (Gao, 2011).

(4) Over-supply and Low Service Levels. In recent years, concerns for safety have led to the installation of surveillance devices in various urban areas, including traffic roads, parks, shopping and office districts, and residential areas, significantly impacting residents' privacy. With the rise of the internet, cities have accelerated the construction of administrative and citizen service networks, along with financial institutions and other commercial networks, resulting in frequent personal information leaks. Moreover, the rapid development of mobile communication public infrastructure has led to over-construction and supply issues.

In the operations and maintenance of urban public infrastructure, operators and enterprises often lack professional personnel and equipment, as well as scientific and automated management technologies. Reliance on manual operations limits the acquisition of real-time and continuous systematic information and the understanding of environmental and structural system characteristics (Wang et al., 2009), resulting in actual service levels falling short of target levels.

5.5.3.2 Reform Measures

The primary focus of urban public infrastructure operation reform is to clearly define the roles of government and the market, standardizing operational processes. The operation rights of public infrastructure suitable for market mechanisms should be returned to enterprises, allowing market regulation to play a full role. Infrastructure requiring government provision should remain under government control, with market mechanisms introduced when conditions mature. The Chinese government has made various attempts, from traditional BOT model trials to large-scale PPP project implementations and the continuous advancement of REITs models, demonstrating its determination and resilience in reform, indicating the future direction of public infrastructure operation reform.

The book argues that as reforms deepen, it is necessary to continually enhance the understanding of urban public infrastructure operations. The goal of urban public infrastructure construction and operation is to meet urban operational needs and serve the public. Therefore, the country should engage the whole society in infrastructure construction, selecting the most efficient enterprises and institutions to build and operate public infrastructure projects, further diversifying operational models, and improving efficiency by subdividing urban public infrastructure operation stages and marketizing highly competitive and exclusive parts. This approach has the following benefits: improving supply efficiency, avoiding the neglect of operational issues, recouping operational costs through charging mechanisms, incentivizing market entities to enhance service quality, preventing excessive government involvement, alleviating fiscal pressures, and reducing corruption.

However, implementing market mechanisms still requires government support. Government departments and state-owned enterprises should work to eliminate bureaucratic management practices in operating public infrastructure, implement performance evaluation systems, and selectively introduce market mechanisms to enhance operational efficiency. For example, it is crucial to supervise and evaluate government officials responsible for managing public infrastructure, establish scientific evaluation systems, and assess whether projects truly serve society and public interests during these evaluations.

References

Aschauer, D. A. (1989). Is public expenditure productive? *Journal of Monetary Economics, 23*(2), 177–200.

Aschauer, D. A. (1990). Why is infrastructure important? *New England Economic Review, 30*(9), 69–112.

Biehl, D. (1991). The role of infrastructure in regional development. In R. W. Vickerman (Ed.), *Infrastructure and regional development* (pp. 1–20). Pion.

Chen, Y., & Wang, D. (2017). Mechanism and countermeasures of social capital participation in the construction and operation of urban and rural infrastructure. *Economic Review, 1*, 101–104.

Cheng, M., & Chen, H. (2012). Study on long-term evaluation of urban infrastructure systems. *Industrial Technology & Economy, 31*(11), 84–88.

Cheng, M., & Pei, X. (2017). Spatial-temporal differences in the efficiency of infrastructure investment in cities above prefecture level in China: based on DEA and Malmquist index model. *Management Review, 29*(6), 225–233.

Chu, Y., & Wang, H. (2019). Research on the correlation between fiscal decentralization, public infrastructure investment, and local government tax and fee structure: An empirical analysis based on provincial panel data in China. *Shandong Social Sciences, 11*, 126–133.

Cohen, J. P., & Paul, C. J. M. (2004). Public infrastructure investment, interstate spatial spillovers, and manufacturing costs. *Review of Economics and Statistics, 86*(2), 551–560.

Cui, G., & Nan, Y. (2009). Discussion on the innovation of urban infrastructure financing modes in relation to the nature of public goods. *Economic Trends, 3*, 39–42.

Ding, C., Liu, M., & Liao, Y. (2015). Official turnover and transportation infrastructure investment: evidence from provincial-level official data in China. *Journal of Financial Research, 41*(4), 90–99.

Estache, A., & Sinha, S. (1999). Does decentralization increase spending on public infrastructure? [Policy Research Working Paper].

Fan, J., & Bai, B. (2004). The impact of infrastructure capital on economic growth: An estimate using a two-level three-factor CES production function method. *Economic Forum, 11*, 10–13.

Fu, Y. (2010). Fiscal decentralization, government governance, and the supply of non-economic public goods. *Economic Research Journal, 45*(8), 4–15.

Gao, J. (2011). Joint supply of urban infrastructure by the government and non-government sectors. *Urban Problems, 7*, 78–82.

Gao, Y., Zhang, M., & You, D. (2016). Evaluation of technological innovation efficiency in the new energy vehicle industry from an urban perspective. *Industrial Technology & Economy, 35*(3), 47–54.

Guo, P., Cao, Y., & Yang, Y. (2021). Research on the estimation of the return on infrastructure capital and its influencing factors. *Southern Economy, 1*, 83–101.

Guo, X. (2008). Research on improving the level of urban infrastructure construction. *Dongyue Tribune, 1*, 160–164.

Huang, C., & Zhang, J. (2014). The impact of urban infrastructure construction on urban scale expansion: an empirical study from an urbanization perspective. *Price Theory & Practice, 9*, 110–112.

Huang, H., Huang, W., & Zhang, Y. (2011). Study on infrastructure evaluation of cities above prefecture level in China. *Economic Geography, 31*(1), 47–54.

Jin, G. (2016). Estimation of China's infrastructure and non-infrastructure capital stock and output elasticity. *Economic Research Journal, 51*(5), 41–56.

Jin, J., & Li, D. (2012). Infrastructure investment and economic development: a spatial econometric study based on Guangdong Province. *Fiscal Research, 6*, 55–59.

Kappeler, A., & Välilä, T. (2008). Fiscal federalism and the composition of public investment in Europe. *European Journal of Political Economy, 24*(3), 562–570.

Li, H., & Li, Z. (2009). The impact of transportation infrastructure investment on enterprise inventory: An empirical study based on panel data of manufacturing enterprises in China. *Management World, 8*, 73–80.

Liu, B., & Liu, Y. (2011). The construction of transportation infrastructure and the reduction of inventory costs of manufacturing enterprises in China. *China Industrial Economics, 5*, 69–79.

Liu, Y. (2010). Transportation infrastructure investment, regional economic growth, and spatial spillover effects: An analysis based on panel data of road and water transportation. *China Industrial Economics, 12*, 37–46.

Lou, H. (2003). *Public infrastructure investment and long-term economic growth*. China Financial & Economic Publishing House.

Munnell, A. H., & Cook, L. M. (1990). How does public infrastructure affect regional economic performance? *New England Economic Review, 30*(9), 69–112.

Oates, W. E. (1972). *Fiscal federalism*. Harcourt Brace Jovanovich.

Ostrom, E. (1990). *Governing the commons: The evolution of institutions for collective action*. Cambridge University Press.

Pereira, A. M., & Roca-Sagalés, O. (2003). Spillover effects of public capital formation: Evidence from the Spanish regions. *Journal of Urban Economics, 53*(2), 238–256.

Qiao, B., Fan, J., & Feng, X. (2005). China's fiscal decentralization and compulsory primary education. *Chinese Social Sciences, 2005*(6), 37–46.

Ren, X., & Zhang, Z. (2010). A spatial econometric analysis of transportation infrastructure and manufacturing location choices. *Inquiry into Economic Issues, 10*, 13–17.

Schwartz, M. A. E. (1996). State infrastructure and productive performance. *American Economic Review, 86*(5), 1095–1111.

Shi, Y., & Li, C. (2010). Analysis of the difficulties in the reform of China's urban infrastructure investment and financing system. *Journal of Central University of Finance and Economics, 7*, 62–65.

Su, S., & Wang, K. (2005). Research on the driving force of infrastructure investment on consumption. *Statistics and Decision, 16*, 85–87.

Sun, Y., Wang, K., & Yao, X. (2015). Economic benefit evaluation of urban public infrastructure based on DEA cross-efficiency model. *China Soft Science, 1*, 172–183.

Tang, H., Wang, Y., Wang, D., et al. (2018). Research on the impact of transportation infrastructure in Western China on manufacturing agglomeration. *China Soft Science, 8*, 137–147.

Tang, W. (2019). Decentralization, externalities, and boundary effects. *Economic Research Journal, 54*(3), 103–118.

Tang, Y., & Chen, Q. (2012). Decentralization, land finance, and urban infrastructure. *Comparative Economic & Social Systems, 6*, 98–110.

Tao, Z., & Sun, Y. (2018). Dynamic analysis of influencing factors of urban infrastructure system supply efficiency. *Research on Financial and Economic Issues, 6*, 131–137.

Wang, K. (2016). Research on the three-dimensional evaluation of urban public infrastructure benefits [Doctoral dissertation]. Tianjin University.

Wang, L., & Wu, W. (2011). Research on the market-based financing of urban infrastructure projects: based on the perspective of insufficient specificity investment. *Urban Development Studies, 18*(1), 120–124.

Wang, L., Yin, D., & Liu, B. (2009). Research on the management and maintenance strategies for the sustainable operation of urban infrastructure. *Modern Finance & Economics (Journal of Tianjin University of Finance and Economics), 29*(11), 63–66.

Wang, X. (2017). Transportation infrastructure, financial development, and household consumption expenditure: Based on spatial panel data of 281 prefecture-level cities. *Consumption Economy, 33*(2), 31–37.

Wang, Y. (2002). On the entry of private capital in infrastructure construction in China. *Reform of the Economic System, 4*, 5–9.

Wei, X. (2010). Infrastructure, spatial spillovers, and regional economic growth. *Economic Review, 4*, 82–89.

World Bank. (1994). *World development report 1994: Infrastructure for development*. Oxford University Press.

Xue, G. (2018). Measurement of urban infrastructure capital stock and output elasticity in China. *Economic Review, 4*, 72–83.

Yan, C., & Gong, L. (2014). Should infrastructure investment be open to private capital? *Economic Science, 6*, 41–52.

Yang, X., Guo, S., & Meng, Y. (2018). Can railway transportation infrastructure promote industrial agglomeration in border areas? *Journal of Yunnan University of Finance and Economics, 34*(10), 62–72.

Yuan, D., Li, D., & Yang, Z. (2017). Does foreign direct investment enhance urban infrastructure performance in China? *The World Economy, 40*(8), 143–166.

Yue, J. (2009). *Research on effective supply of public investment and public goods*. Shanghai: Shanghai Sanlian Publishing House.

Zhang, J., Gao, Y., Fu, Y., et al. (2007). Why does China have good infrastructure? *Economic Research Journal, 3*, 4–19.

Zhao, P. (2012). Determinants of FDI inflows in emerging economies and China's countermeasures. *Economics and Management, 26*(5), 21–25.

Zhou, J. (2019). Research on the development strategies of public welfare logistics infrastructure in the context of "Internet + Circulation." *Journal of Capital University of Economics and Business, 21*(5), 22–33.

Chapter 6
Urban Public Service System and Supply Mechanism

With the rapid urbanization in China, the quality and quantity of urban public services have significantly improved. The expansion of coverage of public services has enhanced regional equality and the diversity of public service providers and supply methods has also gradually increased. However, challenges such as insufficient scale, low quality, and unbalanced development continue to persist in urban public services in China. This chapter, guided by the New Public Service Theory and informed by the development trajectory of urban public services in China, outlines the basic characteristics of public services, identifies current challenges, and offers new perspectives for the reform and development of the public service supply mechanism.

6.1 Urban Public Service System

Since the reform and opening up, China's urbanization has advanced rapidly. By the end of 2019, the urban population in China reached 848.43 million, accounting for 60.60%[1] of the total population. Substantial investments in urban public infrastructure over the past decade have supported the needs for production and living within urban development. However, the supply of urban public services has not kept pace, revealing increasing contradictions between the growing public service demands of urban residents and the imbalance and inadequacy of public service provision. These disparities have become major challenges within China's urban public service supply system.

Throughout the development of China's public service system, the government has consistently prioritized its construction. The goal has been to establish a basic public service system led by the government that meets the survival and development needs of all citizens and is aligned with the level of economic and social development. The

[1] National Bureau of Statistics: *Statistical Bulletin of the People's Republic of China on National Economic and Social Development 2019.*

B. Wu et al., *Effective Supply Mechanism of Urban Public Goods*, Public Economy and Urban Governance in China, https://doi.org/10.1007/978-981-96-2608-3_6

11th Five-Year Plan for National Economic and Social Development of the People's Republic of China was the first policy document marking the government's emphasis on the equalization of basic public services as a governmental priority. Subsequently, the central government has constantly improved the basic public service system, striving for comprehensive coverage and increased equalization between urban and rural areas. The *14th Five-Year Plan for National Economic and Social Development of the People's Republic of China* further emphasized the importance of enhancing the level of urban public services and achieving equalization of basic public services in the context of urban–rural integration.

6.1.1 Connotation and Characteristics of Public Services

6.1.1.1 Concept and Function of Public Services

Currently, there is no unified definition of "public service" among scholars, both domestically and internationally. This concept largely derived from the notion of public goods. While some scholars equate public services with public goods, others draw distinctions to differentiate them from tangible public items. Yet, since certain public services are rooted in public goods, defining their precise scope remains challenging (Tan et al., 2002). The academic community offers a variety of interpretations of public services from diverse perspectives, which include:

(1) Defining public services based on public goods theories: Samuelson defined public goods or services from the perspective of non-rivalry, saying that true public goods or services are those which, when consumed by one person, do not reduce the availability of that good or service to others. Mankiw (2003) referred to public services that exhibit both non-rivalry and non-excludability as pure public services, and those that exhibit only one of these characteristics as quasi-public services. From the externality perspective, the production of pure public services generates positive external effects for all members of society. These definitions illustrate the characteristics of public services without explaining their connotations.
(2) Defining public services based on government or public sector functions: Typically, public services provided by the government or public sectors cannot be adjusted through market mechanisms due to market failures. Zeng Xu (2016) defines public services as the collective public and nonprofit actions taken by the government to address economic, social, and public needs. Sun Chunxia (2010) views them as the government's resource allocation method to resolve issues beyond the market's reach through public institutions. These definitions primarily focus on the providers and foundations of public services, rather than their inherent nature.
(3) Defining public services based on content and form: Some scholars divide public services into basic public services, economic public services, security

public services, and social public services based on their content and form (Li et al., 2006). Basic public services include infrastructure like water, electricity, transportation, and communication. Economic public services provide various productive services for economic activities. Security public services include national defense, police, and fire safety services. Social public services offer educational, healthcare, and social security services, among others (Chen, 2010). Some scholars argue that public services should be understood more narrowly as those organized by the government, including not only foundational services but also social-oriented ones such as elderly care, healthcare, social security, and environmental protection (Liu et al., 2017).

(4) Advocating a broader concept of public services. There are scholars who believe that public services should include not only abstract public goods such as macroeconomic policies and laws and regulations established by the government to correct market failures and ensure the normal operation of the market economy but also public service projects provided by the government to meet citizens' needs for production, living, development, and entertainment (Lu, 2012a, b). Moreover, the *11th Five-Year Plan* outlines the tasks in the public service sector, including compulsory education, public health, social security, social assistance, employment promotion, poverty reduction, disaster prevention and mitigation, public safety, public culture, basic science and frontier technology research, social welfare technology research, and national defense. The government is responsible for utilizing public resources to provide these services. Although many public service projects are listed, the *11th Five-Year Plan* primarily focuses on public services in a narrow sense.

This book defines public services as all types of services provided to meet the needs of society, enterprises, and the public for production and living. Public services are distinct from public goods: the former refers to intangible public products, which can be termed public services, while the latter refers to tangible public products, known as public goods. Both types of public products share the characteristics of non-competitiveness and non-exclusiveness. In practice, these two types of public products often overlap, making it difficult to isolate and decompose them.

6.1.1.2 Characteristics of Public Services

Public services differ from private services and exhibit the following characteristics as a type of public goods:

(1) Non-rivalry in service utilization: Public services can be accessed by individuals, enterprises, or organizations without excluding others from using them. However, increased demand may lead to shortages or reduced quality, resulting in "congestion costs" and supply constraints. To address this, governments often impose limits on service usage, while market supply mechanisms may implement club systems or other strategies to allocate services.

(2) Non-excludability of benefits: Non-excludability means that beneficiaries of public services do not prevent others from enjoying the same services, implying relative service property rights or entitlements for all individuals.
(3) Indivisibility of utility: Public services are designed for society as a whole or specific segment, entitling all members to access and benefit from them. Such services cannot be divided into individual parts for personal ownership; instead, they offer collective benefits. Examples include national defense, transportation services, and environmental management.

These complicate the definition of public service benefits and often require government provision over market supply due to potential market failures. Public services typically involve significant scale economies and initial investment, making private enterprise operations under uncertain returns challenging (Liu et al., 2007). However, many public services do not completely exhibit the characteristics of pure public goods. Therefore, it's common to see both government provision and the involvement from the private or social sector, resulting in quasi-public services.

6.1.2 Major Modern Public Service Theories

Public service theories primarily include New Public Management Theory and New Public Service Theory.

6.1.2.1 New Public Management Theory

New Public Management (NPM) Theory emerged in the 1970s and 1980s, during a time when Western capitalist countries in Europe and America were facing economic stagflation. The drawbacks of government intervention became increasingly evident, as significant fiscal deficits and inefficient or ineffective public service delivery fueled widespread social dissatisfaction. Consequently, reforms such as the "Reinventing Government Movement", "Market-Oriented Government", and "Entrepreneurial Government" were initiated. These reform practices gave rise to theories and management models distinct from traditional public administration, eventually crystallizing into the New Public Management Theory (Jane-Erik, 2004).

Given the various problems associated with government intervention, NPM Theory advocates for marketization, emphasizing the use of market competition mechanisms and efficiency principles to manage public sectors. It calls for a clear delineation of functions between the government and the market, suggesting that the government's role should be "steering" rather than "rowing", thereby reducing government size, decreasing public expenditures, and enhancing work efficiency (Mei, 2006). NPM supports integrating public and market mechanisms, advocating for market-oriented governance that uses competition and performance management to deliver public services that meet citizens' needs (David et al., 1996). In practice,

NPM encourages the diversification of public service supply by involving private enterprises or independent entities as service providers to eliminate monopolies in public service provision. For non-public utility infrastructure, a user-pays model is recommended to meet public service needs most economically (Li, 2002).

6.1.2.2 New Public Service Theory

While NPM Theory focuses on maximizing market interests, often neglecting public interests, its implementation has had limited success in addressing financial crises in Western countries. Traditional industries have continued to decline due to the information technology revolution, exacerbating social inequality and diminishing citizens' willingness to engage in civic matters. In response to these issues, American public administration scholars Janet V. Denhardt and Robert B. Denhardt proposed the New Public Service Theory, which centers on citizens and seeks to promote public interest (Janet et al., 2004).

The New Public Service Theory introduces a framework of citizenship rights, democracy, and public interest service. It asserts that public service should be rooted in dialogue and consultation with citizens to ensure the public interest. Key aspects include:

(1) Government's role as a service provider: The government's role should shift from "steering" to "serving", actively engaging in public affairs and providing services with a focus on service rather than management, thereby empowering citizens;
(2) Pursuit of public interest: The ultimate goal of public service is to serve the public interest, intrinsically linked to individual interests. This shared responsibility of managers and citizens influences personal pursuits. The government should foster a strong legal environment and encourage fair, open dialogues to embed public interest in citizen's minds;
(3) Citizen-centric principle: Within legal and social responsibility constraints, the government must deliver high-quality public services, prioritizing citizens' long-term interests and fostering cooperative relationships;
(4) Priority on people: In providing public services, the government must safeguard citizens' rights and dignity, prioritizing human-centric values alongside work efficiency and respecting individual worth;
(5) Entrepreneurial spirit to citizenship: The governments should function as civil servants contributing to society instead of prioritizing profit, avoiding the perception of public funds as personal property;
(6) Strategic thinking and democratic actions: Policies and projects that meet public needs and promote citizen collaboration and participation are deemed most efficient in execution;
(7) Complexity of accountability: Government and administrative personnel shoulder various responsibilities, ignoring any of which can lead to citizen dissatisfaction and social inequality. The New Public Service Theory prioritizes

citizens, emphasizes serving them, and empowers them, with the core value of pursuing public interest (Janet et al., 2004).

6.1.3 Urban Public Service System

Urban public services are based on public service theory, embodying the general characteristics of public services while integrating with urban features, representing the practice of public services in cities. The basic public service system includes the scope and standards of public services, resource allocation for public services, the operation and management of public service fields and projects, public service supply methods, and performance evaluation. Forming a comprehensive institutional arrangement. The public service system mainly includes the following aspects: (a) Basic Public Services for Ensuring Livelihoods. Services like energy supply and employment support; (b) Public Welfare and Social Security Services. They encompass public education, healthcare, sports and cultural services, and social security; (c) Economic Public Services for Citizens and Enterprises, which facilitate economic activities through industrial and commercial tax services, living platform services, financial support, market transaction services, legal consultations, and technology dissemination; (d) Security Public Services to Ensure Safety, which provide safety guarantee in production, consumer protection, and social stability. The categorization of these services is not rigid, and there are overlaps and interconnections between them.

6.1.3.1 Basic Public Services

Basic public services refer to public products or services essential for national life and the economic and social activities of enterprises and institutions, such as tap water and sewage treatment, energy supply, postal, and telecommunication services. These services play a fundamental role in citizens' lives and production and often exhibit natural monopoly characteristics, making government provision more economically efficient. When supplying these services, governments must prioritize accessibility and availability while avoiding monopolistic practices. Failure to do so can negatively impact citizens' basic survival and living quality, increase economic activity costs, and hinder sustainable economic development, ultimately affecting employment and the overall development level of the country (Gao, 2011).

6.1.3.2 Public Welfare and Social Security Services

Public welfare and social security services provide basic social security for public life and development, enabling citizens to engage in socioeconomic activities, which include basic education, healthcare, science and technology, sports and culture, and public housing. Across the world, public welfare and social security services are recognized as indicators of social development, particularly the completeness of social security service systems, reflecting a nation's commitment to social safety and welfare.

China has now established a relatively comprehensive social security system, including social assistance, social insurance, and social welfare, although the level of social welfare protection is still low, offering only basic services. The 19th National Congress of the Communist Party of China proposed building a multi-layered social security system covering the entire population, integrating urban and rural areas, with clear rights and responsibilities, appropriate protection, and sustainability. Social public services such as basic education, healthcare, and public housing are significant for socioeconomic development and public life. China has implemented a nine-year compulsory education system with enrollment rates reaching the average level of developed countries and is enhancing the quality and integration of compulsory education. China has also established a basic urban healthcare system, including basic medical insurance for urban employees, urban and rural residents, and medical assistance systems.

6.1.3.3 Economic Public Services

Economic public services are provided to citizens and enterprises for economic activities, including industrial and commercial tax services, living platform services, financial services, market environment and transaction services, policy and legal consultations, and technology dissemination and promotion. The quality and quantity of economic public services directly impact the economic development environment. Effective economic public services can reduce economic friction, foster a favorable economic development atmosphere and market order, and promote a virtuous cycle of socioeconomic development.

6.1.3.4 Security Public Services

Public safety is a prerequisite for socioeconomic development and the normal operation of cities, serving as the foundation for orderly social development. A deficiency in the public safety assurance system can lead to disorder and chaos in economic and social activities. Essentially, public safety issues fall within the scope of public goods, being a service that the government must and should provide to citizens.

Security public services broadly involve functions related to safeguarding and supervising citizen and national security. Internally, they focus on economic prosperity, social stability, harmony, and legal fairness. Externally, they address national defense, international peace and stability, and the realization of national interests in international division and competition. Security public services involve various sectors and departments, including national defense and diplomacy, public safety and national security, judiciary and supervision, fire protection and environmental protection, as well as various production safety supervision departments, urban management departments, and regulatory departments for both profit and non-profit organizations. The government is responsible for delivering security public services in areas such as production safety, consumer safety, and social safety, thereby fulfilling its responsibilities in building and supervising the safety service system. Additionally, ensuring consumer, food, and drug safety is a fundamental obligation of the government in constructing the public service system (Gao, 2011; Wang, 2010a, b).

6.2 The Development Status of Urban Public Services in China

6.2.1 The Development Process of Urban Public Services

With the transformation of the economic system and the change in government functions, the scope of urban public services in China has continuously extended, gradually forming a unique urban public service system with Chinese characteristics. Previously, insufficient provision of urban public services, imbalanced urban–rural development, and reliance on a single leading provider significantly hindered the healthy, coordinated, and sustainable development of China's social economy. To meet residents' basic needs for survival and development, China has systematically improved the institutional mechanisms of urban public services, increased public service investment, and sought to establish a sound basic public service system. This includes issuing documents such as the *National Basic Public Service System Twelfth Five-Year Plan* and the *Thirteenth Five-Year Plan to Promote the Equalization of Basic Public Services*. As a result, significant progress has been made in education, employment, healthcare, elderly care, and housing.

The development of China's urban public service system can be broadly divided into the following stages:

6.2.1.1 Urban Public Service System Dominated by the "System of Unit" (1949–1977)

In the early period of the People's Republic of China, the country faced low productivity levels and resource scarcity. To build a socialist economic system, China implemented an administrative planned economy that centralized production, consumption, and resource allocation. This led to a simple and state-managed public service system characterized by egalitarianism and state intervention (Yu, 2011). Influenced by the "System of Unit", "Household Registration System", and "Egalitarianism", the urban public service system developed a centrally planned administrative mechanism.

During the planned economy period, urban enterprises, administrative service units, known as "Danwei, played a crucial role in providing public services. The public service provision model was mainly "state-unit-resident", whereby the government guided the supply and distribution of social public services through administrative agencies and state-owned enterprises. Residents relied on their work units to meet basic public service needs such as education, elderly care, and healthcare, with "Danwei" serving as a vital intermediary (Wang, 2019a, b).

Influenced by Soviet principles of "Communism" and "Egalitarianism", essential public services were equitably distributed in a resource-scarce environment, meeting most urban residents' daily needs. However, this period also revealed limitations. The "system of unit" weakened the social service function of public services, causing significant inequality in public service access for individuals outside these units. Additionally, the limited development of the urban economy meant the government and enterprises could only provide inadequate public services, failing to adequately meet urban residents' needs.

6.2.1.2 Gradual Disintegration of the "System of Unit" in Urban Public Services (1978–1992)

After the Third Plenary Session of the 11th Central Committee, the acceleration of reform and opening up led to the gradual disintegration of the planned economy's public service system. However, restructuring the public service supply model based on the urban–rural dual structure and household registration system faced significant challenges.

The market economy's development and state-owned enterprise reforms were critical factors in changing the public service system and supply mechanism. During this period, public-owned enterprises gradually shifted away from their roles as social welfare providers. In November 1984, the Ministry of Civil Affairs clarified the guiding principle of "social welfare administered by society", and the government began exploring new urban public service systems (Li et al., 2012).

Education service reform served as the turning point for the broader public service system. Between 1966 and 1976, public undertakings, especially education, suffered significant setbacks. Thus, the central government restored the college entrance examination system in 1977 and increased educational investments to develop higher education and establish a modern basic education system with mandatory education. Meanwhile, reforms were made to the outdated medical system, leading to the creation of a socialized medical insurance system that improved public health and healthcare services.

In social insurance, the State Council issued the *Interim Provisions on the Implementation of Labor Contract System in State-Owned Enterprises* in 1986, proposing a social insurance system for workers' retirement pensions. This system required joint contributions from enterprises and workers. In 1991, the State Council released the *Decision on Reforming the Enterprise Employee Pension Insurance System*, introducing a tripartite pension system where the state, enterprises, and individuals share responsibilities, prompting reforms in the enterprise employee pension insurance system.

During this period, urban public services transitioned from single-provider and entirely free services to diversified providers where residents pay for services. This shift improved the efficiency and quality of urban public services to varying degrees. Guided by the principle of "focusing on economic construction", the government's public service functions leaned more towards economic public functions, transitioning from a "governing" to a "developmental" government (Zhu et al., 2005). Consequently, more funds were allocated for productive investments to promote social and economic development, leading to relatively low public service expenditure as a proportion of total fiscal outlays. However, rising demands for material and cultural life among residents imposed higher requirements on the quality and quantity of urban public services, exacerbating supply–demand imbalances.

6.2.1.3 Exploration of Market Mechanisms in Urban Public Services (1993–2001)

As China's socialist market economy system was established, the previously rigid public services could no longer meet the diverse needs of urban residents. This period saw numerous reforms promoting market-oriented, socialized, and localized urban public services.

The primary challenge during the public service marketization process was leveraging enterprises, individuals, and social organizations to provide public services. Academics and government departments recognized that for successful marketization, public service costs had to be reduced, and quality and efficiency improved (Wang et al., 2019). Marketization did not imply government withdrawal but rather maintaining macro-level control, establishing competitive market mechanisms at the micro-level, and strengthening public–private cooperation. The government should transition from a "monopolist" to a "service provider" (Wang et al., 2014). Both central and local governments introduced policies, regulations, and guidelines encouraging private sector growth and facilitating private sector participation in public services. The government also began reforming public institutions' administrative and social service functions, separating market-suitable public service projects from traditional institutions, and introducing market competition mechanisms in certain business activities (Reform et al. Department, Luo Chongpu, 2012). In economic public service domains, enterprises, and social capital began investing and operating; in social public services areas like education, healthcare, and employment, governments started cooperating with enterprises and social organizations to provide services.

In 1994, the implementation of the tax-sharing reform clarified central and local government fiscal powers and responsibilities, advancing the localization of urban public services. The central government handled national defense, key construction, and central-level administrative and service expenses, while local governments took charge of local administrative, infrastructure, agricultural support, social security, compulsory education, and healthcare expenses (Yu, 2011). The central government delegated powers to local governments and selectively applied market mechanisms in public services such as road maintenance, communication, and medical health to attract more social funds and align services with market demands, better meeting the growing needs of urban residents (Li, 2004). However, tax-sharing reform also presented challenges for urban public service development. Different regions' fiscal capacities varied, resulting in significant disparities in public service provision. Economically advanced regions had better education, healthcare, technology, and social security services, while less developed regions faced insufficient fiscal capacity, leading to inadequate and unequal public service provision (Zheng et al., 2014).

6.2.1.4 Continuous Advancement of Equalization of Urban Public Services (2002–Present)

In 2002, the 16th National Congress of the Communist Party of China defined the government's basic functions of "economic regulation, market supervision, social management, and public services". Subsequent periods saw enhanced government roles in social management and public services, transitioning from an "omnipotent" to a "service-oriented" government. Both market-oriented economic reforms and government function changes propelled urban public service marketization reforms in the new era. With accelerating urbanization, China's urban public services developed towards standardization and systemization.

In 2005, the "Recommendations of the CPC Central Committee on Formulating the Eleventh Five-Year Plan for National Economic and Social Development" was issued, which introduced the concept of "public service equalization". The subsequent "12th Five-Year Plan for the National Basic Public Service System" in 2012 focused on defining national public services' scope, standards, and critical tasks, guiding public resource allocation. The 19th CPC National Congress report prioritized education development, accelerated the equalization of basic public services, and established a comprehensive, sustainable, multi-tiered social security system covering all citizens. On March 13, 2021, the *14th Five-Year Plan and the Long-Range Objectives Through the Year 2035* further underscored significantly improving basic public service equalization by 2035. It prioritized filling gaps in basic public services, strengthening non-basic public services, emphasizing the government's primary role in basic public service provision, diversifying providers for non-basic public services, and varying delivery methods.

6.2.2 *Analysis of the Current Status of Urban Public Services in China*

With the continuous development of urban public service theories and practices in China, innovations in government methods, and the increasing quantity and variety of public service products, the level of urban public services in China has been steadily improving. This has gradually led to the formation of a relatively complete public service system, including security services, livelihood services, and socioeconomic services.

6.2.2.1 General Development of Urban Public Services

(1) Urbanization and expansion of service targets. The increasing urbanization has led to a growing non-agricultural population, expanding the scale of urban public service targets. Since the reform and opening up, the dual model dividing urban and rural areas has been gradually dismantled, resulting in a significant migration of rural populations to urban areas, especially after the relaxation of policies converting rural residents to urban residents. By the end of 2019, China's urban population reached 848 million, with an urbanization rate of 60.60% (see Fig. 6.1).

(2) Improvement in infrastructure dependent on public services. Urban infrastructure directly affects residents' satisfaction with their lives. Well-developed urban infrastructure can enhance daily life standards and ensure the smooth execution of various economic activities. With the acceleration of urbanization, significant improvements have been made in urban water supply, gas supply, electricity

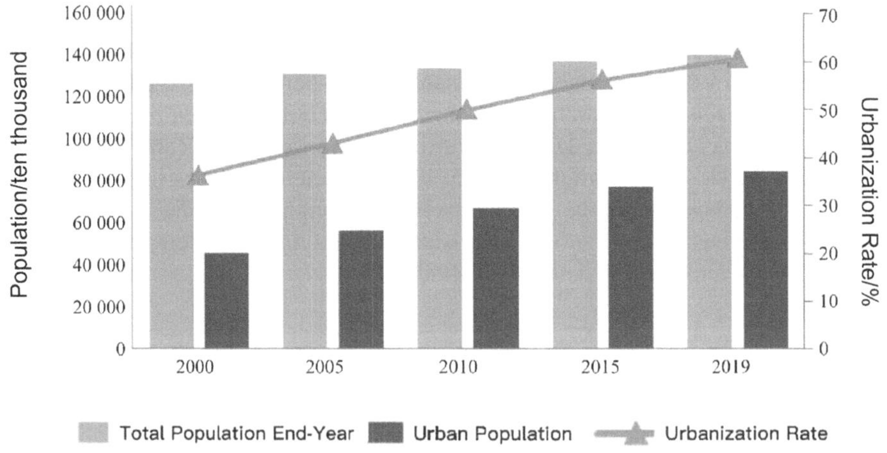

Fig. 6.1 Urbanization development trends in China (2015–2019). *Source* China statistical yearbook

supply, municipal facilities, public transportation, green spaces, parks, and city sanitation.

By the end of 2019, there were 297 prefecture-level cities in China, covering an urban area of 60,300 square kilometers. Table 6.1 shows the development status of urban public utilities in 2019: water supply and gas supply coverage rates were 98.78 and 97.29%, respectively, nearly achieving full coverage. Public transportation has also rapidly developed, with an average of 13.13 public transport vehicles per 10,000 people and a per capita urban road area of 17.36 square meters. Concurrently, the green space per capita reached 14.36 square meters, with an urban green coverage rate of 41.50%. Significant improvements have also been made in urban lighting and waste management capabilities.

(3) Steady development of public services in science, education, culture, and health. As significant areas of urban public service provision, these fields play a crucial role in promoting national economic development and socialist modernization. As shown in Fig. 6.2, China's expenditure on research and experimental development has risen from 2007 to 2019, reaching 2,214.360 billion yuan by the end of 2019, with a growth rate of 12.53%. Although the overall growth rate of research and experimental development expenditure shows a downward trend, it has slightly increased since 2015. Expenditure on education also shows an upward trend, reaching 5,017.812 billion yuan in 2019, with a growth rate of 8.74%. The growth rate of educational expenditure generally shows a downward trend but started to rise again at the end of 2017.

As shown in Table 6.2, in the healthcare sector, by the end of 2019, Chinese cities had 87.81 hospital beds per 10,000 people, 111 health technicians per 10,000 people, and 41 practicing (assistant) physicians per 10,000 people. In the cultural sector, by the end of 2019, there were 3,196 public library institutions, a 99.10% population coverage rate for radio programs, and 3,609 television programs.

Table 6.1 Overview of urban public utilities development

Indicator	2005	2010	2015	2019
Urban area/sq km	32,520.72	40,058.01	52,102.31	60,312.50
Water supply coverage/%	91.10	96.70	98.10	98.78
Gas supply coverage/%	82.10	92.00	95.30	97.29
Public transport vehicles/10 k	8.62	11.20	13.29	13.13
Per capita urban road area/sq m	10.92	13.21	15.60	17.36
Per capita park green space/sq m	7.89	11.18	13.35	14.36
Green coverage in bulit-up areas/%	—	38.60	40.10	41.50
Urban streetlights/10,000	1207.02	1773.99	2422.52	2865.60
Solid waste collection/10,000 tons	15,577.00	15,805.00	19,142.00	24,206.00
Sanitation	64,205.00	90,414.00	165,725.00	281,558.00

Source China statistical yearbook (2006–2020)

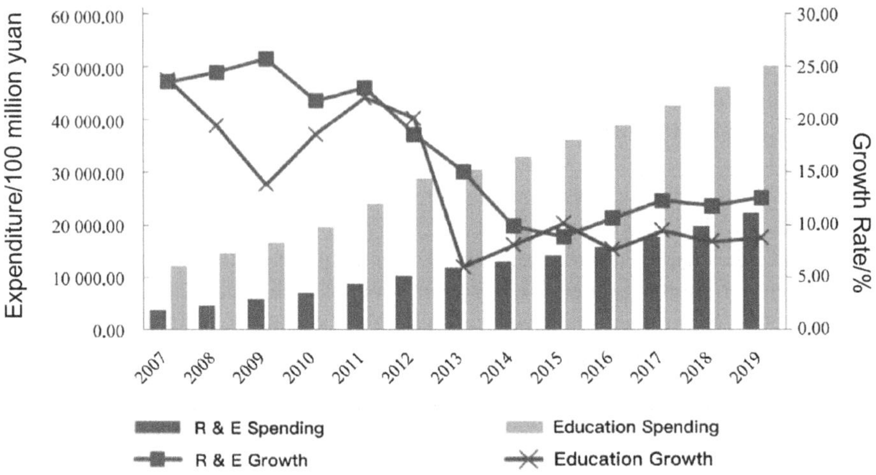

Fig. 6.2 Trends in China's science and education development (2007–2019). *Source* China statistical yearbook

Table 6.2 Overview of development in science, education, culture, and health (2007–2019)

Year	Indicator					
	Med beds/ 10 k	Health technicians/ 10 k	Practicing physicians/ 10 k	Public libraries	Broadcasting coverage	TV channels
2007	49.00	64	26	2799	95.40	3127
2008	51.70	67	27	2820	96.00	3199
2009	55.40	72	28	2850	96.30	3250
2010	59.40	76	30	2884	96.80	3272
2011	62.40	79	30	2952	97.10	3274
2012	68.80	85	32	3076	97.50	3273
2013	73.60	92	34	3112	97.80	3250
2014	78.37	97	35	3117	98.00	3329
2015	82.70	102	37	3139	98.20	3442
2016	84.13	108	39	3153	98.40	3360
2017	87.54	109	40	3166	98.70	3493
2018	87.00	109	40	3176	98.90	3559
2019	87.81	111	41	3196	99.10	3609

Source China statistical yearbook (2008–2020)

Table 6.3 Overview of social insurance system development (Unit: 10k people)

Year	Indicator				
	Urban pension insurance	Urban basic medical insurance	Unemployment insurance	Work injury insurance	Maternity insurance
2000	13,617.4	3786.9	10,408.4	4350.3	3001.6
2005	17,487.9	13,782.9	10,647.7	8478.0	5408.5
2010	25,707.3	43,262.9	13,375.6	16,160.7	12,335.9
2015	35,361.2	66,581.6	17,326.0	21,432.5	17,771.0
2016	37,929.7	74,391.6	18,088.8	21,889.3	18,451.0
2017	40,293.3	117,681.4	18,784.2	22,723.7	19,300.2
2018	41,901.6	134,458.6	19,643.5	23,874.4	20,434.1
2019	43,487.9	135,407.4	20,542.7	25,478.4	21,417.3

Source China statistical yearbook (2001–2020)

(4) Gradual improvement of social security systems. Currently, cities in China have established a social security system covering pension, medical, unemployment, work injury, and maternity insurance. To address living difficulties, the minimum living guarantee system for urban residents has also been implemented. The report of the 19th National Congress of the Communist Party of China (CPC) emphasized the importance of "strengthening the social security system". By the end of 2019, social insurance fund revenue reached 8355.04 billion yuan. The number of participants in urban pension insurance was 434.879 million, of which 311.775 million were active employees and 123.104 million were retirees. Basic medical insurance coverage in urban areas included 1.354 billion people, with expenditures of 2,085.42 billion yuan. Unemployment insurance covered 205.427 million people, and there were 2.283 million recipients of unemployment benefits. Work injury insurance covered 254.784 million people, and maternity insurance covered 214.173 million (see Table 6.3).

In terms of social relief, by the end of 2019, the number of urban residents under the minimum living guarantee reached 8.609 million. The actual beneficiaries of social pension insurance for urban and rural residents reached 160.319 million, with 528,000 community service institutions and facilities nationwide, covering 92.9% of urban community comprehensive service facilities.

6.2.2.2 Level of Urban Public Service Development

To provide a more detailed analysis of the level of urban public services in China, this study focuses on the cities in the Yangtze River Delta region.

(1) Overall Development Level of Public Services in the Yangtze River Delta

Urban public services should primarily meet residents' livelihood and public welfare needs. Taking the cities in the Yangtze River Delta as examples, this study constructed an index system to measure the level of urban public services from aspects such as education, health services, cultural services, urban transportation and communication, energy infrastructure services, and ecological environment services.[2] The levels of urban public services among cities in the Yangtze River Delta are analyzed to reflect the level of public services in economically developed regions of China (Table 6.4).

The data show that apart from cities like Shanghai, Hangzhou, Suzhou, and Nanjing, most cities in the Yangtze River Delta still have relatively low levels of public service development. From 2007 to 2017, many cities' public service levels did not significantly improve, showing considerable regional disparities.

In 2007, the top three cities in the Yangtze River Delta region by public service development level were Shanghai, Hangzhou, and Suzhou. There were 22 cities with public service levels above the average. The bottom ten cities were Huainan, Chizhou, Anqing, Suqian, Xuancheng, Chuzhou, Lu'an, Suzhou (Anhui), Bozhou, and Fuyang. Shanghai, ranking first, scored 8.109 in public service levels, while Fuyang, ranking last, scored 1.034, a difference of 7.075 points. The comprehensive scores of the top ten cities were about three times higher than those of the bottom ten, indicating significant disparities in public service levels among the cities.

By 2017, public services in the Yangtze River Delta region had improved. In comparison to 2007, there were no significant changes in the top ten cities, and Shanghai, Hangzhou, Nanjing, and Suzhou still topped the list. Hefei descended from 7 to 13th, Shaoxing from 8 to 11th, and Lianyungang from 10 to 30th; Zhoushan rose from 11 to 5th, Jiaxing from 12 to 8th, and Huzhou from 16 to 10th. The last ten cities were Xuzhou, Bengbu, Anqing, Chuzhou, Chizhou, Huainan, Lu'an, Suzhou (Anhui), Fuyang, and Bozhou. With Shanghai as the top one, it scored 10.471, and Bozhou, ranking last, scored 0.952, with a difference of 9.519 points. The comprehensive scores of the top ten cities were about four times higher than those of the bottom ten, indicating that although public service improved from 2007 to 2017, inequality in public service provision remained pronounced.

(2) Classified Comparison of Public Service Development Levels in the Yangtze River Delta

Based on the scores from 2007 and 2017, we classify the public service development of cities in the Yangtze River Delta into five levels: low, relatively low, medium, relatively high, and high, which reflect regional changes in public service development.

(1) The development level of urban public services in the Yangtze River Delta region presents a "One Core, Five Circles, Four Belts" pattern. Shanghai serves

[2] City Public Service Development System Data Sources: *China Statistical Yearbook*, *China Urban Statistical Yearbook*.

Table 6.4 Levels of urban public services in the Yangtze River delta

2007			2017		
City	Score	Rank	City	Score	Rank
Shanghai	8.109	1	Shanghai	10.471	1
Hangzhou	6.653	2	Hangzhou	8.553	2
Suzhou	6.547	3	Nanjing	8.345	3
Nanjing	6.200	4	Suzhou	8.216	4
Wuxi	5.908	5	Zhoushan	6.824	5
Ningbo	5.804	6	Ningbo	6.673	6
Hefei	5.043	7	Wuxi	6.489	7
Shaoxing	4.992	8	Jiaxing	5.275	8
Changzhou	4.805	9	Changzhou	5.273	9
Lianyungang	4.799	10	Huzhou	4.949	10
Zhoushan	4.738	11	Shaoxing	4.900	11
Jiaxing	4.650	12	Zhenjiang	4.553	12
Wenzhou	4.601	13	Hefei	4.356	13
Ma'anshan	4.560	14	Quzhou	4.309	14
Tongling	4.540	15	Jinhua	4.205	15
Huzhou	4.422	16	Wenzhou	3.866	16
Nantong	4.406	17	Yangzhou	3.734	17
Zhenjiang	4.357	18	Nantong	3.731	18
Jinhua	4.312	19	Ma'anshan	3.610	19
Huangshan	4.107	20	Tongling	3.494	20
Yangzhou	4.054	21	Taizhou	3.400	21
Wuhu	4.047	22	Huangshan	3.325	22
Quzhou	3.936	23	Wuhu	3.314	23
Lishui	3.852	24	Lishui	3.306	24
Taizhou	3.775	25	Taizhou	3.298	25
Taizhou	3.640	26	Huaibei	2.972	26
Xuzhou	3.530	27	Huaian	2.916	27
Huaibei	3.402	28	Xuancheng	2.836	28
Yancheng	2.970	29	Yancheng	2.831	29
Huaian	2.807	30	Lianyungang	2.757	30
Bengbu	2.804	31	Suqian	2.564	31
Huainan	2.770	32	Xuzhou	2.443	32
Chizhou	2.696	33	Bengbu	2.371	33
Anqing	2.581	34	Anqing	2.330	34
Suqian	2.564	35	Chuzhou	2.276	35
Xuancheng	2.369	36	Chizhou	2.249	36

(continued)

Table 6.4 (continued)

2007			2017		
City	Score	Rank	City	Score	Rank
Chuzhou	2.262	37	Huaian	2.076	37
Lu'an	2.183	38	Lu'an	1.634	38
Suzhou	1.603	39	Suzhou	1.211	39
Bozhou	1.566	40	Fuyang	1.114	40
Fuyang	1.034	41	Bozhou	0.952	41
Average	4.035		Average	4.085	

Source Calculated from data in *China Statistical Yearbook* and *China Urban Statistical Yearbook*

as the regional "core", boasting the highest level of public services, influencing the surrounding cities like Nanjing, Hangzhou, Hefei, Suzhou-Wuxi-Changzhou, and Ningbo metropolitan areas. Leveraging the Shanghai-Hankou-Chengdu, Shanghai-Hangzhou-Ningbo corridors, cities like Shanghai, Nanjing, Hangzhou, Hefei, and Ningbo utilize their comprehensive public service advantages to form the Shanghai-Nanjing-Hefei-Hangzhou-Ningbo development belt. The Shanghai-Hangzhou-Jinhua development belt connects cities with higher levels of public services along the Shanghai-Kunming corridor. Additionally, the Yangtze River Golden Waterway development belt and the coastal development belt emphasize the coordination between land and sea. On the whole, urban public service levels in the Yangtze River Delta region are highest in Shanghai, with a gradual decline from coastal to inland areas, often leading to the emergence of regional development centers, indicating significant disparities in public service access.

(2) The public services in the Yangtze River Delta region display a "Pyramid" structure. Most cities are at the base of the "pyramid", with only a few cities at the top. From 2007 to 2017, Shanghai, Hangzhou, Nanjing, and Suzhou consistently ranked among the highest in urban public services, while cities like Huainan, Lu'an, Suzhou (Anhui), Fuyang, and Bozhou were at the lower end.

(3) Path dependency in the development of Urban Public Services. Most cities have not seen significant shifts in their public services, mainly due to factors like economic development levels, the degree of local government intervention in the economy, the level of urbanization, and the degree of marketization, which are challenging to change significantly in the short term. To generally improve the level and equalization of basic public services in Chinese cities, considerable efforts are still required.

6.2.3 *Issues in Urban Public Service Supply in China*

Since the reform and opening up, China has gradually formed a mechanism for urban public service provision characterized by diversified providers, market-oriented methods, and smooth operations. However, due to historical development factors, the construction of China's urban public service system started late, leading to issues like underdeveloped providers, unclear boundaries between government administrative services and public services, and an imperfect public service provision mechanism.

6.2.3.1 Insufficient Reform Momentum of Single Government Supply Providers

In China, urban public services are primarily provided by the government and public institutions. Local governments, which possess administrative authority within their jurisdictions, are tasked with various administrative duties. As the government transitions into a "service-oriented" entity, providing public services has become a crucial part of its functions. Public institutions, unique to the planned economy period, formed the public service supply units. In this era, the government provided some public services through public institutions, creating a distinctive "government-affair unity" public service supply system (Ning, 2017). Public institutions are active in fields like science, education, culture, and health, typified by public libraries, schools, and hospitals. When providing public services, government public departments often exhibit a robust administrative character, leading to low supply quality, service efficiency, and a lack of diverse, timely service products, failing to meet residents' diverse needs.

Since the 1980s, with the development of China's market economy, the marketization reform of public products has also slowly unfolded. The introduction of market competition mechanisms into the urban public service system has changed the supply providers, gradually forming a diversified public service supply model led by the government, supported by market organizations, and supplemented by social organizations (Yang et al., 2016). These reforms alleviated the fiscal pressure on the government, increased the total supply of public services, and improved supply efficiency. The main change brought by the reform is the gradual reduction of public service projects directly supplied by government administrative departments, with some public service functions transferred to public institutions. Meanwhile, private enterprises and social organizations have also started to enter the public service field, becoming providers of some public services. Fields like education, healthcare, welfare institutions, and transportation services have seen the emergence of a multi-provider system comprising the government, social organizations, and market organizations. However, the government remains the primary provider of urban public services, and developing multiple supply providers is still insufficient. For instance, the professionalization and vocationalization of autonomous organizations, associations, and volunteer agencies are low, and the participation of for-profit organizations in public service provision is minimal. Market operations like leasing and service outsourcing are ineffective, failing to meet residents' diverse and multi-level demands for urban public services.

6.2.3.2 Ineffectiveness in the Public Service Supply Mechanism

The public service supply mechanism, fundamentally the optimal allocation of public resources, involves balancing efficiency and equity, which adjusts based on historical stages. Public service supply operations include decision-making, efficiency, coordination, equity, and responsibility mechanisms, mainly addressing the production issues within the supply mechanism (Yu, 2018).

Under the current system, local government fiscal revenue determines their economic and social public affairs management functions. In China's existing fiscal tax-sharing system, local governments in remote areas struggle to afford local public service provision, while economically developed areas often have ample financial resources, leading to significant spatial imbalances in public service provision. Despite the government's primary role due to market failures, issues like improper regulation, inefficiency, and lack of supervision persist. Although the introduction of market and social organizations has improved public service supply efficiency, lack of collaboration among providers leads to fragmented and dispersed public service operations, hindering the achievement of Pareto optimality. Additionally, public service supply costs are often high due to the absence of a scientific and practical supply performance evaluation mechanism. Vulnerable groups' participation awareness and capability are weak, making achieving indiscriminate basic public service provision difficult. The lack of relevant laws and regulations also means the urban public service supply process lacks responsibility supervision mechanisms.

6.2.3.3 Unclear Responsibility and Standards in Government-Social Organization Cooperation

Government procurement of services is a newly emerging model for social organization participation in public service provision, but it faces many issues in practice. Based on a research project by the Ministry of Civil Affairs and recent situations, the prominent problems include:

(1) There is poor independence of social organizations, with some being government-funded in various ways, functioning as extensions or external organizations of government departments, and thus not independent legal entities.
(2) The specific tasks and standards for procurement are unclear, and the responsibilities of the government and social organizations are ambiguous. In the

process of service procurement, the government often regards social organizations as internal administrative function implementation agencies. Consequently, the service procurement content may not align with actual responsibilities. Additionally, government procurement frequently focuses on emergency tasks, resulting in irregular procedures and arbitrary commissioning. There is also considerable inconsistency in the cooperation between the government and social organizations, sometimes involving the government arranging budgets to purchase workforce without specifying tasks (Liyuan, 2008). This results in social organizations lacking long-term development plans, service work lacking norms, and difficulties in establishing clear work standards.

(3) Social organizations are small in scale and lack sufficient negotiating power when cooperating with the government, making service procurement sometimes a unilateral collaborative behavior. In the provision of public services, social organizations act as contractors but lack the capacity and status to negotiate with the government. Their survival and development heavily rely on government funding, with limited access to other resources and funding channels.

(4) The performance appraisal system for government service procurement is incomplete; the service process lacks a monitoring system, leading to poor service effectiveness and difficulty controlling service costs. In government service procurement projects, the efficiency evaluation often becomes a formality, usually performed by the government departments or third-party evaluations attached to the government departments, lacking authenticity and fairness. Moreover, the evaluation of public service effectiveness lacks specific evaluation systems for different projects and lacks an objective public assessment.

(5) It is difficult for social organizations to exercise their professionalism, whose public services are not easily trusted by the public. As some social organizations essentially become external organizations for government departments, their professionalism in public service provision is restricted. Furthermore, these organizations, despite their undertaking governmental responsibilities, don't have administrative power, making it challenging for them to gain public trust.

6.2.3.4 Disparities in the Levels of Urban Public Service Provision Between Regions

On a national level, introducing market mechanisms into the public service provision field has broken the traditional model of exclusive government supply, leading to improvement in public service provision efficiency. However, some drawbacks of marketization reforms have become apparent. While pursuing efficiency, the market often tends to overlook fairness, exacerbating disparities in public service levels between regions and between urban and rural areas.

After tax-sharing reform, the fiscal revenue gap between local governments has widened. Despite the central government increasing fiscal transfers to central and western regions, disparities in regional actual fiscal revenue persist due to varying economic development levels, land financing practices, and land-based financial impacts, resulting in uneven spatial distribution of public service provision.

In recent years, infrastructure improvements, such as road construction in central and western regions, have narrowed the gap in regional public infrastructure levels. However, except for nationwide unified basic social security, other public service levels have not seen significant changes. For example, in 2019, the per capita local fiscal budget expenditure in Beijing was 33,827.35 yuan, while in Henan Province, it was only 10,265.56 yuan, roughly 3.30 times lower. In terms of pension insurance, the per capita basic pension insurance fund expenditure in Shanghai in 2019 was 11,203.86 yuan, compared to 1,594.30 yuan in Guizhou Province, approximately 7.03 times higher.

Another manifestation of regional disparities in public service provision levels is the irrational allocation of public resources. A significant amount of high-quality education and healthcare resources are concentrated in major cities like Beijing, Shanghai, and Guangzhou, while central and western regions, as well as rural areas, lack educational and healthcare resources, have an underdeveloped social security system, and lower public service levels.

As is stated in the report of the 19th National Congress of the Communist Party of China, "There remain many limitations in the field of people's livelihood.... People face difficulties in employment, education, medical care, housing, and elderly care", and also "in the new era, China must improve people's livelihood, taking measures to solve the problems in people's livelihood, promote social fairness and justice, improve pre-school education, meet people's education needs, create more employment opportunities, access medical services, provide elderly care, address housing issues, and help vulnerable groups". All these lead to increased investment in people's livelihood, improvement of the public service system, the guarantee of the masses' basic livelihood, and the enhancement of the capacity and level of essential public services.

6.2.4 Analysis of Factors Influencing Urban Public Service Development

6.2.4.1 Theoretical Analysis of Factors Influencing Public Service Development

With the gradual advancement of economic construction in China, the construction of an essential public service system closely related to people's well-being has also been accelerating. However, due to uneven economic development, regional disparities, and inadequate assessment mechanisms for administrative departments, there is still a significant gap between the supply level of public services and the public's expectations. Local governments' financial capacity and management capabilities directly influence the level of public services in various regions. Generally, areas with more substantial financial capacity can allocate a higher proportion of their fiscal expenditure to public services, thus providing higher quality public services to their residents. Strong government management capabilities also imply that public services will be provided more efficiently. Since China's tax-sharing reform, there has been a mismatch between the financial and administrative powers of the central and local governments, especially in areas such as basic education and healthcare. The fiscal decentralization system makes it challenging for the government to provide non-economic public services rationally and efficiently.

The government primarily relies on fiscal revenue as the main provider of basic public services. Local governments' fiscal revenue partially comes from taxes, which are influenced by the local economic development level. In recent years, the accelerated urbanization process has led to significant population growth and industrial agglomeration in cities, which in turn has triggered a rapid increase in residents' demand for public services. Consequently, the total supply of public services by local governments has also increased. The provision of urban public services in China relies heavily on government departments and public institutions. Although social capital is allowed to enter public service, there exist many barriers that limit the involvement of enterprises and social organizations in public services, slowing the development of the public service market.

6.2.4.2 Empirical Analysis of Factors Influencing Public Service Development

Empirical research shows that in recent years, with the improvement of economic development levels and the advancement of regional economic integration, the level of public services in cities across China has increased to varying degrees. Local fiscal expenditure, as an important source of funding for public services, is often considered the most direct factor influencing the local level of public services. However, local government fiscal expenditure is usually influenced by the institutional environment. Driven by economic growth goals, local government fiscal expenditure tends to favor economic construction, leading to a lower proportion of investment in public services related to people's livelihood, such as science, education, culture, and health. Moreover, with the acceleration of urbanization, the continuous agglomeration of population and industries in cities impacts the level of public services due to changes in population size, structure, and spatial distribution.

Taking cities in the Yangtze River Delta as an example, we analyze the impact of urban economic development level, local government fiscal expenditure preferences, urbanization level, local government competition degree, and marketization degree on the level of urban public services. With the baseline model (OLS), spatial econometric models are also employed by considering spatial weight factors. The significance of the spatial error model (SEM) and spatial lag model (SLM) is tested using the Lagrange multiplier and robustness test methods. Ultimately, the spatial error model is adopted, and the analysis results are shown in Table 6.5.

Table 6.5 Results of the baseline model and spatial error model regression analysis

Variable	Baseline model		Spatial error model	
	2007 urban public service level	2017 urban public service level	2007 urban public service level	2017 urban public service level
Economic development level	0.0090(0.14)	0.3547**(2.08)	-0.0468 (−1.39)	0.3477**(2.26)
Local government expenditure preference	-0.0022 (−0.53)	-0.0016 (−0.19)	-0.0054 (−1.57)	-0.0034 (−0.45)
Urbanization level	0.0719***(12.05)	0.2065***(8.38)	0.0689***(14.48)	0.2062***(8.70)
Local government competition degree	0.1461***(3.76)	-0.0377 (−0.90)	0.1703***(4.72)	-0.0001 (−0.00)
Marketization Degree	0.1193***(3.74)	0.0172 (1.67)	0.1159*** (4.83)	0.0147 (1.53)
Constant	-1.1530 (−1.21)	-12.0953***(−4.35)	-0.0302 (−0.27)	-11.0928*** (−4.08)
Observations	41	41	41	41
R-squared	0.883	0.766		
R2_a	0.867	0.732		
F-Value	52.97	22.89		
Lambda			0.1664***(3.45)	0.0201**(1.97)
Wald test			11.898***	3.869**
LR test			8.929***	4.382**

Note **, *** indicate significance at the 5% and 1% levels, respectively. Parentheses in the baseline model indicate the t-values of the corresponding coefficients, and parentheses in the spatial error model indicate the z-values of the corresponding coefficients

The analysis of public service levels in 2007 and 2017 reveals that in 2007, there were significant positive correlations between urbanization level, local government competition degree, marketization degree, and public service level. This indicates that improvements in urbanization, an increase in foreign investment proportion, and higher marketization levels promote the enhancement of regional public service levels. In 2017, the coefficients of economic development level and urbanization level were significantly positive, indicating that improvements in economic development level and the acceleration of urbanization processes are conducive to enhancing public service levels. The coefficient of local government fiscal expenditure preference was insignificant, indicating that China's current fiscal expenditure preferences do not have a significant impact on public services.

6.2.4.3 Development of Information Technology and Urban Public Service Provision

The supply level and methods of public services are influenced by economic development level, fiscal budget, and technological factors. The information technology revolution of the 1980s has a substantial impact on the provision of public services.

Big data presents new opportunities for the development of government public service models, leveraging powerful information collection, analysis, and coordination advantages to address issues such as structural imbalances, single supply entities, and inefficiencies in urban public service provision. The application of big data, the internet, and information platforms contributes to the equalization, socialization, and efficiency of public services, forming a supply model where government, market, society, and public entities participate and share responsibilities. This transforms traditional passive, fragmented, and extensive services into proactive, holistic, and precise services. On one hand, the application of big data in government will lead to intelligent administrative reforms. By implementing a "one-stop" government service model, governments can achieve collaborative operations, advance the modernization of governance capabilities, and create innovative governance models such as "e-government" and "electronic public services". E-government plays a positive role in optimizing government business processes, improving work efficiency, enhancing transparency, and improving decision-making. On the other hand, with technological advancements, data acquisition is becoming more convenient, and storage costs are decreasing. Big data is gradually extending to various industries and segments, with increasing applications in public service fields such as education, transportation, healthcare, and public safety. This leads to the formation of a new public service supply model centered on platform interoperability, data openness and sharing, service coordination, and value co-creation.

In recent years, the establishment of communication networks and management information systems in e-government construction has improved social governance levels. With the rapid development of cloud computing and big data, the informatization of public services has become an inevitable choice for enhancing public service quality, broadening supply channels, and reducing supply costs. This also creates conditions for the precision, equalization, and fairness of public services (Tang, 2016; Wu et al., 2020; He et al., 2017).

6.3 Mechanisms for Urban Public Service Supply

Since the reform and opening up, rapid socioeconomic development has increased urban residents' and enterprises' demand for public services. However, systemic constraints of the traditional government-led mechanism of public service provision make it difficult to meet these demands. This discrepancy has stimulated a transition from a purely government-administered supply mechanism to a diversified, market-oriented provision system involving multiple social entities. Currently, China's urban public service provision operates through three approaches: government supply, market supply, and multi-stakeholder cooperative supply mechanism.

6.3.1 Government Mechanisms for Urban Public Service Provision

6.3.1.1 Areas and Content of Government-Provided Public Services

The government must ensure both the coverage and quality levels of public services while focusing on the spatial allocation of public resources to promote regional and urban–rural equity in service provision. Public service equality requires that basic, appropriate, and relatively equal services be offered to the public. In recent years, China has significantly improved its urban public services, forming a more comprehensive system encompassing public education, healthcare, social security, employment, social services, housing security, public culture, and sports (Yang, 2012).

To unify and effectively coordinate basic public service systems across urban and rural areas, China needs to establish a modern public financial system. This involves reforming the fiscal system and increasing financial support for equalizing public services, underscoring the government's primary role in supplying basic public services. Such reforms clarify the responsibilities and fiscal duties of central and local governments and enhance support from central and provincial budgets to grassroots governments, laying the groundwork for achieving fiscal equalization.

Education equity is essential for achieving social equity and has long been a fundamental principle in China's educational policy. Since the introduction of nine-year compulsory education in 1986, as mandated in the *Compulsory Education Law of the People's Republic of China*, the government has continued to prioritize educational fairness. Initiatives such as the elimination of tuition fees for compulsory education in both rural and urban areas, and the introduction of the *Urban and Rural Compulsory Education Funding Management Measures* have increased the efficiency of education funding. Many policies have been enacted to bridge the educational gap between urban and rural, remote, and minority regions, thereby enhancing access to equal educational services.

In healthcare, ensuring public health and easy access to medical services are also crucial for citizen welfare. Recently, the focus of China's public health initiatives has shifted from prevention to a combination of prevention and treatment. While earlier reforms concentrated on urban public health systems, primary healthcare institutions still face challenges. To address issues of expensive and inaccessible medical services, China established a tiered diagnosis and treatment system in 2015, rationalizing the allocation of medical resources between urban and rural areas, supporting rural doctors and clinics, and thus making public health services more accessible and equitable (He, 2019; Wang, 2019).

The social security system is also a fundamental channel through which all citizens can benefit from the country's reforms and development. Currently, China has established a comprehensive and well-functioning social security system. It is based on social insurance, social assistance, and social welfare, emphasizing basic pensions, basic medical care, and minimum subsistence allowances, with philanthropy and commercial insurance serving as supplements. A sound social security system forms the foundation for providing social security services to urban and rural residents. Regarding pension insurance, China has reformed the pension system for government and public institution employees and has promoted a new rural social pension insurance system (Zheng, 2019). In terms of medical insurance, China has implemented systems such as basic medical insurance for urban employees and residents, as well as the new rural cooperative medical system, ensuring adequate medical services for both urban and rural populations.

China also attaches great importance to developing the market employment mechanism, actively guiding the government's role in employment policies, enhancing training efforts for vocational technical personnel, and ensuring the orderly advancement of employment services for urban and rural residents. Efforts are also made to accelerate grassroots cultural development and strive to build a public cultural service system that covers both urban and rural areas. Following the principle that "houses are for living in, not for speculation", the housing security system is rapidly developed. However, the urban–rural dual structure poses significant challenges to equalizing public services between urban and rural areas, particularly in fundamental public services like education and social security. In education, China has established a relatively comprehensive education system encompassing basic education, higher education, vocational education, and private education. However, the primary sources of education funding in China are national financial education funds and public fiscal education funds, with a small portion coming from social investment. As a result, economically developed regions enjoy richer educational resources and higher educational levels, while economically underdeveloped regions face long-term stagnation in educational resources and levels, leading to notable regional disparities. In terms of social security, Chinese cities have established a comprehensive social security system, including pension, medical, unemployment, work injury, and maternity insurance. Rural areas' governments also encourage farmers to participate in the new rural cooperative medical insurance through subsidies. Nevertheless, the overall social security system in rural areas remains at a low level and with limited coverage.

6.3.1.2 Models of Government Provision of Public Services

The provision of public services by the government does not mean that the government is the direct provider of these services. Even during the planned economy period, not all urban public services were directly produced by the government. Thus, the provision of public services by the government refers to the government's complete control over the entire process of public service provision. Under the planned economy system, the government controlled the majority of public resources and provided public goods directly. In the transformation of government functions from "economic-oriented" to "service-oriented", the government's focus on public service provision shifted towards overall planning, organization, coordination, supervision, and evaluation. However, for some public services related to public interest (such as environment, education, and healthcare) and those inappropriate for market-oriented organizations to provide, state-owned enterprises remain the primary providers.

China implements a nine-year compulsory basic education system. The direction and goals of schooling, as well as the admission system, school years, curriculum, textbooks, and teacher qualifications, are all clearly specified by the government, with schools responsible for specific implementation. In terms of education funding, in recent years, China's investment in education has met the requirement of accounting for 4% of GDP. In 2019, the total expenditure on education nationwide was 5,017.812 billion yuan, which was about 5.06% of GDP and approximately 21.01%[3] of the general public budget expenditure. According to China's fiscal system, education funding is shared by the central and local governments based on their responsibilities, with provincial governments responsible for coordination and implementation. Besides funding from general public budgets and government funds, educational funding also comes from enterprise allocations in state-owned and state-holding enterprises, school-run enterprises, and social service revenue. In recent years, the government has developed preschool education, community education, vocational education, and continuing education by purchasing services from social organizations, representing a new initiative in public education service provision. For example, the government uses educational projects tender to purchase education products needed by the public from social organizations (mainly non-profit organizations), then optimizes community education resources through market mechanisms (Xu et al., 2020). In the development of higher education, China also primarily relies on government investment and management, with most higher education institutions funded and operated by central or local governments. Since the reform and opening up, China has carried out a series of reforms on the investment and management mechanisms of higher education institutions, with social capital allowed to establish higher education institutions since the 1990s, with some restrictions on degree awarding and program settings. For public higher education institutions, admission methods, program settings, degree awarding conditions, and teacher qualifications are generally approved or recognized by the Ministry of Education.

In the field of public health and medical services, the government provides administrative management services for matters such as public health and epidemic prevention. The government focuses on health security and residents' health, engaging in preemptive prevention, treatment during events, and post-event monitoring of major diseases, particularly infectious diseases, as well as supervising and regulating food, medicine, and public environmental hygiene and conducting disease-related publicity, health education, and vaccination (Lu, 2012). China's public health services adopt a hierarchical management model: the central government sets public health

[3] Ministry of Finance of the People's Republic of China: *Statistical Bulletin on the Implementation of National Education Expenditure in 2019*.

policies and goals at the macro level, local governments handle specific public health matters, and provincial governments serve as the coordinating channel between the central and local governments, collectively providing efficient and equitable public health services to the populace. Especially after the outbreak of COVID-19, central and local governments at all levels organized anti-epidemic efforts, forming a health and epidemic prevention organization system composed of disease control and prevention centers, leading groups for health and epidemic prevention, and working groups for health and epidemic prevention. This cooperation among party and government departments, professional teams, and grassroots social organizations yielded notable results.

In China, public health and epidemic prevention funding comes from government budgets at all levels. According to statistics, in the 2019 central financial budget, health expenditure was 24.772 billion yuan, accounting for about 1.49% of the central financial total budget; expenditure from local government financial budgets was 1,641.762 billion yuan, accounting for about 98.51%[4] of the local financial total budget. To combat COVID-19, by the end of November 2020, government expenditure on epidemic prevention and control exceeded 400 billion yuan, providing strong support for the fight against the epidemic.

The *Notice on Doing a Good Job in Basic Public Health Service Projects* issued in 2020 stated that the per capita basic public health service funding subsidy in China for 2020 was 74 yuan, and there will be an additional 5 yuan in 2021, which will be fully allocated to rural and urban communities. This funding was coordinated for costs related to community health service centers (stations), township health centers, and village clinics conducting COVID-19 epidemic prevention work, enhancing grassroots epidemic prevention funding guarantees, and improving epidemic prevention capabilities.

In the field of public health services, the government also organizes social forces to provide public health services through procurement. The funds for purchasing public health services are included in the fiscal budget by budget management, and procurement methods include open bidding, invited bidding, competitive negotiations, inquiries, sole source, fixed grants, and reward-based grants.

In the field of medical services, China has long provided medical services mainly through government-invested public hospitals. However, with the deepening reform of the medical system and mechanisms, the country encourages social forces to establish private hospitals and allows some specialist doctors to set up private clinics. In some cities, social capital manages public hospitals, thus forming a multi-stakeholder cooperative supply mechanism in providing medical services, which will be further discussed in subsequent sections.

In the field of environmental public services, the non-excludability and non-rivalrous nature of environmental public goods make it difficult to supply via market mechanisms. Environmental public goods are often regulatory, such as laws and regulations, behavioral norms, and public policies related to environmental protection, which require the government to enforce them compulsively. Therefore, the

[4] National Bureau of Statistics: *China Statistical Yearbook* (2020).

government is the main provider of environmental public goods. Due to the externalities and the contradiction of zero marginal social efficiency, the government cannot be the sole provider. To enhance the efficiency of government provision of environmental public services, China has established multiple provision models centered around government service functions: a government authoritative-led supply model, a government-participation market competition model, and a government-guaranteed volunteer service model (Hua, 2016). Funding for environmental public services mainly comes from fiscal special funds, budgetary allocations, and central and local government split finances.

6.3.1.3 Fiscal Expenditure Mechanisms for Government Public Services

The public service supply is fundamentally supported by national public financial expenditure. From 2000 to 2018, China's general budget expenditure increased from 1,588.65 billion yuan to 22,090.413 billion yuan, roughly a 13-fold increase. Along with the continuous improvement of the fiscal and tax system, the proportion of central and local government fiscal expenditure has also changed. The proportion of central fiscal general budget expenditure dropped from 34.75% in 2000 to 14.81% in 2018, while the proportion of local fiscal general budget expenditure rose from 65.25% in 2000 to 85.19% in 2018. The increasing proportion of local fiscal budget expenditure means local governments have more abundant funds and greater initiative in providing local public services, allowing them to actively and flexibly combine local development conditions to offer more targeted public services.

As can be seen from the history of China's public service reforms, significant progress in public services is closely related to the continuous increase in public service expenditure in the government fiscal budget. The fiscal input into public services by the Chinese government is allocated according to the division of responsibilities between the central and local governments, with both central and local governments formulating their respective fiscal budget allocations. Table 6.6 reflects the central government's expenditure on public service-related projects.

Table 6.6 shows that from 2008 to 2018, the central government's fiscal budget and public service expenditures consistently grew. Significant increases were observed in environmental protection, urban–rural community affairs, and healthcare expenditures, which grew by 4 to 6 times. Other public service expenditures, such as education, social security and employment, public safety, and science and technology, rose by 2 to 3 times. In recent years, central government expenditure has increased significantly in areas such as environmental protection, healthcare, education, social security and employment, and science and technology. In 2018, central government budget allocations included 312.027 billion yuan for science and technology, 204.151 billion yuan for public safety, 173.123 billion yuan for education, 150.368 billion yuan for general public services, 131.371 billion yuan for transportation, and 118.455 billion yuan for social security and employment. Besides increasing the provision of public safety, economic, and livelihood services, the state has also intensified support

Table 6.6 Central government budget expenditure on public service projects (Unit: trillion yuan)

Indicator	2008	2010	2012	2014	2016	2018
Fiscal expenditure	13,344.17	15,989.73	18,764.63	22,570.07	27,403.85	32,707.81
General public service	2344.55	837.42	998.32	1050.43	1209.15	1503.68
Public safety	648.63	875.20	1183.47	1477.76	1741.91	2041.51
Education	491.63	720.96	1101.46	1253.62	1447.72	1731.23
Science and technology	1077.35	1661.30	2210.43	2436.66	2686.10	3120.27
Culture, sports, media	140.61	150.13	193.56	223.00	247.95	281.13
Social security and employment	344.28	450.30	585.67	699.91	890.58	1184.55
Health care	46.78	73.56	74.29	90.25	91.16	210.65
Environmental protection	66.21	69.48	63.65	344.74	295.49	427.56
Urban–rural community affairs	14.33	10.09	18.19	17.18	19.76	86.38
Agriculture, forestry, water affairs	308.38	387.89	502.49	539.67	779.07	592.30
Transportation	913.20	1489.58	863.59	731.16	812.12	1313.71
Other expenditures	413.75	98.32	38.31	129.99	432.17	826.74

Source China statistical yearbook (2006–2019)

for environmental protection and cultural and sports activities, with expenditures of 42.756 billion yuan for environmental protection and 28.113 billion yuan for culture, sports, and media in 2018.

According to China's fiscal system and division of responsibilities, numerous public service projects are managed by local governments, which also bear the expenditure responsibilities. Table 6.7 illustrates the expenditure of local governments on major public service projects.

It can be seen in Table 6.7 that from 2008 to 2018, the fiscal budgets of local governments increased continuously, along with public service expenditures. Significant growth was observed in expenditures for transportation, healthcare, urban–rural community affairs, and science and technology, which grew by 4 to 5 times. Other public service expenditures, such as energy conservation and environmental protection, social security and employment, education, public safety, culture, sports, and media, grew by more than two times. Notably, in recent years, expenditures in education, social security, employment, and healthcare have increased significantly. In 2018, local government public budget expenditures included 3,043.824 billion yuan for education, 2,582.754 billion yuan for social security and employment, and 520.638 billion yuan for science and technology. In addition to increasing the provision of economic and livelihood services, local governments have also

Table 6.7 Main items of local fiscal general budget expenditure (Unit: 100 million yuan)

Indicator	2008	2010	2012	2014	2016	2018
General budget expenditure	49,248.49	73,884.43	107,188.34	129,215.49	160,351.36	188,196.32
General public service	7451.37	8499.74	11,702.14	12,217.07	13,581.37	16,871.01
Public safety	3411.13	4642.50	5928.13	6879.47	9290.07	11,739.97
Education	8518.58	11,829.06	20,140.64	21,788.09	26,625.06	30,438.24
Science and technology	1051.86	1588.88	2242.20	2877.79	3877.86	5206.38
Culture, sports, media	955.13	1392.57	2074.79	2468.48	2915.13	3256.73
Social security and employment	6460.01	8680.32	11,999.85	15,268.94	20,700.87	25,827.54
Health care	2710.26	4730.62	7170.82	10,086.56	13,067.61	15,412.90
Energy conservation and environmental protection	1385.15	2372.50	2899.81	3470.90	4439.33	5870.05
Urban–rural community affairs	4191.81	5977.29	9060.93	12,942.31	18,374.86	22,037.75
Transportation	1440.80	3998.89	7332.57	9669.26	9686.59	9969.05
Housing security	–	1990.40	4068.71	4638.31	6338.77	6299.92

Source China statistical yearbook (2006–2019)

intensified environmental protection efforts, with local fiscal expenditures for energy conservation and environmental protection reaching 587.005 billion yuan in 2018.[5]

6.3.2 *Market (Private) Mechanism for the Supply of Urban Public Services*

At the Third Plenary Session of the 16th Central Committee of the Communist Party of China, the party, for the first time, decided to allow non-public capital to enter infrastructure, public utilities, and other industries and sectors not prohibited by laws and regulations. Subsequently, the government eased market access conditions for the non-public sector economy and further introduced market competition mechanisms in the field of public infrastructure. Private capital began to invest in public infrastructure sectors such as transportation, water, electricity, gas, roads, landscaping, and

[5] Statistical Communiqué of the People's Republic of China on the 2019 National Economic and Social Development.

waste treatment (He Qiaozhi, 2014). After that, China's urban public services sector also started exploring the investment and operation of private capital, encompassing education, employment, housing, culture, and other fields.

With the advancement of market-oriented reforms in China's public infrastructure and public services, the previous government-monopolized model of supplying public goods has been broken. Various profit-oriented and non-profit organizations have gradually participated in producing and supplying urban public services and products. The traditional single-provider model of public service supply has transitioned to a diversified one, with more private capital entering certain public service areas and market supply mechanisms starting to play a role in the public service sector. This situation is directly related to the overall economic and institutional reforms in China. In 2017, the proportion of investment in fixed assets by non-state entities as a share of total social fixed asset investment was 78.31%, non-state urban employment accounted for 85.72% of total urban employment, the paid-in capital of non-state industrial enterprises accounted for 93.54% of the total paid-in capital in industrial enterprises, and foreign capital in non-state industrial enterprises accounted for as high as 99.89% of the total foreign capital in industrial enterprises (see Table 6.8).

In the education sector, the market mechanism was introduced in the non-compulsory education field in the 1990s. On one hand, private capital was allowed to invest in and establish kindergartens and primary and secondary schools. On the other hand, private capital was permitted to set up private colleges and universities while relaxing regulations on educational fees. Private education has become an

Table 6.8 Development overview of China's non-state economy (Unit: %)

Year	Indicator			
	Proportion of non-state investment in fixed assets to total social fixed asset investment	The proportion of non-state urban employment to total urban employment	The proportion of paid-in capital of non-state industrial enterprises to total paid-in capital in industrial enterprises	Proportion of foreign capital in non-state industrial enterprises to total foreign capital in industrial enterprises
2007	71.81	79.25	85.27	99.79
2008	71.82	79.92	85.17	99.86
2009	68.97	80.73	88.16	99.61
2010	66.90	81.21	88.30	99.75
2011	73.52	81.33	89.65	99.90
2012	74.32	81.57	89.68	99.67
2013	75.39	83.36	94.39	99.94
2014	75.59	83.94	95.25	99.94
2015	75.14	84.64	92.97	99.91
2016	78.72	85.11	92.80	99.98
2017	78.31	85.72	93.54	99.89

Source Calculated based on relevant data from the *China Statistical Yearbook* (2008–2018)

essential part of the national education system, having equal legal status with public education. The state vigorously supports and guides private education, promoting its entrance into higher vocational education and vocational training. According to the *2019 National Education Development Statistical Bulletin*, as of 2019, there were 191,500 private schools of all levels and types nationwide, accounting for approximately 36.13% of all schools of the same types and levels; the number of enrolled students was 17,743,300; the number of students in various educational stages was 56,166,100, with the highest proportion in preschool education at about 47.17%, followed by regular primary education at about 16.82%, showing new progress in the development of private education.

Along with the rapid development of private education, legislative work in this area has also achieved significant success. In 2012, the Ministry of Education issued the *Opinions on Encouraging and Guiding Private Funds to Enter the Education Sector to Promote the Healthy Development of Private Education*, encouraging and guiding private funds to enter the education sector. In terms of law enforcement, in December 2019, the Ministry of Education also issued the *Opinions on Strengthening Educational Administrative Law Enforcement Work*, which set out requirements for clarifying the scope of educational administrative law enforcement, enforcing law enforcement responsibilities, improving law enforcement agencies, enhancing the quality of law enforcement personnel, and perfecting law enforcement mechanisms.

In the healthcare sector, the core of market-oriented reforms is to give more autonomy to hospitals through graded management to expand the autonomy of public hospitals to operate on a self-sustaining basis and to break the monopoly of traditional public hospitals by allowing social capital to invest in and operate medical institutions, thus changing the single public ownership model of medical institutions.

The operation, personnel appointment, and profit distribution of private medical institutions are managed in a corporate manner, with most being for-profit institutions, while only a few are non-profit institutions enjoying government subsidies. Following the implementation of the 2009 new medical and health system reform, private capital entered the healthcare sector, breaking the monopoly of public medical institutions. In October 2013, the State Council issued the *Opinions on Promoting the Development of the Health Service Industry*, which proposed easing market access conditions for private capital to enter the medical service industry, accelerating the implementation of policies that treat non-public medical institutions and public medical institutions equally. Subsequently, private hospitals entered a period of rapid development. In April 2014, the National Development and Reform Commission, the National Health and Family Planning Commission, and the Ministry of Human Resources and Social Security jointly issued the *Guideline on Market-Adjusted Pricing of Medical Services in Non-Public Medical Institutions*, allowing non-public medical institutions to set their own medical service prices and encouraging private medical practice. Data from the *China Statistical Yearbook* (2020) show that in 2019, the total national health expenditure was 6,584.139 billion yuan, with social health expenditure accounting for 2,915.057 billion yuan, approximately 44.27% of the total national health expenditure, about 1.62 times the government health expenditure; the number of privately-run village health stations was about

134.6 thousand, approximately 21.84% of the total number of village health stations nationwide; the utilization rate of private hospital beds was 61.4%, with an average of 224 working days per bed per year, and an average hospital stay of 9.4 days for discharged patients, 0.4 days higher than that of public hospital beds.

In the field of social security, China began reforming the social security system towards a market economy system in 1978. After 1998, China initially established a basic insurance system and policy framework under the socialist market economy system, mainly establishing a cost-sharing system for social security involving the government, enterprises, and individuals. In sectors like health insurance, work injury insurance, and maternity insurance, market mechanisms were introduced, with enterprises paying insurance premiums for employees. Enterprise pension insurance was co-financed by enterprises and employees, using individual accounts and operated under market-oriented management. The government departments played a supervisory role. Meanwhile, the government gradually opened up commercial insurance companies to provide commercial insurance in healthcare, pensions, personal accident, and other areas. The combination of commercial insurance with the government's compulsory social insurance has formed a relatively comprehensive social security system.

6.3.3 Multi-Stakeholder Cooperative Supply Mechanism for Urban Public Services

In China's public service reform practice, there are good results in some fields that allow private capital entry, but they also encounter problems. For example, some private capital focuses too much on commercial profits and market-oriented operations, deviating from the functions and nature of public services and even harming the interests of some vulnerable groups. Addressing government failures often leads to market failures. Therefore, to complement the shortcomings of government-provided public services, prevent the excessive privatization or marketization of public services, and mobilize more social capital to participate in the supply of social services, since the mid-1990s, China has encouraged social capital and social organizations to participate in public service undertakings, leading to the formation of a mechanism for the cooperative supply of public services by multi-stakeholders, including the government, market (private) sector, and society.

Countries have accumulated considerable experience in exploring government public sector reforms. According to Savas (2002), cooperation between the government, public sector, and social forces includes various forms, such as collaboration with community citizens and volunteers, cooperation with private enterprises, and working with non-profit organizations. In China, the partners in the cooperation between the government, public sector, and social forces are enterprises and social organizations. In the field of public infrastructure, the government often cooperates with enterprises, as previously discussed. In the field of public services, the government typically uses market mechanisms to cooperate with social organizations and, less often, with enterprises. This is determined by the functions and nature of public services. Moreover, the government can promote cooperation with social organizations to provide public services due to the development of social organizations following the reform and opening up. Since the late 1980s, China has permitted the establishment and development of social organizations. The Ministry of Civil Affairs resumed the registration of social organizations in 1988. Since then, social organizations in China have proliferated, forming a system of social organizations with orderly public participation, comprehensive urban and rural coverage, and various categories (Wang, 2016). As of 2018, the number of social organizations in China was 817,360, and the number of social groups was 366,234, which increased by 664,038 and 235,566, respectively, compared to the year 2000. The number of foundations was 7,034, an increase of 6,059 compared to 2005. The number of private non-enterprise units was 444,092, an increase of 421,438 compared to 2000 (see Table 6.9). Many of these social organizations have participated in the supply of public services, playing a positive role in politics, economy, culture, education, science, and technology, and have become an important force in the supply of public goods in China.

Civil affairs in China have also developed rapidly. As shown in Table 6.10, by the end of 2018, the total number of civil affairs service institutions and facilities registered and managed by civil affairs departments nationwide was 1.876 million, an increase of 3.0% over the previous year. The total donation income of social organizations nationwide was 91.97 billion yuan, an increase of 26.1% over the previous year. The coverage rate of comprehensive service facilities in urban communities was 78.7%. The number of urban minimum living security (Dibao) recipients was 10.07 million.

The diversification of public service providers has improved the quality of public services, with the government acting as the purchaser and regulator of public goods. The diverse supply methods of public services can combine market supply with

Table 6.9 Development overview of China's social organizations

Year	Indicator			
	Number of social organizations	Number of social groups	Number of foundations	Number of private non-enterprise units
2000	153,322	130,668	—	22,654
2005	319,762	171,150	975	147,637
2010	445,631	245,256	2200	198,175
2015	662,425	328,500	4784	329,141
2016	702,405	335,932	5559	360,914
2017	761,539	354,794	6307	400,438
2018	817,360	366,234	7034	444,092

Source China statistical yearbook (2001–2019)

Table 6.10 Development status of civil affairs services in China

Year	Indicator			
	Number of civil affairs service institutions and facilities managed and registered by civil affairs departments/million units	Donation income of social organizations/ 100 million yuan	Coverage rate of comprehensive service facilities in urban communities /%	Number of urban minimum living security recipients / million people
2014	166.8	524.8	81.0	1877.0
2015	176.5	610.3	82.0	1701.0
2016	174.5	786.7	79.3	1480.2
2017	182.1	729.2	78.6	1261.0
2018	187.6	919.7	78.7	1007.0

Source Statistical report on the development of civil affairs (2014–2018)

government supply models based on the characteristics of service recipients and the nation's economic development level, leveraging each model's strengths and compensating for its weaknesses. Currently, social organizations participate in public services in three main ways: government-built and privately managed, privately built, and government-assisted, and privately built and managed. The *Thirteenth Five-Year Plan for Promoting the Equalization of Basic Public Services* proposes promoting the Public–Private Partnership (PPP) model, using various methods such as public bidding, invitation bidding, competitive negotiation, and competitive consultation to fairly select social capital with corresponding management experience, professional ability, financing strength, and good credit status for cooperation. In the implementation of specific projects, the construction and operation management of facilities can be separated, forming flexible participation forms such as BOT, TOT, BBO, contract outsourcing, and government procurement (Yang et al., 2014).

Another important way for the government to cooperate with social organizations in providing public services is through government procurement of services. The scope of government procurement of services in China includes public service areas such as health and medical care, education, community governance, employment, and family planning. Under the support and funding of the government, a number of private non-profit social organizations have been established, obtaining working funds through government procurement services and being specially commissioned by the government to handle public service tasks (Wang, 2015).

6.3.4 Reforms on Urban Public Service Supply Mechanisms

In China's economic system reform, the public service supply mechanisms have undergone significant adjustments, with social organizations assuming more responsibility for public service provision. However, issues such as excessive government restrictions on social organizations and their slow development have limited the role of the market and social organizations in public service provision. To improve public service levels and establish an effective public service supply system, it is necessary to increase the total supply of public resources, optimize the supply structure, and continuously reform the public service supply system and mechanisms.

6.3.4.1 Promote the Transformation of Government Functions to Build a Service-Oriented Government

The reform of the public service supply system and mechanism hinges on the transformation of government functions and adjustments to its roles. The core is to utilize market mechanisms in public services, redefining the relationship between government and society and clarifying the government's role and responsibilities, which include:

(1) A clear understanding of government roles, responsibilities, and functions. A modern government's key responsibility is to mobilize resources to provide sufficient, high-level, and high-quality public services. The government should transition from a "rower" to a "steerer" and, more importantly, to a "service provider". Since the reform and opening up, China's government functions have undergone multiple reforms, including adjustments to institutions, government-enterprise relationships, investment systems, and fiscal mechanisms. These reforms mainly targeted private sectors, with minimal changes in the direct intervention and control of public sectors. Hence, there is an urgent need to deepen the reform of public sector mechanisms. The 19th National Congress of the Communist Party of China proposed "building a service-oriented government that satisfies the people", with the ultimate goal of resolving social conflicts and meeting the increasing demands of the populace in economic, political, cultural, and ecological aspects.

(2) Clarifying government responsibilities in the public sector. In public sectors, it is essential to clarify the government's responsibilities and authority in project approval, investment, production, distribution, and supervision. In most public service areas, the government should shift from being a producer to an investor and regulator. While the government can transfer some production responsibilities and delegate certain administrative powers, it must retain its fundamental responsibility for public service provision as the public representative. Changes in the mechanism or specific supply methods of public services do not mean reducing the government's responsibility for providing these services.

(3) Distinguishing government and SOEs' roles in public service provision. The relationship between the government and state-owned enterprises (SOEs) in public service provision is complex, and their responsibilities are not often clearly defined. Future reforms should clarify the roles and responsibilities of the government and SOEs. Accelerating the classification reforms of SOEs, promoting their de-bureaucratization and de-commercialization, and gradually transforming capable SOEs into enterprises or social organizations will be crucial. By streamlining administration, delegating powers, reforming SOEs, and opening up public sector investments, China can further clarify the relationships among the government, market, and society and the roles of different levels of government and their subordinate units and enterprises in public service provision.

6.3.4.2 Establishing a Public Service System with Multiple Collaborating Entities

Given the broad scope, extensive coverage, and complexity of public service projects in China, their supply process often involves significant uncertainties and complexities, making it challenging for a single department or social organization to provide them independently. Thus, a cooperative approach involving various sectors is necessary. China's public service supply mechanism is gradually transitioning from a government-centric to a socially diversified model. However, as previously mentioned, the government's role in this multi-stakeholder cooperative supply mechanism needs a more precise definition. The government should relax restrictions on public sectors to build a market mechanism for public services. On the one hand, in public service areas where market mechanisms can be effective, the government should deepen institutional reforms and promptly introduce comprehensive policies to open the public sectors. To attract social capital investment, the scope of market operations for public services should be appropriately expanded, allowing social capital participation in environmental protection, social security fund management, etc. Reasonable public service project fee structures and government subsidy systems should be developed, such as implementing fee and subsidy systems in education, healthcare, and public housing to ensure operating enterprises achieve certain profitability and foster a competitive market environment. On the other hand, the marketization of urban public services means resource allocation and enterprise operations will be profit-oriented, with most providers being profit-driven organizations. This could lead to conflicts with public service goals and potentially harm public interests. Therefore, the government should act as a public interest agent in a multi-stakeholder cooperative supply mechanism, clearly defining project production and supply objectives and organizing suitable enterprises and social organizations to participate in investment and operations while fulfilling regulatory responsibilities based on laws and contracts.

6.3.4.3 Constructing Various Public Service Supply Methods Through Institutional Arrangements

Innovating supply methods and tools is critical in the transformation of the public service supply system, serving as the platform for achieving appropriate and effective supply mechanisms. Currently, global practices in public service supply include direct government provision, supply by enterprises, private and social capital, government procurement of services, and public–private partnerships. Different projects adopt different supply methods. China's current public service supply methods primarily involve direct government provision and supply by state-owned enterprises and institutions, with some involvement from private enterprises and social capital. Over the past two decades, the trend has been for the government to cooperate with social organizations through service procurement. However, the scope and projects of services supplied through procurement remain limited, and their impact has not fully materialized. To address this, China needs to innovate its institutional framework and develop targeted public service project property rights and investment financing markets to create conditions for various public service supply methods, establishing a comprehensive public service supply system. Additionally, the government should alleviate financial pressures on social organizations and enterprises participating in public service provision through fiscal tax incentives and subsidies.

6.3.4.4 Strengthening Legal Framework for Government and Social Organization Cooperation in Public Service Provision

Currently, China has some policy documents related to public service supply but lacks national laws and regulations to standardize the rights and obligations of supply entities and their actions. This has led to issues such as unclear rights and obligations of supply entities and irregular property transactions.

To establish a complete public service legal system, it is crucial first to clarify the legal status, rights, and obligations of public service supply entities and relevant participants. Secondly, public service-related laws and regulations should be unified, incorporating various government service procurement contents into the *Government Procurement Law of the People's Republic of China*, standardizing procedures in government procurement of public services and public–private partnerships. Provisions related to fiscal budgets and tax payments in public service supply should be added to the *Budget Law* and various tax laws, specifying the tax responsibilities and benefits of social organizations, enterprises, and individuals involved in public service supply. A robust legal system for public services will help protect the interests of all parties involved and ensure the stable and orderly provision of public services.

6.3.4.5 Strengthening Supervision and Establishing a Performance Evaluation Mechanism for Public Service Supply

In urban public service provision, it is essential for the government to establish a dynamic management and supervision system. Every stage of public service projects, including planning, decision-making, application, review, project initiation, procurement and bidding, contract signing, production or implementation, and service delivery or product distribution, requires dedicated departments to oversee these processes. This ensures alignment with planning objectives and compliance with contractual obligations by the parties involved.

A comprehensive performance evaluation mechanism for public service supply is crucial for adequate provision. The 18th National Congress of the Communist Party of China emphasized the importance of building a service-oriented government that satisfies the people, with public service satisfaction becoming a key performance evaluation indicator. As government reforms deepen, efficiency and fairness in public service provision have become significant social concerns.

The efficiency of urban public service provision directly impacts the sustainability and development of the city, as public departments need to maximize resident benefits with minimal resource input. In practice, government departments often bear the primary responsibility for urban public service provision, with direct investments and ongoing expenditures accounting for a substantial proportion of the urban economy. Given limited fiscal funds, it is crucial to allocate funds to areas with the highest potential benefits. To improve the efficiency of urban public service supply, the government needs to encourage greater participation of market and social organizations in the public service supply. However, in an entirely market-driven mechanism, there is a risk of compromising fairness in urban public service. To ensure equitable access, particularly for residents in remote areas, the country has implemented policies to channel public resources towards these regions. Ensuring the basic physiological and safety needs of social members is fundamental for them to pursue higher social aspirations and realize their potential.

References

Arah, O. A., Klazinga, N. S., Delnoij, D. M. J., & et al. (2003). Conceptual frameworks for health systems performance: A quest for effectiveness, quality, and improvement. *International Journal for Quality in Health Care, 15*(5), 377-398.

Chen, Q. (2010). *Service cities: The return of modern urban functions*. Shanghai People's Publishing House.

Denhardt, J. V., & Denhardt, R. B. (2004). *The New Public Service: Serving, Not Steering*. (Ding, H., Trans.). Beijing: China Renmin University Press.

Gao, C. (2011). On public service provision and China's inclusive development. *Dongyue Tribune, 32*(12), 67–72.

He, J. (2019). 70 years of medical security legislation in New China: Focusing on the system design and progress of tiered diagnosis and treatment. *Law, 2019*(10), 75–92.

He, J., Zhang, H., & Li, Y. (2017). Research on the governance of "Internet + Public Service": Status review, logical framework, and key issues. *E-Government, 2017*(12), 12–21.
He, Q. (2014). *Research on government purchasing public services*. Beijing: Ministry of Finance Fiscal Science Research Institute.
Hua, Z. (2016). Government roles and model optimization in the provision of public ecological environment products. *Gansu Social Sciences, 2016*(2), 251–255.
Ju, H. (2006). *Market mechanisms in public services: Theories, methods, and techniques*. Peking University Press.
Lane, J. (2004). *New Public Management*. (Zhao, C., Wang, L., Cui, Y., et al., Trans.). Beijing: China Youth Publishing House.
Le, Y. (2008). Public service procurement: Contract cooperation model between government and civil organizations—A case study of the Dapuqiao Community Cultural Service Center in Shanghai. *China Nonprofit Review, 2*(1), 143–160.
Li, B. (2002). The practice and evaluation of public service marketization in Western countries. *Management World, 4*, 142–145.
Li, H., & Li, M. (2006). *Media politics*. Communication University of China Press.
Li, J., & Li, Z. (2012). The provision of basic public services in New China: Evolutionary stages and future directions. *Fiscal Research, 1*, 13–16.
Li, Z. (2004). The dilemma and reform ideas of China's public service marketization. *Journal of Northwest Normal University (Social Science Edition), 3*, 67–72.
Liu, X., & Zhao, N. (2007). On determining the reasonable boundaries of the public sector: A discussion on the price formation mechanism of the mixed public sector. *Economic Research, 3*, 45–56.
Liu, X., Dong, X., & Kong, X. (2017). Building a public service purchasing system and deepening the reform of public institutions. *Economic and Management Research, 38*(4), 35–46.
Lu, G. (2012a). On free markets and government intervention. *Contemporary Economic Management, 34*(1), 1–6.
Lu, Y. (2012b). Government responsibility in promoting community health services from the perspective of public goods theory. *Soft Science of Health, 26*(7), 627–629.
Mei, Z. (2006). New public management theory and its reference significance. *Administrative Forum, 1*, 5–8.
Mu, H. (2002). *International comparison of social security*. China Labor and Social Security Publishing House.
Ning, L. (2017). Research on public service purchasing reform from the perspective of the supply-side. *Shandong Social Sciences, 1*, 94–98.
Osborne, D., & Gaebler, T. (1996). *Reinventing Government: How the Entrepreneurial Spirit is Transforming the Public Sector*. (Shanghai CPPCC Compilation and Translation Group, Trans.). Shanghai: Shanghai Translation Publishing House.
Reform Magazine Special Research Department, & Luo, C. (2012). The trajectory and direction of classified reforms in China's public institutions. *Reform, 4*, 5–15.
Savas, E. S. (2002). *Privatization and Public-Private Partnerships* (Zhou, Z., et al., Trans.). Beijing: China Renmin University Press.
Sun, C. (2010). The reform of the urban public service supply mechanism in the United States and its implications for China. *Jianghan Forum, 9*, 45–48.
Tang, J., & Li, H. (2002). Market characteristics and public management costs of public service products. *Economic Issues Exploration, 12*, 30–33.
Tang, S. (2016). Promoting the reform of public service supply through informatization. *Macroeconomic Management, 2016*(10), 25–28.
Wang, C. (2019a). Analyzing the path to effective government provision of public services. *People's Forum, 2019*(34), 71–73.
Wang, Z. (2019b). 70 years of public policy: The development and reform of the social security and public service supply system. *Journal of Beijing University of Technology (Social Science Edition), 19*(5), 25–35.

Wang, D., Wan, Y., & Jiang, S. (2019). *Towards a balanced and sustainable development path: 40 years of public service reform in China*. Shanghai Jiao Tong University Press.

Wang, J., & Fu, J. (2014). The essential characteristics of the public-private partnership system and policy choices for China's urban utilities. *China Industrial Economics, 7*, 96–108.

Wang, P. (2010a). *Government purchasing public services from social organizations: China's experience and global analysis*. Peking University Press.

Wang, Z. (2010b). *Research on rural public safety services in a transforming society*. Hubei People's Publishing House.

Wang, P. (2015). Analysis of the reform mechanism of government purchasing public services from social forces. *Journal of Peking University (Philosophy and Social Sciences Edition), 52*(4), 88–94.

Wu, S., & Zeng, J. (2020). Reflections on the supply-side reform of public services driven by "big data." *Rural Economy and Science-Technology, 31*(3), 276–277.

Xu, Y., & Wang, L. (2020). The model, logic, and strategies of government purchasing community education services. *China Adult Education, 2020*(11), 72–76.

Yang, Q. (2012). Exploring the "meaning" of public services and reconstructing its content. *Legal Science (Northwest University of Political Science and Law Journal), 30*(4), 100–112.

Yang, W., Wang, X., & Zhang, F. (2014). Research on the path of selecting PPP models for public projects: Based on the three-dimensional transaction cooperation framework. *East China Economic Management, 28*(2), 121–126.

Yang, Y., & Xing, W. (2016). Study on the supply-side reform of the public service system. *People's Forum Academic Frontiers, 5*, 70–83.

Yu, H. (2018). *Research on the public service supply mechanism for new residents: An empirical investigation based on Zhejiang Province*. Publishing House of Electronics Industry.

Yu, J. (2011). China's public service system: Development process, social policies, and institutional mechanisms. *Academic Monthly, 43*(3), 5–17.

Zeng, X. (2016). The historical logic of the evolution of the Chinese government's public service function: From the perspective of historical institutionalism. *Dalian Cadres Journal, 32*(9), 38–42.

Zheng, G. (2019). Building a multi-level social security system: Status assessment and policy suggestions. *Social Security Review, 3*(1), 3–29.

Zheng, H., Ye, Z., & Zha, J. (2014). Study on the influencing factors of central-to-local fiscal transfer payments: Empirical tests based on county-level data in China. *Journal of Public Management, 11*(1), 18–26.

Zhu, G., & Sun, T. (2005). "Regulatory-Service" Local Government: Positioning, connotation, and construction. *Journal of Renmin University of China, 1*, 103–111.

Chapter 7
Urban Public Goods Supply Policies and Practices

The government plays a leading role in the development of China's market economy, particularly in the provision of public goods. As the primary supplier, the government makes investment decisions and allocates resources according to specific objectives, principles, and regulations. This process ultimately shapes public policies, which serve as the primary frameworks guiding the government's provision of public goods. Therefore, public policies function not only as a special kind of public good but also as a strategic tool for mobilizing public resources and regulating the supply of public goods.

Differences in economic development, fundamental values, and social and cultural practices across countries lead to variations in public policy formulation. However, the inherent social and welfare functions of public goods bring common principles and methods to the public policies of different countries, especially concerning social stability and welfare distribution.

This chapter, grounded on the basic theories of public policy, analyzes the evolution and characteristics of public policies for the supply of public goods in China and the main factors influencing these policies. By examining policies in public health, public education, and social security, it assesses the effectiveness of China's urban public policies, and offers policy recommendations.

7.1 Public Policy of the Public Sector in China

7.1.1 Evolution of Public Policy in China

Since the reform and opening up, China's public policies have been continuously adjusted.

B. Wu et al., *Effective Supply Mechanism of Urban Public Goods*, Public Economy and Urban Governance in China, https://doi.org/10.1007/978-981-96-2608-3_7

7.1.1.1 Public Policy Reform and Exploration Stage (1978–1992)

This stage began with a reflection on the administrative planned economy mechanisms and the reform and opening up program initiated at the Third Plenary Session of the 11th CPC Central Committee. Public policies were revised to align with the broader goal of reform and the opening up and establishment of a socialist market economy. During this period, China lacked clear systems and implementation strategies for these reforms, leading to a phase characterized by policy mobilization, trial and error, and learning. China faced the dual challenge of dismantling traditional public policies that hindered economic development and social reform while seeking evidence-based public policies suitable for the new development environment and the construction of socialism with Chinese characteristics.

The reform of public policies initially focused on rural policies. The Household Responsibility System in rural areas catalyzed significant changes in rural economic policies. Through both theoretical exploration and practical implementation, the central government established the household contract responsibility system and the dual-layer management system, abolished the unified purchase and sale policy, and formulated a series of rural reform policies. The *Decision of the Central Committee of the Communist Party of China on Economic System Reform,* approved at the Third Plenary Session of the 12th CPC Central Committee specified the reform policy which called for "invigorating the domestic economy and opening up to the outside world". The issue of *The Promulgation of Several Provisions of the State Council on Deepening Enterprise Reform and Enhancing Enterprise Vitality* in December 1986 marked the beginning of urban economic and state-owned enterprise reforms, leading to the implementation of a series of enterprise reform and market-oriented policies, including the state-owned enterprise asset management responsibility system, the contract management responsibility system, and the shareholding system. Correspondingly, policies related to investment, production, consumption, prices, distribution, and employment in the national economy were gradually adjusted.

7.1.1.2 Public Policy Exploration and Innovation Stage (1992–2002)

Following Deng Xiaoping's Southern Tour speech in 1992, China accelerated its transition to a market economy. The 14th National Congress of the Communist Party of China in 1992 set the goal of establishing a socialist market economy. In May 1992, the Political Bureau of the CPC Central Committee approved the *Opinions on Accelerating Reform, Expanding Opening Up, and Striving for a Better and Faster Economic Development*, which advanced economic system reforms and market system establishment. Up to China's accession to the World Trade Organization and the 16th National Congress of the Communist Party of China, public policies under the new socioeconomic system were continually explored and innovated. This ongoing exploration of new economic systems and mechanisms necessitated a dynamic process of public policy formulation, implementation and adjustment.

During this period, China steadily moved away from the traditional planned economy system and dual-track mechanisms, seeking to develop public policy systems compatible with a socialist market economy and modern social structures. In line with these economic reforms, China introduced policies with the aim of establishing a socialist market economy, including fiscal, financial, foreign investment and trade, enterprise reform, and social security policies. Particularly, the 1994 fiscal tax-sharing system reform redefined the fiscal and administrative responsibilities between the central and local governments. Initiatives such as the *Decision of the State Council on Further Deepening the Reform of the Foreign Trade System* and the *Decision of the State Council on Deepening the Reform of the Urban Housing System* facilitated economic system reforms and ensured stable socioeconomic development.

7.1.1.3 Institutionalization Stage of Public Policy (2002–Present)

Following China's accession to the WTO (World Trade Organization) and the convening of *the* 16th National Congress of the Communist Party of China, China entered a new phase of external openness. Economic policy reforms faced the challenge of aligning with international economic regulations while establishing socialist market economy mechanisms and integrating them into the global economic system. Consequently, post-accession public economic policies were fully adjusted to align with international standards. During this time, China also explored systems and policies suited to its socioeconomic reality, leading to the establishment of a distinct public policy and governance system and marking a period of innovation and institutionalization. Key policies were introduced, such as the *Several Opinions of the State Council on Promoting the Reform, Opening, and Stable Development of the Capital Market* and the *Decision of the Standing Committee of the National People's Congress on Abolishing the Agricultural Tax Regulations.* Additionally, systematic policy documents related to foreign economic relations were formulated and implemented, refining relevant laws and gradually forming a comprehensive economic legal system. Through the ongoing reform and opening up, and development of the market economy, China's public policies have entered a phase of institutionalization and governance (Chen, 2009).

7.1.2 Characteristics of Public Policy Evolution Since Reform and Opening up

7.1.2.1 Changes in the Institutional Environment of Public Policy, Continuous Adjustment of Goals and Content

After the founding of the People's Republic of China, an administrative planning management system emerged during the socialist construction process. However, this system became increasingly inadequate as the socialist market economy evolved after the reform and opening up. The need for new systems and mechanisms necessitated the development of an updated policy framework, as the foundational conditions for policy formulation and implementation underwent continuous transformation amid economic reforms. Thus, since the reform and opening up, China's public policies have been in a state of continuous evolution, generally adjusting and innovating in response to social and economic development. In fact, the path of social and economic development in China is different from that of other countries, so the system and mechanism of socialism with Chinese characteristics have no replicable models in the world. Therefore, China must rely on its own exploratory efforts for ongoing improvement. This exploration has evolved from dismantling traditional systems and policies at the outset of the reform and opening up, to establishing policies focused on economic development guided by these reforms, and ultimately to the formulation of systematic public policies aiming at comprehensively building a modern socioeconomic nation. Over time, China has developed a relatively complete and stable public policy system.

7.1.2.2 Shift in Public Policy Focus from Economic Growth to Comprehensive Social Development

After the reform and opening up, China's public policies have primarily focused on economic development, centering around economic objectives. From the early 1980s to the early twenty-first century, the adjustments in China's public policies largely reflected economic policies, effectively creating a new economic policy system in line with the requirements of the socialist market economy system. This system includes various sectors of the national economy, such as resource allocation, production and services, investment and consumption, and income distribution. Particularly, a series of policies have been introduced to support the deepening of reforms in establishing a market economy system, a modern enterprise system, and a foreign economic system.

A fundamental shift in China's public policies has occurred, evolving from an early emphasis on economic growth to a more balanced focus on both economic and social development. Especially in the new era, the rapid development of the public sector has transformed the government's social management system towards multifaceted social governance. Correspondingly, numerous policies in the realm of public goods have been formulated to guide and promote social undertakings, leading to significant progress in areas such as science and education, healthcare, ecological and environmental protection, social security systems, and urban–rural integration. Although some policies have faced challenges during implementation, such as limited impact or constraints imposed by traditional systems and interest groups, the overall trend indicates that public policies are increasingly crucial for promoting social development and establishing a modern social governance framework.

7.1.2.3 The Transition of Public Policy from Regulation to Publicity and People-Centricity

During the planned economy period, China's public policies mirrored the centralized administrative management mechanisms, reflecting government regulation of economic and social activities. Since the reform and opening up, with the development of the market economy and the increasing openness, the content and tools of China's public policies increasingly reflect the transformation of government roles and functions, leading to a greater emphasis on guidance, service orientation, and legal frameworks in policy implementation.

The 17th National Congress of the Communist Party of China emphasized the need to "accelerate the reform of the administrative management system and build a service-oriented government". This initiative focused on improving government responsibilities, the public service system, e-government, and social management and public services. Consequently, the government has accelerated its reform efforts, transforming its functions, enhancing public decision-making, and shifting from direct administrative intervention to indirect regulation. Under the socialist market economy, the transformation of government roles and adjustments in functions enable it to effectively fulfill public service roles (Liang, 2007).

In practice, the introduction of new policies reflects the government's proactive efforts in transforming functions and improving public service levels. For example, in education, the government promotes rural compulsory education to ensure equity and balanced development. In urban housing policy, addressing housing issues is prioritized, with measures to stabilize the real estate market, emphasizing "houses are for living, not for speculation", and increasing public rental housing to alleviate housing pressure among urban residents. In social policy, there is a notable shift from traditional administrative management to grassroots social governance, emphasizing public participation and the equalization of basic public services, especially through comprehensive support policies for low-income families. By adjusting policy content and implementation tools, the government integrates social management into a service-oriented framework.

7.1.2.4 Public Policy Formulation Mechanism Transitioning from Government-Led to Government-Society Cooperation

With the increase in participants in socioeconomic activities and the expansion of the scope of activities, conflicts of interest among various entities arise. When the government acts as the sole decision-maker, public decision-making may fail to reflect real societal realities and achieve effective implementation. To achieve coordinated economic, social, and environmental development, the report of the 17th National Congress of the Communist Party of China stated that "people's democracy is the life of socialism". In response, China has encouraged the participation of democratic parties, social organizations, and the public in public policy-making to enhance the democratic system, affirm that all state power belongs to the people, expand orderly citizen political participation, and fully leverage the positive role of social organizations in broadening public engagement and reflecting public needs. This approach aims to augment societal self-governance functions. Meanwhile, the media's influence in public policy formulation has expanded, with mass media playing an increasingly pivotal role in enhancing transparency in policy and decision-making processes.

7.1.2.5 Strengthened Scientific and Legal Basis in Public Policy Formulation

During the planned economy period, many public policies prioritized political goals, often disregarding the principles of economic development. After the reform and opening up, there was a tendency for some public policies to swing to the opposite extreme, excessively emphasizing economic growth at the expense of social coordination and fairness, thereby widening the wealth gap. In recent years, public policymakers have focused on addressing social problems from the perspective of social fairness. While economic growth remains an important policy goal, social development, social fairness, and environmental protection have also been given equal importance. Policymakers now prioritize public interests, leading to significant achievements in anti-poverty initiatives and the establishment of a framework addressing deeply ingrained issues concerning the well-being of people.

Moreover, with the improvement of China's legal system and the standardization of decision-making procedures, the formulation and implementation of public policies more rigorously align with legal principles, fairness, and transparency in decision-making processes. Government, social organizations, and the public are equally involved in the public policy formulation process, enhancing the seriousness, standardization, and effectiveness of public policies.

7.1.3 Issues and Reform Recommendations for Public Policies in China

Public policy decisions and implementation are influenced by a country's political and economic systems. As previously noted, China's public policies have undergone significant changes after the reform and opening up period, but remnants of the planned economy can still be found. The fundamental decision-making mechanisms have not undergone substantive changes. In a market system that is still influenced by administrative planning, public policy formulation and implementation face challenges from both sides, leading to inefficiencies in decision-making and execution. This book offers the following reform recommendations to address these issues.

7.1.3.1 Reforming Traditional Public Policy Formulation and Implementation Methods, Establishing a Scientific Public Policy Decision-Making and Execution Mechanism

China has not yet fully transitioned from experience-based policy formulation to a modern, scientific approach. The information collection channels during the policy formulation process are relatively narrow, and the transparency of decision-making procedures is low, often leading to a discrepancy between policies and actual societal needs. Currently, public policy formulation tends to be an insular process within administrative departments, with limited communication between the government and stakeholders, restricting opportunities for opinion gathering. During policy implementation, insufficient information disclosure grants excessive discretionary power to government departments, resulting in a reliance on experiential policy formulation and decision-making methods driven by the value preferences of public policy entities. This "trial and error" method, which involves selecting an option among alternatives and judging its effectiveness through feedback, was feasible during the early reform and opening up period when theoretical foundations and decision bases were weak. However, long-term reliance on this method can lead to policy errors and irreversible consequences.

Therefore, China needs to adopt advanced modern public policy theories, technologies, and methods to transform the experience-based policy formulation approach. This involves changing the working methods of government departments, enhancing the professionalism of personnel involved in policy making, and moving away from using administrative orders as policy execution tools. Instead, diverse public policy tools should be actively used, especially leveraging the contributions of social organizations and citizens in specific policy implementation areas to ensure the quick and effective execution of public policies.

7.1.3.2 Improving the Public Policy System and Building a Robust Public Policy Decision Support System

To build a modern public policy system, China needs to establish an integrated framework that includes information systems, advisory systems, decision-making systems, and oversight systems. Despite significant progress since the reform and opening up period, there is still a considerable gap compared to the demands of modern social and economic development. First, under the leadership of the Communist Party, it is essential to clarify the division of responsibilities between the Party and the government in social development and governance. Currently, the separation of powers, functions, and responsibilities between the Party and the government in public policy lack clarity, and the legislative functions of the People's Congress in policy review and decision-making have not been fully utilized, especially in the initial stages of policy demonstration and formulation; Second, although Party and government departments have strengthened efforts to collect public opinions and suggestions, and some policy decisions have been made through consultative meetings and hearings, there is often a disparity between the collected information and actual societal conditions and citizen demands; Third, while policy research institutions and think tanks are designed to support the government planning and consulting, many have yet to fully realize these roles; Finally, there is an imbalanced development between external policy research organizations and internal policy research organizations, with insufficient close contact between official policy research systems and independent policy research entities.

Consequently, the process of public policy formulation, decision-making, and implementation should break the isolation of single government department systems under the unified leadership of the Party, mobilize and integrate social forces, and establish an open and socialized public policy system. This entails enhancing the legal status of the People's Congress and its review role in public policy decisions, as well as making full use of professional policy research institutions and think tanks.

7.1.3.3 Improving the Legalization of Public Policy to Promote Rule of Law in Public Policy

Legalizing public policy is fundamental to democratizing and scientizing policy formulation and implementation, as it serves as the basic safeguard for public policy. Since the reform and opening up, China has achieved significant strides in legal construction, establishing a relatively complete legal system, which lays the legal foundation for the formulation and implementation of public policies. However, there remain significant gaps in laws and regulations regarding information collection and disclosure, formulation procedures, implementation evaluations, and public participation in policy-making. The legal status of certain public policy subjects is not clear, and some administrative policy documents lack proper review by relevant legal departments, resulting in ambiguous administrative decision-making responsibilities. Some government departments do not emphasize the importance of basing public policy on relevant laws and regulations, leading to ineffective legal measures during policy implementation (Li, 2014b).

Therefore, to strengthen its legal framework, China needs to establish a specialized public policy law that clearly defines the responsibilities and procedures in policy formulation, decision-making, implementation, and evaluation. This law would regulate the behavior of all stakeholders involved in public policy. Public policy-making departments at all levels should improve decision-making rules and procedures, establish systems for soliciting public opinions, and set up systems for public disclosure and hearings on major issues. An expert consultation system should be refined, alongside a responsibility system to ensure accountability for decisions made. It is crucial to establish a responsibility and tracking system where "whoever makes the decision is responsible" and to address decision-making errors according to the nature, severity of the issues involved. Additionally, legal education should be strengthened for government departments, relevant institutions, enterprises, and individuals to ensure strict adherence to relevant regulations and procedures during the formulation and implementation of public policies (Tan, 2004).

7.1.3.4 Eliminating the Influence of Special Interest Groups on Public Policy to Protect Public Interests

Public policy substantially impacts socioeconomic activities and the distribution of interests. As a mechanism for interest distribution, it is also the result of interest conflicts and negotiations among stakeholders. The formulation of public policies is often constrained by interest groups during the marketization process. Furthermore, political factors may lead some local governments to prioritize social stability and economic growth, resulting in public policies that do not align with social progress or public interests. In the area of public goods, rapid government investment growth in public infrastructure and social service projects has resulted in the concentration of public resources under the government's control, with some interest groups exerting influence on government decisions to obtain these public resources.

Therefore, public policy formulation and implementation must prioritize a strong awareness of public interests and demands. Effective public policy arises from democratic procedures and standardized policy-making processes, including problem identification, goal setting, policy design and selection, implementation, monitoring, evaluation, and feedback. China should standardize public policy formulation procedures, increase transparency, solicit public opinions, and embrace social supervision.

7.1.3.5 Improving Public Policy Performance Evaluation and Supervision Mechanisms

Supervision during the formulation and implementation of public policies is essential for ensuring the legitimacy, fairness, and implementation of public policies. Therefore, China should establish specialized supervisory bodies dedicated to overseeing public policy formulation and implementation. Although China's current legal system grants the public the right to supervise government decisions, actual public influence on government decision-making is limited. Government decisions often favor officials' or experts' opinions over public opinions, limiting public involvement.

The "Regulations of the People's Republic of China on Open Government Information",[1] issued in 2008, aimed to enhance transparency and accountability in policy-making and implementation. Despite their positive impacts, these regulations have not fundamentally resolved the information asymmetry between the government and citizens, largely due to the administrative system. In times of crisis, the government tends to withhold information to maintain social stability, exacerbating public distrust and discouraging citizen participation in policy-making. To enhance public engagement, the government has adopted methods like opinion collection, policy hearings, and think tank reports, but these have not been standardized or institutionalized. Hearing procedures often lack transparency, often inviting only select participants,

[1] Revised on April 3, 2019, according to Order No. 711 of the State Council of the People's Republic of China.

which undermines the ability of the broader public to voice their opinions and fulfill their supervisory roles.

To improve the supervision mechanism within the People's Congress, China needs to encourage more public participation in overseeing policy formulation and implementation. Feedback from various social groups on public policies should be accepted, with public opinions disclosed and addressed. Additionally, China should develop a scientific and reasonable public policy performance evaluation system tailored to its actual conditions.

7.1.3.6 Enhancing Decision-Making Mechanisms Using Modern Technology

Effective public policy formulation and implementation require a thorough understanding and analysis of the policy environment and target subjects. However, China's public sector has neglected the collection and analysis of fundamental data and information, lacking the capacity to use modern information technology to support decision-making and policy implementation. As public affairs have become more complex, relying solely on experience is insufficient for scientific and accurate judgments.

The rise of big data presents new opportunities to enhance decision-making mechanisms. Modern technology can effectively capture, analyze, and visualize vast amounts of data, revealing patterns and establishing logical connections between problems and solutions. This data-driven approach provides scientific and systematic support for policy formulation, thereby enhancing decision-making accuracy, effectiveness, and predictability. Evidence shows that modern technology can lead to innovative governance decision-making and models, promoting a shift from extensive to refined decision-making, from isolated to collaborative processes. To improve the scientific and effective nature of decision-making, the government must shift from traditional decision-making concepts and methods to the rational use of modern technology, collecting and analyzing basic data to inform decisions, moving away from reliance on traditional experience in decision-making. Specific efforts should include:

(1) Fostering a big data mindset: Government staff must adopt a "data-driven" approach to administration and governance, aligning with modern information technology. The decision-making process should transition from reliance on experience to a scientific framework that emphasizes data analysis and application.
(2) Building integrated government big data service platforms: The government should develop integrated service platforms and unified information interfaces based on modern information technology to facilitate efficient information retrieval, break down departmental information barriers, and enhance scientific-basis for decision-making.
(3) Legislating to remove data barriers: It is crucial to enact laws and regulations that promote orderly and transparent data usage. This includes defining the scope and

methods for applying modern technology and clarifying the responsibilities and rights of government departments regarding information collection and utilization, ensuring the effective implementation of open government information regulations.

(4) Ensuring data security in public policy application: The government must strengthen its information security infrastructure and develop a robust system to guarantee the secure application of modern technology in decision-making, with enhanced capabilities for monitoring, early warning, control, and emergency responses.

7.2 Urban Public Education Policy

7.2.1 Evolution of Public Education Policies and Practices in China

The balanced development of public education is a significant foundation of social equity and a primary objective of China's educational reforms. Since the founding of the People's Republic of China (PRC), the government has prioritized the development of education. Initially, the focus was on the universalization of compulsory education, but political movements caused fluctuations in the progress of both basic and higher education, leading to disparities in compulsory education between urban and rural areas and across regions. Despite limited economic resources after the economic reforms, the nation strengthened its commitment to universal compulsory education, significantly enhancing the level of basic education. However, urbanization exacerbated existing disparities in public foundational education between urban and rural areas. Overall, China's public education policies have evolved from promoting universal access to achieving balanced development.

7.2.1.1 Emphasis on and Universalization of Basic Education (1949–1977)

In the early years following the founding of the PRC, basic education nationwide was significantly underdeveloped, with a net enrollment rate of only about 20% for primary school-aged children. To improve people's education, the government prioritized basic education, highlighting the goal of "planned and stepwise universal education" in five-year plans and mobilizing societal efforts to develop foundational public education. In 1956, the Central Committee of the Communist Party of China proposed universal primary compulsory education and made efforts to expand secondary and higher education. During the 1970s, alongside the push for primary education, there were concerted efforts to broaden access to secondary education through support from central and local governments. This period saw a gradual increase in primary education enrollment, with the net enrollment rate of primary school-aged children rising from 49.2% in 1956 to 96.0% in 1976. By 1976, the gross enrollment rate for junior secondary education reached approximately 69.0%, marking significant progress in secondary education.

7.2.1.2 Universalization of Primary Compulsory Education and Implementation of Nine-Year Compulsory Education (1978–1990)

After the reform and opening up policy, China made great efforts to promote primary education by implementing nine-year compulsory education. In 1982, China's newly enacted *Constitution of the People's Republic of China* mandated the "universalization of primary compulsory education" and called for efforts to expand junior secondary education where conditions permitted. The *Decision of the Central Committee of the Communist Party of China on the Reform of the Educational System* was issued in 1985, and it officially announced the implementation of nine-year compulsory education. In 1986, on the fourth session of the Sixth National People's Congress, the *Compulsory Education Law of the People's Republic of China* (hereinafter referred to as the *Compulsory Education Law*) was debated and approved, which legally established a "nine-year compulsory education system". During this period, significant achievements were made in the development of basic education in China, especially in the universalization of primary compulsory education (Liao, 2019), which included:

(1) an increase in the enrollment rate of primary education, a decrease in the dropout rate, and a certain degree of universalization in junior secondary education. By 1990, the net enrollment rate of school-age children in primary education nationwide reached 97.83%;
(2) significant improvements in school conditions, with the total number of teaching staff in primary schools reaching 6.24 million and full-time teachers in ordinary junior secondary schools 2.47 million in 1990. However, the quality of basic education during this period remained to be improved. In 1990, the retention rate of primary school students was only 71.40%, the universalization and enrollment rate of junior secondary education was relatively low, and there was a shortage of educational resources, including insufficient teacher availability and inadequate basic teaching infrastructure.

7.2.1.3 Improving Quality and Achieving Comprehensive Universalization of Compulsory Education (1991–2009)

During this period, the improvements of the economic development laid the economic foundation for the development of China's education, while the transformation of the social economic system also created institutional conditions for the comprehensive development of basic education, which include:

(1) Universalized nine-year compulsory education: Universalizing compulsory education became a key national development strategy. To implement the Compulsory Education Law, China issued the *Implementation Rules for the Compulsory Education Law of the People's Republic of China* in March 1992, outlining the objectives, principles, steps, and methods for universalizing compulsory education. In February 1993, the Central Committee of the Communist Party of China and the State Council released the *Program for China's Educational Reform and Development*, aiming to achieve the goal of universalizing nine-year compulsory education nationwide by the 1990s. To fulfill the goal, the May 2001 *Decision of the State Council on Basic Education Reform and Development* emphasized increased support for compulsory education in impoverished and ethnic minority areas. In 2004, the State Council passed the *National Plan for Tackling 'Two Basics' in the Western Region (2004—2007)*,[2] introducing measures such as the construction of rural boarding schools, compulsory education projects in impoverished areas, renovation projects for dangerous buildings in primary and secondary schools, rural modern distance education projects, and the special-post teacher plan; Policies like the "one-fee system" and "two exemptions and one subsidy" were implemented to alleviate students' financial burdens. The 2006 revision of the Compulsory Education Law mandated that no tuition and miscellaneous fees be charged for compulsory education nationwide;

(2) Increased investment: Both the central and local governments significantly boosted funding for compulsory education and encouraged social forces to run schools. In the *Notice of the State Council on Deepening the Reform of the Rural Compulsory Education Funding Guarantee Mechanism* issued in December 2005, incorporating rural compulsory education into government fiscal expenditure was recommended. To ensure consistent funding for compulsory education, the 2006 revised Compulsory Education Law specified the shared financial responsibilities between central and local governments;

(3) Reformed teaching and education systems: China deepened reforms in the teaching and education systems to enhance the guidance and management of compulsory education. The May 2001 *Decision of the State Council on Basic Education Reform and Development* proposed improving the management system of rural compulsory education, establishing a system where local governments were responsible under the leadership of the State Council, with tiered management focusing on county-based implementation.

With the joint efforts of the whole society, China's compulsory education in this period saw great improvement, achieving the goal of its overall universalizing. By the end of 2010, all 2,856 counties (cities, districts) nationwide had achieved the "two basics" goal,[3] covering 100% of the population. The conditions for running basic

[2] According to the *Decision of the State Council on Declaring a Batch of State Council Documents Invalid*, this document has been declared invalid.

[3] "Two Basics" refers to the basic universalization of nine-year compulsory education and the basic eradication of illiteracy among young and middle-aged adults.

education schools improved significantly; by the end of 2010, the qualification rate of full-time primary school teachers in China reached 99.52%, and the qualification rate of full-time junior secondary school teachers was 98.65% (Liao, 2019; Zhu, 2012).

7.2.1.4 Achieving Balanced Development of Compulsory Education (2010–Present)

With the universalization of compulsory education achieved, China's focus during this phase shifted to achieving balanced development of basic education in different regions and the integrated development of urban and rural compulsory education.

In July 2010, the CPC Central Committee and the State Council issued the *Outline of the National Medium- and Long-term Education Reform and Development Plan (2010–2020)*, specifying the core tasks of compulsory education as "consolidating and improving the level of nine-year compulsory education" and "promoting the balanced development of compulsory education". Specifically, one task is to address the issues of the imbalanced development of compulsory education between regions and the integrated development of urban and rural compulsory education. In September 2012, the *Opinions of the State Council on Deepening the Balanced Development of Compulsory Education* set the guiding principles, basic goals, and policy measures for the balanced development of compulsory education. The *Opinions of the State Council on Coordinated Promotion of the Integrated Development of Urban and Rural Compulsory Education in County Regions* issued in July 2016 provided specific rules for the integrated reform and development of urban and rural compulsory education; Another task is to increase the financial budget input by central and local governments to improve the running conditions of weak schools in impoverished areas. The *Opinions of the Ministry of Education, the National Development and Reform Commission, and the Ministry of Finance on Comprehensively Improving the Basic Running Conditions of Weak Schools for Compulsory Education in Poverty-stricken Areas* was issued in December 2013, which clarified tasks and policy measures for improving the basic running conditions of weak compulsory education schools in poverty-stricken areas and required advancing the reform of the funding guarantee mechanism for urban and rural compulsory education, coordinating the balanced allocation of urban and rural compulsory education resources.

As a result of long-term efforts, there has been a high level of nine-year compulsory education in China. By 2018, the net enrollment rate of school-age children in primary education reached 99.95%, the gross enrollment rate of junior secondary education nationwide was 100%, and the nationwide retention rate of nine-year compulsory education was 94.20%. The level and treatment of teachers significantly improved, with the student–teacher ratio in primary schools reaching 16.79:1 and 12.79:1 in junior secondary schools by 2018; in 2018, 59.10% of full-time primary school teachers and 86.22% of full-time junior secondary school teachers had bachelor's degrees or above. Meanwhile, the layout of schools in the compulsory education stage became more rational, with 161,800 primary schools and 52,000 junior secondary schools nationwide by 2018. The school infrastructure conditions for compulsory education improved, and by 2019, 94% of schools met the basic national standards for running schools, and 92.7% of county-level units achieved basic balanced development of compulsory education (Liao, 2019).

The evolution of China's public education policies and practices primarily focused on first enhancing the universalization of basic education, then improving its quality, emphasizing the balanced development of regional compulsory education, and promoting the integrated development of urban and rural compulsory education.

7.2.2 Major Public Education Policies in China

The development of education in China is driven by the formulation and implementation of education policies. Public education policies are institutional measures by the country to achieve strategic educational goals, reflecting national education development plans and serving as tools for the government to promote and manage education. Since the reform and opening up, China has continuously adjusted its education policies to promote the development of education and achieve the goals of modern basic education development.

7.2.2.1 Policies for Universalized and Balanced Development of Compulsory Education

In building a socialist society, China increasingly prioritizes basic education resources. The universalization of compulsory education is the most important educational goal, serving as a fundamental measure to promote the strategy of revitalizing the country through science and education and the strategy of prioritizing education development. The development of compulsory education is also a process of exploring and practicing compulsory education policies. As previously noted, the strategic goals of basic education development in China are to universalize compulsory education, achieve balanced regional development of compulsory education, and integrate urban and rural compulsory education. To gradually achieve these goals, China has promulgated and implemented a series of policies, which include: (1) Enacting and revising laws and regulations related to compulsory education; (2) Issuing policies and measures by government departments to promote compulsory education; (3) Reforming the education management system and mechanisms. From the laws and policies over the years, it can be found that the evolution of education policies has shifted from universalizing compulsory education to promoting balanced regional and urban–rural development. This reflects the equitable and equal development of basic education in China. Since the reform and opening up, policies have universalized urban and rural compulsory education and also focused on the balanced development of primary and secondary schools in rural areas and compulsory education in economically underdeveloped areas. In the past decade, policies also focused on compulsory education for children of migrant workers. As a special group in cities, many children of migrant workers cannot enjoy compulsory education in public schools due to differences in household registration and social security systems (Zhu et al., 2017). To solve this problem, the government issued policies in the *Provisional Measures for the Schooling of Migrant Children (1998)* and the *Opinions on Further Improving the Compulsory Education for Children of Migrant Workers (2003).*

7.2.2.2 Policies to Reform the Mechanism of Public Basic Education and Encourage Social Investment in Basic Education

The development of public basic education is a fundamental responsibility of the government, but education is also a crucial aspect of social development that requires support and resources from various societal forces. China's economic development level and fiscal capacity are not sufficient to support high-standard private education investment. Therefore, China needs to encourage social forces to invest in basic education, which is an effective way to enhance the level of basic education through different educational mechanisms.

In 1985, the *Decision of the Central Committee of the Communist Party of China on the Reform of the Educational System* was issued, which mandated that local governments formulate their education policies and arrange their education finances. In 1993, the *Outline for China's Education Reform and Development* was issued by the Central Committee of the Communist Party of China and the State Council, which specified guidelines, principles, and policies for the reform of the education system and mechanisms. The 1999 *Decision of the Central Committee of the Communist Party of China and the State Council on Deepening Education Reform and Comprehensively Promoting Quality Education* stated that basic education was mainly the responsibility of local governments while schools should be run with the support of social forces. In December 2002, the Thirty-First Meeting of the Standing Committee of the Ninth National People's Congress passed the *Law on the Promotion of Private Education of the People's Republic of China*, stating that private education is a component of socialist education. China encourages, supports, guides, and manages private education according to the law, making education a cause of the whole society and opening the door to diversified and pluralistic education (Long & Yi, 2017).

According to the *Law on the Promotion of Private Education of the People's Republic of China*, private education refers to schools run with non-state financial funds, including those run by social organizations and individuals. Private schools are invested in and operated by their sponsors, with policy support from the government. In urban development, the development of private education has its intrinsic reasons, including the inability of existing public schools to meet the educational needs of the children of migrant families, the ability of private schools to meet the needs of some students for individualized education, and the willingness of some parents to choose private schools with superior teaching facilities if economic conditions permit. Private education is an important part of China's education system, contributing experience in running schools and education management. However, private education also faces issues such as excessive pursuit of economic benefits and insufficient investment in facilities. Local governments should analyze the causes of these problems and avoid simply converting private schools into public ones, as this is not conducive to the ecological development of basic education in China. The government should regulate private education while appropriately increasing support for it.

7.2.2.3 Policies for the Integration of Urban and Rural Compulsory Education in the Context of Urban–Rural Integrated Development

In the development of basic education in China, there is a significant gap in educational standards between urban and rural areas. The accessibility and quality of rural compulsory education are major constraints on the overall improvement of the country's basic education level. The primary factors limiting the development of rural compulsory education are insufficient educational funding and inadequate faculty resources. Additionally, with the flow of rural labor, the number of school-age children in rural areas has decreased, making it difficult for school education to achieve scale. To address these issues, in 2015, the *State Council Notice on Further Improving the Funding Guarantee Mechanism for Urban and Rural Compulsory Education* was issued, which called for both central and local governments to increase investment in compulsory education, with a focus on rural areas. The *National Medium- and Long-term Education Reform and Development Plan (2010–2020)* also made it clear that with increasing national education expenditure, more investment should be channeled into rural, remote, impoverished, and ethnic regions. Considering the financial challenges of some provinces and cities, the central government supports the development of educational undertakings in underdeveloped and ethnic areas through increased transfer payments. As a result of these fiscal policies, funding for rural compulsory education has gradually increased over the years. Although there still exists some disparity in education expenditure between urban and rural areas, the gap has significantly narrowed (see Table 7.1).

To address the shortage of faculty resources in rural areas, in recent years, the government has not only increased the salaries of teachers but also strengthened teacher training and implemented policies for appropriate exchanges of school leaders and teachers between urban and rural primary and secondary schools. These measures have enhanced the teaching quality in rural primary and secondary schools.

Table 7.1 Expenditure per student for urban and rural compulsory education

General primary				General junior high		
Year	National	Rural	Difference	National	Rural	Difference
2006	1633.51	1505.51	128.00	1896.56	1717.22	179.34
2007	2207.04	2084.28	122.96	2679.42	2433.28	246.14
2008	2757.53	2617.59	139.94	3543.20	3303.16	240.09
2009	3357.92	3178.08	179.84	4331.62	4065.63	265.99
2010	4012.51	3802.91	209.60	5213.91	4896.38	317.53
2011	4966.04	4764.65	201.39	6541.86	6207.10	244.76
2012	6128.99	6017.58	111.41	8137.00	7906.61	230.39
2013	6901.77	6854.96	46.81	9258.37	9195.77	62.60
2014	7681.02	7403.91	277.11	10,359.33	9258.37	647.51
2015	8838.44	8576.75	261.69	12,105.08	11,348.79	756.29
2016	9557.89	9246.00	311.89	13,415.99	12,105.08	1310.91
2017	10,199.12	9768.57	430.55	14,641.15	13,447.08	1194.07

Unit yuan
Source National Education Finance Execution Statistics Bulletin (2006–2017)

7.2.3 Public Education Policy Performance Evaluation and Future Development Goals

7.2.3.1 Performance Evaluation of Compulsory Education Policy

Through the effective implementation of compulsory education development policies, there have been balanced developments in compulsory education in China. According to the compulsory education evaluation indicators and analysis results by Zhu et al. (2017), indicators of compulsory education development have significantly improved. Specifically,

(1) The balanced development goals of compulsory education stipulated in the *National Medium- and Long-term Education Reform and Development Plan (2010–2020)* have been achieved, with significant improvements in the balanced development of compulsory education between regions and between urban and rural areas;
(2) Over the past decade, with education expenditure accounting for 4% of GDP, the central and local governments have included compulsory education expenditure in the public finance budget, increasing investment in basic education and narrowing the funding gap between urban and rural areas. Since the implementation of the performance pay policy for compulsory education teachers in 2009, the working conditions of teachers and the mechanism for investment in compulsory education have greatly improved, and a fiscal system that legally guarantees the funding of compulsory education has been established;

(3) With the increase in educational funding, there are more standardized educational facilities in schools, and the conditions for running schools have greatly improved. By 2014, the per capita building area of primary schools nationwide had reached 6.85 m^2, and that of junior high schools was 11.99 m^2;
(4) The construction of the basic education faculty team has yielded good results. The *2012 State Council Opinions on Deepening the Balanced Development of Compulsory Education* ensured the implementation of unified staffing standards for urban and rural primary and secondary schools, with focused support for rural primary schools and teaching points. The *2014 Notice from the Central Organization Department, Ministry of Education, and Ministry of Finance on Uniform Staffing Standards for Urban and Rural Primary and Secondary Schools* was issued to resolve the reverse deployment of teacher staffing in urban and rural areas to some extent, stabilizing the rural teacher team.

Meanwhile, since 2010, the state has fully implemented the *National Training Program for Primary and Secondary School Teachers*, with an annual arrangement of financial budgets for teacher training, establishing a teacher training system, increasing the intensity of teacher training, and improving the quality of the teacher team.

7.2.3.2 Progress Evaluation of the Integration of Urban and Rural Compulsory Education

After years of efforts, with the integration of urban and rural compulsory education policies in China, a more balanced development of compulsory education between urban and rural areas has been realized. The policies for the integrated development of urban and rural compulsory education have been effectively implemented, and some basic systems that affect the equalization of urban and rural compulsory education, such as the household registration system, have also been gradually broken down. These policy measures ensure that rural school-age children can attend schools in urban areas, thereby narrowing the gap in basic educational standards between urban and rural areas. Specifically, the national strategy of expanding the rural teacher workforce has gradually addressed the shortage of teachers in rural basic education (see Table 7.2).

Table 7.2 shows that the student–teacher ratio for rural compulsory education is lower than that in urban areas. This is partly due to rural school-age children migrating to urban areas for education, leading to a decrease in the number of students in rural schools. Additionally, the improvement in the treatment of rural basic education teachers has attracted some teachers to work in rural schools. Meanwhile, China's mechanism of rotating teachers between urban and rural schools has gradually been established. In 2014, with the release of the *Opinions on Promoting the Exchange and Rotation of Principals and Teachers within Counties (Districts)* by the Ministry of Education, Ministry of Finance, and Ministry of Human Resources and Social Security, provinces and cities nationwide also issued relevant policies and conducted

Table 7.2 National urban and rural compulsory education student–teacher ratio (2017)

Grade level	Teachers and students	Total	Urban	Towns	Rural
Primary	Teachers	5,944,910	1,865,679	2,161,813	1,917,418
	Students	100,936,980	34,622,854	38,560,500	27,752,636
	Student–teacher ratio	16.98	18.56	17.84	14.47
Junior	Teachers	3,548,688	1,221,327	1,752,616	574,745
	Students	44,420,630	15,671,422	22,315,114	6,434,094
	Student–Teacher Ratio	12.52	12.83	12.73	11.19

Source China Statistical Yearbook (2018)

pilot reforms to promote the mobility of outstanding teachers to rural schools and those with weak faculty resources. This has facilitated the balanced allocation of teacher resources.

At the same time, the layout of primary and secondary schools between urban and rural areas has become more reasonable. In 2012, the *Opinions on Regulating the Adjustment of the Layout of Rural Compulsory Education Schools* was issued by the General Office of the State Council., which specified that county-level people's governments should scientifically formulate special plans for the layout of rural compulsory education schools. In 2013, the *Notice on the Formulation of Special Plans for the Layout of Rural Compulsory Education Schools* issued by the Ministry of Education stipulated that localities should reasonably formulate special plans for the layout of rural compulsory education schools and strictly regulate school merger procedures and behavior to stop the blind merger of rural compulsory education schools, thus safeguarding the right of rural school-age children to attend nearby schools.

7.2.3.3 Future Goals of Public Education Policy

The *China Education Modernization 2035*, issued by the Central Committee of the Communist Party of China and the State Council in 2019, is a strategic document outlining the future direction, tasks, implementation paths, and safeguard measures for public education in China. It emphasizes the need for "one policy for one region" and "sub-regional implementation".

In the *China Education Modernization 2035*, it is stated that it is essential to follow the spirit of the 19th National Congress of the Communist Party of China and the second and third plenary sessions of the 19th Central Committee and fulfill the strategies of strengthening the country through education, with the overall layout of 'Five in One'[4] and the strategic layout of 'Four Comprehensives',[5] to build up the 'Four Confidences',[6] under the leadership of the Chinese Communist Party. The mission of education is to serve the people, govern the Communist Party, the reform and opening up, and construct a socialist modernization construction, to ultimately develop the socialist system with Chinese characteristics and achieve the prosperity of the Chinese nation. We must prioritize the development of education, promote the modernization of educational concepts, systems, content, methods, and governance, improve the quality of education, promote educational equity, optimize the educational structure, and provide support to achieve the goal of building a moderately prosperous society in all respects and the objectives of socialism with Chinese characteristics.

The goal for promoting education modernization, as stated in "China Education Modernization 2035", is: "to achieve education modernization by 2035, positioning China as one of the world's leading countries in education so that China can be into a nation with rich human resources and a wealth of talents". The development goals by 2035 include: "establishing a modern education system that supports lifelong learning for all, achieving high-quality universal preschool education, realizing equitable and balanced compulsory education, universally providing senior high school education, enhancing the service capacity of vocational education, increasing the competitiveness of higher education, ensuring suitable education for children and adolescents with disabilities, and forming a new pattern of educational governance with the participation of the whole society". All these will lead to the establishment of an education system characterized by vertical cohesion, horizontal communication, coordinated development, and mutual integration.

To achieve these educational goals, China must have a clear and unified construction direction, along with the individual characteristics of different regions and levels of education. For regions with different levels of development, China should implement educational development strategies that align with local conditions and educational principles, rather than relying on highly centralized and rigid administrative planning mechanisms. It is essential to empower educational institutions with more autonomy in running schools to enhance their effectiveness.

In the future, while promoting educational development, China should continue to improve the quality of public basic education, elevate the universal level of high school education based on the already achieved universal levels of junior high and primary education, promote the coordinated development of secondary vocational

[4] "Five in One" refers to five-pronged comprehensive strategy China's development. It encompasses the coordinated advancement of five areas of development: (a) economic development; (b) political development; (c) cultural development; (d) social development; (e) ecological civilization development.

[5] These include: (a) building a moderately prosperous society in all respects; (b) deepening reform comprehensively; (c) advancing the rule of law; (d) strengthening Party discipline.

[6] The "Four Confidences" reflect the Chinese government's confidence in its chosen path and governance model. These include: (a) confidence in the path; (b) confidence in the theory; (c) confidence in the system; (d) confidence in the culture.

education and general high school education, and encourage diversified and characteristic development of general high schools. China aims to realize equalization of basic public education services, improve the equalization level of compulsory education, further promote high-quality balance based on achieving a basic balance of compulsory education within counties, advance the equal treatment of migrant children in urban education, expand urban school places, improve the inter-school examination system for children of migrant populations, and ensure targeted assistance for disadvantaged groups by improving the financial aid system for students from economically disadvantaged families, and to provide quality special education.

To achieve the goals of modern educational development, China should promote the modernization of the education governance system and governance capabilities, enhance legal governance in education, construct a complete system of educational laws and regulations, and improve the legal support system for school operations. Additionally, consistent increases in educational, fiscal investment, encouragement of private investments in education, and support for basic education are crucial to developing a multi-stakeholder cooperation supply mechanism for the development of public education.

7.3 Urban Public Health Policies

7.3.1 Evolution of Public Health Policies in China

At the beginning of the nineteenth century, American public health expert Winslow (1920) defined public health as "the science and art of preventing disease, prolonging life, and promoting health through organized community efforts to improve the environment". This definition was recognized by the World Health Organization and the academic community. Public health encompasses a broad range of topics, including food hygiene, maternal and child health, mental health, surveillance of infectious and major diseases, and the prevention and disposal of public health emergencies.

Since the founding of the People's Republic of China in 1949, the living standards of the people have steadily improved. China has prioritized public health services, with policies evolving in conjunction with economic and social development and the country's overall strategic objectives. The evolution of these policies can be delineated into four distinct stages: the Welfare Health Service Construction Stage (1949–1978), the Health Policy Adjustment Stage (1978–2003), the Public Welfare Health Service Construction Stage (2003–2015), and the "Healthy China" Strategic Construction Stage (2015–present) (Li, 2019).

First Stage: Welfare Health Service Construction (1949–1978).

In the early years of the People's Republic of China, the nation faced significant economic and military challenges. The medical and health industries were underdeveloped and the government prioritized the development of the healthcare sector and public health welfare. In 1950, the Central Committee introduced the health work guidelines emphasizing services to workers, farmers, and soldiers, the principle of "prevention first", and the integration of Chinese and Western medicine. In 1952, Premier Zhou Enlai further emphasized the importance of combining health initiatives with mass movements. Under these directives, China's health sector saw rapid advancement, earning the World Bank commended China's praise for achieving the greatest health benefits with minimal investment (Liu, 1999; Zhang, 2010). However, public health policies during this period lacked a systematic and comprehensive framework, and the health sector was still in its formative stage.

Second Stage: Health Policy Adjustment (1978–2003).

The 1978 Third Plenary Session of the Eleventh Central Committee marked the onset of reform and opening up policies, ushering in a new era of socioeconomic development in China. The reform brought significant changes to the management systems and operational mechanisms within the public health sector. Following a period of adjustment, the government re-emphasized the development of public health and medical services. The Ministry of Health's 1990 release of the *Planning Goals for Achieving 'Health for All by the Year 2000' in Rural Areas of China (Trial Implementation)* marked a significant push towards improving public health. Subsequent policies in the *Decision of the Central Committee of the Communist Party of China and the State Council on Health Reform and Development* and other related documents helped foster further development in this sector, resulting in more stable operational conditions. Despite these advancements, challenges such as resource misallocation, weak primary health care, and slow development in the public health sector arose.

Third Stage: Public Welfare Health Service Construction (2003–2015).

The 2003 SARS outbreak and long-standing issues of "difficulty in accessing affordable medical care" prompted the government to reconsider the excessive marketization of the public health sector. The *Opinions of the Central Committee of the Communist Party of China and the State Council on Deepening the Reform of the Medical and Health System* was issued in 2009, and it planned the establishment of a public health service system covering both urban and rural residents. During this period, the government's financial investment in public health services significantly increased, leading to improvements in the public health service system and overall service (Fig. 7.1).

Fourth Stage: "Healthy China" Strategic Construction (2015–Present).

The strategy "Healthy China" was formulated at the Fifth Plenary Session of the 18th Central Committee in 2015. Subsequent policies are included in the *Opinions of the Central Committee of the Communist Party of China and the State Council on Deepening the Reform of the Medical and Health System* (2016) and the *Opinions of the State Council on Implementing the Healthy China Action (2019)*, which set the goals for establishing a health promotion policy system by 2022 and achieving health equity by 2030.

After the outbreak of COVID-19, the Chinese government, besides taking comprehensive anti-epidemic actions, further introduces policies to reform the public health system, pushing China's public health endeavors to new heights.

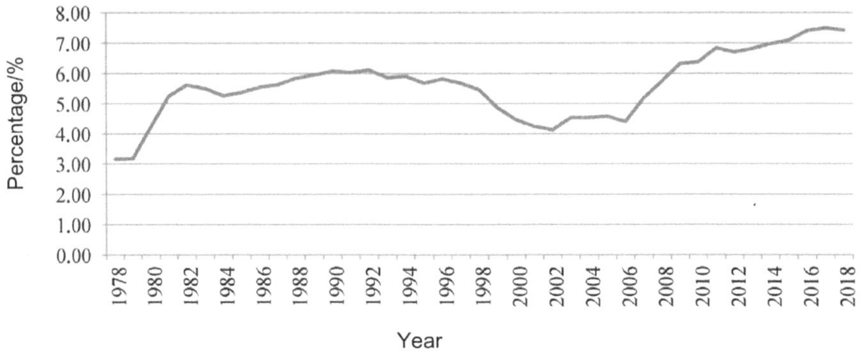

Fig. 7.1 Changes in the proportion of government health expenditure to fiscal expenditure from 1978 to 2018 (*Source China Statistical Yearbook*)

7.3.2 Major Public Health Policies and Practices

Public health encompasses a wide range of activities, focusing on different priorities at different times. Since the founding of the PRC, the country has simultaneously bolstered basic health infrastructure while emphasizing the prevention and control of major infectious diseases and establishing a public health and medical security system.

7.3.2.1 Prevention and Control of Major Infectious Diseases

In China, infectious diseases such as schistosomiasis, filariasis, hookworm, kala-azar, malaria, smallpox, and AIDS have posed significant threats to public health. The central and local governments have undertaken extensive and long-term efforts to control and eradicate these diseases. Measures include widespread vaccination campaigns, community-based prevention and treatment initiatives, and the establishment of comprehensive prevention and treatment systems. The following are discussions on the control of schistosomiasis and AIDS.

(1) Prevention and Control of Schistosomiasis

Schistosomiasis is a parasitic disease that endangers health. It once ravaged various regions in China, leading to barren lands and labor shortages in severely affected areas. In November 1955, the Central Committee of the Communist Party of China established the Schistosomiasis Control Leadership Group to unify the leadership in schistosomiasis endemic areas. In February 1956, the central government made a significant decision to mobilize the entire party and population to eliminate schistosomiasis, setting the policy of "strengthening leadership, comprehensive planning, relying on mutual assistance and cooperation, organizing Chinese and Western medical forces, actively preventing and controlling, and eliminating the disease within seven years". Subsequently, regions formulated overall control plans and established regular reporting systems (Zhuang, 2020).

To achieve the goal of schistosomiasis control, the central government developed a series of policies in the *1956–1967 National Agricultural Development Outline* issued in January 1956, the *Directive of the State Council on Eliminating Schistosomiasis* and the *Notice of the Central Committee on Ensuring the Implementation of the State Council's Directive on Eliminating Schistosomiasis* issued in April 1957, in which the objectives, guidelines, action plans, and time requirements for schistosomiasis control work were clarified. With pilot projects in China's Pingjiang County and Wuxi City as examples, large-scale control of the disease was launched nationwide.

Given the high infection and recurrence rates of schistosomiasis, China developed strategies to completely eradicate the disease, which included:

(1) Establishing disease prevention and treatment institutions and teams: From 1956 to August 1957, 19 disease prevention and treatment institutes, 236 disease prevention and treatment stations, and 1,346 disease prevention and treatment teams were established in endemic areas, training over 17,000 professional control staff, and conducting large-scale control work in 309 counties;
(2) Identifying and treating patients: Patients were found and treated to eliminate the sources of infection;
(3) Eliminating Oncomelania snails: The government launched a campaign of conducting large-scale construction of water conservancy facilities and ecological environment management in endemic areas to eradicate Oncomelania snails, the intermediate host of schistosomiasis, thereby cutting off transmission channels;
(4) Combining Chinese and Western medicine: 16 effective traditional Chinese medicine prescriptions from over 1,000 were selected and combined with Western medicine in treatments;
(5) Conducting extensive public education: The government conducted thorough public mobilization and scientific education in endemic areas to raise awareness and enhance confidence and determination in disease prevention and control;
(6) Supervision and inspection: Supervision and inspection teams were formed, and work reporting systems were established at all levels of government to regularly report progress and issues and coordinate control efforts among relevant departments (Lin & Li, 2005; Zhuang, 2020).

By the end of 1957, significant progress had been made, with 13 counties almost eradicating schistosomiasis, 343 towns and townships eradicating Oncomelania snails, and more than 500,000 patients treated nationwide. By 1958, over 3 million patients had been treated, and Oncomelania snails had been eradicated (New China's Preventive Medicine Historical Experience Editorial Committee, 1988). These marked a great victory and laid a solid foundation for long-term control of schistosomiasis in China.

(2) Prevention and Control of AIDS

In 1985, China reported its first case of AIDS. In view of the highly infectious effect of the disease, China issued policies against it. In 1989, at the Sixth Session of the Standing Committee of the Seventh National People's Congress, the *Law of the People's Republic of China on the Prevention and Treatment of Infectious Diseases* was passed, which, revised in 2004 and 2013, is a comprehensive legal framework for preventing, controlling, and eliminating infectious diseases.

In 1999, the *Opinions of the Ministry of Health on the Management of HIV Infected Persons and AIDS Patients* was issued, which specified that local health and epidemic prevention departments were responsible for organizing epidemiological investigations, establishing personal records, and conducting regular follow-ups. The *Opinions of the Ministry of Health and the State Administration of Traditional Chinese Medicine on the Management of Antiviral Treatment for AIDS* issued in April 2004 emphasized the need to supervise the implementation of relevant laws and regulations and strictly handle medical institutions and personnel refusing to provide services to AIDS patients. In 2006, the State Council issued the *Regulations on the Prevention and Treatment of AIDS*, institutionalizing the "Four Frees and One Care" policy[7] for AIDS patients. In 2013, the National Health and Family Planning Commission, the National Development and Reform Commission, and five other ministries issued the *Notice on Further Promoting AIDS Prevention and Control Work*, requiring localities to include AIDS opportunistic infection treatment in the new rural cooperative medical system by the end of June 2014. In 2017, the General Office of the State Council issued the *13th Five-Year Action Plan for AIDS Containment and Prevention in China*, calling for leveraging traditional Chinese medicine in AIDS prevention and control and developing comprehensive treatment plans combining Chinese and Western medicine.

Currently, AIDS prevention and control in China remains challenging. According to statistics from the National Health Commission, there were 64,170 new AIDS cases and 18,780 deaths in 2018, with the incidence of AIDS increasing from 0.43 per 100,000 people in 2005 to 4.62 per 100,000 people in 2018. In September 2019, the National Health Commission and other departments released the *Implementation Plan for Containing the Spread of AIDS (2019–2022)*, coordinating efforts among the AIDS Prevention Coordination Mechanism Office, health departments, judicial

[7] The "Four Free and One Care" policy includes the following elements: ① Provision of free antiretroviral drugs: Free antiretroviral therapy (ART) is provided to rural AIDS patients and urban AIDS patients with economic difficulties; ② Free HIV consultation and initial screening: Free consultation and initial screening are provided nationwide to individuals who voluntarily accept HIV counseling and testing; ③ Prevention of mother-to-child transmission: Free treatment and consultation are provided to HIV-infected pregnant women to prevent mother-to-child transmission of HIV; ④ Educational support for orphans and HIV-infected minor: Orphans left behind by deceased AIDS patients and HIV-infected minors from economically disadvantaged backgrounds are exempt from miscellaneous fees and textbook fees for compulsory education. Fees for preschool and high school education are reduced or waived; ⑤ Inclusion in government assistance programs: Economically disadvantaged AIDS patients are included in government assistance programs and provided with necessary living allowances according to national regulations. There is also active support for HIV-infected persons and AIDS patients with the ability to work, helping them engage in production and work activities within their capacity.

departments, and education departments. The plan includes six major projects: AIDS prevention education, comprehensive intervention, expanded testing and treatment, comprehensive social governance, elimination of mother-to-child transmission, and student education on AIDS prevention. These all aim to curb the rising trend of AIDS transmission. After decades of efforts, significant progress has been made in AIDS prevention and control in China, particularly in establishing a comprehensive prevention, control, and treatment system.

7.3.2.2 Establishing and Improving the Handling System for Public Health Emergencies

Public health emergencies can cause immeasurable economic losses in a very short time and also trigger social panic. The SARS outbreak in 2003 tested China's system and mechanisms for handling public health emergencies and preventing major infectious diseases.

After the SARS outbreak, the Chinese government mobilized the entire society to fight against the epidemic and controlled it in a relatively short period. During this process, China accumulated experience in handling public health emergencies and issued a series of prevention and control policies, establishing emergency plans and norms and improving the related legal system. In May 2003, the State Council issued the *Emergency Regulations on Public Health Emergencies*, which required all levels of government to formulate emergency plans for public health emergencies and establish an emergency reporting system for such incidents. In 2006, the State Council issued the *National Emergency Plan for Public Emergencies*, categorizing public emergencies into natural disasters, accidents, public health incidents, and social security incidents, which are managed and handled at four levels based on severity and other factors. In the same year, other policies were issued and implemented, including the *National Emergency Regulations on Public Health Information Reporting, Management Measures for Reporting Public Health Emergencies and Infectious Disease Outbreak Monitoring Information, National Emergency Plan for Medical and Health Rescue in Public Emergencies*, and *Guidelines for Community Emergency Plans for Public Health Emergencies*. These policy documents provide guidance for the identification, classification, reporting, monitoring, and emergency response to public emergencies (Sun et al., 2014).

At the end of 2019, following the outbreak of COVID-19, the State Council enacted epidemic prevention and control policies. During the anti-epidemic process, the central and local governments took various measures: expanding medical facilities primarily through the construction of makeshift hospitals, utilizing the power of grassroots communities to hospitalize and treat patients comprehensively, and controlling community spread of the virus while concentrating resources and medical supplies nationwide on the frontline of the epidemic. The Ministry of Finance allocated prevention control subsidies and implemented financial policies such as timely disbursement of unemployment benefits, exemption from personal income tax on protective gear for employees, waiving medical expenses for COVID-19 patients, and providing insurance benefits for medical personnel. With these measures, China effectively controlled the epidemic. The lessons drawn from the fight against COVID-19 include the following:

(1) An epidemic prevention system should be formed, which combines home isolation with centralized quarantine, and community control, and also designated hospitals with temporary hospitals and reserved medical service capacities;
(2) Importance should be attached to ensuring the normal operation of public sectors such as medical resources, living supplies, and transportation during sudden epidemics;
(3) Emergency prevention and control plans for public health emergencies should be formulated and implemented by localities and units;
(4) Unified leadership must be formed in establishing an organizational and institutional guarantee system, particularly relying on grassroots social organizations, mobilizing societal strength to establish a community-based epidemic prevention network, and establishing a cross-departmental and cross-regional comprehensive prevention and coordination mechanism;
(5) Emphasis should be laid on establishing information disclosure and reporting systems based on the Internet and big data technologies, supported by laws and regulations, and setting up a rapid decision-making feedback system.

7.3.2.3 Maternal and Child Health Care Construction

During the early years following the founding of the People's Republic of China in 1949, there were very limited medical and health services. This, together with insufficient knowledge of protection among health institutions and medical personnel, led to frequent maternal infections and high infant mortality rates. During this stage, the focus of maternal and child health work was to promote childbirth methods, specifically the concept of "one lying position and three disinfections".[8]

In 1977, the World Health Organization introduced the global strategic goal of "Health for All by the Year 2000". In response to this call, in 1986, China committed to this goal, leading the Ministry of Health to revise the *Maternal and Child Health Work Regulations*[9] issued in 1980, which defined the tasks and goals of maternal-child health work, providing guidance for the construction of relevant professional institutions and grassroots organizations. In 1990, the Ministry of Health issued the *Opinions on Implementing the Responsibility System for Maternal and Child Health Care* outlining nationwide adoption of this system, which covers adolescent and marital health (premarital checkups), maternal care series, child care series, eugenics series, and family planning technical services. In the same year, the State Council

[8] In the "one lying position and three disinfections" practice, "one lying position" refers to giving birth in a lying position, and "three disinfections" include sterilizing the delivery instruments, the hands of the person assisting with the delivery, and the perineal area of the pregnant woman.

[9] This practice has been abolished according to the *Order on the Abolition of the 'Maternal and Child Health Work Regulations'* and *'Six Other Departmental Rules' (National Health and Family Planning Commission Order No. 2).*

Women and Children Work Coordination Committee was established to organize and guide the protection of women's and children's rights and promote gender equality. It was renamed the State Council Women and Children Work Committee in 1993.

In 1992, China enacted the *Law on the Protection of Women's Rights and Interests*, and in 1994, the *Law on Maternal and Infant Health Care*, followed by their *Implementation Measures* in 1995. These developments marked the transition of maternal and child health work into a phase of legal management and service provision. From 1996 to 2000, China collaborated with UNICEF on maternal and child health work, which rapidly advanced the field. To reduce maternal mortality, the State Council approved the *Implementation of the Outline Program for the Development of Chinese Children (2001–2010)* and the *Implementation of the Outline Program for the Development of Chinese Women (2001–2010)* in 2001, outlining goals, tasks, and policy measures for the early twenty-first century (Li Hongbin et al., 2011).

In September 1982, family planning was a fundamental national policy with the goal of controlling population growth. According to the National Bureau of Statistics, China's birth rate in 1982 was 22.28‰. After implementing the family planning policy, this figure gradually declined, reaching 12.10‰ in 2012. In 2012, China had 100.403 million elderly people aged 65 and above, with an elderly dependency ratio of 12.7% (Cheng & Ma, 2018). Given the decreasing labor force and accelerated aging of the population, at the sixth meeting of the Twelfth National People's Congress Standing Committee, the *Resolution on Adjusting and Improving the Birth Policy* was passed on December 28, 2013, formally ending the one-child policy, which allowed couples, where one spouse was the only child, to have two children. In 2021, the family planning policy was further adjusted to allow couples to have three children.

In 2017, according to the *Decision of the State Council on Amending Some Administrative Regulations*, China revised the *Implementation Measures of the Law on Maternal and Infant Health Care* to further refine the technical standards for hospital deliveries. In 2018, the National Health Commission issued the *Post-Abortion Contraceptive Service Standards*, the *Maternal and Infant Safety Action Plan (2018–2020)*, and the *Healthy Children Action Plan (2018–2020)*, further specifying goals and measures for maternal and child health services.

After years of efforts, significant achievements have been made in maternal and child health work in China. *China's Health Statistics Yearbook* (2015) shows that the maternal mortality rate nationwide was 21.7 per 100,000 in 2014, a 75.56% drop from 88.8 per 100,000 in 1990, meeting the United Nations' target for reducing maternal mortality ahead of schedule. The *National Medical Insurance Agency's 2019 Medical Security Development Statistical Bulletin* revealed that, in 2019, the total number of people covered by maternity insurance reached 214.32 million, an increase of 4.90% over the previous year.

7.3.3 Performance Evaluation of Public Health Policies

The implementation performance of public health policies is an important indicator of a country's level of health services. Performance evaluation of implementation is a crucial driving force for testing policy execution and improving public health standards. The assessment framework of structure, process, and outcomes established by American public health scholar Avedis Donabedian has been widely recognized in academia. Many countries have based their national public health performance evaluation frameworks on this model (Su, 2010). Compared with Western countries, China's public health performance evaluation started later, so some evaluations of public health policies refer to the standards of other countries or the World Health Organization. The following section will introduce the progress of public health policy performance evaluation in China's health system construction, operation of medical institutions, and basic public health service levels.

7.3.3.1 China's Health System Construction Performance Evaluation

In the *2000 World Health Report*, the World Health Organization used indicators such as healthy life expectancy, responsiveness level and distribution, fairness in health financing, and per capita health expenditures to evaluate the health system construction of various countries. The report showed that China ranked 144th in overall performance evaluation and 61st in the overall level of national health status. However, some scholars believe that the evaluation indicator system established by the World Health Organization did not include essential factors such as the economy and culture or reflect the level of health service demand and utilization (Li, 2011a, 2011b).

The performance evaluation of China's health system construction is primarily conducted through the selection of National Health Cities (towns, counties, districts). In 1989, to implement the *Decision on Strengthening Patriotic Health Work*, China launched the National Health City creation activity. The initiatives of constructing National Health Towns (counties) began in 1997, and National Health Districts were initiated in 2000 in the four municipalities directly under the Central Government. To establish evaluation criteria and management methods for National Health Cities (towns, counties, districts), the National Patriotic Health Campaign Committee formulated the *Implementation Details of the National Health City Inspection and Evaluation Criteria* in 1991. Starting in 1999, the committee issued documents such as the *National Health City Standards, National Health City Evaluation and Naming Methods, and the National Health District Standards.* In 2015, the committee revised the *National Health City Standards* and promulgated the *National Health City Evaluation and Supervision Management Measures.* In 2007, 2010, and 2011, the committee issued the *National Health City Evaluation and Naming and Supervision Management Measures, National Health City, District Standards and Their Evaluation and Naming and Supervision Management Measures*, and the *National*

Health City Evaluation and Naming and Supervision Management Measures. In 2014, the *National Health City Standards* were revised again, refining evaluation criteria and improving the evaluation system for National Health Cities (towns, counties, districts) (Ruan, 2015). According to documents from the National Health Commission, till February 2019, the number of National Health Towns had reached 1,452. The evaluation of health cities and health counties has significantly improved local health conditions in China (Ruan, 2015).

7.3.3.2 Performance Evaluation of Medical Institutions

In 1950, the First National Health Work Conference established a three-tier medical and health service network. In 1951, the State Council approved and issued the *Provisional Regulations on the Management of Medical Clinics*.[10] During this period, there were few national policies targeting the management of medical institutions. After the reform and opening up, China began to focus on the assessment and evaluation of medical institutions. In November 1989, the Ministry of Health issued the *Hospital Grading Management Measures*, which classified hospitals into three grades and ten levels according to the *Hospital Grading Management Standards*. In 1994, the State Council issued the *Regulations on the Administration of Medical Institutions*, stipulating that medical institutions without a medical institution practicing license were not allowed to operate independently. In the *Measures for the Evaluation of Medical Institutions*, issued in 1995, more detailed regulations on the standards and processes for evaluating medical institutions were listed. In 1997, the Ministry of Health issued the *Evaluation Standards for Township Health Centers, Evaluation Standards for General Hospitals*, and *Evaluation Criteria for Hospital and Township Health Center Evaluation Conclusions*, which conducted evaluations and grading of hospitals nationwide.

In the twenty-first century, the country has revised policy documents such as the *Regulations on the Administration of Medical Institutions* and the *Implementation Rules for the Administration of Medical Institutions* according to the development level of medical institutions and emerging medical challenges and has established and improved the evaluation system for tertiary hospitals. In 2008, the Ministry of Health issued the *Hospital Management Evaluation Guide*, which laid a foundation for establishing China's hospital management evaluation index system, mainly applicable to tertiary general hospitals. In 2011, the Ministry of Health issued the *Evaluation Standards for Tertiary General Hospitals*, detailing 378 evaluation standards. According to data from the National Bureau of Statistics Information Center, till the end of November 2018, there were 2,498 tertiary hospitals, 8,806 secondary hospitals, 10,477 primary hospitals, and 10,695 ungraded hospitals in China. In 2019, the National Health Commission issued the *National Performance*

[10] Abolished on September 1, 1994.

Assessment Manual for Tertiary Public Hospitals, establishing a performance assessment indicator system with four dimensions, marking a pioneering endeavor in the performance assessment of medical institutions in China.

In addition to the evaluation standards for tertiary hospitals, the country has also developed evaluation standards for newly established hospitals, conducting assessments of the medical facilities and management of newly established hospitals. Furthermore, in 1994, the Joint Commission on Accreditation of Healthcare Organizations (JCAHO) established its Joint Commission International (JCI), to evaluate and accredit medical institutions outside the United States. Till 2017, more than 80 hospitals in China had received JCI accreditation.

7.3.3.3 Performance Evaluation of Basic Public Health Service Levels

The performance evaluation of China's disease prevention and control policies first began in December 2008, when the Disease Prevention and Control Bureau of the Ministry of Health issued the *Basic Responsibilities of Disease Prevention and Control Centers at All Levels and the Performance Evaluation Standards for Disease Prevention and Control Work*. In 2009, the *Performance Evaluation Manual for Disease Prevention and Control Work* was issued, specifying the implementation process and data collection for performance evaluations. In 2013, the *Performance Evaluation Standards for Disease Prevention and Control Work* was issued.

In 2009, the *Opinions of the Central Committee of the Communist Party of China and the State Council on Deepening the Reform of the Medical and Health System* was issued which outlined the tasks to "promote the gradual equalization of basic public health services for urban and rural residents". Subsequently, the country conducted overall assessments and management of basic public health services. In June 2015, the *Notice on Issuing the Guidelines for the Performance Evaluation of National Basic Public Health Service Projects* announced the reference documents for the evaluation indicator systems at the provincial, municipal, and county levels, including five dimensions: organizational management, financial management, project implementation, project outcomes, and additional indicators.

After the outbreak of COVID-19, the Party and the government prioritized public health services, considering the improvement of the public health system as a crucial aspect of health reform and development. Efforts have been made to strengthen various types of professional public health institutions, steadily enhancing public health service levels. The reform of the public health system and mechanisms is beneficial for improving the disease prevention and control system, enhancing the sensitivity and accuracy of evaluation and monitoring, and perfecting the response plan system. It also helps enhance the detection and handling capabilities for major public health emergencies, improve the hierarchical, classified, and triaged treatment mechanisms for major epidemics, and optimize the treatment system for major epidemics. It mobilizes the power of society, especially leveraging the role of grassroots community organizations, to carry out the patriotic health campaign deeply. It also increases government investment in the public health field, focusing efforts on basic research and key technology breakthroughs, and improves the legal and regulatory framework for public health, ensuring the legal protection system for public health (National Health Commission, 2020).

Over the years, China has built a relatively systematic network of grassroots medical and health institutions and disease control institutions. These institutions undertake the responsibility of providing basic medical and public health services. By the end of 2019, there were 2,755 counties (district, county-level city)-level disease prevention and control centers, 16,175 county-level hospitals, 36,000 township health centers, and 616,000 village clinics nationwide, achieving the goal of having a comprehensive hospital, a traditional Chinese medicine hospital, and a disease prevention and control center in every county, a township health center in every township, and a health clinic in every administrative village. At the same time, the number of personnel in the county (district, county-level city) level disease prevention and control centers reached 126,800, with 1.445 million medical personnel in township health centers, 503,000 practicing (assistant) physicians, 1.446 million medical personnel in village clinics, and 435,000 practicing (assistant) physicians. These increases in institutions and personnel have made healthcare more accessible, with over 80% of residents able to reach a medical facility within 15 min.

7.3.4 Reform of Public Health Policies

Since the reform and opening up, China's public health services have significantly improved, and the medical and healthcare sectors have developed significantly. Statistics show that in 1978, China had only 169,700 medical and health institutions, with 2.0417 million beds and 2.4639 million health technicians. By 2019, these numbers had grown to 1.014 million, 8.92 million, and 10.1 million, respectively, with annual growth rates of 4.46, 3.66, and 3.50%. Progress in medical institutions, equipment, personnel, and service levels is inseparable from the promulgation and implementation of public health policies. However, due to imbalanced economic development and fiscal limitations, the medical security level for residents remains relatively low, with disparities in urban and rural public health investment, resource distribution, and basic medical insurance systems.

In the 1980s, traditional public medical systems were challenged in the face of the impact of the market economy. Government investment grew slowly, with the health sector lagging behind and medical institutions experiencing significant losses. In 1985, the Ministry of Health released a report stating that it was essential to promote public health system reform. Similar to other urban public sectors, health institutions nationwide implemented accountability systems, such as administrative leadership responsibility, post responsibility, quota-based contracts, and task indicators. Autonomy for hospitals or pharmaceutical enterprises gradually increased, and pricing for instruments and drugs moved toward market determination (Li et al., 2008). In 1992, the *Ministry of Health's Opinions on Deepening Healthcare Reform* specified the market-oriented direction of medical and health system reform, with the government gradually relaxing control over medical service supply. In 1997, the *Central Committee and the State Council's Decisions on Healthcare Reform and Development* called for increased health investment, diversified health financing, and the establishment of effective competition mechanisms. In 1998, the basic medical insurance system for urban employees was established. The 2000 guidelines for urban medical reform aimed at the simultaneous advancement of various reforms. To reduce urban–rural disparities in public health services, the 2006 Eleventh Five-Year Plan of the People's Republic of China and the CPC Central Committee's decisions on constructing a harmonious socialist society proposed improving public finance systems and achieving equalization of basic public services, including public health services. In December 2008, the State Council established a leadership group to deepen healthcare system reform. In 2009, opinions by the Central Committee and the State Council and the 2009–2011 healthcare reform implementation plan were issued. The 2012 annual report on deepening healthcare reform outlined key directions, focusing on improving primary healthcare, refining the new rural cooperative medical care system, promoting the national essential drug system, and enhancing the safety and quality of medical services. With these reforms, China's basic medical service provision system improved, with insurance coverage expanding to most urban and rural residents through urban employee insurance, urban resident insurance, and the new rural cooperative medical scheme. Pilot programs for major disease insurance for urban and rural residents were extended nationwide, and basic drug systems in primary healthcare institutions showed significant reform effects.

In the *Outlines for the Thirteenth Five-Year Plan of the People's Republic of China*, it is proposed that a basic medical and health system should be established, which will cover urban and rural residents and can promote healthcare system and market reforms. The *2016 Government Work Report* called for coordinated reforms in healthcare, medical insurance, and pharmaceuticals. Consequently, various localities undertook public health and medical system reform practices. For instance, Shanghai piloted a family doctor contract service system and launched the "1 + 1 + 1" contract model, allowing patients to annually voluntarily select one community health service center, one district center medical institution, and one tertiary hospital (Duan, 2017). Anhui province piloted the "three strengths" coordination between medical administration, health supervision, and the new rural cooperative medical care, enhancing reporting on fees for designated healthcare institutions to maximize fund usage efficiency. Sanming City in Fujian province established a medical security fund management center to sever financial ties between hospitals and drug suppliers, curbing excessive medical treatment. These policies explored the "three medical linkages[11]" from community, urban, and county perspectives.

In October 2016, the CPC Central Committee and the State Council issued the *Healthy China 2030 Planning Outline*, which set the goal that by 2030, the health indicators of Chinese residents should rank among the top countries. In 2019, China initiated the *Healthy China Action Promotion Committee and formulated the*

[11] The "Three Medical Linkages" refer to the integration of medical services, medical insurance, and pharmaceuticals.

Healthy China Action (2019–2030), which specified specific goals and action plans, including strengthening organizational leadership, conducting monitoring and evaluation, establishing performance assessment mechanisms, improving support systems, and enhancing public awareness.

With continuous economic development, China increasingly emphasizes healthy lifestyles for individuals. Public health reform will focus on effectively implementing public health policies to benefit more people. The COVID-19 pandemic highlighted the severe impacts of health emergencies on public health and the socioeconomic sphere, prompting the need for further improvement in public health systems and accelerating healthcare reforms.

(1) Public health policies must be effectively implemented. The government should provide financial subsidies to economically backward regions and support central special funds for healthcare infrastructure. Performance evaluation of public health policies should be strengthened, with strict supervision and inspection of policy implementation to prevent inaction or perfunctory actions by local government officials due to fiscal pressure or neglect.
(2) Public health systems and mechanisms should be improved. The government should reform public health systems to address issues such as aging populations, increased population mobility, and urban–rural divides, promoting equalization of basic public health services among urban and rural residents. Reforms in medical insurance reimbursement systems and the establishment of a medical service information platform are needed to address cross-regional healthcare challenges.
(3) Public health funding should be increased. The government should increase the proportion of public health spending within its government budget, establishing fixed ratios to ensure the conduct of basic public health services. Government budgets at all levels should be allocated for public health under strict supervision of budget execution, including regular audits, and performance evaluations.
(4) The construction of "Healthy China" should be prioritized. The government should strengthen hygiene inspection and supervision of food, drugs, health products, and cosmetics, enhance the ability to identify public health risks, and avoid sudden public health events. Additionally, it is necessary to raise national awareness of the importance of public health through educational programs and public service advertisements.

7.4 Urban Social Security Policies

7.4.1 Evolution of Social Security Policies in China

Social security is a vital institution through which the government addresses social issues economically, safeguards citizens' basic subsistence rights, and enhances the quality of life and social welfare of people. Since the founding of the People's

Republic of China in 1949, the social security system has progressed from traditional to modern forms.

From 1949 to 1979, the social security system was based on traditional models aligned closely with the planned economy, characterized by national insurance and collective security. As China's economy and society rapidly developed, the traditional social security system began to show limitations such as low protection levels, egalitarianism, closed operations, and a lack of personal responsibility. Following the reform and opening up policy initiated in 1979, China's social security system gradually improved. The modern social security phase has integrated market mechanisms into the traditional administrative planning system, emphasizing shared responsibilities and risks among the government, enterprises, and individuals, balancing rights and obligations, and promoting fairness and social operations (Tang, 2008).

During the planned economy period, China's social management distinguished between urban and rural areas and social classes. The household registration system contributed to significant differences in labor, social security, and public services between urban and rural residents. Urban residents' social security rights vary depending on their employment status, and they are categorized into public sector personnel, enterprise personnel (state-owned and collective enterprises), and non-employed residents. The government implemented varying social security policies based on these employment categories, while rural residents relied on rural collective organizations for basic social security, education, and healthcare, which were funded by local economic resources and individual contributions. Strict control on mobility between urban and rural residents ensured compliance with these policies, resulting in significant disparities in social security levels and access (Wang, 2019).

After the reform and opening up, a socialist market economy was established, which transformed urban–rural economic relations, increased mobility, and highlighted the inadequacies of the planned economy in a market context. Starting in the 1980s, China gradually began to build a modern social security system. A key factor for this change was the substantial financial losses in state-owned enterprises (SOEs) and the resulting widespread unemployment. In the 1990s, approximately 60 million workers from SOEs and urban collective enterprises were laid off, placing immense strains on the traditional "unit-based" social security system, which became unsustainable for enterprises.

To address the challenges faced by the unemployed and stabilize social development, the government established a social security system for the unemployed, initiating a series of social security reforms. In terms of pensions, since 1984, China has piloted a basic social pension insurance system for contract workers in economically developed coastal areas, applying social pooling to retirement expenses for fixed enterprise workers. In public healthcare, the Ministry of Health and the Ministry of Finance jointly reformed the traditional public healthcare system in 1984. For unemployment insurance and female employee protection, in 1986, China implemented a waiting insurance system for SOE workers, and in 1988, the State Council issued *Regulations on Labor Protection for Female Workers*,[12] initiating the maternity insurance system (Zheng, 2018).

The 16th Party Congress Report in 2002 proposed combining social pooling with personal accounts in urban areas to improve basic pension insurance and medical insurance for urban employees, enhance unemployment insurance, and establish minimum living standards for urban residents. It also called for exploring pension and health insurance for rural areas based on local conditions. In 2007, the 17th Party Congress Report emphasized the need to accelerate the establishment of an urban–rural comprehensive social security system and public health service system, enabling equal employment opportunities and integrated socioeconomic development between urban and rural areas. The 18th Party Congress Report in 2012 further highlighted coordinated urban–rural social security development, aiming for comprehensive coverage, basic protection, multi-level, and sustainable social security systems to enhance fairness, adaptability, and sustainability fully. Over the past decade, the government has increased social security expenditures within the public finance budget, improving the system of shared responsibilities and costs between enterprises and individuals. With an initial modern social security system, the 19th Party Congress Report in 2017 emphasized the goal of building a multi-tiered social security system covering all citizens with clear responsibilities, adequate protection, and sustainability. This marked the beginning of a new phase in enhancing social security levels and developing an integrated urban–rural social security system.

7.4.2 Social Security System and Its Practices

China has now developed the world's largest social security system, including social insurance, social assistance, social welfare, and special care and resettlement systems.

China's social insurance system comprises medical insurance, pension insurance, unemployment insurance, work injury insurance, and maternity insurance (see Table 7.3). Since the promulgation of the *Labor Protection Ordinance* in the 1950s, long-term efforts have established a social insurance system with Chinese characteristics. The *Social Insurance Law*, passed in the 17th meeting of the Standing Committee of the National People's Congress in 2010, legally ensured the execution of the social insurance system.

The table shows that by 2019, total pension insurance participants reached 96.748 million, with a coverage rate of 69%. Basic medical insurance participants numbered 135.436 million, nearly a 97% coverage rate, effectively achieving universal medical insurance coverage.

While social assistance has long existed in various forms in China, a formalized aid system has gradually taken shape since the founding of the People's Republic of China in 1949, primarily aiming to meet the basic living needs of recipients. The *Interim Measures on Social Assistance* specified eight assistance programs:

---

[12] Abolished on April 28, 2012.

Table 7.3 Social insurance coverage in China (2015–2019)

Year	Urban employee pension insurance	Urban–rural resident pension insurance	Basic medical insurance	Unemployment insurance	Work injury insurance	Maternity insurance
2015	35,361	50,472	66,570	17,326	21,404	17,769
2016	37,862	50,847	74,839	18,089	21,887	18,443
2017	40,199	51,255	117,664	18,784	22,726	19,240
2018	41,848	52,392	134,452	19,643	23,868	20,435
2019	43,482	53,266	135,436	20,543	25,474	21,432

Unit 10 k people
Source Compiled from the 2019 *National Economic and Social Development Statistical Bulletin*

minimum living security, support for persons in extreme poverty, disaster relief, medical assistance, education assistance, housing aid, employment aid, and temporary assistance. In recent years, China has strengthened the integration of social assistance and poverty alleviation policies, significantly raising standards and expanding coverage. From 2015 to 2019, the registered impoverished population decreased by 50.24 million, with the poverty incidence dropping from 5.7 to 0.6%. By 2020, all 832 impoverished counties nationwide had been alleviated from poverty (Song & Kang, 2021). By November 2019, China established a comprehensive social assistance system covering urban and rural areas, benefiting 43.335 million low-income individuals, 4.716 million extremely poor individuals, and it allocated 33.51 billion yuan in aid and support funding, assisted 861,000 vagrant and beggar individuals, and achieved nearly complete rescue coverage. From 2015 to 2019, the urban low-income population decreased by 8.4 million while the rural low-income population declined by 14.48 million, with an average annual decrease of 110,000 in extremely poor population (Li et al., 2021).

The social welfare system aims to enhance national welfare and improve material and cultural living standards, covering social allowances, housing welfare, educational welfare, occupational welfare, and social services. It focuses on vulnerable groups such as the disabled, women, the elderly, and children, thereby enhancing their quality of life.

The special care and resettlement system targets military personnel and their families, offering benefits such as preferential treatment, pensions, old-age care, and employment resettlement. The government has significantly increased fiscal allocations for this system, frequently adjusting benefits and living allowances for preferential care recipients.

Additionally, social services, affordable housing, compulsory education, elderly services, and other welfare undertakings have comprehensively developed. By the end of 2019, 35.791 million elderly individuals received subsistence allowances, and there were 8.036 million social service beds available (Dong & Shen, 2021).

7.4.3 Adjustment and Reform of Social Security Policies

Since the reform and opening up, China's social security system has undergone continuous changes and developments, evolving to reflect China's realities and characteristics. However, there remains a considerable gap between the levels of social security and the aspirations and needs of the population, as well as the intended goals of social security. Flaws and issues within the social security system urgently persist, highlighting the urgent need for comprehensive reforms to improve its effectiveness.

7.4.3.1 Define the Policy Orientation of Social Security and Transition from High-Speed to High-Quality Development

China's current social security system already covers a wide range of services and has implemented a series of policies to ensure residents' basic needs of living. Nevertheless, the overall level of social security remains relatively low, characterized by imbalances and insufficiency. Hence, future social security policies should aim to meet the evolving needs of the population and address the limitations of the existing system.

The report from the 19th National Congress of the Communist Party of China emphasized a people-centered development approach, advocating for "improving people's livelihood and social fairness and justice". It also emphasizes the need to ensure that children are well raised, educated, and adequately employed, that the sick receive medical care, the elderly are provided for, housing is available, and the vulnerable groups are supported. The goal is to "build a comprehensive, nationwide, and multi-tiered social security system that is urban–rural coordinated, clear in responsibilities, adequately guaranteed, and sustainable". To achieve these objectives, China's social security system must shift from high-speed expansion to high-quality development, which requires policy adjustments, including:

(1) Improving the social security system, which should focus on system construction, operational mechanisms, and functions;
(2) Coordinating services: It is essential to achieve nationwide coordination and urban–rural integration in basic pension, basic medical insurance, major disease insurance, unemployment and work injury insurance systems and urban and rural social assistance systems;
(3) Establishing a unified platform: It is necessary to create a national social insurance public service platform to enhance public participation in insurance, improve the system's sustainability, streamline management, expand coverage, and minimize disruption in insurance;
(4) Refining functions: It is crucial to strengthen functions of social security related to income adjustment, employment promotion, and social safety, to achieve higher-quality development;
(5) Targeting vulnerable groups: alongside the expanding of coverage, it is important to address the needs of the high-risk and most-needed groups, such as gig

workers, freelancers, and migrant workers who have yet to access basic pension insurance;
(6) Promoting legal framework: It is necessary to ensure basic security through robust legal administration and foster favorable conditions for a multi-tiered social security system (Song & Kang, 2021).

7.4.3.2 Strengthen Social Security System Construction to Address Imbalance and Insufficiency

To establish an effective social security system, China needs to create efficient operational mechanisms, leverage market mechanisms, and design social security programs tailored to the needs of beneficiaries, expanding appropriate insurance types and coverage.

Current imbalances and deficiencies in the social security system manifest in several ways (Zheng, 2019):

(1) Disparities in the structure and projects of social security, where national projects dominate the system, while corporate supplemental security systems are underdeveloped, with limited personal and family investment in social security;
(2) Regional and urban–rural imbalances in social security levels with local government-driven projects showing significant variations that exacerbate urban–rural economic disparities;
(3) Imbalance in government investment, focusing more on social insurance than social assistance and welfare;
(4) A mismatch between government and market mechanisms in project design, funding, and services;
(5) Management imbalances, where there is an excessive focus on benefit adjustments rather than improvement in supply structure and efficiency.

To address these challenges, clear development goals and intensified reforms are essential.

7.4.3.3 Rational Planning of Social Security Costs

The successful implementation and sustainability of the social security system depend on the government's financial capacity and social funding effectiveness, with its social impact closely tied to its costs. Key challenges include high social insurance costs and insufficient personal account incentives. To tackle these issues, a systematic approach is essential. It is necessary to adjust cost policies to alleviate enterprise burdens, utilize market mechanisms for resource allocation and management and improve the investment returns of social security funds. It is also vital to improve personal account incentives to address sustainability concerns, as emphasized by the CPC Central Committee. Lowering the nominal contribution rate can also boost participation and enhance the financial sustainability of the system.

7.4.3.4 Maintaining an Appropriate Level of Social Security and Adhering to the Principle of Actuarial Balance

China's social security system should align with its economic development. While improving social security levels, the system must operate within its capacity, taking into consideration demographic changes, social culture, economic conditions, and fiscal constraints. This approach seeks to align social security benefit standards with economic realities and establish a dynamic adjustment mechanism (Long et al., 2020). In implementing the social security system, the principle of "actuarial balance" must be upheld, which aims to balance annual social security contributions with benefit expenditures, and ensure that the goals and means of social insurance plans are consistent. With household incomes on the rise, the government should align the contributions and benefits of insured individuals, increase central government transfer payments and dedicated investments in social security. It is also essential to formalize the principle of "actuarial balance" through legislation.

To ensure financial sustainability, efforts should focus on advancing the rule of law, establishing constraints on social insurance, and reinforcing the system's integrity (Zheng, 2018).

References

Chen, Q. Y. (2006). *Public policy analysis*. Peking University Press.

Chen, T. (2009). Changes in China's public policy since reform and opening up. *Huxiang Forum, 22*(4), 10–13.

Cheng, Z., & Ma, J. (2018). Evolution of China's population aging and coping strategies. *Academic Exchange, 2018*(12), 101–109.

Dong, K., & Shen, G. (2021). The centennial changes of China's social security system under the guidance of the Party. *Administrative Management Reform, 5*, 21–35.

Duan, Y. (2017). Exploration of the urban community family doctor contract service model. *Medical Frontier, 7*(25), 36–37.

Li, C. (2011a). Research and practice of disease prevention and control performance evaluation in China [Master's thesis]. Fudan University.

Li, C. (2011b). Research on the reform of China's universal medical insurance system under the background of the new medical reform [Doctoral dissertation]. Fourth Military Medical University.

Li, M. (2014b). Research on the problems and countermeasures in China's public policy. *Frontier Economy and Culture, 7*, 43–45.

Li, J. (2019). From "system" to "life": The evolution of China's public health policy over the past 70 years. *Chinese Journal of Public Health, 35*(10), 1281–1284.

Li, L., Jiang, Y., & Chen, Q. (2008). 30 years of health reform in China under the background of reform and opening up. *China Health Economics, 2*, 5–9.

Li, J., Zhai, T., & Feng, Y. (2021). Current situation, problems, and countermeasures of urban poverty governance in China. *Social Governance, 3*, 57–67.

Liang, B. (2007). *Research on China's public policy formulation in the new era*. Lanzhou University Press.

Liao, Q. (2019). The development history and achievements of compulsory education in New China for 70 years: Also on universal education. *Journal of Southwest University (Social Science Edition), 45*(5), 5–13.

Lin, J., & Li, L. (2005). Review and current status of schistosomiasis prevention and control. *Strait Journal of Preventive Medicine, 2005*(1), 22–23.

Liu, S. (1999). Implementing a prevention-oriented approach to promote people's health. *Chinese Journal of Preventive Medicine, 1999*(2), 6–7.

Long, C., & Yi, C. (2017). Basic public service equalization, balanced development of compulsory education, and public policy optimization: Analysis of China's compulsory education policy change and path. *Journal of Xiangtan University (Philosophy and Social Science Edition), 41*(6), 14–20.

Long, Y., Wang, Y., & Ning, Y. (2020). Goals and key measures for the development of social security during the "14th Five-Year Plan" period. *Economic Trends, 8*, 105–118.

Ruan, S. (2015). Comprehensive evaluation study on the establishment of national health cities [Doctoral dissertation]. Shandong University.

Song, F., & Kang, S. (2021). Achievements, problems, and prospects of social security construction during the "13th Five-Year Plan" period. *Journal of Hebei University (Philosophy and Social Science Edition), 46*(4), 138–146.

Su, H. (2010). Research on the performance evaluation indicator system of China's public health service system [Master's thesis]. Huazhong University of Science and Technology.

Sun, M., Wu, D., Shi, J., et al. (2014). Policy changes in emergency response to public health emergencies in China: 2003–2013. *China Health Policy Research, 7*(7), 24–29.

Tan, J. H. (2004). Discussion on strengthening the scientific, democratic, and legal construction of government decision-making. *Journal of Yunnan Administrative College, 2*, 44–46.

Tang, J. (2008). An analysis of China's social security policy. *Dongyue Tribune, 1*, 12–34.

Wang, Z. (2019). 70 years of public policy: The development and reform of the social security and public service supply system. *Journal of Beijing University of Technology (Social Science Edition), 19*(5), 25–35.

Winslow, C. E. (1920). The untilled fields of public health. *Science, 51*(1306), 23–33.

Wu, P. (2014). Research on the effective supply mechanism of rural public goods from the perspective of urban-rural coordination [Doctoral dissertation]. Southwestern University of Finance and Economics.

Zhang, Y. (2010). Risk perception, social learning, and paradigm shift: Policy changes triggered by public health emergencies since 2003 [Doctoral dissertation]. Fudan University.

Zhang, Y., & Zhang, L. (2018). Exploration of the transition from medical security system to health security system under the background of Healthy China. *China Health Policy Research, 11*(1), 2–5.

Zheng, B. (2018). 40 years of social security in China: Experience and reform orientation. *Chinese Journal of Population Science, 4*, 2–17.

Zheng, B. (2019). Reform orientation and basic principles of China's social security system. *Economic Research Reference, 12*, 127–128.

Zhu, D., Li, P., & Song, N. (2017). Report on the balanced development of compulsory education in China: Evidence from the third-party evaluation of the "Education Planning Outline." *Journal of East China Normal University (Education Science Edition), 35*(1), 63–77.

Zhu, H. (2012). Analysis of gender and regional differences in education levels of Chinese residents. *Social Scientist, 10*, 42–45.

Zhuang, J. (2020). Historical experience and lessons from the prevention and treatment of schistosomiasis in New China. *China Administrative Management, 2020*(3), 143–146.

Afterword

As noted in the preface of this series, our research on social economic issues has highlighted the growing significance of the public goods sector in China's economic activities and there is increasing public attention to the operational efficiency of public infrastructure and the quality of public services. After over 40 years of reform and opening up, the public goods sector has undergone substantial changes in both growth and institutional transformation. However, despite profound research in other areas of economics, there are limited studies on the public goods sector. In China, public economics does not constitute a separate academic discipline; instead, it is typically categorized under fiscal studies within applied economics.

The Institute for Economic Development at the School of Business of East China University of Science and Technology (ECUST), established in the mid-1980s, has long been home to scholars conducting research on public economics. Notably, Professor Cai Jiangnan and Professor Xu Bin translated *Lectures on Public Economics* (by Atkinson & Stiglitz, 1992). Over the years, faculty members from both the School of Business and the School of Social and Public Administration at ECUST have undertaken numerous research projects on public economics, contributing significantly to the field. In 2011, the School of Business at ECUST offered a doctoral program in applied economics, which includes training in public economics for graduate students. In 2016, ECUST partnered with the Shanghai Development Research Center to establish the Shanghai Public Economics and Social Governance Research Center, which, with a focus primarily on the theoretical and practical applications of public economics, undertakes multiple projects and regularly hosts academic seminars, becoming an open platform for scholarly exchanges in the field of public economics.

The book is the product of collaborative research and group discussion among faculty and doctoral students from the Institute of Economic Development at the School of Business, East China University of Science and Technology, and the Shanghai Public Economy and Social Governance Research Center. In 2017, we received a grant for the project titled "Research on Effective Supply Mechanisms of Urban Public Products" under the Scientific Research Innovation Programs of the Shanghai Municipal Education Commission. Over the past few years, we have

B. Wu et al., *Effective Supply Mechanism of Urban Public Goods*, Public Economy and Urban Governance in China, https://doi.org/10.1007/978-981-96-2608-3

regularly held seminars on urban public economics, with the participation of scholars both from home and abroad. These academic activities have significantly contributed to the writing of this book.

The project was planned by the chief editor Baijun Wu, who outlined the structure, wrote the first chapter, reviewed and revised the remaining chapters. Other contributors include Zhen Li who wrote chapter two and part of chapter four; Maogang Tang who authored chapters three and four; Cao Zhiwei who contributed chapter five while Lv Tingting authored chapter six. And chapter seven was co-authored by Gao Shan Lingyun, Li Mengqi, Qiu Zhen, and Xi Yuting.

We would like to extend our gratitude to the Institute of Social Sciences at ECUST and the Shanghai Public Economics and the Social Governance Research Center for their providing an exceptional academic exchange environment that facilitates the completion of the book, and also to the National Social Science Foundation and the Scientific Research and Innovation Program of Shanghai Municipal Education Commission for their financial support. This book is a product of the Key Project of the National Social Science Foundation "Research on Improving Development Mechanism of Urban–Rural Integration" (21AZD036), and the project "Research on Effective Supply Mechanisms of Urban Public Products" (201701070002E00008) under the Shanghai Education Commission Scientific Research Innovation Plan in 2017. This book, as a volume of Research on Innovation of Urban Public Economy and Social Governance series, is also funded by the Chinese National Publishing Fund and Shanghai Publishing Projects for Universities Serving National Strategies. Thanks also go to the East China University of Science and Technology Press for their support.

We welcome all feedbacks and suggestions for the book. Thank you.

Baijun Wu

Early Autumn 2021, Shanghai

The manufacturer's authorised representative in the EU is Springer Nature Customer Service Centre GmbH, Europaplatz 3, 69115 Heidelberg, Germany. If you have any concerns regarding our products, please contact ProductSafety@springernature.com

Printed and bound by CPI Group (UK) Ltd, Croydon, CR0 4YY
01/10/2026
02225938-0003